Rosida Storkino
Chicago, Fall 2016

Real and Imagined

HARVARD EAST ASIAN MONOGRAPHS 376

Real and Imagined

THE PEAK OF GOLD IN HEIAN JAPAN

Heather Blair

Published by the Harvard University Asia Center
Distributed by Harvard University Press
Cambridge (Massachusetts) and London 2015

© 2015 by The President and Fellows of Harvard College
Printed in the United States of America

The Harvard University Asia Center publishes a monograph series and, in coordination with the Fairbank Center for Chinese Studies, the Korea Institute, the Reischauer Institute of Japanese Studies, and other facilities and institutes, administers research projects designed to further scholarly understanding of China, Japan, Vietnam, Korea, and other Asian countries. The Center also sponsors projects addressing multidisciplinary and regional issues in Asia.

Portions of chapter 3 appeared previously in Heather Blair, "Rites and Rule: Kiyomori at Itsukushima and Fukuhara," *Harvard Journal of Asiatic Studies* 73, no. 1 (2013): 1–42, and are reprinted with permission. The quotation of Edwin A. Cranston's translation of *Man'yōshū* 1.38 in chapter 3 is from *The Gem-Glistening Cup*, volume 1 of *A Waka Anthology* (Stanford: Stanford University Press, 1993), and is also reprinted with permission.

This publication uses the multilingual "Brill" typeface. With over 5,100 characters covering Latin, IPA, Greek, and Cyrillic, this typeface is especially suitable for use in the humanities.

For more information, please visit brill.com/brill-typeface

Library of Congress Cataloging-in-Publication Data

Blair, Heather Elizabeth.
Real and imagined : the Peak of Gold in Heian Japan / Heather Blair.
pages cm. — (Harvard East Asian monographs ; 376)
Includes bibliographical references and index.
ISBN 978-0-674-50427-1 (hardcover : acid-free paper)
1. Kinpu, Mount (Nara-ken, Japan)—History. 2. Mountains—Japan—Religious aspects—History—To 1500. 3. Landscapes—Japan—Religious aspects—History—To 1500. 4. Sacred space—Japan—History—To 1500. 5. Japan—Kings and rulers—Biography. 6. Fujiwara family. 7. Pilgrims and pilgrimages—Japan—History—To 1500. 8. Japan—History—Heian period, 794–1185. 9. Japan—Politics and government—794–1185. 10. Japan—Religious life and customs. I. Title.
DS894.69.N3695K462 2015
952'.184—dc23

2014032676

Index by June Sawyer

♾ Printed on acid-free paper

Last figure below indicates year of this printing
22 21 20 19 18 17 16 15

This book is dedicated to my father, Bill, who died before it was finished, and to my daughter, Madrona, who was born after it began.

Contents

Maps and Figures

Maps

Figures

Acknowledgments

It may be, as the sociologist Maurice Halbwachs remarked, that we locate memories "with the help of landmarks that we always carry within ourselves."[1] Inasmuch as this book is about place, it is important to note that I have conducted my research not only by reading but also by walking. Using texts as a tracking device, I have visited the sites described by Heian-period pilgrims. My experiences in the mountains have changed my thinking in ways both subtle and obvious. Walking the slopes, looking for springs, and losing the trail: these activities have produced bodily, affective memory in me. They have given me an interior landscape in which to locate my own recollections, and this has become a medium through which I construe the cultural memory and conventional practices of Heian pilgrims. Any historical project has a subjective bent, and mine has been shaped by my time in the mountains.

This book would never have come to completion without the help of many generous people. I cannot thank all of them here, but my gratitude is both strong and sincere. Among my teachers, I would like to extend particular thanks to Ryūichi Abé, who has been a constant source of wisdom and support, and David Lurie, who taught me how to read *kanbun*. My colleagues Manling Luo, Kevin Martin, and Kevin Tsai provided humor and criticism when I needed both. Rick Nance and Ed Drott gave generously of their time to provide insightful comments on

1. Halbwachs, *On Collective Memory*, 175.

large portions of this book. Anna Andreeva and Carina Roth let me know that I am not the only one absorbed by medieval religious landscapes, mountains, and gods. I have been very grateful for their comments, suggestions, and camaraderie. Many thanks to Theresa Quill, who created the maps for this book, and to Allison Darmody, who helped format the bibliography. I also owe a debt of gratitude to the staff at Harvard University Asia Center and Westchester Publishing Services for their editorial support.

During research in Japan, I have benefitted from the assistance of many scholars who gave unstintingly of their time despite the many other demands on their attention. Katō Tomoyasu sponsored me during my dissertation research at the University of Tokyo's Historiographical Institute and provided generous assistance. Uejima Susumu gave perceptive guidance and kind instruction, first at Harvard University, and then at Kyoto Prefectural University and Kyoto University. From the day I met Nemoto Seiji, he has always asked provocative questions—I am grateful to him for pushing me and for doing so with a smile. I first admired Kawasaki Tsuyoshi from afar for his clear, well-designed research; as I have gotten to know him, he has also proven tremendously insightful and kind. I very much appreciate his and Chikamoto Kensuke's ongoing assistance and support. I owe many thanks also to Tsuboi Gō, whose patient and thoughtful help enabled me to articulate my work on the *Gōki* in Japanese. Toda Fusako helped me when I was first learning to read handwritten manuscripts; without her, I would never have made it through the Meiji-period manuscript of the *Gōki* fragment, a text discussed in the pages that follow.

My family and friends have been part of this book as well. My father, Bill Blair, accompanied me on a hike through the Ōmine Range in 2006 and contributed several of the photographs that appear in this book. It was a wonderful trip, and I am deeply glad that he was there to share it with me. Andrew Reichman climbed "the forbidden peak" to take photographs for me in November 2005. By asking questions and photographing outhouses and signs about trash, my father and Andrew helped me see aspects of the landscape to which my own preconceptions had blinded me. My husband, Craig Coley, and my mother, Sandra Hernshaw, accompanied me on a pilgrimage to Kumano in 2006. That too was a splendid journey, and I thank them for their willingness to go on an adventure with me. I am profoundly grateful to my husband for his unfailing support. I depend upon his patience, kindness, and generosity on a daily basis. I extend many thanks to my mother for actually reading my prose. Thanks, mom!

Finally, I would like to express my thanks to organizations that have provided me with funding during the years I have worked on this book. A Fulbright Institute of International Education grant, which included support from the Japan-U.S. Educational Commission (JUSEC), and a Kennedy Traveling Fellowship from Harvard University provided support during my dissertation research. At various stages in my writing, I have received support from the Whiting Foundation, the Andrew W. Mellon Fellowship of Scholars in the Humanities at Stanford University, and Indiana University. A postdoctoral research fellowship from the Japan Society for the Promotion of Science (JSPS) permitted me to complete the revision of this manuscript.

Note to the Reader

Following standard usage, names for historical individuals are given surname first, with a connective "no" for people who lived prior to 1185 (e.g., Ōe no Masafusa); by convention, the connective "no" is omitted for those who lived from 1185 onward (e.g., Kujō Michiie). Because there is some disagreement about the pronunciation of Heian-period women's names, both pronunciations are given in the text (e.g., Fujiwara no Shōshi, alt. Akiko). Birth and death dates are provided at the first mention of a historical figure. Dates accord with those given in *Heian jidai-shi jiten.* In cases where that dictionary provides no entry for an individual, dates follow those given in *Kokushi daijiten* or in Hirabayashi and Koike, *Gojūonbiki sōgō bunin sōreki sōran.* Ages given in the text conform to premodern convention, according to which a person is one year old at birth. Names for buddhas and bodhisattvas are given in Sanskrit due to that language's status as *lingua franca* in the field of Buddhist studies; hence, Śākyamuni and Maitreya, not Shaka and Miroku.

Citations to canonical Buddhist materials refer to the East Asian Buddhist canon, for which the standard edition is *Taishō shinshū daizōkyō* (hereafter cited as *T.*). The titles of sutras and other canonical works are rendered in English in the main body of the text; however, in the notes, Chinese titles and references to the *Taishō* canon are given, together with Japanese titles at first mention. English translations are provided for the titles of premodern Japanese sources at first use, but the Japanese titles are used thereafter. Entries from premodern annals and diaries are cited by date, with era name first, followed by month and day; the abbreviation "i" stands for intercalary month. Citations for the volume and page number of the modern edition are given in parentheses. Thus, an entry from the *Midō kanpakuki* for the seventeenth day of the intercalary fifth month of Kankō 4 is cited as follows: *Midō kanpakuki,* Kankō 4.i5.17 (1:222). The diaries cited in this book were originally written on scrolls; the term *uragaki* denotes material written on the back of a manuscript.

To make the source material more accessible to readers who do not understand classical Chinese and Japanese, whenever possible, I have included references to published translations of premodern works in the notes. Unless otherwise marked, passages from premodern works quoted in the text are my translations; however, I have also provided references to alternative translations to facilitate comparison.

Transliterations of Japanese terms follow the modified Hepburn system, yielding Kinpusen, not Kimbusen, and *kanpaku,* not *kampaku.* Japanese characters are given in the index. When relevant terms are given in multiple languages, the abbreviations C. (Chinese), J. (Japanese), and Skt. (Sanskrit) are used. Transliterated Sanskrit has been retained for a number of Buddhist terms, such as *dhāraṇī*; however, when terms (for instance, sutra or mandala) have entered general English usage, as measured by the inclusion of a relevant definition in *Merriam-Webster's Collegiate Dictionary,* they have been rendered in roman type with no diacritics.

Abbreviations

alt.	alternate (used to indicate an alternate name or pronunciation)
C.	Chinese
DNBZ	*Dai Nihon bukkyō zensho*
DNK	*Dai Nihon kokiroku*
GR	*Gunsho ruijū*
i.	intercalary month
J.	Japanese
KSS	*Kinpusenji shiryō shūsei*
NE	*Nihon no emaki*
NKBT	*Nihon koten bungaku taikei*
NST	*Nihon shisō taikei*
Skt.	Sanskrit
SNKBT	*Shin Nihon koten bungaku taikei*
SNKBZ	*Shinpen Nihon koten bungaku zenshū*
SS	*Shugendō shōso*
SZKT	*Shintei zōho kokushi taikei*
T.	*Taishō shinshū daizōkyō*
ZGR	*Zoku gunsho ruijū*
ZNE	*Zoku Nihon no emaki*
ZST	*Zōho shiryō taisei*

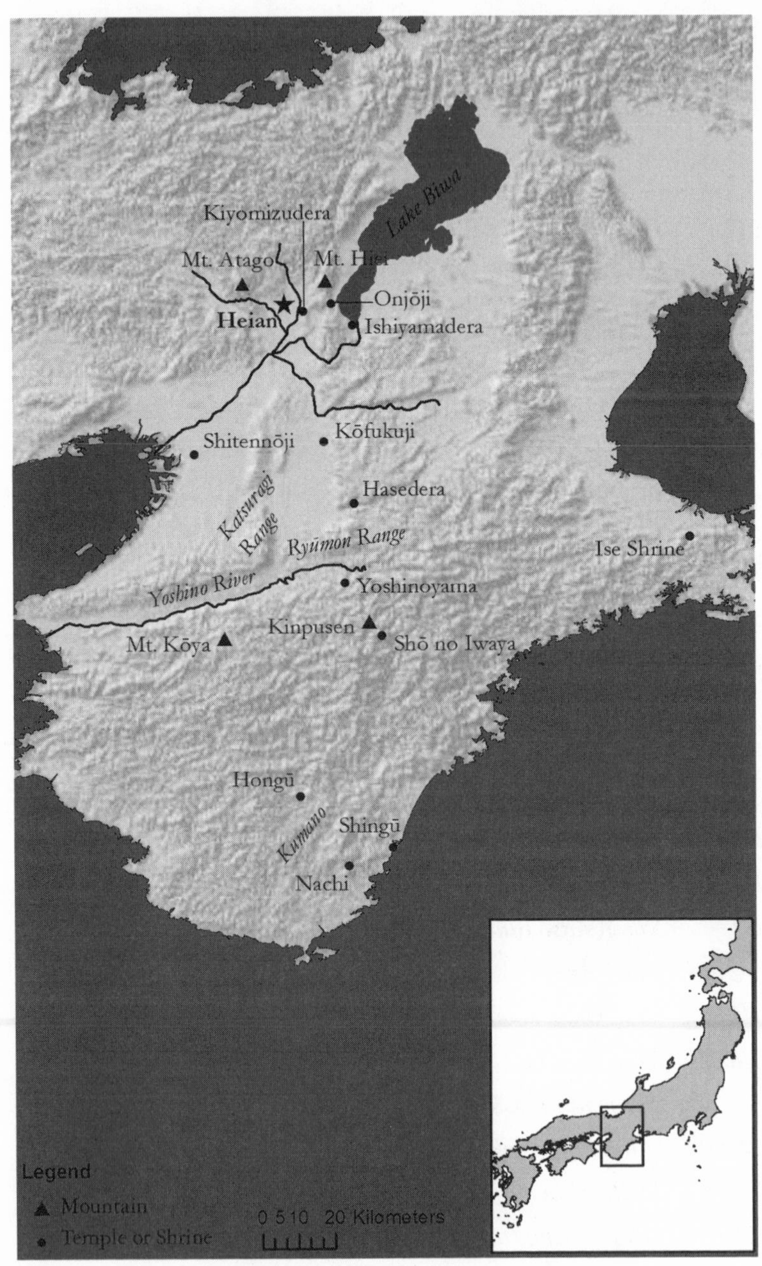

MAP 1 Kii Peninsula, with an inset map of Japan. (Note: coastlines and watercourses are contemporary.) Map by Theresa Quill, Indiana University Bloomington.

Introduction

> [The Japanese immigrant monk Hongshun (Kanho, n.d.)] said that some 500 *li* south of the Japanese capital stands the Peak of Gold. Upon its summit is the bodhisattva Vajra Zaō, foremost in miracles. Upon the mountain, there are pines and cypresses, renowned flowers and tender grasses. In several hundred temples, great and small, dwell those who practice the lofty Way. Women cannot climb it. Even today, men who want to climb it abstain from liquor and meat and sex for three months, and then all their wishes are fulfilled. It is said that this bodhisattva is a transformation-body of Maitreya, like Mañjuśrī at Mt. Wutai.
>
> —Yichu (n.d.), in *Shishi liutie* (Six volumes for Buddhists)[1]

A long day's walk south of the village of Yoshinoyama in western Japan, Kinpusen, the Peak of Gold, rises up out of the northern reaches of the Ōmine Range (map 1). Even today, much of the Ōmine region is wilderness, home to boar, bear, monkey, deer, and countless smaller birds and beasts; however, it has also long been a haunt of humans and gods. In 2004, Kinpusen, alternatively known as Sanjōgatake, Ōminesan, and Mitake, was included in a newly designated UNESCO World Heritage Site.[2] This book tells the story of how the mountain first rose to cultural prominence during the Heian period (794–1185).

Archaeological remains indicate that religious practice was under way at Kinpusen by the Nara period (710–84). According to narrative sources, during the early 800s holy men who combined Buddhist devotion with Daoist-style longevity practices and the worship of indigenous gods (*kami*) traversed the Ōmine Range, gaining special powers through ritual practice. During the 900s, Kinpusen gained fame as the

1. *Shishi liutie* (459). This text dates to the 950s.
2. UNESCO, "Sacred Sites and Pilgrimage Routes."

haunt of a fierce local deity named Zaō, the King of the Treasury, and by midcentury, male members of the high aristocracy had begun to make pilgrimages to the mountain. Accordingly, Kinpusen came to play an important role in the ritual and political life of the ruling elite.

The mountain's fortunes shifted dramatically at the end of the eleventh century, however. Armed conflict between religious institutions was becoming increasingly common, and Kōfukuji, a powerful temple located in the Nara Basin, was working to bring temples and shrines across the province of Yamato under its sway. Being located at the far southern end of the province, Kinpusen became a prime target for these campaigns. In 1093, Kōfukuji forces marched on Kinpusen and defeated the mountain monks in a series of battles, disrupting established patronage patterns and bringing the mountain into closer contact with the religious establishment of Nara, the "southern capital" (*nanto*). In the ensuing hundred years, Kinpusen's infrastructure developed significantly; meanwhile, proponents of mountain practice produced texts in which they sought to codify traditions, construct transmission lineages, and canonize itineraries through the Ōmine Range. In the wake of the Genpei War, which convulsed Japan between 1180 and 1185, well-known monks connected with the Nara revival, including Kōfukuji hierarchs, took an active interest in Kinpusen and the surrounding Ōmine region. Ascetically inflected mountain pilgrimage became a recognized mode of Buddhist practice around which sectarian identity gradually coalesced; in this respect, it bore a strong similarity to monastic discipline (*ritsu*), meditation (*zen*), and Pure Land devotion. Toward the end of the Kamakura period (1185–1333), a discrete religious movement known as Shugendō, "the Way of practice," emerged from interchange between communities associated with powerful lowland temples and the Ōmine region.

In conceptualizing the roles that Kinpusen played in premodern religious culture, I draw loosely on Henri Lefebvre's theoretical formulation of perceived, conceived, and lived space, which has been put to good use in other studies of sacred mountains in East Asia.[3] Since the

3. Lefebvre, *The Production of Space,* esp. 39–41; Ambros, *Emplacing a Pilgrimage,* 23–38; Robson, *Power of Place,* 7–8. Foucault's threefold conceptualization of space in terms of utopia, dystopia, and heterotopia has also been applied to East Asian mountains (see Foucault, "Of Other Spaces"; and Moerman, *Localizing Paradise,* 2, 234–37).

1970s, geographers like David Harvey and Edward Soja have elaborated upon Lefebvre's model; in this book, I refer primarily to the triad of real, imagined, and real-and-imagined space articulated by Soja.[4] Real space (or as Soja often calls it, Firstspace) is what we see and touch: in the case of Kinpusen, this means the granitic outcroppings and ridges, beech and cryptomeria, and shrines and steles lining the paths. Knowledge privileging this physical, material mode of spatiality has traditionally been concerned with the "surface plottings" of classical cartography, although research on the social and historical production of material landscapes has been on the rise. Imagined space (or Secondspace) refers to the realm of representation: this is what and how we think of our world. At an extreme, imagined space may be "entirely ideational, made of projections into the empirical world from conceived or imagined geographies."[5] In Heian Japan, courtiers envisaged Kinpusen as a realm of immortals, where "meditation monks sip upon the mists" and where "morning clouds and evening rains are deep blue and boundless."[6] This kind of representation has no a priori relation to physical reality, yet it can exert profound influences on human perceptions of real space.

Despite their differences, the real and imagined dimensions of spatiality are interdependent, hence the third term, real-and-imagined space. As embodied creatures, we necessarily operate in real-and-imagined space at the same time that we live with it: our actions depend upon and shape our world. In turn, our world shapes our lives.[7] For the purposes of this book, real-and-imagined space designates the ground for religious practice as well as its results. Pilgrims, for instance, climbed a very real Kinpusen; meanwhile, through financial endowments, they contributed to the growth and institutionalization of the mountain's built environment. During their journey and after their return, they wrote and spoke about the mountain, thereby enhancing its

4. Soja, *Thirdspace,* esp. 74–82; Harvey, *The Condition of Postmodernity,* 218–21.

5. Soja, *Thirdspace,* 77, 79.

6. For meditation monks, see memorial quoted in *Go-Nijō Moromichiki,* Kanji 5.8.17 (2:168). For clouds and rain, see *Gōtotoku nagon ganmonshū* 3.5 (426).

7. Lefebvre, Soja, and others maintain that the introduction of a third term opens up ontological and epistemological binaries, resulting in analyses that emphasize both/and openness, rather than either/or closure. On this point, compare Soja, *Thirdspace,* 139–44; and Bhabha, *The Location of Culture,* 53–56.

reputation and disseminating a particular spatial imaginary. By burying sutra manuscripts upon the peak, they altered the physical landscape, while projecting themselves into an imagined future when, in a distant rebirth, they would return to the mountain in the presence of Maitreya, the future buddha, and their scriptures would rise up out of the earth. In practice, then, the real and imagined interfused. It is the historical, human reception and construction of Kinpusen as a real-and-imagined place that is the focus of this book.

It was through pilgrimage that Kinpusen developed into a culturally significant landscape. When courtiers began to make the journey in the mid-900s, pilgrimage itself was a new practice among laymen. With no inns, topographical maps, or ready supply of food en route, travel of any sort was difficult and, if one traveled in any comfort, expensive. Consequently, pilgrimage remained largely an elite endeavor or a specialized mode of ascesis for some centuries.[8] As discussed in chapter 1, early evidence for lay pilgrimage to Kinpusen is fragmentary; nonetheless, it is clear that whereas other early pilgrimage sites, such as Ishiyamadera and Hasedera, were comparatively accessible, Kinpusen was the first destination requiring more than a week of travel to be frequented by nobles. It attracted a full range of male aristocrats, from comparatively low-ranking literati, to provincial governors, to senior aristocrats. Following upon Kinpusen's success, aristocrats began to travel to Mt. Kōya in the eleventh century and to the Kumano area, which is home to three shrines, Hongū, Shingū, and Nachi, in the twelfth. Like Kinpusen, both Mt. Kōya and Kumano are located on the Kii Peninsula (see map 1). These "three Ks," often referred to by Heian writers as the "southern mountains" (*nanzan*), were the most important remote pilgrimage destinations for the male elite from the 900s into the Kamakura period.[9] All three remain active centers today.

Pilgrimage was certainly a devotional activity, but it was also saturated with political significance. The most eminent members of the

8. For a classic study of the development (and difficulties) of pilgrimage in the context of the history of travel and transport, see Shinjō Tsunezō, *Shaji sankei*. For an overview of Japanese pilgrimage in general, see Reader and Swanson, "Pilgrimage."

9. Wakamori, *Shugendōshi kenkyū*, 78. For use of the phrase "southern mountains" to refer explicitly to Kinpusen, see, for example, *Shōyūki*, Eisō 1.2.11–12 and 4.4–5, Chōwa 5.18–20 (1:161, 172, 4:200).

ruling elite traveled to Kinpusen. In this respect, two phases in Heian history are important for the purposes of this book: the Fujiwara regency and the *insei,* literally "rule by retired emperors." In the second half of the ninth century, it became increasingly common for an emperor to reign with a regent, usually his maternal uncle or grandfather. In the ensuing decades, this custom was institutionalized and the office of regent was monopolized by one patriline within the Fujiwara family's Northern House. Accordingly, the period from the mid-900s until the late eleventh century is known as the regency (*sekkan seiji, sekkan jidai*). Although the regents were far from the sole players on the political scene, or even at court, their close ties to the emperor and the Council of State, together with their command of extensive landholdings and clientage networks, made them tremendously influential.[10]

Retired Emperor Shirakawa (1053–1129, r. 1072–86) is widely recognized as the primary architect of the *insei* (1086–1221), a political order in which retired emperors achieved political ascendancy. Although the regency and Fujiwara control of it endured as formal institutions for hundreds of years, their importance was relativized when Shirakawa, who had stepped down from the throne in favor of his son in 1086, began to assert control over matters of state. Despite the upheavals of the Genpei War, retired emperors continued to dominate the political scene up through the early Kamakura period. Their ascendancy came to a definitive end only with the Jōkyū Disturbance, when Retired Emperor Go-Toba (1180–1239, r. 1183–98) mounted a failed challenge to the military government in 1221. Changes in the power balance notwithstanding, a high level of continuity obtained between the regency and the *insei*: like the regents, the retired emperors' influence was based on their clientage networks, landholdings, and relationship with reigning emperors.[11]

10. On the establishment of the regency, see Piggott and Yoshida, *Teishinkōki;* and essays by Morita Tei and Sasaki Muneo in Piggott, *Capital and Countryside.* The Japanese literature in this area is immense; helpful overviews include Ishigami and Katō, *Sekkan seiji to ōchō bunka*; and Hotate, *Heian ōchō.*

11. For the political history of the *insei,* see, for instance, Hurst, *Insei*; Adolphson, *The Gates of Power*; and Motoki, *Inseiki seijishi no kenkyū.* For the *insei* as an outgrowth of regency trends in shared rulership, see Ihara, *Nihon chūsei no kokusei,* esp. 191–232; and Uejima, *Nihon chūsei shakai,* esp. 147–227.

Both the regents and retired emperors headed vertically integrated conglomerates, which the influential historian Kuroda Toshio referred to as power blocs (*kenmon*). In Kuroda's view, interdependent, and often fractious, rapprochements between blocs associated with the court, religious institutions, and warrior houses were the signal characteristic of medieval rule.[12] Institutional historians have shown that power blocs took full form during the *insei*; consequently, even though Kuroda's analysis has been critiqued, refined, and reinterpreted, it has led to a reconceptualization of the Middle Ages as beginning with the *insei*, rather than the Kamakura period.[13] I follow this line of thought in this book: I frame Kinpusen's integration into Kōfukuji's power bloc during the late eleventh century as one instance of a much larger trend in the formation of a medieval religious landscape, that is, a landscape dominated by power blocs.

Together with the accrual of estates and the creation of administrative structures, ritual performance was central to the growth of a power bloc. In the following chapters, I maintain that Japan's most powerful men and women built their lordship through flexible, ritual-cum-political systems; for analytical purposes, I refer to these as ritual regimes. Put briefly, I argue that ritual regimes were anchored in distinctive sets of sites, rites, and texts associated with specific patrons or lineage groups. From 969 to 1090, at precisely the time when the Fujiwara regents enjoyed political preeminence, they made Kinpusen into their signature pilgrimage destination: from generation to generation, members of their patriline climbed the Peak of Gold. By contrast, when retired emperors overshadowed the regents during the *insei*, they resorted to Kumano in a gesture of political and ritual change. Through spatial synecdoche, the regents mantled themselves with Kinpusen's religious authority; the retired sovereigns, with Kumano's. At the same time that ritual regimes provided a framework for spatio-religious symbolism, they also contributed to the articulation of clientage relationships within a power bloc. Membership in

12. For a classic exposition of the characteristics of a power bloc, see Kuroda, "Chūsei kokka to tennō," in *Kuroda Toshio chosakushū*, 1:3–46. Kuroda's analysis has been furthered and adapted by a range of scholars; the most important study in English is Adolphson's *The Gates of Power*.

13. See, for instance, Rekishigaku Kenkyūkai and Nihonshi Kenkyūkai, *Chūsei no keisei*.

the retinue of an eminent pilgrim, for instance, demonstrated social and political intimacy, whereas the provision of logistical and financial support expressed clientage. Externally, ritual regimes provided a platform for interaction with other power blocs. When Retired Emperor Shirakawa visited Kinpusen in 1092, for instance, he not only contested the regents' symbolic claims to the mountain, but also made it clear that he sought to form his own constituency there. At the same time, by taking a hand in Kinpusen's affairs, he positioned himself over and against the power-bloc temple Kōfukuji, which had already begun to make the claim that Kinpusen was properly one of its client institutions.

Given its immersion in political culture, Heian-period travel to Kinpusen and the Kii Peninsula fits with the observation of the anthropologists John Eade and Michael Sallnow that pilgrimage is often a matter of competition.[14] Pilgrims to the southern mountains vied with each other in their gifts to the gods and expressions of piety. Together with the explicitly hierarchical organization of pilgrimage parties, this contravenes Victor Turner and Edith Turner's classic theoretical model, according to which pilgrims experience *communitas*, a liminal state of "anti-structure" in which social boundaries dissolve, only to be reinstantiated upon the pilgrims' eventual return home.[15] Nonetheless, the Turners' conceptualization of pilgrimage as a rite of passage resonates with the Heian situation, for spatial practices, which included talking and writing about place, as well as traversing and inhabiting it, were integral to the production and maintenance of social identities. Regents and retired emperors legitimated and majestified themselves through their journeys; as pilgrims, they were making themselves at the same time that they were making the mountain. The sociologist Ian Reader, who has written extensively about pilgrimage in Japan, has shown quite vividly that pilgrims, institutions, and stories are constantly making and remaking the real-and-imagined landscape.[16] Without pilgrims, Kinpusen would not have looked the same, to either the physical or the mind's eye.

14. See Eade and Sallnow, *Contesting the Sacred,* 1–29; and Coleman and Eade, *Reframing Pilgrimage,* 1–25.

15. Turner and Turner, *Image and Pilgrimage*; Turner, "Pilgrimages as Social Processes."

16. Reader, *Making Pilgrimages.*

In order to illuminate the relationship of pilgrimage to other modes of practice, especially political activity and manuscript production, in the following chapters I often employ the term "traces" (*ato,* or in compound, *seki* or *jaku*). Across a range of genres, Heian-period writers consistently designated physical entities that provided access to the past and the divine as traces; these could be manuscripts, footprints, gods, or even human remains. By appropriating the notion of traces as an interpretive lens, I mean to bring into focus a broader, integrative project in Heian discourse and religious practice. Persistent references to traces, I argue, indicate that the political and the religious, walking and writing, functioned as cognate domains. Traces played a central role in political culture, where precedent (*rei,* or sometimes *ato*) provided the reigning standard for law, governance, and etiquette. They also anchored theological imagination, which posited that *kami* are manifest traces (*suijaku*) of buddhas and bodhisattvas. Footprints were called "foot traces" (*ashiato, sokuseki*); manuscripts and calligraphy, "hand-traces" (*shuseki*). This terminological consistency was no coincidence. Whatever category traces belonged to, they tended to operate as what we might today call ostensive signs, which show what they represent because they are of a substance with it.[17] Put differently, a trace was not so much a representation as a condensation or replication of the person or god who produced it. A manuscript, for instance, could operate as a physical, satisfying, and ritually potent instantiation of its scribe and/or author.[18]

Broadly speaking, Heian-period men and women felt that traces were important because they localized and materialized what would otherwise be inaccessible temporally or geographically.[19] In this respect, it is significant that Heian writers often paired the term "trace" with the verb "to seek out or inquire" (*rei o tazunu*). Because sacred sites

17. I borrow this usage from Fabio Rambelli, who has it by way of Umberto Eco. As Rambelli notes, icons and Buddhist relics have also long functioned as important types of ostensive signs (Rambelli, *Buddhist Materiality,* 79, 123–24; see also Sharf, "On the Allure of Buddhist Relics").

18. For correlations between scripture and the bodies of its copyists and authors, see Eubanks, *Miracles of Book and Body,* as well as chapter 5 of this book.

19. This position stands in decided contrast to the Derridean conceptualization of "the trace" (*la trace*) as a mark of unbridgeable absence that "properly has no site" (Derrida, *Margins of Philosophy,* 24). In the Heian period, traces were represented as persisting in, springing from, and actually making place.

were often framed in terms of traces left by founder-figures, pilgrimages can fruitfully be construed as inquiries into traces. In her analysis of the European Santiago de Compostela pilgrimage, the cultural anthropologist Nancy Frey has commented that through their journeys pilgrims engage in dialogue with the past.[20] The same was eminently true of pilgrims in Heian Japan.

The fact that traces offered access to the past and the divine helped to mediate formal and categorical differences among traces. In the ensuing chapters, I argue that in the Kinpusen cult and in Heian religious culture more generally, texts, rituals, and places became mutually constitutive. For instance, when the regents and retired emperors went to Kinpusen, they copied Buddhist sutras and buried them upon the summit. Purposely leaving traces on the page and in the earth, these men were simultaneously making text and marking place. This book, then, is a history of religious practice in a particular place, but it is also a history of practices of place-making.[21]

To write the history of Kinpusen as a real-and-imagined place during the Heian period, I have worked almost exclusively with Heian-period sources. This might seem unexceptional, and indeed unexceptionable, but in fact it departs from dominant trends in the Japanese- and English-language literature. To date, Japanese research has favored structural analyses, while English-language research has focused primarily on contemporary practices, with some attention to medieval developments.[22] In this respect, it is telling that of the seven hundred

20. Frey, *Pilgrim Stories,* 17–46, 221–22. The pilgrim's dialogical, interpretive project is thus similar to the historian's as discussed by LaCapra in "Rethinking Intellectual History."

21. The term "practice" is commonly used in Buddhist studies to refer to devotional and meditative activities. Without excluding this usage from my discussion, I intend the word more in the sense developed by Pierre Bourdieu (for instance, in *Outline of a Theory of Practice*) and applied by Sherry Ortner and others (see, for instance, Ortner, *High Religion*). Practice, then, may be understood as activity limited and made possible by the social structures within which it occurs and characterized by inequalities of power and authority. I have borrowed the phrase "place-making" from Basso, *Wisdom Sits in Places.*

22. Miyake Hitoshi's Japanese-language research has been particularly influential. See, for example, his *Ōmine shugendō no kenkyū*; *The Mandala of the Mountain*; and *Shugendō: Essays.* In English, see, for example, Swanson, "*Shugendō* and the Yoshino-Kumano Pilgrimage." For the Middle Ages, see Royall Tyler, "Kōfukuji and the Mountains."

pages of Shudō Yoshiki's authoritative institutional history of the temple Kinpusenji and its eponymous mountain, fewer than sixty are explicitly devoted to the years prior to 1185.[23] There is certainly more to be said. Furthermore, researchers have consistently based their representations of Kinpusen's early history on sources produced at a time when Shugendō was coalescing as a discrete religious movement.[24] In this historiographical mode, early and mid-Heian practices appear as proto-Shugendō. By viewing Kinpusen and the ritual and textual activities focused on it as part of the broader religious and political culture, however, we gain a richer, more nuanced understanding of Japanese religious history. It also begins to appear that Shugendō emerged from rupture, not continuity. In fact, toward the end of this book, I argue that the emergence of Shugendō groups was predicated upon Kinpusen and Kumano's loss of institutional independence and that Shugendō organizations themselves became a source of division and disruption.

The present project is also distinguished by its focus on the activities of laypeople. In the field of religious studies, most research on premodern Japan has concentrated on monks and, to a much lesser extent, nuns. In addition, researchers have preferred to examine the doctrinal—and less often, the ritual—practices of specific schools, for instance the Buddhist Tendai or Shintō Watarai school.[25] These endeavors are important and worthwhile, but the fact remains that discussions of the activities of the laity, the vast demographic majority in any period of history, have been far fewer.[26] In this book, I take up the

23. Shudō, *Kinpusenji shi,* 25–81.

24. The most important later texts to be taken as reflections of Heian circumstances are the *Kinpusen sōsōki* and *Kinpusen zakki,* both of which date to circa 1300. A third key source is the *Kumano gongen kongō Zaō hōden zōkō nikki.* Although often cited as a reliable report, this last text has been shown to be as much a work of fiction as a record of facts (see Kawasaki, "*Kumano gongen kongō Zaō hōden zōkō nikki* to iu gisho"). For examples of the uses to which these sources have been put in the secondary literature, see Royall Tyler, "Kōfukuji and the Mountains," 177–79; and Miyake Hitoshi, *Ōmine shugendō no kenkyū,* 275–77.

25. On Tendai, see, for instance, Groner's studies, *Saichō* and *Ryōgen*; as well as Stone, *Original Enlightenment.* On the eponymous school, see Teeuwen, *Watarai Shintō.*

26. For the Heian period, Ruppert, *Jewel in the Ashes*; and Moerman, *Localizing Paradise* are notable for analyses of both lay and clerical religiosity. See also Ambros, "Liminal Journeys" for laywomen's pilgrimages, and Yiengpruksawan, *Hiraizumi,*

practices of elite laymen, not because their activities are inherently more interesting or important than commoners', but because they are particularly well documented.

In addition to its political significance, several other aspects of lay religiosity bear emphasis. Perhaps most strikingly, laypeople did participate in doctrinal innovation. Clear evidence of this is to be found in *honji suijaku* discourse, which identified buddhas and bodhisattvas with *kami* and which was central to Kinpusen's local theology. Most of the extant early examples of *honji suijaku* interpretation came from the hands of male literati, not monks. Laypeople were also major players in the realm of ritual innovation, a point exemplified by sutra burial. This practice emerged around the year 1000 and became central to lay pilgrimage to Kinpusen. Furthermore, laypeople exercised their ritual agency consciously, even conscientiously. This is particularly visible in the form and function of the practices that I analyze as ritual regimes, which show how successful the nonmonastic elite could be in shaping religious activities to suit their own ends.

Among the many laymen who were active at Kinpusen, three play starring roles in this book: Fujiwara no Michinaga (966–1027), Fujiwara no Moromichi (1062–99), and Retired Emperor Shirakawa. (It should be noted that Michinaga and Shirakawa later took the tonsure; at the time of their Kinpusen pilgrimages, however, they were still laymen.) The reasons for choosing these men as dramatis personae are threefold. First, each represents a specific phase in the history of politics and pilgrimage. Second, each made at least one journey to Kinpusen. And third, the historical and archaeological record for these three pilgrims is comparatively rich, in contrast to scant documentation for others.

Even today, Michinaga is famous as the regent extraordinaire: he represents the high tide of the Fujiwara regency, and it was he who cemented his family's connection to Kinpusen, as well as its participation in pilgrimage more broadly. Michinaga made one successful trip to

---

"The Eyes of Michinaga," and "The Phoenix Hall at Uji" for temple-building projects pursued by members of the Fujiwara family. Relevant discussions also occur in essays by William McCullough, Helen Craig McCullough, Stanley Weinstein, and Allan Grapard in Shively and McCullough, *Heian Japan*.

Kinpusen in 1007 and planned two others, which he was forced to cancel, in 998 and 1011. Moromichi, Michinaga's great-grandson, was well regarded in his own day, but in historical perspective, he played the role of the twilight regent. Moromichi assiduously maintained his family's traditions, including pilgrimage to Kinpusen, visiting the mountain in 1088 and 1090. With Moromichi's untimely death in 1099 at age thirty-seven, followed by the death of his father two years later, the regents' position eroded significantly. Into the gap stepped Retired Emperor Shirakawa, who exerted influence first as the father and then the grandfather of two successive reigning emperors. During the decade following Moromichi's death, Shirakawa declined to make Moromichi's heir, Tadazane (1078–1162), regent, creating the first formal gap in the regency in a century. Having traveled to Kinpusen in 1092, where he emulated and competed with the regents, Shirakawa began to make repeated pilgrimages to Kumano during the second decade of the twelfth century, when his political ascendancy was assured. In this way, Shirakawa eclipsed Kinpusen, making Kumano a signature site for himself and his descendants.[27]

The arc of Kinpusen's rise and fall as an elite pilgrimage destination thus illustrates the more general move from the ancient regime and its statutory codes (*ritsuryō*), which persisted into the early Heian period, through the royal court state (*ōchō kokka*) over which the regents presided, and into the increasing factionalization of the *insei*. During Kinpusen's close association with the Fujiwara regents, its institutions functioned on a more-or-less independent basis. By contrast, in the early *insei* period, Kōfukuji forcibly integrated Kinpusen into its growing domain, thereby ushering the mountain into the Middle Ages, by which I mean an institutional and political order dominated by power blocs.

It is possible to analyze these developments in detail because royals, aristocrats, and officials customarily keep daily records (*nikki*) of their activities. Happily, both Michinaga and Moromichi's journals, including their accounts of their Kinpusen pilgrimages, have been largely preserved. In addition, materials from their sutra burials happen to

27. For Kumano during the *insei,* see Moerman, *Localizing Paradise,* esp. 139–80.

have been excavated from the mountain. These include votive texts, as well as fragments of sutras that the regents copied out in golden ink on indigo-dyed paper. In Moromichi's case, we have most of a prayer that he wrote out on plain paper to bury with his sutras, whereas in Michinaga's, we have a votive inscription from the gilt bronze tube in which he buried his scriptures. We have no text written by Retired Emperor Shirakawa about Kinpusen, but during research at the Historiographical Institute at the University of Tokyo in 2005–7, I found manuscript copies of a fragment of a journal written during the 1092 pilgrimage by one of Shirakawa's retainers, most likely Ōe no Masafusa (1041–1111). In addition, the same journey is briefly described in the unofficial annal *Fusō ryakki* (Brief history of the East); a prayer written by Masafusa on Shirakawa's behalf also survives. These sources are central to the following discussion. In telling us how individual elite pilgrims represented their own actions, these texts make it possible to develop a tightly focused history of religious practice at one particular site.

This book falls into three parts. The three chapters of part 1 focus on Heian-period representations and cultural memory of Kinpusen, that is, the mountain imagined. In chapter 1, I chart out the mountain's spatial imaginary, which was rooted in a conceptual duality through which *ritsuryō* ideology defined the capital over and against the mountains. With the emergence of lay pilgrimage in the tenth century, members of the elite began to subvert this divide, appropriating the mountain's wild, otherworldly charisma and expanding the domain of the civilized center. In the second chapter, I introduce Kinpusen's pantheon, focusing on its king, Zaō. Resolutely local, Zaō and the other mountain gods embodied the combinatory quality of the entire mountain cult: they mixed the attributes of buddhas and *kami*, while simultaneously exemplifying ideals associated with Daoism. In this respect, Kinpusen stands as a vivid example of the twin processes of indigenization and Buddhicization that have marked the spread of Buddhism throughout Asia and around the world. Chapter 3 centers on the concept of ritual regimes as a theoretical model of the religious practices of Heian elites. In ritual regimes, the most eminent nobles and royals used integrated sets of sites, rites, and texts to strengthen their rule and display their righteousness. Ritual regimes were shaped by the twin dynamics of emulation and competition. Thus, when Kinpusen became the signature pilgrimage site for the Fujiwara regents during the eleventh century, the mountain took on great political significance. Conversely, this meant that it was bound to become a victim of political change during the *insei*, as the retired emperors sought to establish distinctive ritual regimes of their own.

Based on close readings of eleventh-century pilgrims' journals and votive texts, part 2 focuses on pilgrims' engagement with the real mountain and their contributions to Kinpusen as a real-and-imagined place. To date, very little information on what Heian-period pilgrims actually did has been available to Western-language readers; here, I reconstruct the protocol of the journey to Kinpusen, including the process of sutra burial. Chapter 4 maps out the ritualized itinerary followed by the regents Fujiwara no Michinaga and Moromichi. Chapter 5 takes up the segmented, complementary rites that they conducted at the summit. Whereas pilgrims undertook sutra burials to advance personal religious agendas, they paired these observances with conventional dedications of huge corpora of scriptures, which operated as rites of state protection.

In chapter 6, I tell the story of Retired Emperor Shirakawa's 1092 journey to Kinpusen, which paradoxically contributed to both Kinpusen's institutional growth and destabilization. On the one hand, Shirakawa laid the groundwork for direct patronage by building, staffing, and endowing a cloister in the Yoshinoyama area, which, unlike the summit of Kinpusen, was habitable year-round. On the other, his resolute promotion of mountain monks and his involvement in Kinpusen's administration provoked Kōfukuji's partisans, who were convinced that by rights it was they who ought to control Kinpusen's affairs. This chapter is based on the above-mentioned journal fragment, which provides the most detailed extant record of ritual protocols at the peak. Analysis of this source illuminates the details of the pilgrimage process as well as the complex frictions between Shirakawa, Kōfukuji, and Kinpusen.

Part 3 examines the religious culture of Kinpusen in the wake of the eleventh-century boom in elite pilgrimage. Chapter 7 chronicles the wars of 1093–94, which resulted in Kinpusen's defeat and subsequent integration into Kōfukuji's power bloc. This conflict profoundly affected the mountain's religious culture. Although Kinpusen monks violently resisted Kōfukuji's suzerainty until 1145, during the second half of the twelfth century the two institutions entered a phase of comparative amity, with a sizeable portion of Kinpusen's community adopting Kōfukuji's interests as their own. Around the same time, however, proponents of mountain practice also sought to resist assimilation through textual strategies. These are taken up in chapter 8, which analyzes texts produced during the twelfth and thirteenth centuries about Kinpusen and the broader Ōmine region. Known as *engi,* these materials combine origin narratives with litanies of deities and sites. They construct lineages, codify rituals, and define territory. Importantly, although *engi* about Ōmine testify to a concerted effort by partisans of the southern mountains to assert their own, distinctive religious identity in reaction to their newly subordinate institutional status, the texts themselves were clearly disseminated through networks dominated by power-bloc institutions. This juxtaposition points to the hybrid, multivocal quality of *engi* and their representations of the Ōmine region.

In the epilogue, I conclude that the ruptures of the twelfth century, followed by integration into the sphere of the post-Genpei Nara revival, created the matrix from which Shugendō groups emerged in the late Kamakura period. Most twentieth-century research on Shugendō was conducted in the field of folklore studies, wherein the existence of religious practitioners known as "those who lie down in the mountains" (*yamabushi*) has been loosely equated with the existence of Shugendō. Although literary and historical sources do show that *yamabushi* were common figures on the Heian-period religious scene, these men were not organized into discrete groups with their own hierarchies, doctrines, and sectarian consciousness. As historical research during the past two decades has shown, discourse in which Shugendō figured as an independent "Way" (*dō, michi*) came into use around the year 1300. Thus, although it is possible to trace out connections between Shugendō and Heian-period pilgrimage to Kinpusen, it is important to recognize that the two phenomena belong to two, very different historical contexts.

Before turning to the ways in which Heian-period men and women imagined Kinpusen, it is worth noting that their practices and mine are in some ways parallel. The four processes of walking, writing, reading, and remembering are at the core of this book. For Heian pilgrims, these came together in the deposit and discovery of traces. They have also been fundamental to the research and writing for this book, which is, after all, a trace that I have left, with both my writing hands and my walking feet.

PART I

The Mountain Imagined

CHAPTER ONE

Affective Landscape

> Kinpusen is the realm of the assembled immortals, the dwelling of the myriad sages. Passing over the floods and tides, it crossed to the East; mounting the clouds and rainbows, it ascended the heights. . . . As I give thanks for the dawn frost at good fortune's summit, how quickly auspicious omens appear! The divine response has already come.
>
> —Minamoto no Masazane (1059–1127), dedication for a bell; text attributed to Ōe no Masafusa[1]

One could describe Kinpusen as an upwarped mountain standing at 34° latitude and 136° longitude, with an elevation of 1,719 meters, but that would not satisfy a pilgrim or a devotee. For the past twelve centuries, men and women have been interacting with Kinpusen's physical terrain in ways that create an ever-emerging array of meanings for the mountain. In order to consider these processes of place-making, we need to examine what I call the affective landscape. Loosely speaking, affective landscape is analogous to the imagined dimension of spatiality, but in this chapter I wish to draw particular attention to its ties to pilgrims' devotional sensibilities. Shaped by cultural memory—both the "cool" information and "warm" dispositions communicated and reworked among generations of potential pilgrims—the affective landscape was (and is) capable of evoking, overlaying, and even occluding the physical terrain.[2] By engaging with and contributing to the affective landscape, Heian pilgrims

1. Dedicatory prayer dated Chōji 3, seventh month, *Honchō zoku monzui* 7 (*SZKT*, 29.2:117).
2. For the notion of cultural memory, see Assman, *Religion and Cultural Memory*.

construed the meanings of their journeys, before, during, and after travel.[3]

Consider the example of the successful courtier Minamoto no Masazane, who visited Kinpusen in the entourage of Retired Emperor Shirakawa in 1092 and then returned to the mountain on his own in 1106. In the hundred years preceding Masazane's journeys, pilgrimage to Kinpusen had become quite common among male aristocrats. Like his peers, Masazane planned his pilgrimage carefully, commissioning a noted literatus to write a prayer to be formally recited during offering rites at the peak. His 1106 prayer reads in part:

> From thought to thought, I am sincere. I have observed abstentions and precepts for one hundred days. Traveling on and on, I stride forward, single-mindedly accumulating a store of merit for this world and the next. And now I do not object to the mountain clouds; rather, I welcome the valley moon. The path climbs up to the sky, and from the consecrated boundaries, I enter into mystery. Above, I walk upon the rainbow; below, I hear the thunder. It is as if the mountainside were split and the temple put into the crevice. As though turning my feet sideways [to navigate a difficult path], I match my steps to the traces. I am gladdened: my vow is already fulfilled. I am touched: my old bones keep enduring.[4]

At first glance, this prayer might appear to describe Masazane's response to his journey, but it was really written in a subjunctive mood, as a prescription for the effort he would exert and the awe he should feel. At home in the capital, Masazane and his literary proxy took what they knew of Kinpusen and imagined how it would be to stand at the summit of the mountain. The prayer thus charted out Masazane's affective landscape at the same time that it narrated his hoped-for transformation from a courtier into a holy man. First he would engage in a

3. In much the same vein, Ian Reader refers to a pilgrimage route's "emotional terrain," which he defines as a combination of objects of worship, narratives about the pilgrimage route and destination(s), and "the material objects, signs and traces that pilgrims have left along the route to mark their presence and influence later pilgrims" (Reader, *Making Pilgrimages*, 39).

4. *Gōtotoku nagon ganmonshū* 3.5, inferred date of Kashō 1.7.18 (426). I have followed Yamasaki's emendations to the Rokujizōji manuscript here.

lengthy course of purifications in preparation for his pilgrimage. With this prerequisite fulfilled, he would be able to respond to the otherworldly landscape as if he belonged there, welcoming the moon-glow in what might otherwise seem a frightening wilderness. By following in the footsteps of previous pilgrims, Masazane imagined, he would be able to traverse the nearly impassible physical and conceptual distance between the city and the mountain. He anticipated that, like a Buddhist holy man, he would accumulate a great store of merit, and, like a Daoist immortal, be able to walk upon rainbows. The life of the text in which he expressed these hopes exceeded Masazane's own. Because the prayer had been composed by the respected literatus Ōe no Masafusa, it was subsequently preserved as a model of prose style. As a consequence of its status as a literary exemplum, it continued to shape notions of how members of the elite could and should imagine Kinpusen.

To reconstruct pilgrims' affective landscape in greater detail, in the following pages I turn to a broad range of source materials. For the most part, these are brief references or short anecdotes preserved in annals, law codes, stories, votive texts, and poetry. This type of survey is more methodological necessity than choice: traces of cultural memory about Kinpusen during the tenth and eleventh centuries are preserved only in bits and pieces. From the thirteenth century onward, members of the religious community at the mountain did generate historical and ritual compilations about Kinpusen, but those were produced within the context of later institutional developments. During the mid-Heian, it was nonspecialists who were writing about Kinpusen, and their point of view—which of course framed what they saw—was grounded in the city of Heian and the old "southern capital," Nara.[5] Being literate, these writers were socially privileged; some of them were monks or laywomen, but in most cases, they were laymen connected with the court.[6]

5. As the geographer J. Nicholas Entrikin notes, our understanding of place is always "perspectival" because as embodied creatures, we are always located: our perceptions originate from a particular place (Entrikin, *The Betweenness of Place*, 24).

6. Early literature, such as the *Nihon shoki, Man'yōshū,* and *Kaifūsō,* contains plentiful references to Yoshino, but not to Kinpusen. One possible exception is *Man'yōshū* 13.3293 (*SNKBT,* 3:266), which is often cited as the earliest direct reference to Kinpusen because it includes the phrase "Yoshino's Golden Peak" (*Miyoshino no mikane no*

The following discussion of Kinpusen's affective landscape and its relationship to pilgrimage practices during the Heian period begins by charting out a binary opposition between city and mountain that structured the spatial imaginary of the late-Nara and early-Heian *ritsuryō* legal codes. Moving forward into the tenth and eleventh centuries, which saw the emergence of the royal court state, the coalescence of the Fujiwara regency, and the beginnings of lay pilgrimage, this chapter then provides an analysis of stories about heroic mountain practitioners as exempla produced for, and in many cases by, Heian elites. Elite writers actively imagined Kinpusen as an alternative world from which pilgrims could gain wisdom and charisma. Importantly, they also defined the mountain by social stricture: by the mid-900s a systematic ban on women was in place at Kinpusen. The exclusion of women figured Kinpusen as categorically different in social terms, thereby maintaining the alterity of mountain space in the face of the growing presence of lay, male urbanites. This chapter closes with a consideration of how one elite pilgrim, Fujiwara no Moromichi, the heir apparent to the regency, engaged with Kinpusen's affective landscape. Well-established mnemonics clearly shaped Moromichi's expectations and experiences; at the same time, when he wrote about the mountain, he laid down traces in cultural memory for others to discover and follow.

Oppositions under the Ritsuryō

For members of court society, Kinpusen's affective landscape grew out of a more general spatial imaginary in which the city, which stood for civilization, order, and culture, figured opposite the mountains, which were associated with the wild, the dangerous, and the divine. Similarly, the courtier appeared as the antithesis of the mountain holy man. The

take). There is, however, a general consensus among folklorists that this poem actually refers to Aogane-ga-mine, a mountain that stands near the contemporary Kinpu Jinja at the northern end of the settlement in Yoshinoyama (Gorai and Inoue, *Yama no shūkyō*, 121; Miyake Hitoshi, *Ōmine shugendō no kenkyū*, 60–61).

opposition between mountain and capital was expressed in the criminal and civil law codes that structured society and politics from the late seventh through the ninth century. This theoretical duality was persistent, but it was also open to subversion, and eventually to mediation, by some of the most powerful members of society. The practice of lay pilgrimage began to develop during the 900s in the conceptual and social gap between the mountain and the city. By going to the mountains, courtiers temporarily put themselves out of place in a sociospatial transgression that contributed to the maintenance of their own political ascendancy by affording them an opportunity to appropriate the charisma and piety of holy men, as well as rights to mountain practice and mountain space. Inasmuch as pilgrimage to Kinpusen questioned and complicated the relationships of notional opposites, its social dynamics corresponded to the mountain's narrative theology and ritual customs. Kinpusen's was a distinctive cult that valorized Zaō, a local deity who, as discussed in chapter 2, was understood to be both a buddha and a *kami* (and sometimes a king and a dragon, as well). As a socially and conceptually in-between place where conventional binary categories opened up, Kinpusen provided a real-and-imagined site where alternative ways of being, acting, and thinking became possible.[7]

Under the *ritsuryō*, and indeed, as far back as the historical record goes, what we would now call multiple religious affiliations were the norm in Japan: men and women consistently mixed elements from Confucian, Daoist, and Buddhist traditions with *kami* worship and local practices. Religious culture was not, however, an undifferentiated blend, in part because categories served the ideological interests of the state. Conceptualizing Buddhism, *kami* worship, and expertise in the Way of Yin and Yang as three distinct domains, the *ritsuryō* government established separate administrative agencies to oversee them. Buddhist monks and nuns were subject to the monastic board of overseers known as the Office for Monastic Affairs (*sōgō*), as well as to the Bureau for Foreign and Buddhist Affairs (*genbaryō*). Meanwhile, the

7. In theoretical terms, the mountain can thus be construed in terms of what Homi Bhabha called third space; Edward Soja, Thirdspace; or Michel Foucault, heterotopic space (see note 7 in the introduction; and Foucault, "Of Other Spaces").

Council for Kami Affairs (*jingikan*) was charged with the creation and maintenance of a centralized network for *kami* worship, designed to extend the state cult across the realm and bring local practices under central influence. Through the Bureau of Yin and Yang (*onmyōryō*), the government sought to monopolize continental learning in the fields of astronomy, divination, prognostication, and time-keeping.[8]

In this context, mountains appeared as a problematic sphere precisely because they were difficult to regulate. Religious mountain practice tended to obviate the conceptual boundaries the state had so carefully erected, and geographic inaccessibility made oversight difficult. Furthermore, mountain practice was understood to generate supernatural powers, which could easily escape official control.

To illustrate the threat—and the attraction—of mountain practice under the *ritsuryō,* there is perhaps no better example than the narrative persona of E no Ozuno (n.d.), later known as En no Gyōja. Revered since the Kamakura and Muromachi (1336–1573) periods as the founder of Shugendō, in the *ritsuryō* imagination, E appeared as an outlaw. His story is a classic romance, and he continues to be known today as a mysterious, dangerous, and therefore fascinating character. The first record of his career appears in the *Shoku nihongi* (Continued chronicles of Japan), a court annal that was presented to the throne in 797, at the very beginning of the Heian period. Here, we learn that E no Ozuno lived in the Katsuragi Mountains at the end of the seventh century (see map 1). E, according to the text, was widely believed to compel demons and spirits to fetch his water and firewood, and to bind those who disobeyed him with mantras. His disciple, Karakuni no Hirotari (n.d.), brought charges against him, perhaps because the Code for Monks and Nuns (*sōniryō*) placed the use of mantras under legal control. Even

8. On *ritsuryō* oversight of Buddhism, see Abé, *The Weaving of Mantra*, 76–83; and Piggott, "Tōdaiji," 29–37. In the Japanese literature, the extent to which the *ritsuryō* order produced a real "state Buddhism" is subject to considerable debate; for instance, compare Inoue, *Nihon kodai no kokka to bukkyō,* to Yoshida, *Nihon kodai shakai to bukkyō*. On the Jingikan, see Mori, "Ancient and Classical Japan." On the Bureau of Yin and Yang, yin-yang masters and their technologies, see Yamashita, *Heian jidai no shūkyō bunka*; Ooms, *Imperial Politics and Symbolics,* 86–96; and Bock, *Classical Learning and Taoist Practices.*

though the *Shoku nihongi* referred to the allegations as slander (*zan*), implicitly exonerating E of nefarious intent, it also reported that he was convicted of treachery and exiled to Izu in eastern Japan. Clearly, in this court-centered narrative, E's expertise in spells and theurgy posed a serious threat to the state.[9]

As other storytellers embroidered upon this brief account, E gained an explicit association with Kinpusen, a more developed Buddhist and Daoist pedigree, and an ever-greater reputation, becoming a stock figure in short, semi-vernacular tales (*setsuwa*). A diverse style of literature with sources ranging from continental belles lettres to gossip, *setsuwa* circulated orally, but they also passed through the hands of literate (which is to say, elite) compilers and redactors on their way to the page.[10] The *Nihon ryōiki* (Accounts of the numinous and strange from Japan), compiled in the early 800s by a Nara monk named Keikai (alt. Kyōkai, n.d.), is the earliest extant collection of *setsuwa* and exemplifies the didactic qualities of the genre. It slightly postdates the *Shoku nihongi* and casts E as a semi-lay Buddhist practitioner (*ubasoku*), who

> lived by putting his faith in the three jewels [=the Buddha, the Dharma, and the *sangha*]. He wished to ride upon five-colored clouds, to fly beyond the heavens, to join hands with guests in the immortals' palace, to sport in the million-year park, to lie in flower gardens, and to suck upon life-nourishing *qi*. Therefore, when he was some forty years old, he went to live in a cavern, dressed himself in vines, and ate pine needles; he bathed in pure-water springs, purified himself from the filth of the world of desire, practiced the rite of the Peacock Mantra, and attained strange powers. He achieved mastery and had demons and spirits at his beck and call. He summoned a number of demons and spirits and bade them, "Build a bridge, that I may go from the Peak of Gold (*Kane no mitake*) in Yamato Province to the Peak of Katsuragi (*Katsuragi no mitake*)."

9. *Shoku nihongi,* Monmu 3.5.24 (*SZKT,* 2:4).

10. For analyses of *setsuwa* literature, see Michelle Li, *Ambiguous Bodies*; and Eubanks, *Miracles of Book and Body.* For well-known Heian collections, see Dykstra, *Miraculous Tales*; Kamens, *The Three Jewels*; Kyoko Nakamura, *Miraculous Stories*; and Ury, *Tales of Times Now Past.*

As the story continues, readers learn that Hitokotonushi, the tutelary *kami* of the Katsuragi area, resented E's dominion and slandered him in an oracle delivered to the court. Acting upon Hitokotonushi's accusations, the court sent men to arrest E. When he eluded them, they seized his mother instead, whereupon E promptly gave himself up. Thereafter, he dutifully spent his days in exile in Izu, though at night he climbed Mt. Fuji to engage in religious practices. When his exile ended, he flew up to the heavens, only to be rediscovered years later in Silla by Dōshō (629–700), a monk who did, in fact, travel to the continent.[11]

This story's longevity and many adaptations testify to its popularity: variants are preserved in sources dating from the Heian period to the present day. In fact, entire books have been written about E no Ozuno, his apotheosis as En no Gyōja, and his narrative career.[12] For the present, several elements in E's story are of interest: the political ramifications of his activities, their hybrid and esoteric character, and their location.

First, there is the matter of plain legality. E was understood to be Buddhist, but he was in clear violation of the government's Code for Monks and Nuns on several points. The law expressly forbade private ordination and made it clear that ordained Buddhists were to study sutras, ritualize on behalf of the state, and live quiet, disciplined lives within the walls of officially recognized temples.[13] Though many *ubasoku* were in fact Buddhist monastics-in-training who sought official ordination, others, like E, appear to have pursued quasi-monastic life-

11. *Nihon ryōiki* 1.28 (*SNKBT,* 30:41–43, 220–21; for an alternative translation, see Kyoko Nakamura, *Miraculous Stories,* 140–42).

12. Other Heian-period versions of E's (or En's) biography can be found in *Sanbōe* 2.2 (*SNKBT,* 31:89–92; translation in Kamens, *The Three Jewels,* 191–96); *Honchō shinsenden* (*NST,* 7:258–59, 581; translation in Kleine and Kohn, "Daoist Immortality," 148–52); *Fusō ryakki,* Monmu 3.5.24 and Monmu 5, first month (*SZKT,* 12:69–72); and *Konjaku monogatarishū* 11.3 (*SNKBT,* 35:16–18). For books on En, see Keenan, "En no Gyōja"; Miyake Hitoshi, *En no gyōja to shugendō*; and Zenitani, *En no gyōja denki.*

13. On private ordination see *Sōniryō,* article 22 (*NST,* 3:222–23). Note that the earliest extant version of the *Sōniryō* comes from the *Ryō no gige,* an early Heian commentary on the 718 Yōrō Code. For the relationship between this recension and the earlier Taihō code, see Futaba, *Kodai bukkyō shisōshi kenkyū,* esp. 167–76.

styles outside state-recognized institutions.[14] E's ordination status was not the only problem. When the *Shoku nihongi* reported that he was accused of trickery (*yōwaku*), the implication was that he was flouting the Code's prohibition on prognostication, which, the court worried, might be used to beguile laypeople or to form close relationships with them.[15] E also used mantras, which were also known as "spells" (*ju,* alternatively pronounced *majinai*); the Code restricted use of this oral technology to curative rites.[16] Furthermore, E lived in the mountains, which, as article 13 of the Code for Monks and Nuns shows, was another serious issue:

> Monks and nuns are to engage in meditation and to practice the Buddhist path. Their hearts delight in tranquility and they do not interact with laypeople. If they wish to take up residence in the mountains and engage in special dietary practices, then their temple administrators (*sangō*) must sign their request. If the petitioner is in the capital, the Office of Monastic Affairs will pass the application to the Bureau for Foreign and Buddhist Affairs. If he or she is outside the capital, the temple administrators will pass it to the provincial and district offices. The authorities will verify and record it, and submit it to the Council of State. Following [receipt of] official permission, the provincial and district officials with jurisdiction over the mountain residences must always know where the monastics are in the mountains. Monks and nuns are not permitted to move to other sites.[17]

Clearly, E was not playing the government's game. He was not a proper monk, he was not engaging in proper practice, he was not in his proper place, and he had not followed proper protocol. He was also not alone. If Buddhists had not already been heading to the mountains in

14. On the administrative procedures through which *ubasoku* could and did apply for permission to be officially ordained, see Satō Fumiko, "Ubasoku kōshin no jitsuzō."

15. *Sōniryō,* articles 1 and 2; see also articles 5, 13, and 22 (*NST,* 3:216–22). See also Bialock, *Eccentric Spaces,* 92–95; and Ooms, *Imperial Politics and Symbolics,* 147–51.

16. *Sōniryō,* article 2 (*NST,* 3:216).

17. *Sōniryō,* article 13 (*NST,* 3:219; for an alternative translation, see Piggott, "Tōdaiji," 269–70).

the seventh and eighth centuries when the *ritsuryō* codes were composed, the government would have felt no need to legislate in this way. Just as clearly, by the ninth century Kinpusen had come to epitomize potentially problematic mountain sites in collective imagination and the legal record. The authors of the *Ryō no gige* (Explanation of the code), an 833 commentary on the Yōrō Code, cited Kinpusen in article 13 as the paradigmatic example of mountains where monks and nuns might go into extralegal or illegal retreat.[18]

Second, there is the matter of moral and categorical turbidity. E's dark side was never exorcised from cultural memory, and his allegiances remained decidedly opaque. His use of mantras (or spells) was illegal and potentially seditious: because such techniques generated power without predetermined ends, they could be directed against the state. Furthermore, his religious practices retained pronounced hybrid and esoteric qualities. Even the overtly Buddhist *Nihon ryōiki* tempered E's Buddhist characteristics (his faith in the three jewels and practice of the Peacock Mantra) with Daoist-style longevity practices. Like Chinese immortals described in Daoist classics such as the *Zhuangzi* and *Baopuzi* (The master who embraces simplicity), E wore and ate wild plants, subsisted upon wind and dew, commanded demons and spirits (J. *kijin*; C. *gui shen*), and took to the skies in flight.[19] E's ritual practice was believed to be tremendously effective, but it also bucked official prescriptions and defied official control. Later in the Heian period, the type of combinatory religious profile exemplified by E became a key part of the personae of Ōmine's mountain men.

18. *Ryō no gige*, commentary on article 13 (*SZKT*, 22:85). Note, too, that from an official vantage, E's subjugation of Hitokotonushi may have appeared as lèse majesté because this god was understood to have become a protector of the royal house during the reign of Emperor Yūryaku in the 400s (see *Kojiki* 3, Yūryaku tennō [*SNKBZ*, 1:346–49]; *Nihon shoki*, Yūryaku 4, second month [*SNKBZ*, 3:158–60]).

19. Bialock reads E's activities in precisely this light, attempting to recover a "Daoist" (sub)text from the narrative (*Eccentric Spaces*, 92–95). In the *Zhuangzi*, Jie Yu is said to have encountered an immortal from Mt. Guye who sucked upon the wind, rode upon clouds and mist, and wandered beyond the four seas. *Zhuangzi* 1, lines 28–29. On demons and spirits in the *Baopuzi*, see note 61.

Finally, there is the question of the landscape that E inhabited. The narrative record always associated E with mountains, with the Katsuragi Range and Kinpusen being his most consistent haunts. Despite reduced visibility from air pollution in the present day, when the weather is clear one can see Kinpusen from the peak of Mt. Katsuragi and vice versa. Similarly, the distance between them can be traversed on foot in two to three days. In human scale, then, these two mountains belong to the same territory and view shed. Historically, their proximity to the Nara- and Heian-period capitals made them a useful source of alterity, such that Katsuragi and Kinpusen became a convenient, wild other for civilized, metropolitan subjects.

Toward the Mountains and Lay Pilgrimage

In 794, the city of Heian, which later became Kyoto, was established according to *ritsuryō* norms as the antithesis of Kinpusen or any other mountain. A civilizing order was expressed in the very design of the city, which imposed a Chinese-style grid of streets onto low-lying, often marshy terrain between the Kamo and Katsura Rivers.[20] Nonetheless, the new city depended upon mountains for fuel, water, and building materials, making deforestation a serious concern.[21] Mountains also provided orientation and geomantic protection. The capital's main axis ran due south from Funaoka, a steep hill located just north of the city limits. Mt. Atago loomed to the northwest, and Enryakuji, a Buddhist complex at Mt. Hiei, fended off evil influences from the directional "demon gate" to the northeast (see map 1). Great hills marched along the city's limits in the east and west, such that Heian was enclosed by mountains in every direction but the south.

20. On changing the capital and the establishment of the city of Heian, see Toby, "Why Leave Nara?" On the city of Heian, see William McCullough, "The Capital and Its Society"; and the indices to McCullough and McCullough, *A Tale of Flowering Fortunes*. Useful illustrated reference works include Kodaigaku Kyōkai, *Heiankyō teiyō*, and Kyōtoshi, *Yomigaeru Heiankyō*.

21. Totman, *The Green Archipelago*, 13–20, 28–33.

This direction drew the gaze of the ruling elite. In East Asia, the verbal phrase "to face south" meant to reign as king: sovereigns occupied the symbolic north. The royal gaze thus tended south, toward the flat, settled lands of the Nara Basin, the cradle of the *ritsuryō* conceptual order and the old Heijō and Fujiwara capitals. Even farther south lay Yoshino, literally the "good land." Though the area along the Yoshino River had long been settled, members of the court knew it as a fishing and hunting ground. During the late seventh and early eighth centuries, it was a favored destination for royal progresses (see chapter 3). Divided from the Nara Basin by the low Ryūmon Mountains, the Yoshino River drainage thus formed a cultural borderland, beyond which a tangle of much higher peaks rose. These southern mountains included Kinpusen, Mt. Kōya, and Kumano.

The Yoshino area exemplifies the combinatory qualities of the montane religious imaginary in ways that show that even under the *ritsuryō,* mountains (and the powers they conferred) were objects of desire as well as anxiety. Geographical conceptions of the area known as "Yoshino" varied historically, but for the purposes of the present discussion, I use the toponym to refer to the southern slopes of the Ryūmon Mountains, which overlook the Yoshino River, as well as the northern side of the river valley directly opposite. I use the term "Yoshinoyama" to refer to the settled area stretching southward along the ridge between the contemporary Yoshinoyama cable-car station and the present location of the Kinpu Shrine (see map 1).

Long before the Heian period, ostensively Daoist personae and practices figured prominently in representations of Yoshino. Michael Como has argued that the Yoshino River drainage and its surrounds were home to several lineages with close ties to the continent, and that as a result Sino-Korean medicinal technologies and ritual practices, many of which had loose connections with Daoism, were adopted and adapted in the area early on.[22] By surveying shrines and rivers with names referring to cinnabar and by analyzing local mineral levels, Matsuda Hisao has shown that, like the Uda district further east and Mt. Kōya to the west, the Yoshinoyama area is comparatively rich in mercury, a key component in alchemical longevity

22. Como, *Weaving and Binding,* 55–83.

elixirs.[23] Although botanical or alchemical practices in Yoshino remain ill-documented and subject to speculation, as early as the seventh century, Japanese literati were imagining the greater Yoshino area as a habitat for Daoist immortals.[24] For instance, Prince Kadono (669–705) composed the following poem, which, according to the headnote in the *Kaifūsō* (Fond recollections of poetry) was set in the Ryūmon Mountains:

I call my palanquin, sport by mountains and waters,
Forever forget all thought of court caps.
How can I attain the Way of Wang Qiao,
Harness a crane, go to Penglai? Yingzhou?[25]

Within the world of the poem, the courtier leaves behind rank and office, instead opting to follow in the footsteps of the immortal Wang Qiao, who was said to have ridden off upon a white crane after learning the Dao at Mt. Song. As the locus of composition, the Ryūmon Mountains thus became the point of departure for a journey to the famous immortal isles of Penglai and Yingzhou. Here the Yoshino drainage opened, at least in imagination, onto classic, fantastic Daoist utopias.

Yoshino was imagined not only as a realm of immortals but also a Buddhist heartland. Judging by accounts in the *Nihon ryōiki,* there were a number of small temples and buddha halls in the area, but the best known is Hisodera, which is situated on the southern slope of the Ryūmon Mountains, overlooking the Yoshino River.[26] This temple has also been known as Hisosanji, Yoshinodera, and Genkōji; today it is called Sezonji. As shown by Sonoda Kōyū, during the 700s it enjoyed a reputation as a mountain retreat for well-respected monks who supported and were

23. Matsuda, *Niu no kenkyū,* 69–173, esp. 153–66. On cinnabar and Daoist valences in religious culture at Kinpusen and Yoshino, as well as possible ties to Mt. Wutai, see Hakamada, "'Kinpusen jōdo' keisei." In English, see also Hino, "The Daoist Facet of Kinpusen," though note that there is no direct material or textual evidence that Kinpusen was ever an active center for mining.

24. Wada Atsumu, *Kodai Nihon no girei,* 221–52.

25. *Kaifūsō* 11 (*NKBT,* 69:83–84).

26. For Hisodera's history, see Tsuji Hidenori, *Narachō sangaku jiin,* 7–39; and Horiike, *Nanto bukkyōshi no kenkyū,* 2:527–44.

supported by state-recognized temples.[27] Both Daoxuan (J. Dōsen, 702–760), a Chinese *vinaya* master who took up residence at Daianji when he emigrated to Japan, and Shin'ei (d. 737), a respected (and possibly Chinese) scholiast who resided at Gangōji, integrated stints of practice at Hisodera into urban, even cosmopolitan, careers.[28] According to the *Shoku nihon kōki* (Latter continued chronicles of Japan), Gomyō (750–834), an eminent monk who trained at Gangōji, performed austerities in the "Yoshino Mountains" prior to his ordination. Later in his career, he is said to have spent the first half of the month "deep in the mountains" and the latter half at Gangōji, where he engaged in doctrinal studies. Today Gomyō is known primarily as an expert in Hossō doctrine, but in the mountains, he practiced the esoteric *Kokūzō gumonjihō,* a rite in which the practitioner contemplates the bodhisattva Ākāśagarbha (J. Kokūzō) in order to gain faultless memory.[29]

Links between mountain sites and urban monasteries, between Chinese and Japanese monks, and between notionally exoteric and esoteric practices carried over into the Heian period. Noting that the number of mountain temples increased dramatically from the late Nara period onward, Tsuji Hidenori has linked the establishment of "Heian Buddhism" to the migration of mountain practice (*sanrin shugyō*) from the "back" to the "front" of religious culture.[30] Kūkai (774–835) and Saichō (767–822), revered as the respective founders of the Shingon and Tendai traditions, spent years in the mountains early in their careers. By his own account, Kūkai, like Gomyō, practiced the *Kokūzō gumonjihō* in wilderness settings.[31] Both he and Saichō traveled to China, received official recognition for their teachings upon their re-

27. Sonoda, "Kodai bukkyō sanrin shugyō," and Tsuji Hidenori, *Narachō sangaku jiin,* 7–39.

28. For Daoxuan at Hisodera, see Saichō's *Naishō buppō soshō kechimyakufu,* which cites a biography probably composed around the time of Daoxuan's death and attributed to Kibi no Makibi (695–775) (*Dengyō Daishi zenshū,* 1:211–12; see Groner, *Saichō,* 251–55, for a review of textual criticism on this source). For Shin'ei, see *Fusō ryakki,* Tenpyō 2.10.17 (*SZKT,* 12:90), which cites the *Enryaku sōroku* (now dispersed) and refers to Shin'ei as a Chinese monk. In this text, Hisodera is referred to as Genkōji.

29. For Gomyō's biography, see *Shoku nihon kōki,* Shōwa 1.9.11 (*SZKT,* 3:29–30); and Sonoda, "Kodai bukkyō sanrin shugyō," 30–31.

30. Tsuji Hidenori, *Narachō sangaku jiin,* 449.

31. *Sangō shiiki,* preface (*NKBT,* 71:84–85); Hare, "Reading, Writing, and Cooking."

turn, and fostered the growth of mountain monasteries that eventually became powerful religious conglomerates.[32] As mountain practices gained credence, the reputation of E no Ozuno, the mountain practitioner par excellence, changed as well. In his 984 collection *Sanbōe* (Pictures of the three jewels), the courtier Minamoto no Tamenori (d. 1011) positioned E as one of Japan's Buddhist founders by placing his biography between those of the culture heroes Shōtoku Taishi (574?–622?) and Gyōgi (668–749).[33] None of these men conformed to *ritsuryō* ideals of "proper" Buddhist practice: Shōtoku was a layman, and E an *ubasoku,* while Gyōgi was famous for his interactions with the laity. The norms for monastic practice and religious identity were clearly being reset.[34]

As part of this process, the government began to put the mountains—and mountain practitioners—to work in rites of state protection. The Council for Kami Affairs developed lengthy rosters of regional shrines, asserting rhetorical control of local gods by conferring court rank upon them.[35] By the mid-ninth century, the government was assiduously propitiating mountain *kami,* including those of the Yoshino area, during regularly scheduled rites, as well as in special observances held at times of agricultural stress. Notably, these occasions blended *kami* worship with Daoist-inflected practices; for instance, in 859 and 863, the court dispatched yin-yang masters to conduct rites at

32. For Kūkai and Saichō's careers, see Abé, *The Weaving of Mantra*; and Groner, *Saichō.*

33. *Sanbōe* 2.1 (*SNKBT,* 31:89–92; translation in Kamens, *The Three Jewels,* 191–96).

34. For examples of holy men whom the Heian-period *setsuwa* literature portrays as being active at Kinpusen and Ōmine, see *Nihon ryōiki* 3.6 (*SNKBT,* 30:137–38, 266; translation in Kyoko Nakamura, *Miraculous Stories,* 230–31); *Sanbōe* 2.16 (*SNKBT,* 31:120–22; translation in Kamens, *The Three Jewels,* 230–31); *Hokke genki* 1.10, 1.11, 2.44, 2.49, 2.60, 3.92, 3.93 (*NST,* 7:65–69, 107–9, 116–117, 128–29, 172–75, 518–20, 532–33, 535, 539, 554; translation in Dykstra, *Miraculous Tales,* 39–42, 70–71, 76–77, 114–16); *Honchō shinsenden,* biographies of En no Ubasoku, Yōshō, a monk from Ōmine, an immortal from Ōmine, and Nichizō (*NST,* 7:258–59, 265–66, 270–71, 274–75; 581, 583–85; translation in Kleine and Kohn, "Daoist Immortality," 148–52, 166–68, 174–75, 181–82); *Konjaku monogatarishū* 12.27, 12.40, 13.1, 13.3 13.21, 13.28, 14.43 (*SNKBT,* 35:150–52, 192–93, 198–201, 204–7, 237–39, 246–47, 363–65).

35. An early-tenth-century recension of these lists is preserved in *Engi shiki* 9 and 10 (*SZKT,* 26:179–320; see 190–91 for shrines in Yoshino district).

"the high mountains of Yoshino" in order to prevent insect damage to crops.[36] By the late 900s, the government had designated a set of seven "high mountains," including Kinpusen, as locations for Buddhist repentance rites to be carried out every fall and spring.[37] All seven of these mountains were located within the home provinces of the Kinai, but Kinpusen was much the farthest from the capital. Thus, the Peak of Gold came to represent the far reach of a new, increasingly civilized mountainscape.

At the same time that the court sent offerings and ritualists out to the mountains, it also drew mountain practitioners into its service. For example, according to the *Fusō ryakki,* the monk Jōsū (866–944) asked the court for permission to return to Kinpusen after seventeen years in service to the throne. Jōsū explained that in 899 he had left a promising career at Tōji, an important temple in the capital, and "gone into seclusion in the area around Kinpusen." In 927, however, he was summoned to court, where he was appointed protector monk (*gojisō*) to Emperor Daigo (885–930, r. 897–930).[38] By Jōsū's day it had, in fact, become so common for mountain practitioners to enter court service that the *Shingishiki* (New ceremonial), a collection of ritual rules compiled at the end of the reign of Emperor Murakami (926–67, r. 946–67), made a categorical pronouncement that mountain practice qualified a monk to serve as a palace chaplain (*naigubu zenji*).[39] Meanwhile, mountain monks were providing ritual services to aristocratic households, in some cases establishing multigenerational relationships with their patrons.[40] For laypeople to go to the mountains themselves, however, was another matter. Mountain pilgrimage, and indeed, pilgrimage more generally, only began to enter the religious repertoires of the lay

36. *Nihon sandai jitsuroku,* Jōgan 1.8.3, Jōgan 5.second month (*SZKT,* 4:36, 105).

37. *Kuchizusami* (*ZGR,* 32.1:64). The other six "high mountains" were Mts. Hiei, Hira, Atago, Ibuki, Kabu, and Katsuragi. The Muromachi-period Buddhist compendium *Shakke kanpanki* repeats the same set of mountains and asserts quite plausibly that the court had supported esoteric masters (*ajari*) at these sites, charging them with the performance of penance rites on behalf of the state (*Shakke kanpanki* 1, "Ajari" entry [*GR,* 15:46–47]).

38. *Fusō ryakki,* Tengyō 6.7.5 (*SZKT,* 12:223).

39. *Shingishiki* 5 (*GR,* 5:69).

40. See, for instance, Groner, *Ryōgen,* 71–93.

elite in the context of changes to political organization and shifts in sovereignty.

Some structures established under the *ritsuryō*, most notably the Council of State, continued to play a role in governance throughout the Heian period, and the emperor certainly remained the ultimate source of political authority. From the mid-ninth century onward, however, trends toward shared rulership became increasingly pronounced. It became more and more routine for men from the Fujiwara family to serve as regents to the emperors beginning in the mid-800s. Being senior aristocrats, regents were members of the Council of State, but they also enjoyed the right to review palace documents (*nairan*). Accordingly, they were able to exert significant control over policy and executive governance. They were not, however, forces unto themselves: they had to work with, and sometimes around, members of their own family, the royals, and other nobles high and low. Under the early regents, especially Fujiwara no Tadahira (880–949), a new political order emerged. This is known among Japanese scholars as the royal court state. In a series of reforms, the court arranged for associated groups—provincial governors and military houses—to carry out taxation, local administration, and military operations on what was essentially a contract basis.[41] The result was a smaller political center, complemented by an extended network of interdependent stakeholders. Meanwhile, the office of regent became the hereditary prerogative of one patriline within the Fujiwara family's Northern House. The regents themselves grew to be more independent of the Council of State, at times growing so powerful that both Heian writers and contemporary historians have likened them to kings in their own right.[42]

41. See note 10 in the introduction, as well as essays by Piggott and Hurst in Adolpson, Kamens, and Matsumoto, *Heian Japan,* 35–101. On the military, see Friday, *Hired Swords,* 70–166; and Farris, *Heavenly Warriors,* 120–251.

42. For the regents' increased independence from the Council of State, see Yoshikawa, *Ritsuryō kanryōsei no kenkyū,* 401–26. For Michinaga's sovereignty (*ōken*) and its relation to ritual, see Uejima, *Nihon chūsei shakai,* 147–89. For a Heian-period comparison of Michinaga to a Buddhist wheel-turning king, see *Ōkagami,* "Michinaga" (*SNKBZ,* 34:314–15); translation from Helen McCullough, *Ōkagami,* 191. This passage is discussed in chapter 3 of this book.

The regents were instrumental in furthering liturgical changes that went hand in hand with their growing political influence. In a shift that had roots extending back to the Nara period, state-supported *kami* worship had come to focus on a system of what Okada Shōji has called "public festivals," in which the court sent envoys to convey royal prayers and offerings to important shrines on scheduled festival days. From this mode of practice emerged a growing set of institutions eventually known as the Twenty-Two Shrines, which served as liturgical centers for state protection. All of these shrines were located in the home provinces; because most had ties to the royal family or leading noble lineages, they were also socially close to the political center.[43] Fujiwara no Kaneie (929–90), whose direct descendants held the office of regent throughout the eleventh century, played an instrumental role in shaping *kami* worship in such a way as to amplify his family's consequence. By Kaneie's day, both regents and reigning emperors were making progresses to the Kamo Shrine, where a princess of the blood served as priestess.[44] In addition to visiting Kamo himself, Kaneie arranged for the reigning emperor to make a much longer progress to Kasuga, the Fujiwara family's ancestral shrine in Nara, thereby inaugurating a new tradition emphasizing imperial ties to the regents. Furthermore, he oversaw the integration of several other shrines with close ties to the regents' house into the emergent set of twenty-two shrines.[45]

Although they did not have direct ties to state ceremonial, multiday pilgrimages to temples gained currency around the same time and among the same social groups. The habits of one of Kaneie's wives, known to posterity as Michitsuna's Mother (d. 995), are illustrative of changes in pilgrimage practices and their potential for combining personal devotion with public display. Though she commented that her

43. Okada, *Heian jidai no kokka,* esp. 51–166, 217–47, 325–61; Grapard, "Institution, Ritual, and Ideology."

44. For pilgrimage as an outgrowth of notionally private offerings sent to the ever-increasing set of official shrines, see Mitsuhashi, *Heian jidai no shinkō,* 47–143.

45. Uejima, *Nihon chūsei shakai,* 149–50; see also Ruppert, "Royal Progresses to Shrines," 190.

own mother had only ever gone as far as Kiyomizudera, which was located just across the Kamo River from the capital, Michitsuna's Mother traveled to Ishiyamadera and Hasedera.[46] Kaneie's most eminent children, the dowager empress (*kōtaigō*) Senshi (alt. Akiko, Higashi Sanjōin, 962–1001) and the regent Michinaga, became enthusiastic pilgrims as well, and sometimes traveled together. They visited Ishiyamadera and the Iwashimizu Hachiman Shrine near the capital, as well as Shitennōji and Hasedera farther afield.[47]

Although the regents did not originate the custom of pilgrimage to Kinpusen, they certainly popularized it among laymen. Retired Emperor Uda (867–931, r. 887–97), who took Buddhist orders after abdicating the throne, is said to have gone to the mountain in 900 and 905. Uda's pilgrimages are reported in the generally reliable *Nihon kiryaku* (Abbreviated records of Japan); however, the entries simply note his departures.[48] It was Kaneie who, in 969, made the earliest lay pilgrimage to Kinpusen on record. This clearly set a compelling precedent, for other male members of the elite began to travel to Kinpusen in growing numbers.[49] For instance, Fujiwara no Sanesuke (957–1046), a prominent courtier and dedicated diarist, noted pilgrimages made by a number of his contemporaries, including Fujiwara no Fuminobu (n.d.), governor of Owari Province, and Tachibana no Takachika (n.d.), a secretary to the Council of State.[50] These

46. Shinjō Tsunezō, *Shaji sankei*, 9.

47. For Senshi and Michinaga's joint pilgrimage to Shitennōji and the Iwashimizu and Sumiyoshi shrines in 1000, see *Midō kanpakuki*, Chōhō 2.3.20–25 (1:54); and *Nihon kiryaku*, Chōhō 2.3.26 (*SZKT*, 11:194). For Senshi at Hasedera, see *Nihon kiryaku*, Shōryaku 2.10.15 (*SZKT*, 11:172); and *Eiga monogatari* 4, "Mihatenu yume" (*SNKBZ*, 31:196; translation in McCullough and McCullough, *A Tale of Flowering Fortunes*, 1:165). For Michinaga at the same temple, see *Shōyūki*, Chōtoku 3.9.20 and Manju 1.11.16 (2:41 and 7:59). For several of Senshi's multiple pilgrimages to Ishiyamadera, see *Nihon kiryaku*, Shōryaku 3.2.29, Chōtoku 1.2.28, Chōtoku 3.8.8 (*SZKT*, 11:172, 181, 188); and *Ishiyamadera engi*, scroll 3, *dan* 1 and 2 (*NE*, 16:26–37, 121–22).

48. *Nihon kiryaku*, Shōtai 3, tenth month and Engi 5, ninth month (*SZKT*, 11:6, 10). Note that the first entry has Uda going to "the southern mountains"; in later sources, this is explicitly identified as a pilgrimage to Kinpusen.

49. *Kagerō nikki* 2.77 (*SNKBT*, 24:104; translations in Seidensticker, *The Gossamer Years*, 77; and Arntzen, *The Kagerō Diary*, 183–85).

50. *Shōyūki*, Eiso 1.4.4–5, Chōgen 4.8.1, 8.20 (1:172; 9:15, 26).

notices indicate that men from all ranks of court society were going to Kinpusen. Furthermore, as discussed in chapters 3 through 5, between 969 and 1090 the regents observed an intergenerational custom according to which nearly every regent traveled to Kinpusen either before or during his time in office.

Annals and diaries tell us frustratingly little about what early pilgrims to Kinpusen did at the mountain, why they went, or what they prayed for. For instance, when Sanesuke spent three nights praying to the gods of Kinpusen in 989, he commented only that his prayers centered on a "personal matter" (*shinjō no koto*).[51] In order to gain some sense of how these men and their contemporaries imagined Kinpusen, it is useful to examine the narrative record, where references to Kinpusen became more frequent as more and more laymen traveled to the mountain. Some anecdotes valorized Zaō, Kinpusen's primary deity, whose category-crossing reputation will be discussed in the next chapter. Many others chronicled the exploits of miracle workers who were simultaneously immortals and Buddhists and who lived charmed lives apparently untouched by the strictures of natural law or *ritsuryō* morality. These were the heroes of Ōmine, the men who gave the peaks their glamour. As exemplars and foils, they shaped the affective landscape for elite laymen at a time when old courtly anxieties were giving way to a more optimistic desire to participate in mountain practice on a personal, physical level.

Mountain Heroes

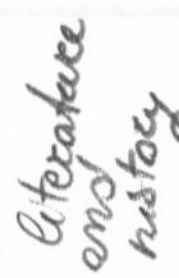

Depictions of Kinpusen in *setsuwa* were inflected by rumor and fancy, but they also derived from and contributed to firsthand experience. Importantly, although *setsuwa* tend to focus on the activities of monks and immortals, aristocratic pilgrims to Kinpusen took a hand in collecting and redacting these stories. For instance, Ōe no Masafusa, who traveled to Kinpusen in 1092, is reputed to have compiled the biographical collection *Honchō shinsenden* (Biographies of immortals in our

51. *Shōyūki*, Eiso 1.2.11–13 (1:161).

country), which includes profiles of several religious practitioners from the Yoshino-Kinpusen area. Masafusa also circulated other stories about the mountain and wrote prayers for fellow pilgrims, including the one for Minamoto no Masazane quoted at the beginning of this chapter.[52] Broadly speaking, then, elite pilgrims were both receivers and transmitters of mountain lore. In telling tales about the wonders of the southern mountains, they were building up their own traditions and articulating their own fantasies.

The most prominent class of practitioners in Heian stories of Ōmine were specialists in the *Lotus Sūtra* (*jikyōsha*).[53] These men were often portrayed as having special powers, as one of the earliest such anecdotes shows. This story from the *Nihon ryōiki* tells of a monk who lived in Yoshino at Amabenomine, a mountain likely located near the contemporary settlement at Yoshinoyama (see map 1). Though he was quite virtuous, this monk had such a strong craving for fish that he sent his disciple to buy some. As the lad was returning home, suspicious bystanders smelled the contraband and forced him to open his bag. Lo and behold, there were only sutra scrolls in the youth's satchel: the fish had turned into the *Lotus Sūtra* in order to protect the master's reputation. As the tale's redactor, Keikai, opined: "We are given to understand that he saved himself with the Dharma. Regarding food, though one may eat poison, it shall turn to sweet dew; although he ate fish, he committed no wrong. The fish transformed into sutras: Heaven was moved and adjusted the Way. This was a strange event."[54] Strange it might have been, but it also instructed readers in the benefits of religious practice in the mountains. Men like E no Ozuno and the nameless *Lotus* devotee might commit transgressions, but they would not, even could not, be punished.

As both audience members and storytellers, pilgrims had a recursive, dialogic relationship with this kind of narrative. The story of the fish-craving holy man of Amabenomine had a long afterlife: variants

52. For the textual history of *Honchō shinsenden* and its authorship, see Sugawara, *Nihon shisō to shinbutsu shūgō*, 129–47.

53. On *jikyōsha* as a distinct class of religious practitioner, see Kikuchi, *Chūsei bukkyō no genkei*.

54. *Nihon ryōiki* 3.6 (*SNKBT*, 30:137–38, 266; for an alternative translation, see Kyoko Nakamura, *Miraculous Stories*, 230–31).

and similar tales became stock material, shaping the ways in which the southern mountains were imagined and remembered in the narrative record.[55] With its setting, this story in particular fed notions that the *Lotus Sūtra* (and scriptures more generally) could work miracles and that men who practiced in the Ōmine Range were extraordinary. Other narratives suggested that mountain men enjoyed such great blessings that they could even obviate the inevitability of old age and death.

This conviction played out dramatically in the story of Yōshō (869–901?), a well-known Buddhist monk turned immortal. Yōshō's story is preserved in multiple variants, the earliest of which appears in the *Hokke genki* (Records of miracles of the *Lotus Sūtra*), a collection of *setsuwa* redacted by a Tendai monk named Chingen (n.d.) in the first half of the 1040s.[56] The variants agree that Yōshō began his religious career as a *Lotus* specialist at Mt. Hiei, but later decided to move to an old immortals' dwelling at Kinpusen. He studied longevity techniques in Yoshino, gradually altering his diet until he could subsist upon nothing but a single chestnut a day. A twelfth-century account from the *Konjaku monogatarishū* (Collection of tales of times now past) had an ascetic from Yoshino comment: "Yōshō became an immortal. He had neither blood nor flesh; he had distinctive bones and marvelous hair. Two wings grew from his body, and he flew through the air like a *kirin* (C. *qilin*) or a phoenix."[57] Yōshō dramatically embodied two concerns for lay pilgrims. First, his career illustrated the power of the *Lotus Sūtra* to secure benefits here and now; pilgrims routinely offered and buried

55. For parallels and variations, see, for example, *Sanbōe* 2.16 (*SNKBT,* 31:120–22; translation in Kamens, *The Three Jewels,* 230–32); *Hokke genki* 1.10 (*NST,* 7:65–66, 518; translation in Dykstra, *Miraculous Tales,* 39–40); *Konjaku monogatarishū* 12.27 (*SNKBT,* 35:150–52). By way of comparison, see *Konjaku monogatarishū* 12.7 (*SNKBT,* 35:111–12), in which a mackerel peddler is revealed to be a holy personage whose fish turn into the *Flower Ornament Sūtra.*

56. *Hokke genki* 2.44 (*NST,* 7:107–9, 532–33; translation in Dykstra, *Miraculous Tales,* 70–71).

57. *Konjaku monogatarishū* 13.3 (*SNKBT,* 35:205). For other variants, see *Honchō shinsenden,* biography of Yōshō (*NST,* 7:265–66, 583; translation in Kleine and Kohn, "Daoist Immortality," 166–68); *Fusō ryakki,* Engi 1, eighth month (*SZKT,* 12:172–73). For extended analysis, see Sugawara, *Nihon shisō to shinbutsu shūgō,* 169–96.

this scripture at the peak, as discussed in chapters 2 and 5. Second, Yōshō gave hope of immortality to pilgrims, who tendered prayers for long life to the mountain pantheon (see chapters 5 and 6). In Yōshō, then, aristocratic pilgrims could see their practices exemplified and their prayers fulfilled.

Safety from evil influences was another desirable prerogative attributed to Kinpusen's holy men. The story of a monk and habitual pilgrim-wanderer named Giei provided inspiration in this vein: in the trackless wilderness of the peaks, Giei came upon a hermit who combined Yōshō's longevity and *Lotus*-centered practice with E no Ozuno's ability to command a supernatural entourage. Giei himself had visited "every holy site in the land" but got hopelessly lost when he tried to walk from Kumano to Kinpusen. Coming upon a lovely house tucked away in the mountains, he saw a youthful monk "chanting the *Lotus Sūtra* in a sublime voice that touched the depths of Giei's being." Every time the monk finished reading a chapter of the sutra, the scroll he had been using would magically roll itself back up. Finally, the holy man noticed that he was being watched, and had his attendants serve Giei a meal. When the hermit confided that he had been there, quite alone in the mountains, for some eighty years, Giei expressed his amazement. To explain his apparent youth, the hermit cited passages from the *Lotus Sūtra* that promise those who recite the scripture the service of celestial lads and protection from illness and old age.[58]

At first, the hermit hesitated to let Giei stay the night, but he relented on the condition that Giei depart promptly the next day and remain completely silent in the meantime.

> Soon after dark, an eerie little breeze sprang up. From his hiding place, Giei watched supernatural beings arrive in all sorts of extraordinary forms. Some had the heads of horses, oxen, or birds, while some were shaped like deer. They crowded in with offerings of incense, flowers, nuts, fruit, and drink, and after placing all these good things before the hut they prostrated themselves in perfect order with palms pressed together.

58. *Miaofa lianhua jing* (*Lotus Sūtra*; J. *Myōhō renge kyō*), *T.* 262 (9:39b17, 54c26).

The creatures listened piously as the hermit recited the sutra all night long. In the morning, once again the hermit used the *Lotus Sūtra* to explain his circumstances, pointing out that it has Śākyamuni pledge that if those who recite this scripture "are in empty and silent places, I will send celestials, dragon kings, *yakṣas,* demons and gods to be their audience and listen to the Dharma." The hermit then sent his awestruck guest on his way, guided by a magical, flying water jar.[59]

In this story, the *Lotus Sūtra* was brought to bear to explain what appear elsewhere as naturalized characteristics of Ōmine and its mountain men: longevity, solitude, and retinues of demons and spirits. In historical terms, the lineage of these qualities exceeded the *Lotus Sūtra* and the Buddhist tradition narrowly construed. At the very least, they have traditionally been imputed to Daoists, too. For instance, the term "demons and spirits" (C. *guei shen*; J. *kijin*), glossed in the translation as "supernatural beings," is quite common in stories of Ōmine practitioners, and describes the retinues of sutra reciters as promised in the *Lotus Sūtra.*[60] It also appears in Daoist classics, occuring some fifty times in the *Baopuzi,* where Ge Hong (283–343) describes his own teacher as follows: "Master Yuan was a great immortal. He was able to harmonize yin and yang; he commanded demons and spirits, wind and rain; he hitched his carriage to nine dragons and twelve white tigers."[61]

Just how we ought to understand the extent of Daoism's impact in Japan is a topic of ongoing research and debate. Neither ecclesiastical Daoist hierarchies nor discrete schools, such as Lingbao or Shangqing, ever formed in Japan. Nonetheless, as already mentioned, the Bureau of Yin and Yang did perform divination and engage with other technologies associated with Daoism, and Daoist classics were well known, es-

59. *Konjaku monogatarishū* 13.1 (*SNKBT,* 35:198–201; translation from Royall Tyler, *Japanese Tales,* 141–43). For an earlier version, see *Hokke genki* 1.11 (*NST,* 7: 66–69, 518–19; translation in Dykstra, *Miraculous Tales,* 40–42). For the *Lotus Sūtra* citation (which is my translation), see *Miaofa lianhua jing, T.* 262 (9:32b10–11).

60. For other references to *kijin* in the context of Ōmine, see *Konjaku monogatarishū* 11.3, 12.40, and 13.1 (*SNKBT,* 35:17, 192, 200). For the *Lotus Sūtra,* see previous note.

61. Incidence of "*kijin*" calculated via word search in the *Scripta Sinica* database. For the passage on Master Yuan, see *Baopuzi* 4 (1:76). Also note that Ge Hong states that ingestion of cinnabar will result in mastery of demons and spirits in *Baopuzi* 4 and 11 (1:75, 203).

pecially among scholars and literati. Masafusa, for instance, routinely made allusions to the *Zhuangzi* and *Laozi* in dedicatory prayers he wrote for other aristocrats. Longevity practices were also of general interest, and, as mentioned above, some researchers have suggested that areas along the Yoshino River valley, including Yoshinoyama, were associated with cinnabar.[62] Judging from the *setsuwa* literature, during the early and mid-Heian period, longevity practices generally focused on dietary restrictions and moral cultivation rather than alchemy. More importantly, as the stories of E no Ozuno, Yōshō, and Giei show, there was no hard-and-fast divide between Buddhist holy men and Daoist immortals.

In the mid-eleventh century, when the first extant version of Giei's story was written down, the narrative record was still reinforcing convictions that longevity and mastery over natural and supernatural phenomena were the signal traits of Ōmine's mountain practitioners. At the same time, the ominous political overtones that had surrounded E were dissipating with the attenuation of the *ritsuryō* order. This created a conceptual space wherein leading members of the royal court were able to engage in mountain practice and to turn their activities to their own advantage, rather than against the court.

Other Worlds

The written record indicates that in addition to stories of supernatural holy men, a rich tradition of imagining Kinpusen as geographically alien or cosmologically remote arose around the same time that lay pilgrimage began. Narratives invested the mountain with the ability to make alternative realities available in the here-and-now, calling into question Japan's territorial relationship to Asia, while subordinating orders of political precedence to a moral hierarchy. In addition, the mountain was seen to open onto heaven and hell, even as it reordered and expanded the everyday world.[63]

62. See note 23, as well as Como, *Weaving and Binding*, 63–66.

63. For analysis of Kumano as a Foucauldian heterotopia that inverted and relativized conventional socio-spatial categories, see Moerman, *Localizing Paradise*, esp. 233–41.

From the 900s on, members of the upper echelons of Heian society were of the opinion that Kinpusen was, in fact, part of a foreign country. Even more strikingly, they claimed that it had actually flown to Japan. Emperor Daigo's fourth son, Prince Shigeakira (906–54), wrote in his journal that Jōsū, the monk who petitioned the throne for permission to return to Kinpusen after serving Daigo as a protector monk, had told him that the mountain had flown to Japan from China.[64] This piece of lore was well known in literary circles. When Ōe no Masafusa composed a prayer on behalf of Retired Emperor Shirakawa, he wrote: "Kinpusen is the dwelling-place of Vajra Zaō. At first, it was west of the western sea, but it mounted five clouds and came flying. Now it soars up south of the southern capital. It shelters the realm and brings benefit."[65] Similar formulae appeared in other texts, in some cases linking Kinpusen to Mt. Wutai in China.[66] By the twelfth and thirteenth centuries, writers were also claiming that once upon a time Kinpusen had been the southeast corner of Gṛdhrakūṭa, the mountain in northern India where Śākyamuni had preached the *Lotus* and many other Mahāyāna sutras. It had, they said, broken off and flown to Japan.[67] Accordingly, pilgrims to Kinpusen could claim that they were actually traveling to China, which many saw as the archetype of civilization, or to India, "the land where the Buddha was born."

Such geographic transpositions localized pan-Buddhist cosmology, reimagining nominally peripheral locations as centers in their own right.[68] As we shall see in chapter 2, this strategy was integral to the lo-

64. *Kokon chomonjū* 2.42 (*NKBT,* 84:79–80); *Shozan engi* (*NST,* 20:110, 350). For Jōsū's connections to Kinpusen, see note 38.

65. *Gōtotoku nagon ganmonshū* 2.1, dated Kanji 2.7.13 but emended to Kanji 6.7.13 (249). For reference to Kinpusen as a flying mountain in *waka* circles, see Yamamoto Kenji, "Kinpusen hirai denshō," 3–4.

66. For Masafusa's role in popularizing Kinpusen's reputation as a flying mountain, see Li Yujuan, "Kinpusen hiraisetsu." For comparisons to other texts, see *Gōtotoku nagon ganmonshū* (247). For similarities in the representation of Kinpusen and Mt. Wutai, see Yamamoto Kenji, "Kinpusen hirai denshō"; and Hakamada, "'Kinpusen jōdo' keisei," 74–82.

67. See, for example, *Shozan engi* (*NST,* 20:90, 131, 342, 359), as well as *Kumano sansho gongen Kinpusen kongō Zaō engi* (47, 56).

68. Toni Huber's analysis of Tibetans' creative imagination of India, the classical Buddhist center, as a dramatically other realm resonates here (Huber, *The Holy Land Reborn*).

cal ethos of Kinpusen's non-normative cult, but it is important to note that neither the gesture of transposition nor the notion of flying mountains was unique. In China, for instance, the mountain above the temple Lingyinsi in Hangzhou was known as the Peak That Came Flying (Feilaifeng); by the eighth century, it was said to be "one of the peaks of Gṛdhrakūṭa." Further afield, Tibetans have claimed that the Himalayan Mountains flew to their present locations.[69] In Japan, other mountains, such as Mt. Miwa in Yamato, have been identified with Gṛdhrakūṭa; other, more remote sites in the Buddhist cosmos have also been localized. For instance, in the Kumano region, Nachi was understood to open onto Potalaka, Avalokiteśvara's paradise, while Hongū often figured as Amitābha's Pure Land.[70] Again, these identifications resonated with continental habits: in China, Mt. Wutai was known as the domain of Mañjuśrī, and Mt. Emei, that of Samantabhadhra.[71] These imaginary geographies, both domestic and foreign, created an intertwining network of transposition and replication.

The most spectacular representation of Kinpusen as a central point in the Buddhist cosmos is decidedly political and deserves sustained attention because it sheds light on how the construction of the mountain as another world affected pilgrimage practices. Organized around the death, visionary travels, and revival of a holy man who may have been a historical figure or simply a fictional narrative persona, "Dōken shōnin myōdoki" (The holy man Dōken's record of the dark realms) uses knowledge gained at the mountain to invert the political order and ritually reconstruct the status quo. In this respect, the narrative mimics the twin potentials of the classical mountain practitioner, who could at once threaten sedition and offer healing. The "Record" is extant in two versions, which are part of an extensive intertextual network. The first takes the form of a lengthy citation in an entry for 941 in the Heian court annal *Fusō ryakki.* The second, which I treat here as a variant, was copied into the eighteenth-century compendium *Kitano*

69. Shahar, "Lingyin Si," 213–22; Buffetrille, "One Day the Mountains."

70. On Miwa, see Royall Tyler, "The Path of My Mountain," 170–76; on Kumano, see Moerman, *Localizing Paradise,* esp. 63–75, 92–117.

71. Birnbaum, *Studies on the Mysteries,* and "Light in the Wutai Mountains"; Hargett, *Stairway to Heaven.*

bunsō (Literature of Kitano) from a manuscript owned by Eikyūji, a temple in the Nara Basin.[72] Although the dating of these texts remains a subject of debate, the *Fusō ryakki* version must have been composed sometime between the year 941, when the narrative is set, and circa 1100, when the *Fusō ryakki* was completed. This period coincides with the regency and the height of aristocratic pilgrimage to Kinpusen.

In 941, according to the story, a monk named Dōken went into retreat in the Ōmine Range, as he had often done during the preceding twenty-six years. Deep in the mountains, he settled into a cave. This is now commonly believed to have been Shō no Iwaya (Mouth Organ Cave), a rock shelter located some four kilometers south of Kinpusen. There Dōken kept silent and fasted for three weeks, performing esoteric Buddhist rites at his altar until one day he died. After leaving the cave, he immediately encountered a monk who gave him a reviving draught of water from the Himalayas. A senior monk then appeared and led Dōken up to the summit of Kinpusen, where they "looked out upon the whole world, the entire earth." The land itself was made of radiant gold. In the north, a high-ranking monk sat enthroned upon a golden peak. This monk introduced himself as Zaō, a transformation-body (*keshin*) of Śākyamuni, and the mountain as Kinpusen, his pure land. After uttering an oracular speech, Zaō permitted Dōken to depart in the company of Dajō Itokuten (the Ministerial Celestial of Might and Virtue), the apotheosis of Sugawara no Michizane (845–903), a famous statesman and scholar who had died in 903 in unjustified disgrace.[73] Conducting Dōken on a tour of his celestial domain, the Ministerial Celestial explained Zaō's oracle: Dōken should change his name to Nichizō and dedicate himself exclusively to mountain practice. The celestial also noted that after his own death as Michizane, he had been fixated on revenge; more recently, however, his anger had begun to fade, thanks to the Buddhist teachings.[74]

72. *Fusō ryakki,* Tengyō 4.third month (*SZKT,* 12:219–22); *Kitano bunsō,* excerpted in *Shintō taikei, jinja-hen,* 11:61–75. For translations, see Royall Tyler, *Japanese Tales,* 144–49; and Hino, "The Daoist Facet," 287–93. Note that neither Eikyūji nor the manuscript describing Dōken's exploits once preserved at that temple survives today.

73. For Michizane's historical career in politics and literature, see Borgen, *Sugawara no Michizane*; and Wa-Kan Hikaku Bungakukai, *Sugawara no Michizane ronshū.*

74. In the *Kitano bunsō* variant, at this point the Ministerial Celestial takes Dōken to Tuṣita Heaven to meet the spirits of several of Michizane's contemporaries.

A second micronarrative (paralleled in the *Kitano bunsō* variant) ensues. According to this account, Dōken visited Āvici Hell, where he encountered Emperor Daigo. After explaining that his own faults and his failure to honor Michizane had brought him to this pass, Daigo cried: "Oh, misery! Oh, sadness! You must report my words to the emperor. Quickly, save me from anguish. . . . Also, tell the regent to erect ten thousand stupas to save me from torment." The *Fusō ryakki* account ends here, but the variant in *Kitano bunsō* closes with advice on how to propitiate the Ministerial Celestial. This is tendered by the Celestial of Replete Virtue, who appears to be the apotheosis of Emperor Uda, Daigo's father and Michizane's patron.

Both spectacular and scandalous, Dōken's story contributed dramatically to the cultural memory of Kinpusen. The fact that it is attested in multiple variants and genres, from illustrated handscrolls to musical treatises, testifies to its popularity.[75] The regents were almost certainly a, if not the, initial target audience for this story. In 941, the year in which the *Fusō ryakki* entry is set, the regent was Fujiwara no Tadahira, an important figure in the development of the regency as an institution, and brother and successor to Fujiwara no Tokihira (871–909), the man generally credited with having engineered Michizane's exile. Over the course of the first several decades of the tenth century, there emerged a public consensus that Michizane's angry spirit was bringing widespread misfortune to the state. In response, Tadahira and his family took a leading role in pacifying and worshipping Michizane as the deity Tenjin. They maintained an interest in his shrine at Kitano over multiple generations and ensured its integration into the roster of state-recognized institutions that later became the Twenty-Two Shrines.[76] The regents may also have taken a hand in compiling the *Fusō ryakki*. In his studies of the annal, Horikoshi Mitsunobu has argued that it was likely Fujiwara no Moromichi, scion of the regents' house and two-time

75. For a timeline of sources on Nichizō, see Yamamoto Satsuki, "Dōken (Nichizō) denshō no tenkai," 97–98. For collections of such sources, see *Dai Nihon shiryō,* 1.7:838–59; Mori and Wada, *Kokusho itsubun* (*shintei zōho*), 513–20; and/or *Shintō taikei, jinja hen,* 11:55–56, 61–75, 406–9, 413–14.

76. Namiki, "Sekkanke to Tenjin shinkō;" see also Borgen, *Sugawara no Michizane,* 308–25; and note 45 in this chapter.

Kinpusen pilgrim, who commissioned it.[77] If this supposition is correct, then the choice to include Dōken's story in the *Fusō ryakki* may be partially explained by the regents' long-standing investments in pacifying Michizane and venerating Kinpusen's gods. The Dōken account surely provoked anxiety by hinting that the political order was vulnerable to supernatural and karmic retribution and by converting (and inverting) the political into a moral hierarchy.[78] Although broadcasting a royal's damnation approached lèse-majesté, in the end, the story leveraged Daigo's plight to show that a mountain monk could resolve the ills of this world and the next by serving as communicant between the gods and the court. According to the story, if the regents would but heed Kinpusen's gods, and if they would turn to the mountain as a source of divine intelligence, then they would be able to maintain their political ascendancy and the health of the state. As discussed at greater length in chapters 3 through 5, during the 150 years between Michizane's apotheosis as Tenjin and the compilation of the *Fusō ryakki*, the regents did just that. Read in this context, the narrative persona of Dōken/Nichizō illustrates the political significance of mountain practice and its potential to mediate between the mountains and the court, the divine and the human, and the dead and the living.

Women and Monsters

When laymen began to travel to Kinpusen, they blurred the old distinction between the capital and the peaks and between courtiers and holy men. Nonetheless, pilgrimage depended on conceptual binaries in order to retain its significance as a boundary-crossing exercise that yielded special powers and blessings. Thus, a second-order exclusion was put into place: women were banned from Kinpusen. This social and ritual

77. Horikoshi, "*Fusō ryakki* senja kō" and "*Fusō ryakki*."

78. For interpretations of Nichizō's story in light of political change and upheavals associated with Fujiwara no Sumitomo (d. 941) and Taira no Masakado (d. 940), see Kawane, *Tenjin shinkō,* 100–107; and Uejima, *Nihon chūsei shakai,* 235–38.

proscription shored up constructions of the mountain as an other world in the face of institutional growth.

"Women's boundaries" (*nyonin kekkai*), territorial proscriptions on women, were quite common in premodern Japan, first appearing in the ninth through eleventh centuries. Mountains dominated by major Buddhist temples, such as Enryakuji at Mt. Hiei or Daigoji at Mt. Kasatori, were closed to women, as were mountains like Mt. Fuji and Hakusan, which are now best known for their *kami* cults. For the most part, these bans dissolved in the nineteenth and twentieth centuries in processes affected by economic necessity and changing social norms. More recently, they became technically illegal under the postwar constitution.[79] The complex reasons behind the creation of these bans are subject to ongoing debate. One interpretive camp, led by Ushiyama Yoshiyuki, argues that *nyonin kekkai* originated with Buddhist *vinaya* rules, which prohibit monks and nuns from living with persons of the opposite sex. By contrast, Katsuura Noriko argues that such bans grew out of the misogynist tenor of continental ideology—Buddhist, Daoist, and Confucian—that permeated Japanese elite culture in the 800s and 900s, giving rise to a pervasive conviction that women were impure.[80]

In the case of Kinpusen, both arguments are plausible, but in the context of pilgrimage practices, the ban on women also appears as an attempt to enforce the radical alterity of the mountains. Although there is no direct evidence for how elite male pilgrims understood *nyonin kekkai,* by observing the ban, they contributed to its reification. In pushing women into the role of the excluded other in the 900s, men made it possible to imagine themselves as a single group united by gender, and not divided by class or ordination status.

Today, Kinpusen is the only mountain in Japan to maintain the old ban on women year-round. As a result, cultural memory has made it into *the* no-women mountain. Fittingly enough, some of the earliest

79. For overviews of bans on women, see Suzuki Masataka, *Nyonin kinsei*; and Sekimori, "Sacralizing the Border." For a focused study of the dismantling of Mt. Fuji's ban, see Miyazaki, "Female Pilgrims and Mt. Fuji."

80. For the *vinaya* rules argument, see Ushiyama, "The Historical Development." For the argument that ideologies of female impurity drove *nyonin kekkai,* see Katsuura, "Josei to kegare kan"; for the role of continental learning, see Katsuura, "Nihon kodai ni okeru gairai shinkō-kei san'e"; and "Nana, hasseiki shōrai Chūgoku isho."

evidence for *nyonin kekkai* is associated with Kinpusen. In the tenth-century Chinese encyclopedia *Shishi liutie*, quoted in the epigraph to this book's introduction, the monk Yichu reported what his Japanese acquaintance Kanho had told him: "Women cannot climb" Kinpusen. "Even today, men who want to climb it abstain from liquor and meat and sex for three months, and then all their wishes are fulfilled."[81] Some years later, in 1051, a woman who identified herself as a member of the Ki family and who probably hailed from Ki Province, commissioned a votive bronze, which she sent to the mountain. In her inscription, she wrote that she hoped to be reborn male so that she could come into the divine presence at the peak (see chapter 2). Clearly, the ban affected the soteriological hopes and physical practices of real women, as well as the mountain's broader reputation: it defined and delimited Kinpusen's social landscape.

Structurally, the *nyonin kekkai* at Kinpusen and other mountains is related to rituals of consecration, which are simultaneously rites of exclusion. The establishment of a Buddhist zone of practice—whether an altar or a temple—conventionally begins with the formation of a *kekkai*, literally "binding a realm." By binding a site, a ritualist establishes dominion and expels unwanted influences from the newly defined interior space. For instance, when Kūkai founded Kongōbuji on Mt. Kōya, thirty-odd kilometers west of Kinpusen, he included the following declaration in his liturgy.

> Reverently, I pray: may the buddhas rejoice, may the celestials keep watch, and may the good spirits pledge to bear witness to this. For seven leagues in every direction—east, west, north and south, to the four corners, above and below—all evil demons and spirits be gone from within my boundary. Any good spirit who would bring benefits may dwell here should it so wish.[82]

At Kinpusen, male ritualists bound the realm, consigning women to the exterior of the *kekkai* as demonic, dangerous others.

81. *Shishi liutie* (459).

82. *Seireishū* 9.99 (*NKBT,* 71:411). Cf. 9.100, in which Kūkai uses similar language in a dedication for an altar at Mt. Kōya.

As Katsuura has argued, issues of purity and pollution subtended the definition of women as persona non grata. By the time the *Kojiki* (Record of ancient matters) and *Nihon shoki* (Chronicles of Japan) had been compiled in the early eighth century, purity was a matter of central concern to *kami* worship. By the ninth century, Buddhist, Daoist, and Confucian biases against women were beginning to make it an ideological and ritual axiom that to be female was to be polluted.[83] In many cases, it became the male ritualist's prerogative and duty to expel or expunge the polluting, the demonic, and the feminine. In a story from the *Shozan engi* (*Engi* of many mountains), a set of narrative and ritual materials copied circa 1200, En no Gyōja travels south from Mino'o, a site in contemporary Osaka, along the western coast of the Kii Peninsula, and then eastward through the mountains to Kumano. The setting thus correlates not to Kinpusen but rather the route that elite pilgrims followed to Kumano during the eleventh and twelfth centuries. Despite the spatial remove and comparatively late date, the story is striking for its dramatization of gendered ritual expulsion. As En made his way to Kumano, he had to cross a river of filth and blood, after which a woman in labor blocked his path. He then encountered a man-eating demon-fish, a horse-eating crone, and a four-horned female monster. To clear the way, En recited *harae* purification formulae, scattered salt, and uttered mantras: using the technology of *kami* worship (itself inflected by Daoist practices) and esoteric Buddhism, he purified the landscape and made it a male preserve.[84] The narrative thus teaches its audience that En held rights to the mountains, whereas the ravenous and bloody, the female and demonic, were interlopers to be put to flight. In point of historical fact, Kumano was actually open to women, but the emphatic tone of the narrative suggests that the presence of real women made (male) obsessions with purity all the more acute.

83. Katsuura, "Nihon kodai ni okeru gairai shinkō-kei san'e." For more general accounts of gender bias in Japanese Buddhism, see, for instance, Nishiguchi, *Onna no chikara*; Taira, "Kyū bukkyō to josei"; and Faure, *The Power of Denial*, esp. 219–324.

84. *Shozan engi* (*NST*, 20:105–108, 348–49). On the influence of continental religious culture on *kami* worship, see Como, *Weaving and Binding*; on *harae* and religious hybridity, see Teeuwen and van der Veere, *Nakatomi Harae Kunge*.

In the socially real complement to this kind of storytelling, aristocratic male pilgrims were expected to take a concerted interest in purity. Custom demanded that they engage in a regimen known as "the long abstentions" (*chōsai*) for roughly seventy days prior to departure and for the duration of the journey itself, a total of eighty-odd days. Pilgrims had to guard their purity carefully: a contact pollution could spoil their abstentions and force the cancellation of the pilgrimage.[85] Canons of official ceremonial indicate that by the 900s childbirth, pregnancy, and menstruation had joined death as conditions of impurity. Women could only resolve pollution brought on by reproductive processes by observing a fixed period of seclusion.[86] Given that most premenopausal women would menstruate at least once during the months-long pilgrimage preparations, it follows that they could not meet the standard requirements for a journey to Kinpusen.

In later centuries, proponents of Shugendō explicitly framed mountain pilgrimage as a rite of rebirth and placed a strong emphasis on religious lineage. In this context, mountain practice and *yamabushi* lineages took on the role of sacrifice, as analyzed by Nancy Jay: they provided an exclusively male means of ritual reproduction meant to supersede biological maternity.[87] In the mountains, which were implicitly feminized as sites for rebirth, men would receive initiations anointing them members of an all-male line. Birth imagery also came to play a central role in ritual. Today, for instance, when *yamabushi* reach the peak of Kinpusen, they crawl through a rock formation identified as a womb, emerging ritually enlightened and reborn.[88] Although ritual practice has opened to women at other sites, at Kinpusen it is still

85. *Midō kanpakuki,* Kankō 8.3.2, 9, 11 (2:95–96).

86. Both pregnancy and menstruation required women to withdraw from the palace during times of ceremonial abstinences (*sai*) and festivals (*matsuri*). Miscarriage, abortion, and birth also brought pollution (see *Engi shiki* 3 [*SNKT,* 26:68–69; translation in Bock, *Engi-Shiki,* 1:116–17]).

87. Jay, *Throughout Your Generations.*

88. Kitamura, *The Autumn Peak of Haguro,* and McGuire and Abela, *Shugendō Now,* include footage relating to rebirth. For written analyses of rebirth symbolism, see Earhart, *A Religious Study,* esp. 129–30; Miyake Hitoshi, *Shugendō girei no kenkyū,* 73–76, passim; and Swanson, "Shugendō and the Yoshino-Kumano Pilgrimage," 78. Hardacre, "The Cave and the Womb-World," provides an account of women's alternative practices.

predicated upon the removal of real women from the scene of ritual reproduction.

As mentioned above, *vinaya* rules also shaped the ban on women. The story of a woman named Toran, which is preserved in numerous variants, illustrates this point. According to the *Honchō shinsenden,* which was compiled around the year 1098, Toran was a nun who lived to be more than one hundred years old. The storyteller, likely Ōe no Masafusa, wrote:

> She lived at the foot of Mt. Yoshino and practiced assiduously day and night. She wanted to climb Mitake [=Kinpusen]; however, there was a violent thunderstorm, and she could not get there after all. The land of this mountain is strewn with gold. Vajra Zaō guards it, waiting for the advent of Maitreya. Moreover, it is a land of the precepts. Therefore women are not allowed to pass.[89]

As discussed in chapter 2, Zaō was closely associated with Maitreya, and Kinpusen's very name suggested that it was a realm of gold. Like the other characters populating the *Honchō shinsenden* biographies, Toran was unusual; however, unlike male Ōmine practitioners, she was unable to overcome conventional rules. The story makes it clear that this was due to her sex. More specifically, her status as anathema derived from Kinpusen's quality as a "land of the precepts," indicating that in some eyes, it was *vinaya* rules that prevented female pilgrims from climbing Kinpusen. In point of fact, although the *vinaya* does bar women from male monastic residences, the application of such a rule to an entire mountain significantly exceeded the letter of the monastic law. As though to point out the extent of the adaptation, in Toran's case it was neither gods nor buddhas who enforced the ban; instead, the narrative endowed the precepts with the natural force of the thunderstorm.

Other versions of this story take on a punitive cast by claiming that Toran, who usually appears as a religious specialist in her own right, turned to stone. Given that *nyonin kekkai* were often marked with large stones, and that barren women were "stone women," this is particularly

89. *Honchō shinsenden,* biography of Toran (*NST,* 7:260, 581; for an alternative translation, see Kleine and Kohn, "Daoist Immortality," 154–55).

telling. As punishment for not resigning herself to her gendered fate—a life of sexual reproduction in the valleys—these versions of the Toran story literally turned her into an object lesson. Similar stories were told about other women at other mountains, showing that there was a perceived need for such warnings. In asserting that Toran, unlike Giei's hermit or the holy man of Amabenomine, was subject to both natural and social law, these stories reified the ban on women; at the same time, they testified to women's real-and-imagined defiance.[90]

Kinpusen's ban was and is subject to constant renegotiation. Today, women are known to flout it fairly consistently, some privately and others publicly.[91] Toran's story suggests that this was the case in premodern times as well. At least as the narrative and lyric record would have it, not all boundary-crossing women went the way of defeated gorgons. A song from the late-twelfth-century *Ryōjin hishō* (Treasured selections of superb songs) celebrates the activity of *miko* at Kinpusen (and as far as I have been able to ascertain, *miko* were always female communicants with the gods):

The *miko* at the Peak of Gold,
The drum she beats, beats up, beats down:
Delightful!
Let's go, too!
Bing, bang, bong it echoes,
Echoes on.
The drum she beats—how does she beat it?
The sound will never end.[92]

90. For the motif of women barred from mountains in later literature, see Matisoff, "Barred from Paradise"; Faure, *The Power of Denial,* 219–49; and Moerman, *Localizing Paradise,* 205–8.

91. See Suzuki Masataka, *Nyonin kinsei,* 44–52 for a discussion of women who publicized their intent to climb Kinpusen in protest of the ban. On a more private level, one avid hiker whom I met in 2005 expressed ambivalence that many women now seem to share about Kinpusen's customs. First she commented that she thought the ban should be maintained because "it is tradition." Then she paused and added, "But I climbed it." She explained that she had participated in a winter ascent by snowshoe. Over all, her motivations for climbing the mountain seemed to be tied more to a love of mountaineering than politics or religious conviction, but that makes her combined affirmation and breach of the ban no less complex.

92. *Ryōjin hishō* 265 (*SNKBT,* 56:76; for an alternative translation, see Kim, *Songs to Make the Dust Dance,* 6). Some seventy-five years after Go-Shirakawa completed

This song entered court circles in the twelfth century, when it was collected by Retired Emperor Go-Shirakawa (1127–92, r. 1155–58), as was another mentioning a crone who "watched" at Kinpusen for hundreds of days, hoping to see a manifestation of Maitreya. Although she failed, the song claims, a pair of male monks who came after her succeeded.[93] The fruitlessness of the crone's religious practice certainly reinforced gender prejudice, but as narrative personae, both she and the *miko* show that Heian audiences found the presence of women at the peak plausible despite the customary ban.

Real women found other, less transgressive ways to insert themselves into mountain practices. They arranged to be buried at mountains, a practice that drew no opposition, apparently because bones were desexed and degendered by death. They sought rebirth as males so that they could, at long last, make their way to the top. And they sent proxies to conduct pilgrimages and make offerings on their behalf at the forbidden peaks.[94] In these ways and in their activities as writers and conversation partners, women contributed to the shared, affective landscape of Kinpusen. The court lady Sei Shōnagon (b. 966?), for example, included an anecdote about Kinpusen in her famous compendium *Makura no sōshi* (The pillow book). Seeking to convey the mood of a woman left behind in the city, Sei wrote:

> Moving things: A filial child. A well-born young man's preparatory abstentions for Mitake [=Kinpusen]. The dawn prostrations he performs, having set himself apart, are so very moving. Thinking of him, his dear one imagines that she hears him when she wakes. Wondering how he

Ryōjin hishō, the Kamakura-period *Jikkinshō* compiler recorded a tale about Genshin (942–1017), famous as an early proponent of Pure Land devotion. In this story, Genshin is impressed by an "accurate *miko*" at Kinpusen who lives up to her reputation for reliability (*Jikkinshō* 6.37 [*SNKBZ*, 51:274]).

93. *Ryōjin hishō* 264 (*SNKBT*, 56:76; translation in Kim, *Songs to Make the Dust Dance*, 93–94).

94. Nishiguchi Junko, for example, considers the interment of women's remains at mountain temples in "Where the Bones Go." For an example of prayers for rebirth, see chapter 2 of this book. For an example of sutra burial conducted on behalf a nun at Mt. Kōya, see Dolce, "Reconsidering the Taxonomy of the Esoteric"; Nakamura Gorō, "Kyōzuka"; and Wakayamaken Kyōiku Iinkai, *Kōyasan okunoin no chihō*, esp. 103–14 and 218–36.

> looks as he makes his pilgrimage, she is careful and concerned, and it is so wonderful when he returns safely from the pilgrimage. But the look of his formal hat is just a bit off. Also, one knows that even those who are terribly lofty still make the pilgrimage in exceedingly plain clothing.[95]

This young man "set himself apart" in a gesture that required his woman to stay behind, allowing Kinpusen to rise in her mind's eye—and that of Sei and her audience—as an ineluctably different world. Sei, of course, was imagining the woman imagining her man, and really, that was precisely the point: Kinpusen was available to most women only through acts of fantasy. The very fact that women persisted in imagining it from afar only added to its cachet.

Conclusion

In the 700s and 800s, the southern mountains appeared to high-ranking residents of the capital as an ominous and remote wilderness zone populated by religious virtuosi who would have been out of place in the city. In this context, it was unthinkable that a courtier would find his way through the mountains, much less struggle to the peak of Kinpusen. But with the erosion of *ritsuryō* ideology, the opposition between mountain and capital loosened. Under the regency, elite lay pilgrimage called into question the tension between the civil center and the wild periphery; consequently, the need to maintain Kinpusen as a symbolically other world became more pressing. With more and more noblemen going to the mountain, the long abstentions and the prohibition on women circumscribed Kinpusen with ritual and social cordons, keeping it separate as a place of longevity and magic, a pure land, a foreign realm, and a portal to other worlds.

Pilgrims were active participants in the creation and maintenance of Kinpusen's affective landscape. The regent Fujiwara no Moromichi provides a good example of these processes. Prior to his departure from the capital in 1088, Moromichi commissioned a prayer for his pilgrim-

95. *Makura no sōshi* 114 (*SNKBT,* 25:153; for an alternative translation, see McKinney, *The Pillow Book,* 119).

age. A partial, holograph manuscript of this text was excavated from Kinpusen, where Moromichi buried it, and is now preserved in a private collection. As material object, literary text, and ritual performance, this prayer created place. In copying the text out in his own hand, Moromichi inscribed a representation of the mountain that he accepted as his own. He had the vow solemnly recited in a mountaintop rite, further discussed in chapter 5; in doing so, he publicly declared his views. Finally, he buried the manuscript in situ, together with sutras he had copied. Here, I wish to call attention to how the affective landscape, which Moromichi first encountered in his native habitat (the capital), informed his experience at the real mountain. Writing in the city and reciting at the mountain, Moromichi addressed himself to Zaō, the primary god of Kinpusen: "The disappearing summits are ten thousand spans high: treading upon autumn clouds, I lose my stride. The long slopes wind on and on: drenched in burning sweat, I exhaust my spirit. With no regard for the difficulty of advancing or retreating, I seek only your mysterious assistance, which never fails."[96] Here Moromichi—through words written by a literary proxy—articulated his devotion in terms of his determined progress through an otherworldly landscape. He was quite conscious that he would be out of place, away from home, at his physical limits, dependent upon a mountain god.

Writing in his diary at Kinpusen, Moromichi expressed his responses as though they were in fact a force of nature. Describing his approach to the peak, he wrote: "I gazed on it intently, mindful of Vajra Zaō, who instructs the throngs of people. Thunder rolls at the bottom of the valleys; wisps of cloud hang about the edges of the mountains."[97] The strategic projection of emotion and mood into landscape is a much-vaunted hallmark of traditional Japanese poetry, and here, Moromichi's parallel prose makes it clear that he was indeed poeticizing. With thunder, he evoked the danger and difficulty of the climb; with wisps of clouds, the ethereal, immortal heights that he and his fellow pilgrims had attained. Although noblemen's diaries were often dry affairs,

96. Prayer for Fujiwara no Moromichi's pilgrimage to Kinpusen, dated Kanji 2.7.27 (*KSS*, 331; also published in *Heian ibun*, supp. doc. 280 [*komonjo hen*, addenda vol., 63–64]).

97. *Go-Nijō Moromichiki*, Kanji 2.7.25 (1:202).

Moromichi's journal entries on his arrival at Kinpusen were drenched in affect. This emotive quality is emphasized by repetition and a rhetoric in which sensibility takes the landscape as its vehicle. On the back of the manuscript for the entry just cited, Moromichi wrote again:

> Around the hour of the cock, we arrived at the base of Hanging Key Peak. Looking up to heaven, there was nowhere for my heart to rest. But being mindful of Zaō, I had no fear. I tried to fathom this: perhaps I am someone who was born before [with a karmic connection to Zaō]. Boundless and fathomless! With our hands and feet we climbed the stony mountain. Taking the measure of the realm, we looked around: the manifold mountains were like jewels.[98]

Here Moromichi sounded a refrain worthy of Zhuangzi as he praised the limitless scope of Kinpusen's mountainscape. When he reached the summit, he paused to play king of the mountain, surveying his realm. At the price of burning sweat and an exhausted spirit, Moromichi had become a temporary holy man.

Even after he returned to the capital, Moromichi continued to carry this affective landscape with him. He sent news and prayers to Kinpusen when he was unwell, and gifts when he received auspicious omens. In 1091 a typhoon blew down the worship hall (*raidō*) that stood before the sanctuary enshrining Zaō. Kinpusen's senior monks Kyōshō (d. 1107) and Kōsan (d. 1096) sent word of the disaster directly to Moromichi, who exclaimed in his journal, "I sigh sadly with terrible pain; my tears fall like rain." With apparent approbation, he also quoted the memorial sent by Kōsan. In metered, parallel phrases, this text read in part:

> As for Treasure Mountain [=Kinpusen], its miracles are foremost in the realm.
> As for Zaō, he is lord of the teachings, beyond compare in the Land of the Sun.
> The blue cliffs soar up to heaven; the halls are wreathed in clouds.
> Sacred niches look out upon the valleys; meditation monks sip upon the mist.[99]

98. *Go-Nijō Moromichiki,* Kanji 2.7.25, *uragaki* (1:202).
99. *Go-Nijō Moromichiki,* Kanji 5.8.16 and 17 (2:168).

Doubtless Moromichi's feelings were sincere, but his emotions and their expression—indeed, his entire perception of the mountain—were shaped by cultural memory. Both a creator and heir to Kinpusen's affective landscape, Moromichi reinforced and depended upon the mountain's position as the capital's other, even as he traversed the distance between.

CHAPTER TWO

The Local Pantheon

In a scripture it says, . . . "When the entire Dharma body is transmigrating through the five realms, we call it 'sentient beings.' And when this Dharma body is practicing the six perfections, we call it 'the bodhisattvas.' And when this Dharma body returns and exhausts its source, we call it 'the buddhas.'" Now, when we consider its unfurling traces, we say that this Dharma body "softens its light and mingles with the dust," and we understand it as the radiance of the *kami*.

Thus, although the substance of original grounds and manifest traces is the same, in terms of their benefits, which embrace particular needs, at any given time one may be better and the other worse. In terms of benefitting our country, the guise of unfurling traces is the best! Once upon a time, when En no Gyōja was practicing in the Yoshino mountains, Śākyamuni's image appeared, but En said, "In this form it will surely be difficult to teach the beings of this country. Do hide yourself." Next Maitreya's form appeared. "This still isn't suitable," said En. Then, when Zaō Gongen appeared in the fearsome guise we know today, En said, "*This* one can teach our country." And now [Zaō] unfurls his traces. When practitioners' faith in him is profound, when they revere him single-mindedly, when they are sincere, there is a sympathetic resonance, and they receive his benefits.

—Mujū Ichien (1226–1312), *Shasekishū* (Collection of sand and pebbles)[1]

Processes of localization and combination were fundamental to Kinpusen's cult. Nowhere is this more obvious than with the mountain pantheon. The gods were very much of the mountain they inhab-

1. *Shasekishū* 1.3 (*SNKBZ*, 52:32–33; for an alternative translation, see Morrell, *Sand and Pebbles*, 80–81). The scriptural reference is unclear. On the notion of sympathetic resonance in Buddhist doctrine, see Sharf, *Coming to Terms*, 77–133.

ited; they were also understood to be at once *kami* and buddhas. We have already seen that Kinpusen provided elite, lay pilgrims with a wild source of grace and charisma. By examining the pantheon in light of interpretive and votive practices, this chapter explores how a resolutely local, idiosyncratic cult could command the attention of the central elite. This is not to imply that a localizing or combinatory ethos was unique to Kinpusen. On the contrary, the gods' ties to a particular place and their embodiment of multiple theological categories exemplified a more general heterogeneity in premodern Japanese religious culture. Distinctive cults developed in other regions across the archipelago, resulting in a highly differentiated religious landscape anchored in what Allan Grapard has called "shrine-temple multiplexes."[2] In these composite institutions, the worship of *kami*, buddhas, and other divine figures intertwined. Each site had a unique pantheon and devotional customs legitimated by local myths.

In accounting for this endemic particularism, local and institutional histories have assumed a prominent position in the religious historiography of Japan.[3] Due to the character of the available source material, however, in this and the following chapters, I attend less to the activities of locals (people who lived at or near Kinpusen) than one might expect or wish. In chapter 6, I do introduce a manuscript that includes an aristocratic interlocutor's record of statements made by a mountain monk, but that account is both heavily filtered and extremely rare. Though we know little about the activities of the mountain's resident population during the Heian period, it makes sense to characterize elite pilgrims as participants, not interlopers, in Kinpusen's religious culture. At the very least, they contributed to Kinpusen as a real-and-imagined place by shaping the environment at the peak and maintaining the mountain's broader reputation.

What is at stake, then, is less the religious habits of a stable, geographically bounded community than practices that emerged from social flows through a particular site. For this reason, it may be helpful to think of Kinpusen's cult less as local religion than as localizing religion.

2. Grapard, *The Protocol of the Gods,* 3–11.

3. For representative works, see Ambros, *Emplacing a Pilgrimage*; Moerman, *Localizing Paradise*; Thal, *Rearranging the Landscape*; and Yiengpruksawan, *Hiraizumi.*

People who wrote about the mountain were adamant that its configuration of sacred elements was unique, site-specific, and therefore powerful. The most vivid example of this tendency is to be found in narratives of the origins of Kinpusen's primary god, Zaō, the King of the Treasury, who was said to have sprung from the very rock of the peak. Zaō shows that localization went hand in hand with doctrinal and ritual hybridity. He was very much a Buddhist deity, but he was not at all an orthodox figure, nor was he exclusively Buddhist. In this respect, Kinpusen's pantheon illustrates the ways in which a proselytizing religion may permeate indigenous religious culture. Buddhist ideas stretched into new forms at Kinpusen, while indigenous elements continued to animate religious activity even as they metamorphosed.

The rest of this chapter develops a portrait of Zaō by considering his combinatory and locative power in several modes. The discussion begins with Zaō's hybrid character and his role in the development of *honji suijaku* discourse, which synthesized the categories of *kami* and buddha. It then turns to the range and variability of what I call narrative theology. During the Heian period, Kinpusen's partisans did not produce theoretical treatises; they did, however, tell stories in which they disclosed their convictions about who Zaō was and how he came to be. In the last part of the chapter, I examine the devotional culture of Kinpusen, specifically the practices of burying sutras and offering images. The ritual logic of these practices resonated with Zaō's narrative theology, amplifying his identity and expressing his relationships with the broader pantheon.

Localized Combinations

Zaō almost certainly first evolved at Kinpusen as a chthonic figure. According to myths of his origins, he erupted from the mountain, such that he was of a substance with the peak over which he presided. In visual terms, Zaō's iconography remained fairly fluid, but he generally had a wrathful visage and hair that stood up in three peaks (fig. 2.1). He went bare-chested and held a vajra in his upraised hand. Often he

FIGURE 2.1 Cast and incised bronze plaque depicting Zaō Gongen, excavated from Kinpusen, twelfth century. 21.5 cm diam. Nara National Museum. Photograph by Morimura Kinji, reproduced by permission of Nara National Museum.

raised the leg on the same side of his body, ready to stamp out ignorance and iniquity, and he sometimes sported a third eye in the middle of his forehead. Zaō thus looked very much like wrathful, esoteric Buddhist deities, especially wisdom kings and vajra lads; however, a deity sharing his name and description appeared nowhere in the canon of Buddhist scriptures, ritual manuals, or iconographies.[4] Instead of being determined by translocal Buddhist orthodoxy, Zaō seems to have

4. For Zaō's resonances with canonical texts and iconographies, see Ikawa, "Zaō gongen zō"; Konno, " 'Zaō gongen' no shutsugen"; and Satō Torao, "Kongō Zaō gongen genryū." Amanda Goodman has also pointed out that more hieratic images of Zaō bear strong resemblances to images of the "Ten Wrathfuls" (Skt. *daśakrodha*) found at Dunhuang (conversation with the author, April 2011).

been always and already a hybrid figure who dwelt in the interstices between the categories of "*kami*" and "bodhisattva."[5] In fact, his Heian devotees called him by both names, and by new, combinatory epithets as well.

In the passage from *Shasekishū* quoted in the epigraph for this chapter, the well-known scholiast and Zen cleric Mujū Ichien cast Zaō as a model for the integration of indigenous *kami* and translocal buddhas. Mujū was engaging with a theoretical model that had first been articulated centuries earlier and that researchers today refer to as *honji suijaku,* literally, "original grounds and unfurling traces." Put briefly, beginning in the tenth century, devotees, scholars, and ritualists began to think of *kami* as the unfurling traces (*suijaku*) of buddhas or bodhisattvas, whom they identified as the gods' original grounds (*honji*). The notion that buddhas and *kami* share a fundamental identity but diverge in their embodiments proved to be tremendously influential. Despite nineteenth-century efforts to eradicate it, it continues to inform some sectors of Japanese religious culture even today.[6] As Mujū's account shows, for many premodern thinkers, privilege did not reside with the apparently originary member of the *honji suijaku* binary—the buddhas and bodhisattvas—but rather with their traces, the local gods.

Considered in Mahāyāna terms, when traces adapted themselves to local exigencies they embodied the ideals of compassion and expedient means. From the vantage of *kami* worship and local cults, traces mediated a rapprochement wherein Buddhist ideology could be reworked into a local idiom and used for expansive purposes. As En would have it in Mujū's story, neither the buddha of the past nor the buddha of the future would suit the Japanese; a transformation was required. That transformation was Zaō, and he was known variously as an unfurling

5. Or, as Homi Bhabha put it in his interpretation of the contemporary artist Renée Green's auto-commentary, "the interstitial passage between fixed identities," which "opens up the possibility of a cultural hybridity that entertains difference without an assumed or imposed hierarchy" (Bhabha, *The Location of Culture,* 5).

6. Teeuwen and Rambelli's *Buddhas and Kami* gives a sense of the variation and duration in these interpretive practices.

trace (*suijaku*), provisional manifestation (*gongen*), and transformation-body (*keshin*). In fact, Zaō and his devotees were in the vanguard of *honji suijaku* interpretive strategies.

Together with other cults characterized by a localizing, combinatory ethos, Kinpusen's operated alongside more normative religious subcultures. In this respect, Mt. Kōya and its main temple, Kongōbuji, provide an instructive comparison. Mt. Kōya became an important pilgrimage destination beginning in the eleventh century, and stories about its founder, Kūkai, by then known as Kōbō Daishi, were instrumental in expanding the mountain's cult.[7] These narratives focused on two episodes. In the first, the Daishi "opened the mountain" to Buddhist practice, arriving with a writ from the court granting him the right to establish a monastery at Mt. Kōya. When Kūkai declared his purpose to the local *kami*, the water goddess Niu and the hunter Kōya Myōjin, they offered him their land and support. Kūkai accepted.[8] In these accounts we have no violence, no protest, only the apparently uncomplicated recognition of the superiority and worth of what Kūkai brought to the mountain. This was nothing less than an orthodox tradition steeped in ritual, authorized by lineage, and structured by a great corpus of canonical texts and images, all shining with the gloss of recent transmission from the continent. In point of fact, as Kūkai built Kongōbuji, the "Temple of the Vajra Peak," he imagined Mt. Kōya as an architectonic mandala-realm, using the new spatial and visual culture of esotericism to make the universal and transcendent perceptible in material form.[9]

7. On the revival of Mt. Kōya, see Londo, "The 11th Century Revival"; on the role of narrative, see Shirai, *Inseiki Kōyasan,* 11–58.

8. Though widely cited, a writ from the Council of State, dated Kōnin 7.7.8 and granting Kūkai permission to found Kongōbuji, is preserved only in comparatively late, narrative sources (see "Dajō kanpu Kii kokushi" in *Kōya goshuin engi* [426–27]; for other sources, see *Shingonshū nenpyō,* 14). Some accounts have Niu grant Kūkai her land through an oracle (see, for instance, *Daishi ongyōjō shūki* [178]). For Kūkai's encounter with Kōya Myōjin, see, for instance, *Konjaku monogatarishū* 11.25 (*SNKBT,* 35:70–73).

9. On Kūkai's construction of esoteric Buddhism (*mikkyō*) as orthodox, see Abé, *The Weaving of Mantra*; on his promulgation of esoteric visual culture, including mandala, see Bogel, *With a Single Glance.*

At the same time that pilgrimage to Kinpusen was becoming increasingly popular among the aristocracy in the eleventh century, legends began to circulate that Kūkai had entered *samādhi* instead of dying. More and more often people said that he was seated in eternal meditation in the Okunoin at Mt. Kōya, where he awaited the coming of Maitreya. Such accounts formed a second nexus of institution-building narratives, answering Mt. Kōya's need for a distinctive, local deity who could not be effectively accessed elsewhere. Despite his apotheosis as a semi-divine figure, Kūkai retained his reputation as an eminent monk; in his case, cultural capital and cultic stature went together. The strategies of the Ninnaji monk Saisen (1025–1115) made this particularly clear. On the one hand, by writing an influential tract on Kūkai's eternal meditation, Saisen amplified Kūkai's reputation for miracles. On the other, by producing an unprecedented set of commentaries on Kūkai's treatises and by editing the *Seireishū*, Kūkai's collected literary works, Saisen secured his patriarch's reputation as a great intellectual and literary master.[10] Due to such efforts, Mt. Kōya became known as a magical, yet civilized, place.

By contrast, En no Gyōja, who gradually came to be revered as Kinpusen's religious founder, was ritually powerful but politically dangerous. He operated outside state-sanctioned hierarchies and used hybrid ritual technologies to bring forth a deity who was unique, not universal. Unlike Mahāvairocana, the cosmic buddha celebrated by Kūkai, Zaō appeared in nary a sutra and worked to localize, not totalize. This is not to say that Zaō was not Buddhist, but rather that his identity embraced extra-Buddhist characteristics without necessarily subordinating them. His devotees put it best. On a pilgrimage to Kinpusen, the successful courtier Minamoto no Masazane offered a prayer that read in part: "The transformations of the *kami* are boundless. They are the purport of ten thousand words and the tracks of one thousand wheels. The buddhas' responses are fathomless. It is the bodhisattva Zaō who combines these two."[11] Zaō's devotees loved him as a metamorphic god and celebrated his ability to embody multiple theological categories.

10. Ruppert, "Saisen, 'Kōbō Daishi' "; Horiuchi, *Saisen kyōgaku no kenkyū.*

11. *Gōtotoku nagon ganmonshū* 3.5, inferred date of Kashō 1.7.18 (426).

Setting the Terms

Any time a religion enters a new context, both the religion and the context change. Buddhism's geocultural spread has involved the composition of new scriptures, accommodations to diverse political orders, and combinations with other religions. This last mode of adaptation has often proven to be an interpretive challenge for the field of Buddhist studies because it begs the question of just what the boundaries of Buddhism are. Indeed, recent books and series referring to Buddhisms in the plural reflect a growing perception of the need to account for variation, difference, and particularity—in short, the local qualities—of what is now a global religion.[12] Not surprisingly, different emphases color research in different geocultural areas. For instance, among scholars who work on the Theravāda, Robert Redfield's paradigm of great and little traditions remained influential for much of the twentieth century, though interest has now shifted to questions of how the criteria for being Buddhist are produced and negotiated.[13] By the same token, China specialists spent much of the last hundred years exploring the so-called Sinification of Buddhism, while current research has turned to specific interactions between religious movements and the ways in which those interactions have produced local religious cultures.[14]

In the case of Japan, interdependent processes of Buddhicization and indigenization profoundly shaped premodern culture and are collectively referred to as "the amalgamation of *kami* and buddhas" (*shinbutsu shūgō*). In the tremendously influential analysis advanced by Tsuji Zennosuke in the early twentieth century, this amalgamation

12. For example, Princeton University Press and University of California Press both have series titled "Buddhisms."

13. For applications of Redfield's ideas, see Obeyesekere, "The Great Tradition"; and Spiro, *Buddhism and Society*. For more capacious definitions of Buddhism and attention to the role of local religion in shaping Buddhist thought and practice, see, for instance, Holt, *The Buddhist Viṣṇu*, and *Spirits of the Place*.

14. For Sinification narratives, see Zürcher, *The Buddhist Conquest*; Gregory, *Tsung-mi*; and Yü, *Kuan-yin*. For interaction and combination, see Mollier, *Buddhism and Daoism*; and Teiser, *The Ghost Festival*. For local religiosity, see Robson, *Power of Place*; and Brook, *Praying for Power*.

appeared as a single, teleological process resulting in full combination. According to Tsuji, it also proceeded in distinct phases, in which *kami* were reinterpreted first as sentient beings in need of salvation, next as Dharma protectors, and then as emanations and/or embodiments of buddhas and bodhisattvas. More recent scholarship has shown that processes of amalgamation were more multifarious than this schema suggests and were even open to reversal. In addition, researchers now recognize that Buddhism and *kami* worship were far from the only elements in the mix, for local cults, continental learning, and ideas and practices that can loosely be described as Daoist contributed significantly to premodern Japanese religious culture.[15]

Zaō's cult was clearly bound up with the amalgamation of *kami* and buddhas, and more specifically, with *honji suijaku* interpretive strategies, which gained currency from the eleventh century through the end of the Heian period. Generally speaking, *honji suijaku* thinking advanced a monistic ontology according to which any deity could be shown to be an embodiment of a bodhisattva or a buddha. This emphasis on identity and interconnection fit comfortably with East Asian correlative cosmology, which grounds diverse phenomena in shared metaphysical principles. It also harmonized with Mahāyāna Buddhist concepts such as nonduality, which affirms the radical equality of all existents, or *tathāgatagarbha,* the idea that buddhahood inheres in every sentient being (or at the limit, any being).

The phrase *honji suijaku* is, in fact, a twentieth-century neologism coined to describe a premodern discourse that reimagined *kami* as traces (*jaku*) that translocal, transcendent buddhas and bodhisattvas "unfurled" (*sui*) in Japan. These trace-deities were often understood as "transformation bodies" (Skt. *nirmāṇakāya;* J. *keshin*), a standard term for the flesh-and-blood forms that buddhas assume in order to teach the unenlightened. In *honji suijaku* discourse, the concept of transformation bodies drifted semantically, coming to refer to *kami,* who were understood to participate in the buddhas' saving activity by manifest-

15. Tsuji Zennosuke, "Honji suijaku setsu." The introduction to Teeuwen and Rambelli, *Buddhas and Kami,* provides a good overview of the topic in English. For Chinese and Korean influences on *kami* worship and combinatory religious culture, see, for instance, Tsuji Hidenori, *Hachiman gūji*; and Como, *Weaving and Binding.*

ing in local forms in compassionate response (*ōke*) to the specific needs of Japan's residents. Especially when these gods were mountain deities, devotees often referred to them as provisional manifestations (*gongen*).

As far back as the historical record for Zaō's cult goes, Kinpusen's proponents were involved in the development and application of these terms and concepts. The earliest reliably dated reference to Zaō points to *honji suijaku*'s continental connections and pan-Mahāyāna resonances, as well as its centrality in the imagination of Kinpusen's cult. In his mid-tenth-century encyclopedia, the Chinese cleric Yichu stated that Zaō and Maitreya shared a fundamental identity. "The bodhisattva Vajra Zaō," he wrote, resides upon the summit of Kinpusen as "a transformation-body of Maitreya, like the Mañjuśrī of Mt. Wutai."[16] Yichu was operating at a remove from the emergent sphere of Japanese *honji suijaku* theory, but his ready acceptance of a local deity as a great bodhisattva shows that the assumptions informing *honji suijaku* discourse were neither isolated nor peculiar. In fact, Yoshida Kazuhiko has argued compellingly that much of Japan's amalgamation of *kami* and buddhas developed out of continental patterns.[17]

If Zaō was readily recognizable to Chinese eyes as a transformation-body, he was also an early exemplar of important categories in domestic *honji suijaku* usage. The relevant terms had deep roots in doctrine, but gained currency among laypeople, who began to use them as early as the ninth century.[18] A 937 document from the Daizaifu, the government

16. *Shishi liutie* (459); for a translation, see the epigraph to the introduction. Note that D. Max Moerman cites two Shugendō texts, the *Ryōi* (alt. *Reii*) *sōjō e'in giki* and *Ōmine dōjō shōgon jizai gi*, as earlier examples of the identification of Maitreya and Tuṣita with Zaō and Kinpusen (Moerman, "Archaeology of Anxiety," 271n82). Although these texts bear dates that correspond to 900 and 909, their content is so heavily esotericized that they more likely date to the Kamakura and Muromachi periods. Further research is necessary, but to me it seems safest to read these as products of Kinpusen's cult in later centuries.

17. Yoshida, "Tado Jingūji," "Suijaku shisō no juyō."

18. Tsuji Zennosuke called attention to an 859 petition from a monk named Eryō (802–860?) that includes the term *suijaku* (or *ato o taru*) (Tsuji, "Honji suijaku setsu," 154; *Nihon sandai jitsuroku*, Jōgan 1.8.28 [*SZKT*, 4:37]). More recently, Yoshida Kazuhiko has argued that a prayer dating to 798 provides earlier evidence that the term *suijaku* was moving into general use (Yoshida, "Suijaku shisō no juyō," 207–9; see also *Heian ibun* 17, dated Enryaku 17.8.26 [*komonjo hen*, 1:9–10]).

headquarters in Kyūshū, provides an example of *honji suijaku* language when it was still comparatively rare. The acting governor at the time, Tachibana no Kin'yori (877–941), and his senior clerk directed local monks to transfer construction of a pagoda containing one thousand copies of the *Lotus Sūtra* from Usa to Hakozaki. The eminent *kami* Hachiman, who, like Zaō, was also known as a bodhisattva, was enshrined at both sites. Thus, wrote Kin'yori, "the grounds of that shrine [=Usa] and this shrine [=Hakozaki] are different, and yet the unfurling traces of the provisionally manifest bodhisattva [=Hachiman] are still the same."[19] In effect, the governor was advancing the argument that provisional manifestations (*gongen*) are unfurling traces (*suijaku*), capable of appearing at multiple sites while maintaining a single identity. In what appears to be the next documented use of the terms *gongen* and *suijaku,* the literatus Ōe no Masahira (952–1012) referred to "the unfurling traces of the provisional manifestation of Atsuta," or Atsuta Gongen.[20] This usage suggests that the term *gongen* was fast becoming an epithet. In 1007, Fujiwara no Michinaga, Kinpusen's most famous pilgrim, buried sutras at the summit in a gilded bronze tube with an inscription that includes the phrase, "Hail to Śākyamuni, lord of the teachings, and Zaō, his provisional manifestation," or, "Zaō Gongen."[21] From then on, this class of deities swelled rapidly, with the mountain gods of Kumano, Sannō, and Hakusan joining Zaō and Atsuta as well-known *gongen.*[22]

Whereas Zaō became a *gongen* rather early, it took some time for his devotees to begin to think of him as a trace. The first clear reference

19. Memorandum from the Dazifu, dated Jōhei 7.10.14 (*Dai Nihon komonjo, iewake* 4, *Iwashimizu* 481 [2:230–32]).

20. Prayer dated Kankō 1.10.14 and attributed to Ōe no Masahira, in *Honchō monzui* 13 (*SNKBT,* 27:352).

21. Prayer inscribed on a sutra tube buried by Fujiwara no Michinaga, dated Kankō 4.7.11 (*KSS,* 236–37; also published in *Heian ibun,* inscription 86 [*kinseki-bun hen,* 88–90]).

22. For Hiei's Sannō, see "Hieizan fudangyō engi," attr. Fujiwara no Akihira (989–1066) and dated Eishō 6.4.22, in *Honchō zoku monzui* 11 (*SZKT,* 29.2:186). For Kumano, see *Heian ibun* 1250, dated Ōtoku 3.11.13 (*komonjo hen,* 3:1243). A list of *honji* for the Kumano deities given by Minamoto no Morotoki (1077–1136) is a *locus classicus* for *honji suijaku* at Kumano, but does not feature the term *gongen*; see *Chōshūki,* Chōshō 3.2.1 (*ZST,* 17:179). For Hakusan, see *Heian ibun,* supp. doc. 287, dated Kanji 8.11.12 (*komonjo hen,* addenda vol., 66).

to Zaō in this light dates to 1088, when Fujiwara no Moromichi declared in the same prayer discussed in the previous chapter, "I bow down before Zaō, the sacred traces."[23] (Given the syntax, this could just as easily mean, "I bow down before Zaō's sacred traces.") By the late Heian period, narratives were variously identifying Zaō as a trace of Maitreya, Śākyamuni, or an Indian monarch, while still others simply stated that he had "unfurled his traces" upon the peak.[24]

Most of the uses of *honji suijaku* terminology mentioned here came from the hands of laymen, indicating that they were part of a shared body of religious discourse and practice that can fruitfully be understood as vernacular religion.[25] Lay involvement is particularly noteworthy given that the central terms—*honji, suijaku, gongen, keshin,* etc.—derived largely from canonical sutras and the Tiantai/Tendai commentarial tradition. Although these literatures are conventionally deemed the province of Buddhist monastics, we know that some members of the Japanese aristocracy did actively engage with them. For instance, Michinaga, who advanced the notion that Zaō is a *gongen,* occasionally studied the Tendai classics.[26] Furthermore, the term *gongen* occurs in the *Sūtra of Golden Light,* which was recited annually at court and was thus known to lettered clerics and laymen alike.[27]

23. Prayer for Fujiwara no Moromichi's pilgrimage to Kinpusen, dated Kanji 2.7.27 (*KSS,* 331; also published in *Heian ibun,* supp. doc. 280 [*komonjo hen,* addenda vol., 63–64]).

24. See, for instance, *Kumano sansho gongen Kinpusen kongō Zaō engi* (32); and *Kumano sansho gongen Kinpusen kongō Zaō gokibun* (75).

25. Here I follow the lead of Hank Glassman and Keller Kimbrough, who have recommended the term "vernacular Buddhism" as an alternative to "popular religion" so as not to imply an absence of elite participation. Glassman and Kimbrough, "Vernacular Buddhism."

26. In 1004, while he was in the middle of a series of thirty lectures on the *Lotus Sūtra,* Michinaga read from Zhiyi's *Miaofa lianhua jing wenju* (*Commentary on the Lotus Sūtra*; J. *Myōhō renge kyō mongu*), *T.* 1718 (34:1–149). In 1005, when he was starting another series of thirty lectures on the *Lotus,* he read from Zhiyi's *Miaofa lianhua jing xuanyi* (*Subtle Meaning of the Lotus Sūtra*; J. *Myōhō renge kyō gengi*), *T.* 1716 (33:681–814). (*Midō kanpakuki,* Kankō 1.7.8 and Kankō 2.5.4 [1:99, 144, 324]).

27. For use of the verb *quanxian* (J. *gongen*) to refer to the buddhas' manifestation in transformation bodies, see *Jinguangming zuishengwang jing* (*Sūtra of Golden Light*; J. *Konkōmyō saishōō kyō*), *T.* 665 (16:406c9).

Among the likely sources for *honji suijaku* terms and ideas, perhaps the most important was exegesis of the *Lotus Sūtra,* especially two influential Tiantai commentaries.[28] Both are attributed to the patriarch Zhiyi (538–97) but were redacted by his disciple Guanding (561–632). Of the two, the *Subtle Meaning of the Lotus Sūtra* is more often discussed in the secondary literature, for it makes a famous distinction between the first fourteen chapters of Kumārajīva's translation of the *Lotus,* which it classifies as "trace" teachings, and the latter fourteen chapters, which it classifies as "original" teachings. In the Tiantai interpretive universe, origin and trace map onto the epistemological, ontological, and hermeneutical categories of the true and the provisional. The *Subtle Meaning* also stipulates that for all their differences, origin and trace should be understood as nondual, because like other perspectives or phenomena, they interpenetrate. Thus, Zhiyi and Guanding adjure us, "Origin and trace, amazing though it may be, are one."[29] Although the second of these exegetical texts, *Commentary on the Lotus Sūtra,* has been largely ignored in research on *honji suijaku,* it is important because it includes multiple references to "unfurling traces." Here we find such dicta as: "Let us interpret origin and trace. The buddhas of the three treasuries must enter nirvana, but in their compassion, they unfurl their traces and produce bodies to abide in the world."[30] Japanese interpreters, including laypeople, saw *kami* as precisely this sort of contingent, yet abiding, body. In turn, they saw Zaō as an exemplar of this type of incarnation.

For all its ties to Buddhist discourse, *honji suijaku* thinking also resonated with other elements in the broader sphere of East Asian religious culture. As some have speculated, Zaō's antecedents may stretch

28. Note that although Tsuji Zennosuke emphasized the "Measureless Lifespan Chapter" of the *Lotus Sūtra* as a source for *honji suijaku* thought, the chapter does not employ the actual terms *honji* and *suijaku* (*Miaofa lianhua jing, T.* 262 [9:42a29–44a4]). For doctrinal sources for *honji suijaku* discourse not covered by Tsuji, see Yoshida, "Suijaku shisō no juyō," 203–6.

29. *Miaofa lianhua jing xuanyi, T.* 1716 (33:764b22–23). On the role of *hon* and *jaku* as interpretive categories in Tendai circa the twelfth century, see Stone, *Original Enlightenment,* 168–75.

30. *Miaofa lianhua jing wenju, T.* 1718 (34:5a16–17).

back to continental Daoism.[31] In the passage quoted at the beginning of this chapter, Mujū Ichien asserted that trace-deities like Zaō result from processes in which "the Dharma body 'softens its light and mingles with the dust.'" Here Mujū combined buddha-body theory with a figure that Tendai exegetes had borrowed from Daoist classics. According to the fourth chapter of the received *Daodejing* (Classic of the Way and its virtue), in relation to the myriad creatures, the Dao "blunts their sharpness; untangles their tangles; softens their light; merges with their dust."[32] This intertextual resonance was not isolated: other thinkers used the idea of traces in applications that were not, or were not solely, Buddhist. In his foundational commentary on the *Zhuangzi,* for example, Guo Xiang (252–312) relied quite heavily on the concept of traces, which for him were the tracks that spontaneous, sagely activity leaves in our world.[33]

In Japan, Heian-period thinkers and writers applied the idea of traces to real-and-imagined space by stipulating that traces were constituent features of holy places. The idea that physical traces left by heroic religious specialists made the past present was clearly in force at Kinpusen by the end of the eleventh century. During a 1092 pilgrimage, the courtier and literatus Ōe no Masafusa described the precinct in front of the mountaintop Zaō Hall as "the traces of En no Gyōja's practice of the Way."[34] This comment provides the earliest evidence that En was understood as having brought Zaō forth at the peak, a view that

31. Working from secondary source material, Wakamori Tarō asserted that during the Tang, the bodhisattvas Avalokiteśvara and Vajra Zaō served as the attendants of the Great Prime Heavenly Worthy; he also noted Zaō's ability to grant longevity (see Wakamori, *Shugendōshi kenkyū,* 63–65). Hayami Tasuku maintained that Zaō was connected to the god of Mt. Tai; however, serious problems with this argument have been pointed out by Saitō Tōru (see Hayami, *Heian kizoku shakai,* 239–42; and Saitō Tōru, "Fujiwara no Michinaga," 19–20).

32. *Daodejing,* verse 4 in the Wang Bi text; translation lightly adapted from Ivanhoe, *Daodejing of Laozi,* 4. Zhiyi picked up this usage as well; see, for instance, his *Mohe zhiguan* (*Great Calming and Contemplation*; J. *Maka shikan*), *T.* 1911 (46:80a16).

33. On Guo Xiang's interest in traces, see Brackenridge, "The Character of Wei-Jin Qingtan"; Ziporyn, *The Penumbra Unbound*; and Fukunaga, "Chūgoku shūkyō shisōshi," 57–58.

34. "*Gōki* fragment."

later became an article of faith for Shugendō practitioners.[35] For present purposes, the more important point is that by imprinting Kinpusen with his own traces, En sealed the mountain as a sacred site. His traces paralleled the activity of Zaō by making the past, if not the future, accessible from the here-and-now. This was not an isolated gesture. In a prayer celebrating the reconstruction of Hashidera, an obscure temple that had fallen into ruin, Masafusa wrote: "One can see no halls, and yet still within the rustic court one can sense the sacred traces" of Gyōgi, the famous holy man credited with founding the temple.[36] Similar claims that miraculously enduring traces define and sanctify place abound in the visual and literary record.[37]

Play and Variability

The interpretive practice of identifying local gods with buddhas was characterized by play, not systematic fixity, and this bears emphasis. Researchers have often referred to *honji suijaku* as a paradigm,[38] which implies that a totalizing theological structure determined divine form, in the same way that a grammatical paradigm drives a noun's morphology. This is problematic. If we expect regular, systematic relationships to have obtained between buddhas and *kami*, we will be frustrated and liable to conclude, as Susan Tyler has put it, that the correlations drawn by premodern thinkers "do not ring true" or that the interpenetration of *kami* worship and Buddhism was "irrational, medieval, and outlandishly complicated."[39]

35. For En as Zaō's theurge, see *Konjaku monogatarishū* 11.3 (*SNKBT,* 35:17). This collection was compiled circa 1120, marking the beginning of the dissemination of this particular micronarrative in the written record.

36. *Gōtotoku nagon ganmonshū* 2.4, dated Kanji 5.12.17 (274).

37. See, for example, *Ippen shōnin eden,* scroll 2, *dan* 7, line 2 (48, 358), in which Shitennōji figures as an "ancient trace" where Śākyamuni once preached, or *Daigoji engi,* according to which the search for an appropriate site to build a temple involves "seeking out traces" (*DNBZ,* 117:246).

38. Matsunaga, *Philosophy of Assimilation*; Teeuwen and Rambelli, *Buddhas and Kami,* 1–53.

39. Susan Tyler, *The Cult of Kasuga,* 8, 94.

A more fruitful approach begins with the recognition that while *honji suijaku* relationships were both associative and patterned, they were rarely singular and hardly ever fixed. One trace could have multiple grounds, and one ground could have multiple traces; different interpreters could propose entirely different sets of identifications, and they could express them through a range of vehicles. In addition to the visual representation of *honji suijaku* relationships, Allan Grapard has highlighted the use of paronomasia, punning, and graphic puzzles; Susan Tyler, dreams; and Irit Averbuch, dance.[40] In the case of Kinpusen, the historical record indicates that narrative and devotional practice played the most significant roles in expressing the identities and relationships among the local pantheon during the Heian period.[41]

Narratives represented Zaō as Maitreya, Śākyamuni, and an Indian monarch, and hinted that he might be a dragon. Far from being mutually exclusive, these identities were interlinked. Although the story adumbrated by Mujū became canonical within the later Shugendō community, Zaō's identities also proliferated. The compiler(s) of the *Kinpusen sōsōki* (Record of the founding of Kinpusen) rattled off a list of Zaō's original grounds circa 1300: "For the past, Śākyamuni. For the present, Thousand-Armed [Avalokiteśvara]. For the future, Maitreya. Or some say Mahāvairocana. Or some say Kṣitigarbha."[42] It was in the Heian period that this kaleidoscopic range with its totalizing temporal reach began to form.

The earliest firmly datable reference to Zaō in the Japanese historical record links him to Maitreya through Kinpusen's association with gold. In the *Sanbōe,* a collection of didactic stories written to educate a princess in 984, the aristocratic man of letters Minamoto no Tamenori wrote that the creation of the Great Buddha of Tōdaiji had ground to a halt in the eighth century because there was no gold with which to gild

40. On visual culture, see Nagasaka, *Shinbutsu shūgōzō*; and essays in Sanford, LaFleur, and Nagatomi, *Flowing Traces.* On other modes of interpretation and representation, see Grapard, "Linguistic Cubism"; Susan Tyler, *The Cult of Kasuga*; and Averbuch, "Dancing the Doctrine."

41. Do note that other strategies became important later on. For instance, linguistic play and esoteric interpretive rubrics are clearly in evidence in later texts, such as the fourteenth-century *Kinpusen himitsuden.*

42. *Kinpusen sōsōki* (*SS,* 3:362; *KSS,* 45).

the monumental image of Vairocana. When prayers were tendered to "Zaō of Golden Peak," the god replied: "This mountain's gold is to be used for Maitreya's world. I am only guarding it. It would be impossible to give you any." He then advised the court on how to find an alternative source.[43] Fittingly, Zaō's name, which means King of the Treasury, helped him to assimilate into Maitreyan visions of the future. Scriptures maintain that when Maitreya is reborn from Tuṣita Heaven into our world as the next buddha, there will be a great transformation: "the land will be flat and pure, like a crystalline mirror," and gold and other treasures will be so abundant that they are piled up into mountains.[44] Sutras assert that until that time, Śākyamuni's disciple Mahākāśyapa will reside within a mountain in northern India, keeping the historical buddha's robe in trust.[45] In the imagination of the tenth-century Japanese court, Zaō played a similar role by keeping the Peak of Gold safe for Maitreya. By the eleventh century, some people were of the opinion that Zaō *was* Maitreya, and by the twelfth, popular entertainers were singing of Kinpusen as a "land of forty-nine mansions," a common epithet of Tuṣita Heaven.[46] From this family of resonances, it became clear that Zaō could manipulate time: he could make the Maitreyan future present.

Soon Zaō's devotees were asserting that he could do the same for the past by embodying Śākyamuni. In the story of Dōken/Nichizō's

43. *Sanbōe* 3.22, rites held in the sixth month (*SNKBT,* 31:195; for an alternative translation, see Kamens, *The Three Jewels,* 328). Note that a reference to "the bodhisattva Vajra Zaō" occurs in the biography of Shōbō (832–909), which is attributed to Ki no Yoshihito (n.d.) and may date to 937 (see *Daigoji engi* [*DNBZ,* 117:249]; and *Shōbō sōjō den* [*ZGR,* 8.2:720]). In addition, the *Shozan engi* includes a story widely accepted as a citation from a 932 entry in Prince Shigeakira's diary, the *Rihōōki* (alt. *Ribuōki*), mentioning "the bodhisattva Vajra Zaō" as the lord of Kinpusen (see *Shozan engi* [*NST,* 20:110, 350]; and/or *Kokon chomonjū* 2.42 [*NKBT,* 84:79–80]). "Dōken shōnin myōdoki," discussed in this chapter and chapter 1, may also date to the tenth century.

44. *Foshuo Mile da chengfo jing* (*Sūtra of Maitreya's Great Buddhahood*; J. *Bussetsu Miroku dai jōbutsu kyō*), *T.* 456 (14:429a18, b19–20).

45. *Foshuo Mile da chengfo jing, T.* 456 (14:433b11–c14.); cf. *Foshuo Mile xiasheng jing* (*Sūtra of Maitreya's Descent and Birth*; J. *Bussetsu Miroku geshō kyō*), *T.* 453 (14:422b12–c13.).

46. *Genji monogatari,* "Yūgao" (*SNKBT,* 19:117–18; translation in Royall Tyler, *The Tale of Genji,* 1:64); *Ryōjin hishō* 264 (*SNKBT,* 56:76).

FIGURE 2.2 Nichizō's encounter with Zaō, who appears as a bodhisattva, detail from *Kitano Tenjin engi emaki*, thirteenth century. Ink, color, and cut gold on paper, 28.8 cm ht. Image © The Metropolitan Museum of Art. Courtesy of Art Resource, NY.

visionary journey at Kinpusen, introduced in chapter 1, the eminent monk who sits upon a throne of seven jewels at the summit declares: "I am the bodhisattva Zaō, the King of the Treasury, a transformation-body of [Śākya]muni. This land is the pure land of Kinpusen."[47] As discussed in chapter 1, cultural memory associated Kinpusen with Gṛdhrakūṭa, a mountain often understood by Mahāyānists to be Śākyamuni's pure land. Eschewing Zaō's wrathful iconography, one thirteenth-century illustration of this episode plays visually upon Zaō's identity with the buddha of the past by portraying him as a monk (fig. 2.2).

Zaō developed other identities, which rippled outward from his association with Śākyamuni and the terrestrial magic trick that brought India to Japan. For instance, Zaō was occasionally said to have been an

47. "Dōken shōnin myōdoki," in *Fusō ryakki,* Tengyō 4, third month (*SZKT,* 12:220).

ideal, wheel-turning king (Skt. *cakravartin*; J. *rin'ō, tenrin'ō*) from Vārāṇasi. In a twelfth-century *engi* narrative, we find the following discussion, which is distinguished by its level of detail:

> The three bodies of Kinpusen's Kongō Zaō, Vajra King of the Treasury, are the great kings of the country of Vārāṇasi. As *kami* and as humans, they are not the same or equal. For the benefit of myriad beings, upon the courts of Rājagṛha, at the foot of Mt. Daṇḍaka, and in the vicinity of the Deer Park, through seven generations of descendants of the golden wheel-turning sage king, the bodies of Kongō Zaō appeared in these three places.
>
> He forsook the country of Vārāṇasi; if one distinguishes among those same dwelling places, the sacred sites where he did good deeds are as innumerable as accumulated dust-motes. As he crossed the River of Sand, his feet never rested upon the earth, and the Congling Mountains shot towering upward. He crossed the waves of the seven rivers and the nine seas, and walked . . . the peaks of the lofty mountains.[48] He passed through the borders of the worst realms, where there is no Way. He sprang forth in the district of Yoshino in the country of Great Japan, and unfurled his traces upon the peak for the sake of the myriad beings in the sixty provinces [of Japan], for their security in this life and good rebirth in the next.
>
> Why have I passed through the borders of the worst realms where there is no Way? For the sake of myriad beings have I walked forth. Why did I walk forth, o myriad beings? Was it not for repentance, through practice and through principle? For no other reason did I spring forth and unfurl my traces upon the peak.[49]

In this account, Zaō retained a connection to Śākyamuni by incarnating at Mt. Daṇḍaka, where the Buddha engaged in his pre-enlightenment asceticism; at the Deer Park in Sārnāth, where the Buddha embarked upon his teaching career; and at Rājagṛha, where the Buddha often expounded the Dharma. Nevertheless, this narrative maintained that Zaō was not Śākyamuni but rather a king who

48. A two-character sequence of nonstandard graphs, which are very difficult to construe, is elided here.

49. *Kumano sansho gongen Kinpusen kongō Zaō engi* (43–44).

incarnated in multiple bodies through multiple generations, traveled across the Gobi Desert (the River of Sand), and ultimately sprang forth at Kinpusen, where he settled by unfurling his traces. The most striking portion of the passage may be the last paragraph, where the narrative voice shifts into a confessional first person. There Zaō testifies to his dedication to Japan's salvation, which he frames in terms of a Tendai-style repentance that proceeds through both the contemplation of principle and ritual activity in the provisional realm of phenomenal existence. As a contrast to Mujū's representation of Zaō in *Shasekishū,* this characterization marks one limit—comparatively secular, royal, and Indian—to the god's narrative persona.

In another turn toward the edges of Zaō's character, the idea that he was in some sense (also) a dragon connected to notions that he was particularly fond of the *Lotus Sūtra*. Dragons live in water, control rainfall, and reside in caves; thus, in terms of climate and topography, the Ōmine Range is ideal dragon country. During the Heian period, pilgrims routinely made offerings near the peak at a shrine to the Eight Dragon Kings. These deities appear in the *Lotus Sūtra* as leaders in the Buddha's audience at Gṛdhrakūṭa.[50] An eleventh-century biography of a *Lotus*-reciter named Denjō (d. 849?) celebrates Zaō's fondness for the *Lotus Sūtra* at the same time that it connects him to dragons. While Denjō was in seclusion upon the peak, he is said to have dreamed of a deity—probably, but not explicitly Zaō—in "the form of a *yakṣa* crowned with a dragon."[51] The archaeologist Sugaya Fuminori is convinced that Kinpusen's mountaintop hall was built around a fissure known as the "mouth of the dragon." Because the inner sanctum generally remains closed, descriptions of it are exceedingly rare; however, when government

50. Today, these gods are enshrined at Ryūsenji in the village of Dorogawa at the western foot of Kinpusen. Both they and a dragon goddess from Mt. Nanao have been the focus of new religious movements during the twentieth century (Suzuki Masataka, *Nyonin kinsei,* 57–70).

51. *Hokke genki* 3.93 (*NST,* 7:174–75, 554; for an alternative translation, see Dykstra, *Miraculous Tales,* 115–16); cf. *Konjaku monogatarishū* 14.17 (*SNKBT,* 35:317–19). The date given in *Hokke genki* for Denjō's death is 849 (Kashō 2). See also *Konjaku monogatarishū* 12.36, where Zaō features among a set of imposing *kami* who come to hear recitations of the *Lotus Sūtra* (*SNKBT,* 35:183).

inspectors commanded entry in the early Meiji period, they noted that when they struck a low wall around "the dragon hole," it sounded hollow.[52] Heian-period sources do not mention a dragon hole, but by the 1300s, Zaō was indeed understood to have emerged from such a lair. In one of several accounts of En no Gyōja's theurgy recorded in the fourteenth-century *Kinpusen himitsuden* (Secret transmissions about Kinpusen), En calls Zaō forth from a "treasure rock" in "Blue Dragon Pond," which is a "dragon-hole pond" located underneath the altar in the inner sanctum of the mountaintop Zaō Hall.[53]

In sum, Kinpusen's Heian-period narrative theology formulated the following propositions: Zaō was a *kami,* a buddha, a bodhisattva, and/or all of the above; he was purposely brought forth by the great thaumaturge En no Gyōja; he was a manifestation of Maitreya, the buddha of the future, and/or of Śākyamuni, the buddha of the past; his mountain was a realm of gold; he was extremely fond of the *Lotus Sūtra*; and he was associated with dragons. His realm was closed to women, as discussed in chapter 1, and his mountain was said to have flown to Japan from India or China. As we shall see shortly, Zaō had his apotheosis when he sprang from the living rock of Kinpusen's peak. Finally, as Masazane pointed out, it was Zaō's ability to combine the qualities of buddhas and *kami* (and, we might add, kings and dragons) that made him special. Others echoed this assessment, celebrating Zaō's simultaneous embodiment of multiple categories and personalities. A popular song, collected in the twelfth century by Retired Emperor Go-Shirakawa, lyrically exclaims:

Peak of Gold: in all the world
To Vajra Zaō-Śākyamuni-Maitreya,
To Inari, to Yawata, to Konoshima, too,
There's never a time that people won't go![54]

52. Sugaya, "Kumano to Ōmine shinkō," 101; Blair, "Zaō Gongen," 28.

53. *Kinpusen himitsuden* (*KSS,* 26–27). By comparison, discourse about dragon holes has been much more prominent and consistent in the local cult at Murōji (see Fowler, "In Search of the Dragon"; and *Rearranging Art and History,* 15–21).

54. *Ryōjin hishō* 263 (*SNKBT,* 56:76).

Located very close to the capital, Inari, Iwashimizu (Yawata), and Konoshima were among the select Twenty-Two Shrines. In comparing Zaō to court-revered *kami* and identifying him with the past and present buddhas, this song demonstrates that he was at once protean and resolutely local. He wielded the power of the buddhas with the particularity of the *kami*, and was best reached in his home terrain.

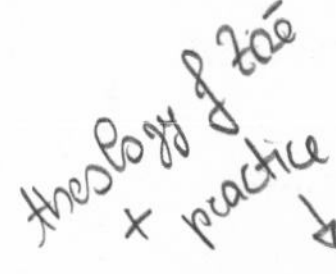

Buried Sutras

Pilgrims to Kinpusen were in the vanguard of sutra burial, a new mode of practice with a ritual logic that complemented Zaō's narrative theology. At Kinpusen in 1007, Fujiwara no Michinaga conducted the first firmly datable sutra burial in Japan. The early date and abundance of Kinpusen's sutra mound (*kyōzuka*) suggest that the mountain cult exerted a significant influence on sutra burial, which became popular throughout Japan and endured into the nineteenth century.[55]

Inasmuch as Buddhists at other times and places have interred scriptures, Japanese sutra burial is not unique. The earliest-known burials of Buddhist texts occurred in Gandhāra during the first centuries of the common era, though whether these were carried out in the course of funerary rituals, to preserve or dispose of manuscripts, or for some other reason is unclear.[56] The manuscript cache at Dunhuang provides a striking example of a library enmured, but again, the reasons for which these texts were sequestered are subject to ongoing debate.[57] Tibetan Treasure texts were understood to have been hidden (and were sometimes physically buried) in order to be discovered in the future; these provide a source of revelation that may diverge considerably from received tradition.[58] In East Asia, it became common practice to inter

55. For more on sutra burial, see chapter 5; and, for instance, Seki, *Kyōzuka no shosō*; Miyake Toshiyuki, *Kyōzuka ronkō*; Hosaka, *Kyōzuka ronkō*; and Moerman, "Archaeology of Anxiety."

56. Salomon, "Why Did the Gandhāran Buddhists Bury Their Manuscripts?"

57. Rong, "The Nature of the Dunhuang Library Cave."

58. Gyatso, "The Logic of Legitimation," and *Apparitions of the Self*, 147–61; Aris, *Hidden Treasures*.

scriptures under—or to install them inside—the heart pillars of pagodas as an analogue of more conventional buddha relics.[59]

Despite all these similarities, no direct historical connection between continental practices and Japanese sutra burial has been substantiated.[60] In fact, the differences are quite pronounced. Far from being new compositions like Tibetan Treasures, the texts used in Japanese sutra burials were canonical. Unlike the materials from Gandhāra and Dunhuang, which show signs of lengthy use prior to their interment, manuscripts used in Japan were made to be buried. Finally, unlike relic texts secreted in stupas, they were placed directly in the earth, outside the walls of any architectural structure, and they were produced and offered independently of building projects.

Received explanations of sutra burial tie it to anxiety that the Dharma was coming to an end (*mappō*); however, the *mappō* thesis cannot fully explain sutra burial at Kinpusen. Although *mappō* thought was indeed a factor in Heian religious culture, the intents and purposes driving sutra burial varied considerably across time and place, as D. Max Moerman has shown.[61] Furthermore, as William Londo has remarked, the Heian archaeological and documentary records for Kinpusen do not evince an explicit concern with the end of the Dharma.[62] In light of Zaō's narrative theology, at least two other reasons can be adduced for sutra burial's integration into the Kinpusen cult.

First, Zaō's name and status linked him to textual practices. As mentioned above, Zaō was literally King of the Treasury. In Japanese, the "three baskets" (Skt. *tripiṭaka*) that comprise the Buddhist canon become "the three treasuries" (*sanzō*). In more concrete terms, the repositories in which temples keep their textual treasures are known as sutra treasuries (*kyōzō*) or simply treasuries (*hōzō*). It follows that

59. Shen, "Realizing the Buddha's *Dharma* Body"; Tsiang, "Embodiments of Buddhist Texts"; Boucher, "The *Pratītyasamutpādagāthā* and Its Role." See also chapter 5.

60. For a review of hypotheses, see Seki, *Kyōzuka no shosō,* 53–79; for a more recent discussion, which brings in rock-carved sutras and veneration of relics, see Kikuchi, *Kamakura bukkyō e no michi,* 106–33.

61. Moerman, "Archaeology of Anxiety."

62. Londo, "The Idea of Mappo," 118–19.

the domain of the King of the Treasury would be an appropriate place to lay up stores of scriptures.

Second, both Zaō and buried sutras were understood to spring from the earth. Narratives of Zaō's apotheosis often maintain that he "sprang forth" (*yūshutsu* or *wakidasu*) from the peak. Although many of these stories are late, the micronarrative of Zaō's eruption dated back to at least the eleventh century: in 1090, Fujiwara no Moromichi noted that he stopped during his pilgrimage to show his reverence at "the rock that produced Zaō."[63] Today, this outcropping near the summit is known as "the springing-forth rock," and, as Suzuki Shōei has noted, it is physically and conceptually homologous to boulders (*iwakura*) understood to be embodiments and/or seats for *kami*.[64]

If Zaō acted like a *kami* by emerging from the peak and settling upon an *iwakura*, he also acted like characters in the *Lotus Sūtra*. Chapters 11 and 15 of the Kumārajīva translation feature well-known episodes of "springing forth" (C. *yongchu*; J. *yōshutsu*). Although the verbs used for Zaō (涌) and in the *Lotus* (踊) are not identical, they are graphically and semantically similar; moreover, the former often glosses or replaces the latter in scriptural variants, commentarial literature, and popular usage.[65] In the eleventh chapter of the sutra, the wonderful stupa of the buddha Many Jewels (Skt. Prabhūtaratna; J. Tahō) emerges from the earth in front of Śākyamuni's seat. The audience learns that, technically speaking, Prabhūtaratna entered *parinirvāṇa* eons ago. Through the power of a vow made during his lifetime, however, his relics appear in his stupa whenever and wherever the *Lotus Sūtra* is preached. Moreover, if beings wish it (and of course they do), his relics transform, and he appears in the living flesh to bear witness.[66] Later, in the fifteenth chapter, myriad bodhisattvas

63. *Go-Nijō Moromichiki,* Kanji 4.8.10, *uragaki* (2:6).

64. Suzuki Shōei, "The Development of Suijaku Stories."

65. For Prabhūtaratna's stupa and the bodhisattvas who spring from the earth, see *Miaofa lianhua jing, T.* 262 (9:32b18, c7 and 39c29–40a1). One example of a shift in orthography is Zhanran's (711–82) reference to the "Emerging from the Earth Chapter" in *Fahua xuanyi shiqian* (*Explanation of the Subtle Meaning of the Lotus*; J. *Hokke gengi shakusen*), *T.* 1717 (33:826a5).

66. *Miaofa lianhua jing, T.* 262 (9:32b16–34b22).

spring from the earth to hear the *Lotus Sūtra* and praise Śākyamuni and Prabhūtaratna.[67] Not surprisingly, the sutra most often buried in Japan was the *Lotus*.

Sutra burial thus combined myths of Zaō's eruption with motifs from the heart of Mahāyāna orthodoxy and put them to work in localized, non-normative practice. Pilgrims were convinced that their manuscripts would eventually spring forth, reenacting the eruptions of Zaō, Prabhūtaratna, and the subterranean bodhisattvas. In the votive inscription from his 1007 sutra burial at Kinpusen, Fujiwara no Michinaga expressed his intent to be reborn in Amitābha's Land of Bliss at the end of his present life, and then to return to this world when Maitreya becomes a buddha and teaches the Dharma. "The scrolls of the sutras that I bury in this place," he wrote, "will naturally spring forth, causing the assembled throngs to perform good works."[68] Michinaga also noted that he buried the *Lotus Sūtra* "to repay the kindness of the Lord Śākyamuni, to meet Maitreya directly, to draw near to Zaō, and to bring me to enlightenment." The gesture of interring scriptures thus intensified Zaō's identifications with the buddha of the past and the buddha of the future, as well as the devotee's connection with all three.

Votive Bronzes

In addition to burying sutras, Kinpusen's pilgrims offered bronzes on which they had traced images of the mountain's pantheon. Excavations at the summit conducted during premodern sutra burials, early-modern construction and repair work, and modern archaeological digs have unearthed hundreds upon hundreds of artifacts, including caches of bronze and copper mirrors and plaques (see figs. 2.1 and 2.3). In archaeological and art-historical research, these are analyzed into four

67. *Miaofa lianhua jing, T.* 262 (8:39c29–40b3). In their discussions of Michinaga's sutra burial, Hosaka Saburō and Inokuchi Yoshiharu have also noted the resonance with these scriptural episodes (Hosaka, *Kyōzuka ronkō,* 14; Inokuchi, "Fujiwara no Michinaga no maikyō," 14–15).

68. For the prayer inscribed on Michinaga's sutra tube, see note 21 and chapter 5.

overlapping subgenres: mirrors (*kagami*), incised mirrors (*kyōzō*), flat-backed plaques (often referred to as *mishōtai*), and hanging plaques (*kakebotoke*). It is the latter three types, which bear images of the pantheon, that concern us here. Incised mirrors, which average about ten centimeters in diameter, were cast with embellishments on their backs, and began to be produced in the decades prior to the year 1000. Plaques with flat backs, some with flanges allowing the plaque to be set into a plinth for display, range from twenty to thirty centimeters in size and seem to have developed during the eleventh century. *Kakebotoke,* which are designed to be suspended, are usually of the same approximate size and often bear relief and repoussé figures. Images of this type began to appear around the twelfth century.[69]

Kinpusen's exceptionally rich archaeology indicates that votive bronzes were central to the mountain's cult, and it has even been argued that the subgenre of *mishōtai* plaques originated there.[70] In a classic catalogue of Kinpusen's archaeology produced in 1937 for the Imperial Museum (now Tokyo National Museum), Ishida Mosaku and Yajima Kyōsuke described and classified hundreds of representational objects—*kyōzō, mishōtai, kakebotoke,* and fragments thereof. This sample is not comprehensive, for more excavations were carried out after the catalogue was published. Moreover, Ishida and Yajima did not distinguish artifacts by date in their analysis. Nonetheless, their data are striking: images of Zaō comprise a consistent majority, while images of local *kami*, buddhas, and bodhisattvas form significant minorities in the material record.[71] Zaō was king of the mountain, but just as clearly, he was part of a broader pantheon.

In form and function, bronzes combined traditions of *kami* worship with Buddhist imagery and devotion. They also represented a rapprochement between continental and indigenous custom. Unincised mirrors had long been traded as prestige goods, and in Japan, mirrors incised

69. For more on these genres, see Yamato Bunkakan, *Kyōzō no bi*; Naniwada, *Kyōzō to kakebotoke*; and Tōkyō Kokuritsu Hakubutsukan, *Kyōzō.*

70. Morioka, "Kakebotoke kigen kō."

71. Ishida and Yajima, *Kinpusen kyōzuka ibutsu*, provides two substantially different sets of statistics. The chart on page 40 analyzes *kyōzō,* while that on page 299 may include different types of artifacts. Nevertheless, Zaō retains pride of place in both data sets.

with images of buddhas and bodhisattvas date back to the tenth century. Their production was almost certainly inspired by Song and Liao prototypes, as well as the use of mirrors in Buddhist ritual and language.[72] At the same time, mirrors were important to *kami* worship. They featured prominently in the court's mythology of the sun goddess, who was represented as the ancestor of the imperial line in the eighth-century *Nihon shoki* and *Kojiki.* During the Heian period, both incised and unincised mirrors were used as votive objects, especially at sites where buddhas and *kami* combined, and ancient mirrors commonly number among shrines' treasures. For instance, a large cache of unincised mirrors has been excavated at Nagoya's Tado Shrine, where one of the first shrine-temples (*jingūji*) had been built in the mid-eighth century.[73] As *honji suijaku* interpretive patterns developed, images incised on mirrors or plaques were often used to represent the original grounds of *suijaku* deities. When these images were placed in the sanctuaries of *gongen* or other hybrid gods, *kami* and buddha literally reflected each other in a visual extension of their theological relationships. By the same token, the prevalence of images of both Zaō and *kami* at Kinpusen indicates a willingness to represent deities in their native, trace bodies rather than in the guises of their original grounds.

The sheer number of bronzes suggests that they functioned primarily as votive offerings. As king of the Peak of Gold, Zaō was literally in his element when represented in metal. Such images were fairly portable, making them attractive to pilgrims, even those of comparatively limited means. Information about the Heian-period mountaintop hall is scant, but we do know that in the late eleventh century, multiple wood images of Zaō were arranged in front of a curtain that closed off the chancel (*moya*) from view.[74] Metal images may have been used in the same way. Some may have been displayed, and it is also possible that some were enshrined; at the very least, in the nineteenth century,

72. Shen, "Image in a Mirror"; Naitō, "Kyōzō no seiritsu"; Yamato Bunkakan, *Kyōzō no bi.*

73. Mainichi Shinbunsha "Jūyō Bunkazai" Iinkai Jimukyoku, *Jūyō bunkazai,* 29:93–94. For the importance of *jingūji* in the history of *shinbutsu shūgō,* see Yoshida, "Tado Jingūji"; and Tsuji Hidenori, *Hachiman gūji,* 375–422. On visual representation, see Kanda, *Shinzō,* 10–13.

74. For the mountaintop Zaō Hall in the late eleventh century, see "*Gōki* fragment."

a number were kept in the closed inner sanctum.[75] Finally, they may have been buried as offerings, as suggested by the number of bronzes excavated from the peak. Votive interment would have fit perfectly with the custom of sutra burial and Zaō's reputation as a chthonic deity. That is, pilgrims may have intentionally placed images of the god, rendered in his own element, within his own ground.

Images of Zaō varied significantly in terms of iconography and style, and as I have argued elsewhere, this representational flexibility matched Zaō's theological character: he was a changeable deity who played with norms rather than living by them.[76] By contrast, although the images of buddhas and bodhisattvas varied stylistically, they tended to cleave to iconographic standards, indicating that they were part of a larger, orthodox Mahāyāna culture. Images of *kami*, too, gravitated toward common representational norms: for the most part, the figures depicted wear courtly garb and look very much like high-ranking laypeople, with a few adopting the guise of a monk.[77] Judging from extant materials, then, iconographic variation was directly proportional to a deity's categorical fluidity.

Most of the images of *kami* seem to depict three deities who also appear in the written record as important local figures. These are Komori, Katte, and Kinpu, alternately known as Mikumari, Yamakuchi, and Konshō; official histories show that these gods were enshrined in the Yoshino area by the 800s.[78] Shrines to them still stand in the village of Yoshinoyama—Katte in the middle of town, Mikumari at the southern reach of the settlement, and Kinpu at the beginning of the march into the higher mountains.

75. "Kinpusenji shinbutsu daihenkaku no ki," entry for Meiji 7.8.7, Kinpusenji kiroku, part 15 (Murakami, Tsuji, and Washio, *Meiji ishin shinbutsu bunri shiryō,* 3:365–66). See also Blair, "Zaō Gongen," 28.

76. Blair, "Zaō Gongen," 9–12.

77. On standard iconography for *kami,* see Kanda, *Shinzō*; and Kageyama, *Shintō bijutsu.*

78. In 840 the Yoshino Mikumari shrine was granted the junior fifth rank lower (*Shoku Nihon kōki,* Jōwa 7.10.7 [*SZKT,* 3:112]). Between 852 and 854, the court granted the "god of Kinpu" the junior third rank, the title of *myōjin,* and offerings for the Ainbe Matsuri (*Montoku jitsuroku,* Ninju 2.11.9, Ninju 3.6.10, and Saikō 1.6.1 [*SZKT,* 3:42, 53, 61]). In 859, the court promoted the same deity to the senior third rank and promoted the Yoshino Mikumari and Yoshino Yamakuchi deities to senior fifth rank lower (*Nihon sandai jitsuroku,* Jōgan 1.1.27 [*SZKT,* 4:17]).

Of these three, Mikumari/Komori appears to have been the most popular among mid- to late-Heian pilgrims, although the early-Heian court granted her ranks that were persistently lower than those of Katte and Kinpu, both of whom are male. Aristocratic diaries show that she was enshrined at the summit of Kinpusen by the beginning of the eleventh century, and among the seventy-four images of *kami* in Ishida and Yajima's survey, twenty depict her.[79] In the simplest terms, Komori is a goddess, but like many other *kami*, she instantiates what Allan Grapard has called a "singular plurality."[80] The Kinpusen bronzes often represent her as a triad, either three women or one woman attended by a monk and a male courtier (fig. 2.3). Her character is multifaceted, as well, with each of her major personae anchored in a particular name. On the one hand, she is Mikumari, Division of the Waters, a watershed *kami* like the Niu goddesses, who are enshrined nearby at Kawakami and Mt. Kōya. As early as the year 700, the court was praying to Mikumari for rain, and in the 900s, hers was one of four Yamato watershed shrines in receipt of government patronage.[81] The goddess's connection to the water supply and agricultural fertility likely mediated the turn into a second identity as Komori, protector of children. Heian pilgrims called her by this name, and even today she continues to preside over pregnancy, childbirth, and the rearing of children.[82] But the goddess was capable of granting other wishes, as well.

In a rare votive inscription, the donor of an eleventh-century *mishōtai* depicting Komori lodged a distinctive request (see fig. 2.3):

> A female disciple from the Ki Clan humbly addresses herself to you:
>
> I offer a representation of the three Komori deities. For years, the Ki Clan has made pilgrimages to approach you; however, I have not come. There-

79. Ishida and Yajima, *Kinpusen kyōzuka ibutsu*, 79.

80. Grapard, "Linguistic Cubism."

81. In 698, the court addressed prayers for rain to "the *kami* of the Mikumari Peak in Yoshino" (*Shoku nihongi*, Monmu 2.4.29 [*SZKT*, 2:3]). The *Engi shiki* indicates that circa 900 Mikumari was included in the court's Toshigoi and Amagoi festivals (*Engi shiki* 3, 8, and 9 [*SZKT*, 26:56, 161, 190; translation in Bock, *Engi-Shiki*, 1:107, 2:70, 119]).

82. During several visits to the shrine between 2000 and 2007, I observed written prayers for pregnancy and votive offerings of model breasts meant to ensure a good milk supply. Do note, however, that the shrine's current administrators refer to the goddess(es) as Mikumari, not Komori.

FIGURE 2.3 Cast and incised bronze plaque depicting Komori, excavated from Kinpusen, 1051. 24.2 x 25 cm. Courtesy of Tokyo National Museum.

> fore, I dedicate this representation in order to transform my female body, that I may become male and make a pilgrimage to approach you, and also that I may receive favor when the Merciful Lord comes to this world.
>
> Eishō 6 (1051), fifth day of the eighth month
> A female disciple of the Ki Clan[83]

The petitioner was likely a member of the local gentry from nearby Ki Province. Though she made no mention of water, fertility, or children, she was certainly concerned with issues of gender and sex. Her desire

83. For a transcription of the inscription, see *KSS*, 238.

to come into closer contact with Komori, and by extension with Zaō and Maitreya, put her into conflict with Kinpusen's territorial ban on women. Knowing this, she hoped that the merit from her offering would help her to be reborn male so that she could climb the mountain herself. Ideologies of women's impurity had gained significant ground in Japan by this time, and prayers for male rebirth were not uncommon. Mahāyāna sutras included many narratives of male-to-female sex changes, setting canonical examples for petitioners' hopes.[84] In all probability, the Ki woman gave the plaque to a male proxy to offer on the mountaintop on her behalf; notably, instead of turning to Zaō, she sought help from the only female member of the local pantheon.

By the Kamakura and Muromachi periods, it was being said that the Katte deity was Komori's husband, but less is known about him than his sometime wife. During the early Heian, the court worshiped him alongside Mikumari as Yamakuchi, "Mouth of the Mountains."[85] Today, his shrine in Yoshinoyama is located near the Zaō Hall, and he may be rooted where he stands, at the gateway to Kinpusen. Yamakuchi's other name, Katte, literally "Victor," suggests that he had a martial character. Mid- to late-Heian pilgrims made no note of a shrine to Yamakuchi or Katte at the peak, and the archaeological record suggests that he played at best a minor role at Kinpusen itself. Among the bronzes unearthed from the peak, Ishida and Yajima identified only three candidates—all in armor—as Katte. At the shrine in Yoshino, however, at least two wood sculptures, both depicting armored deities, survive, and during the Kamakura period, Katte appears to have gained fame as a military god.[86]

A considerable number of bronzes representing a courtier (a classic form for male *kami*) have also been found at the peak.[87] Some of these

84. On the trope of sex-change, see Schuster, "Changing the Female Body." See also chapter 1 for further discussion of impurity in the context of the ban on women.

85. See note 78.

86. For martial visions of Katte during the Muromachi period, see *Kinpusen himitsuden* (*KSS,* 18–19, 39). For wooden sculptures depicting him in armor, see Tōkyō Kokuritsu Hakubutsukan and Kyūshū Kokuritsu Hakubutsukan, *Kokuhō: daijinja ten,* 190–91 (pl. 215). For bronze images excavated from the peak, and the possibility that a deity depicted as an equestrian was Katte's *wakamiya,* see Ishida and Yajima, *Kinpusen kyōzuka ibutsu,* 77–79.

87. According to Ishida and Yajima, fully half of the seventy-four images of *kami* to which they had access show male courtiers (Ishida and Yajima, *Kinpusen kyōzuka ibutsu,* 79).

images may be alternative representations of Katte/Yamakuchi, but many, if not most, portray Konshō, also known as Kinpu or Kane no Mitake. In terms of court-conferred rank, this deity was preeminent among the local *kami,* and his name suggests that he was the tutelary deity of the mountain. Much later, during the Meiji period, the government actually mandated that he replace Zaō as the head of the local pantheon. That policy was short-lived, but it resulted in an expansion of Kinpu/Konshō's shrine and reinforced his status as an eminent local god.[88] During the Heian period, however, elite pilgrims seem to have taken little interest in him, for they left him out of their journals and their prayers. This silence, paired with the significant number of images of courtly male *kami* from the peak, suggest that Kinpu may have represented a local tradition that was too staid to attract the interest or devotion of the urban elite but that did have its own regional constituency.

By contrast, men who came from the capital were very interested in another divine collective that is all but absent from the visual record. These were the Thirty-Eight, whose shrine at the summit received significant attention, but about whom we know very little. At present, the one known Heian-period visual representation of this group can only be identified by inference. It appears on a great bronze that once stood at the peak of Kinpusen and that measures nearly a meter across. Now damaged, the bronze is incised with an image of Zaō surrounded by a group of armed, grotesque figures (fig. 2.4). In its original, symmetrical form, the image almost certainly included a full complement of thirty-eight attendants.[89] Apparently a martial bunch of local origin, these gods may belong to the pan-Buddhist class of local spirits who have transformed into Dharma protectors.

None of these deities—Zaō, Komori/Mikumari, Katte/Yamakuchi, Konshō/Kinpu, or the Thirty-Eight—was canonical. They appeared neither in the Buddhist scriptures nor in indigenous court mythologies. Rather, they grew up as local phenomena. Zaō, as we have seen, was

88. Blair, "Zaō Gongen," 26, 30.

89. Though owned by the Tokyo temple Sōjiji, the bronze is now curated by the Tokyo National Museum. For a fuller discussion of its iconography and history, see Blair, "Zaō Gongen." Also note that one of eighteen *shinzō* kept at the Mikumari Shrine in Yoshinoyama is understood to depict the Thirty-Eight as a single male figure; this image dates to the Kamakura period, however (Oka, *Shinzō chōkoku no kenkyū,* 232).

FIGURE 2.4 Cast and incised bronze plaque depicting Zaō Gongen and the Thirty-Eight, formerly kept at Kinpusen, 1001. 68 x 76 cm. Photograph by Morimura Kinji, courtesy of Nara National Museum. Reproduced by permission of Nishiarai Daishi Sōjiji, Tokyo.

literally of the peak. Even as his cult began to spread in the mid-Heian period, he retained his autochthonous identity—he belonged to Kinpusen as much as Kinpusen belonged to him.[90] Komori, Kinpu, and Katte were gods of the place in their own right, and were not worshiped elsewhere. Fittingly, the Thirty-Eight also stayed close to home.[91]

Kinpusen's divine community was undeniably parochial, for it resided in what appeared to metropolitan eyes as the hinterland. But during the mid-Heian period it was also at the forefront of new devo-

90. On the spread of Zaō's cult, see Hatta, *Reigen jiin to shinbutsu shūgō*, 209–35.

91. Note, however, that as a result of Kinpusen's annexation by Kōfukuji, the Thirty-Eight were enshrined at Kasuga in the mid-twelfth century (see chapter 7). With the later spread of Shugendō, their cult further expanded. For instance, there is an early-seventeenth-century shrine to the Thirty-Eight on the grounds of Ishiyamadera.

tional activities like sutra burial and theological developments like *honji suijaku*. Its flexible, combinatory aspects captured the imagination of sophisticated urbanites: pilgrims made great gifts to the category-crosser Zaō, the shadowy collective of the Thirty-Eight, and Komori, whom they represented as both a laywoman and a monk. By contrast, they seem to have had little to no interest in Kinpu, who was truer to an exclusive type, and they made no mention of worshiping any buddhas or bodhisattvas at the mountain other than Śākyamuni and Maitreya, who were closely connected to Zaō.[92] The categorical poles of *kami* and buddha defined the conceptual limits of Kinpusen's pantheon, but it was the play in the space between—the hybrid, the combinatory, and the local—that was most compelling.

Conclusion

As the images on votive bronzes show, a theological triangle structured the pantheon at Kinpusen: *kami* were clearly distinguishable from buddhas and bodhisattvas, and Zaō played the mediating role of the third term. Inhabiting the space between *kami* and buddhas, Zaō engaged with but never obviated their differences, for aspects in his own personae could shift rapidly or come into simultaneous play. This protean, kaleidoscopic god exerted a centripetal force on members of the local pantheon, binding them together into a local community that began to resemble a kinship group, such that by the fourteenth century the Thirty-Eight were said to be the servants of Zaō and the offspring of Komori and Katte.[93]

Two late-Heian representations of the pantheon illustrate how pilgrims perceived the gods and brought them into the sphere of their

92. A number of bronzes excavated from Kinpusen represent Avalokiteśvara and Amitābha; however, we have virtually no textual evidence for their worship during the Heian period.

93. *Kinpusen himitsuden,* which dates to the 1330s, states that the Thirty-Eight are Komori's children, and that Komori is the wife of Katte (*KSS,* 19). *Tamakisan gongen engi,* which dates to circa 1350, includes a more elaborate backstory, in which Katte goes to Izumo and Komori sends some of their children to serve En no Gyōja (149).

own practices. These stand as examples of how the imagined and the real intertwined in place and practice. One of these representations, a mandala, is visual, while the other, a prayer, is at once a literary and a liturgical text. The mandala (fig. 2.5) was excavated from the peak and takes the form of an incised, gilt plate, the center of which is inscribed with a circular moon-disc and fitted with a thin metal aureole. At one time, this almost certainly framed a sculpted image of Zaō. Chased images of five *kami*, one buddha, and two bodhisattvas surround this now-absent Zaō.

This array gave formal expression to the relationships among the local gods. First of all, it engaged all three points of the theological triangle—*kami*, buddha, and trace—and represented them hierarchically. Zaō, the trace par excellence, was situated at the center. As Ronald Davidson has put it, "Maṇḍalas are implicitly and explicitly articulations of a political horizon in which the central Buddha," or, in the present case, the trace deity, "acts as the [Supreme Overlord] in relationship to the other figures of the maṇḍala."[94] Here Zaō, King of the Treasury, not only mediates between but also reigns over local *kami* and great bodhisattvas: the traces, as Mujū exclaimed, "are the best." On this point, it is important to note that although Zaō's physical absence from this image may recall Derrida's analysis, wherein the trace marks an unbridgeable absence, his absence is due to historical chance.[95] For Heian devotees, Zaō was very much alive, accessible, and literally kicking: by unfurling as a trace upon the peak, he brought the temporally and physically remote into the here-and-now.

The arrangement of other deities around this ironically empty center proceeds by hierarchy and kinship. Designated by their cardinal positions as the second tier of the pantheon, Śākyamuni, one of Zaō's original grounds, and Kinpu, the primary tutelary *kami*, balance each other at the top and bottom of the mandala. Katte and Komori occupy the subordinate lateral positions in the cardinal tier, with their children (*wakamiya*) in the lower corners. As Śākyamuni's subordinates, two

94. The brackets mark a replacement of "Rājādhirāja" with Davidson's own translation of the term as "Supreme Overlord" (Davidson, *Indian Esoteric Buddhism,* 131, 371–72n64).

95. Derrida, *Of Grammatology,* 61, 66.

FIGURE 2.5 Schematic drawing of a mandala in chased bronze depicting the local pantheon, excavated from Kinpusen, now held by Ōminesanji, Nara Prefecture and on loan to the Tokyo National Museum, late Heian period. Drawing by Lily Rushlow.

manifestations of Avalokiteśvara, Cintāmaṇi and Ārya, occupy the corners to his right and left.

This mandala exemplifies the open quality of Kinpusen's cult. No other examples of this particular array survive, suggesting that an anonymous patron and artisan adopted an esoteric Buddhist rubric and then selected an idiosyncratic set of deities to suit their own taste. Whereas the mountain's Heian-period narrative theology addressed the relation of the other deities to Zaō, the idea that Avalokiteśvara was one of Zaō's original grounds entered the written record only in the Kamakura period. Thus, the mandala may point to a case of mythic innovation, an expression of personal devotion to Avalokiteśvara, or both. More importantly, the mandala's creators were unconstrained in making this choice. Zaō's play as *kami,* buddha, king, and/or dragon provided space for his devotees to select, order, and interpret the pantheon as they saw fit. To some extent, this is true in any religious situation: across the world, believers and practitioners find ways to duck the prescriptions of ecclesiastical authorities in order to create personally satisfying devotional worlds. For Heian pilgrims, the theological flexibility characterizing Kinpusen's local religious culture was undoubtedly part of the mountain's appeal.

In language, pilgrims voiced a different sense of the pantheon. Once again, Fujiwara no Moromichi provides a good example, this time of how Kinpusen's gods came together in the mind and activity of an ardent devotee. As noted in chapter 1, pilgrims commissioned liturgical prayers well before they set out from the capital, which means that these texts have a strong subjunctive tone. Rendered in heavily stylized, literary prose by hired writers, they can in no way be taken as unmediated expressions. Because they were designed to be read out loud before an audience of clerics and laymen, liturgical prayers belonged to the sphere of public discourse. For these reasons, these texts express a more-or-less shared sense of who the gods should be, and this makes them all the more informative as traces of theological imagination at and about Kinpusen. The prayer for Moromichi's 1088 pilgrimage began by enumerating scriptures he offered and buried at the peak (see chapter 5). In the second part of the prayer, Moromichi evoked Kinpusen's affective landscape (see chapter 1). He then addressed the mountain pantheon:

> I go forward in order to consider Śākyamuni's precious teaching of the single vehicle; I go back in order to form a karmic tie with the three future assemblies of [Maitreya,] the Merciful One. The power of my prayer is supreme and I do not doubt that I will meet him in person. Ah! Ever guarding longevity as lasting as gold and stone, I revere the miraculous powers of Vajra Zaō. Clearing away the eight major and nine minor misfortunes, I depend upon the divine favor of the Thirty-Eight. If there should be evil influences from the five demons, the Eight Great Dragon Kings will clear them away. If there should be treason among our retainers, the mountain deities will extinguish it. . . .

> But in my heart I have a prayer: Zaō, please bestow your response. Bowing low before your precinct, I finally offer thanks due from a previous life. I pray reverently to the great bodhisattva Zaō, the Thirty-Eight, the Eight Great Dragon Kings, the mountain deities, and the Dharma-protecting deities. Each of you, bestow upon me the mysterious response of your divine spirit, and without fail shine upon the sincere heart of your disciple. Your merit is fathomless; your benefits are boundless. Respectfully I address myself to you.[96]

In this portion of the prayer, Moromichi traversed what is by now familiar terrain: he cast Zaō as a trace connected to both Maitreya and Śākyamuni. At the same time, he called upon the Dragon Kings and the Thirty-Eight. Although he made no mention of Komori on this occasion, in a second pilgrimage two years later, he feted her with offerings of her own (see chapter 5).

As one of a long line of pilgrims from the regents' house, Moromichi sought out and reenacted the precedents of his ancestors at Kinpusen. This lineage-based orthopraxy was informed by a profound concern to discover and create signs of the past and the divine. From generation to generation, the regents engaged in shared ritual protocols at a mountain marked by En no Gyōja's traces; they celebrated Zaō as a trace deity; and they left their own textual traces in the form of journals and buried scriptures. In the process, they wove the real-and-imagined Peak of Gold into the fabric of their political ascendancy, a process that is the subject of the next chapter.

96. Prayer for Moromichi's pilgrimage (see note 23).

CHAPTER THREE

Ritual Regimes

> Those privileged to see him close at hand revered him; those who watched at a distance paid homage from afar. Many of them would have been happy to become trees and shrubs in the vicinity of the Buddha Hall!
>
> —*Eiga monogatari* (*Tale of Flowering Fortunes*)[1]

As a real-and-imagined place, Kinpusen proved immensely attractive to members of the ruling elite during the eleventh century. In order to understand how a two-week journey to a remote mountain peak fit into the religious lifestyles of elite laymen, we need to explore both the devotional and political dimensions of the journey and its destination. The second part of this book focuses on the three people who have left us the best evidence for Heian-period pilgrimage to Kinpusen: Fujiwara no Michinaga, Fujiwara no Moromichi, and Retired Emperor Shirakawa. This chapter examines spatial dynamics, structure, and strategy in their ritual practice, with the aim of situating these men and the Peak of Gold in the larger context of Heian religious culture.

Ritual pervaded the lives of Heian aristocrats. As in other societies, ritual performance contributed to authority and expressed social precedence, providing a key medium for the production of power. For these reasons, members of the high elite were concerned with ritual protocol to an extent that may, in the words of William McCullough, "baffle or appall the casual modern observer."[2] Indeed, one early-twentieth-century historian excoriated Heian courtiers as a bevy of "pampered minions and bepowdered poetasters" whose ritualizing was a sign of

1. *Eiga monogatari* 15, "Utagai" (*SNKBZ,* 32:185; translation from McCullough and McCullough, *Tale of Flowering Fortunes,* 2:501).

2. William McCullough, "The Capital and Its Society," 180–81. On regency ritual, governance, and courtiers' diaries as a source for both, see Piggott and Yoshida, *Teishinkōki,* 8–78.

their degeneracy.[3] This type of dismissal occludes more than it illuminates. As Norbert Elias has shown, if we are to understand a court society, we must understand its ritual, from its etiquette to its grand spectacles.[4] Researchers working on the Heian period have already noted that religious and state ideology were mutually supporting, and that scripture was used to legitimate particular political agendas.[5] To further illuminate the interdependence of ritual and politics, in this chapter I present a theoretical model of what I call ritual regimes, flexible patterns of practice through which members of the high elite strengthened their rule and displayed their piety. This model accounts for elite engagement with Kinpusen, and shows that ritual—whether directed at the *kami,* buddhas, angry ghosts, natural forces, or other human beings—was integral to political life. As the anthropologist and historian David Kertzer has quipped, "There can be no politics without symbols, nor without accompanying rites."[6]

In the following pages, I turn first to the question of why elite laypeople took the trouble to go to Kinpusen, and then to a schematic assessment of their ritual lifestyles more generally. In laying out the ritual regimes model, I argue that Kinpusen played an important role in the regents' enactment of their political ascendancy. By extension, when the retired emperors began to eclipse the regents in the early twelfth century, they effectively replaced Kinpusen with Kumano. In shifts such as these, we see striking examples of the spatial and ritual dimensions of politics.

Of Kinpusen and Kings

Between 969 and 1090, from generation to generation, members of the regents' patriline made the pilgrimage to Kinpusen, marking the mountain as "theirs." They did not, however, go to Kinpusen for fun. In his

3. Murdoch, *A History of Japan,* 1:230. In the same passage, Murdoch more famously referred to Heian aristocrats as "an ever-pullulating brood of greedy, needy, frivolous dilettanti."

4. Elias, *The Court Society,* and *The Civilizing Process.*

5. Kuroda, "Ōbō to buppō" (in *Kuroda Toshio chosakushū* 2:185–96), "Imperial Law and Buddhist Law"; Deal, "The *Lotus Sūtra*"; McMullin, "The *Lotus Sutra* and Politics."

6. Kertzer, *Ritual, Politics, and Power,* 181.

work on transportation history, Shinjō Tsunezō has pointed out that prior to the Edo period (1603–1867), travel involved austerity, not recreation.[7] Indeed, both fiction and diaries make much of the tribulations of the road. High-ranking aristocrats rarely traveled more than two days' journey from the capital, with the exception of occasions upon which junior nobles were sent to Ise as royal envoys. Provincial governors might be dispatched to far-flung posts, and military commanders sallied forth to quell uprisings and pirates, but in the eyes of the high elite, that sort of travel was déclassé. The higher one's status, the closer one stayed to the capital. In this respect, Kinpusen and the two-week journey required to reach it were remarkable.

Why, then, did elite pilgrims in general and the regents in particular make the effort to go to the southern mountains? Perhaps the simplest answer is that Kinpusen was a kingly mountain. Several factors contributed to its majesty: what I call cardinal ideology; its reputation as a realm of gold; its literary and historical associations with rites of kingship; the sheer extremity of the pilgrimage; and the cultural mnemonics, discussed in chapters 1 and 2, that cast the mountain as an otherworldly realm and Zaō as a category-crossing deity.

The appeal of the southern mountains was rooted in part in cardinal ideology. In coining this term, I mean to designate a loose system of directional values based on continental geomancy, five phases theory, and social custom. The Japanese had long since absorbed and adapted Chinese notions of kingship; thus, in lexical usage, "to face south" meant to be or become king.[8] Like the palace and the throne, buddha halls and buddha images were oriented toward the south. Directional consciousness structured etiquette and ritual: the lord faced south, the subject north; the host faced east, the guest west. The old capitals that had preceded the city of Heian—Asuka, Fujiwara, Heijō, and Nagaoka—had all been oriented toward the south. Because these cities were located within the Nara and Yamashiro Basins, a southerly bearing brought urban pilgrims first to Yoshino and then to the heights of the Ōmine Range. Thus, Kinpusen as the southern mountain par excellence was an apposite terminus for regal and Buddhist journeys.

7. Shinjō Tsunezō, *Shaji sankei*, 4.

8. On continental influence on early Japanese models of sovereignty, see Piggott, *The Emergence of Japanese Kingship.*

In keeping with its royal reputation, premodern writers repeatedly figured Kinpusen as a mountain of precious metal, despite a lack of evidence that it actually bears lodes of gold.[9] The didactic collection *Hōbutsushū* (Collection of treasures), which was compiled around the Jishō era (1177–81), waxes particularly fulsome: "There are five phases in heaven, and gold is among these. There are seven treasures on earth, and gold is first among them. We call the Buddha a golden man, and as for *kami*, there is Kinpusen. We call the emperor the sacred king of the golden wheel."[10] In this text, gold's preeminence ranged across categories, beginning with the cosmological five phases and the seven treasures often invoked in sutra literature.[11] Gold also emblematized the Buddha, as well as the *cakravartin,* the ideal Buddhist king. Thus, in the course of showing that gold governs a full ontological range, from the inanimate to the divine, the *Hōbutsushū*'s compiler, Taira no Yasuyori (n.d.), marked Kinpusen and Zaō as kingly because they were golden. In economic practice, too, gold reigned supreme, for it was bound up with the prerogatives of Japanese kingship. The emperor held rights to the cache of gold kept in the palace stores, and, at least in theory, had the authority to control foreign trade, where transactions were based on gold and silver standards.[12]

In using place to symbolize their bloodline and perpetuate their political legacy, the Fujiwara regents used a strategy remarkably similar to that adopted by earlier members of the ruling elite. Yoshino, Kinpusen's gateway, was closely associated with the sovereign Tenmu (d. 686, r. 673–86), who established his own lineage as a stem dynasty when he wrested the succession from his nephew in a brief civil war in 672.[13] Prior to the conflict, Yoshino had been important to Tenmu's mother,

9. For examples, see *Sanbōe* 3.22 (*SNKBT,* 31:195; translation in Kamens, *The Three Jewels,* 328); and *Uji shūi monogatari* 2.4 (*SNKBT,* 42:45–46; translation in Mills, *A Collection of Tales,* 167–68).

10. *Hōbutsushū* 1 (*SZKT,* 40:16).

11. Both the terms used to describe the seven treasures and their interpretation have varied, but gold does tend to occur first in such lists. For example, see the brief discussion of the seven treasures in Pure Land texts in Gomez, *The Land of Bliss,* 318.

12. Hotate, *Ōgon kokka,* 278–88; von Verschuer, *Mono ga kataru kōekishi,* 146–47.

13. For more on the politics of succession, as well the reigns of Tenmu and his descendants, see Piggott, *The Emergence of Japanese Kingship.* On the war, see Duthie, "The Jinshin Rebellion."

who reigned under the names Kōgyoku and Saimei (594–661, r. 642–45 and 655–61). She had maintained a residence in Yoshino, and during the war, the area became a strategic haven for her son. After he succeeded in establishing his reign, Tenmu made Yoshino a site for peace by compelling his own sons to take an oath there, forswearing violence among themselves. The next sovereign, Jitō (645–702, r. 686–97), who was Tenmu's wife as well as his niece, made more than thirty royal progresses to Yoshino, tracing and retracing the path linking it to the new capital, Fujiwara. Jitō's aim seems to have been to recall Tenmu's majesty and to prolong his peace. Her precedent was certainly compelling: up through the 730s, sovereigns who were Jitō and Tenmu's direct descendants continued to travel to Yoshino.[14] Whether by intent or happenstance, the regents adapted this custom of repeated, lineage-based journeys to serve their own purposes more than two centuries later.

The classical trope of "surveying the realm" (*kunimi*) also contributed to the religious culture in which the regents participated. The stereotypical *kunimi* involved a sovereign climbing a mountain to survey the land below in a ritualized gesture of lordship, though the forms and valences of *kunimi* actually varied significantly.[15] During the years around 700, Yoshino had been inscribed in cultural memory as a site where royals engaged in this type of practice. In one of his well-known poems about the area, the famous poet Kakinomoto no Hitomaro (n.d.) represented Jitō as she gazed out over Yoshino, compelling the fealty of the land and its gods:

She who is a god
In action godlike has ordained
That by Yoshino,
Where seething waters deepen into pools,

14. Duthie, *Man'yōshū and the Imperial Imagination*, 243–74. Yoshino progresses for the sovereigns Monmu (683–707, r. 697–707), Genshō (680–748, r. 715–24), and Shōmu (701–56, r. 724–49) are reported in the *Shoku nihongi*, Taihō 1.2.20 and 27, Taihō 2.7.11, Yōrō 7.5.9, Jinki 1.3.1, and Tenpyō 8.6.27 (*SZKT*, 2:9, 15, 96, 100, 140).

15. For an interpretation along classic lines, in which *kunimi* appears as a single, fixed ritual form, see Ebersole, *Ritual Poetry*, 23–32. By contrast, Torquil Duthie argues that *kunimi* was, in fact, more fragmented in both concept and practice (Duthie, "Envisioning the Realm").

Lofty halls shall rise,
Lifting high above the stream;
And when she climbs aloft
That she may gaze upon her land,
Fold upon fold
The mountains standing in green walls
Present as tribute
Offered by the mountain gods
In springtime
Blossoms worn upon the brow,
And when autumn comes
Deck themselves in yellow leaves.[16]

Although explicit reference to *kunimi* faded from the historical and literary record in the early and mid-Heian period, the regents' journeys to Kinpusen resonated with past rhetoric and practice. When he arrived at the peak in 1088, Fujiwara no Moromichi wrote, "Taking the measure of the realm, we looked around: the manifold mountains were like jewels."[17] Standing at the southern boundary of his own experience, deep in the mountains, Moromichi was in a very real sense surveying his domain.

The journey to Kinpusen was, in fact, so difficult and dangerous that it simultaneously tested the limits of sovereignty and personal endurance. This made Kinpusen the perfect site from which to make symbolic claims of lordship. In more ways than one, it was the farthest most elite pilgrims had ever been from home. Travelers had been ambushed and killed en route to the mountain, and the upland paths were (and are) physically challenging, especially in bad weather.[18] For men used to the flatlands of the capital, the pilgrimage could be downright punishing. Furthermore, pilgrims had to earn the right to

16. *Man'yōshū* 1.38 (*SNKBT,* 1:40–41; translation from Cranston, *The Gem-Glistening Cup,* 1:94–95). See also note 15 for a discussion by Ebersole.

17. *Go-Nijō Moromichiki,* Kanji 2.7.25, *uragaki* (1:202).

18. For instance, Fujiwara no Sanesuke noted that the Owari Governor Fujiwara no Fuminobu was attacked on his way back from Kinpusen in 989 (*Shōyūki,* Eiso 1.4.4–6 [1:172]). Similarly, Genjo (d. 1032), who was overseer of Kinpusen at the time, was murdered in the mountains in 1032 (*Sakeiki,* Chōgen 5.6.20 [*ZST,* 6:351]; *Nihon kiryaku,* Chōgen 5.6.18 [*SZKT,* 11:282]).

be present at the mountain by abstaining from meat, sex, and wine for three months prior to their departure from the capital (see chapter 4). When they set out from home, they donned "pure robes," most likely of undyed hempen cloth, putting aside the splendid garments that were so much a part of court life and its intricate status system. After an initial boat ride out of the capital, they walked the entire way.[19] With this physical and symbolic departure, elite men began to traverse their realm, an undertaking that strengthened their right to assert control over it.

As discussed in chapter 1, Kinpusen was identified not only with the limits of the civilized world, but also with other worlds. It was said to be a portion of Gṛdhrakūṭa, and it was construed as a Japanese version of Mt. Wutai. Members of the elite were conversant with these ideas, and may well have imagined their journeys opening onto a pan-Asian, Buddhist cosmos.[20] Thus, by going to Kinpusen they figured themselves not only as lords of their own land but also as citizens of the world at large.

Pilgrimage to Kinpusen, then, exemplified what David Kertzer has called "virtues of ambiguity,"[21] for pilgrims were free to pick and choose from a polyvalent semiotic field. The regents in particular used pilgrimage to generate solidarity among their line without ever having to produce any iterative consensus about what the pilgrimage "meant." Participants or observers might see Kinpusen pilgrimage as family duty, *kunimi*, ascetic journey, rite of lordship, and/or reenactment of ancient precedent. In this respect, the combinatory quality of Kinpusen's pantheon is especially salient. As discussed in chapter 2, the mountain gods developed in dialogue with, but were not determined by, Buddhist canons of orthodoxy. Meanwhile, they had deep roots in the imagery and rhetoric of *kami* worship, as well. The regents then, were free to imagine Zaō as a bodhisattva, *myōjin*, or *gongen*—and as their protector and patron.

If pilgrimage allowed for interpretive play, it also created opportunities for public enactments of piety. Departures and returns to the capital, for instance, functioned as great spectacles that were subjects of general interest. Although we have no descriptions of who turned

19. For a detailed discussion of the protocol for Kinpusen pilgrimage, see chapter 4.

20. On Masafusa's role in disseminating these ideas, see Li Yujuan, "Kinpusen hiraisetsu."

21. Kertzer, *Ritual, Politics, and Power*, 57–76.

out to observe departures for Kinpusen, Moromichi wrote that when his father set out for Mt. Kōya in 1099, vendors sold wares to the many onlookers, creating what he perceived as a nuisance.[22] Clearly, the people of the capital took a lively interest in the journeys of the high aristocracy. Even after eminent pilgrims had departed, they remained conspicuous by their very absence from the spaces of the capital. Pilgrimage, then, was a grand performance, and its proper execution demanded skill and training in the field of ritual.

Ritual Lifestyles

Before and after their pilgrimages, the aristocratic men who went to Kinpusen were immersed in a constant round of ritual activity ranging from what we would today consider etiquette, to court ceremonial, to large-scale rites held at religious institutions. Heian writers recognized the parallels between what appear to contemporary eyes as political and religious action: they referred to the executive functions of government as *matsurigoto,* and to the regularly scheduled festivals that feted the *kami* as *matsuri.* They often called the reigning sociopolitical order "the kingly law" (*ōbō*) and understood it to be interdependent with Buddhist teachings (*buppō*).[23] Thus, activities in shrines and temples and in the halls of state were rhetorically homologous.

At the most intimate level, courtiers constantly ritualized their bodies and their domestic activities. Fujiwara no Morosuke (908–60), one of the founding fathers of the Fujiwara regency and an early expert in court ceremonial, wrote a famous testament in which he instructed his descendants in proper conduct. Providing a template for daily behavior, Morosuke wrote:

> When you arise, first recite the name of the star for the year of your birth seven times. (Do so in a low voice. . . .)[24] Next, take a mirror and look at

22. *Go-Nijō Moromichiki,* Kōwa 1.2.13 (3:258).

23. See note 5, as well as Abé, *Weaving of Mantra,* 420–22; and Adolphson, *The Gates of Power,* 272–73.

24. In the passage I have elided, Morosuke listed the names of the stars in the Big Dipper, each of which correlates to one or two years in the twelve-year zodiac cycle.

> your face. Look at the calendar so that you know whether the date is auspicious or not. Next, take up your toothbrush; then, facing west, wash your hands. Next, chant the names of the Buddha and invoke the *kami* from the shrines that you ought always to revere. Next, record the events of the previous day. (On days with many events, you should record them during the day). Next, eat your rice porridge. Next, comb your hair. (You should comb it every three days; do not comb it daily.) Next, cut your fingernails and toenails. (Cut your fingernails on a day of the ox; cut your toenails on a day of the tiger.)[25]

Morosuke's admonitions continued at some length. As this passage shows, they bound astrology, calendrical divination, and the worship of *kami* and buddhas to exquisitely detailed rules of deportment, producing physical discipline and ritualizing domestic life.

In the public sphere, too, ritual reigned supreme. High-ranking aristocrats participated in a ceremonial schedule of annual observances (*nenjū gyōji*) modeled in part upon the calendar of the Chinese court. When aristocrats went to the palace or to the offices of the Council of State, when they participated in private or public banquets, exchanges of poetry, musical concerts, or dance performances, their behavior was governed by canons of etiquette and ceremonial. They had to dress and comport themselves properly. They had to sit or stand in prescribed places suited to their social stations. In fact, aristocrats recorded seating arrangements at banquets and religious assemblies in great detail, for seating expressed social hierarchies. This was a court society, and behavior was governed by punctilio of the highest order.

Explicitly Buddhist rites occurred on a monthly, if not weekly, basis. Sutra readings, lectures, and esoteric rites were held at court according to seasonal schedule and occasional need. Aristocrats sponsored and attended similar rites at their mansions and family temples, as well as at great complexes like Enryakuji, a virtual city of Tendai cloisters at Mt. Hiei, just northeast of the city. Many of these were large-scale rites: by the eleventh century, the reigning and retired emperors were sponsoring offerings staffed by one thousand monks.[26] On the other hand,

25. *Kujō ushōjō yuikai* (*NST,* 8:116, 296; for an alternative translation, see Sansom, *A History of Japan,* 1:180).

26. On thousandfold rites, see Kan, "Inseiki ni okeru butsuji." Hayami Tasuku made the influential argument that multiplication and enlargement were among the

nobles could and did commission smaller, private rites for personal concerns. As we shall see, they also took to sponsoring splendid temples and articulating new ritual forms.

In the realm of *kami* worship, the court routinely sponsored the dispatch of offerings to the set of institutions that came to be known as the Twenty-Two Shrines. When envoys set out, they processed through the streets of the capital, making the corporate piety of the court visible and public. Royal and regental gifts and progresses to shrines became increasingly frequent, and spectacular, occasions.[27] As noted in chapter 1, pilgrimage grew more popular among the nobility beginning in the late tenth century. Sites that were several days distant, such as Hasedera, joined shrines and temples near the capital, such as Ishiyamadera and Iwashimizu, as destinations for the high elite. Farther still, the southern mountains—first Kinpusen, then Mt. Kōya, and finally Kumano—became popular pilgrimage sites that required their devotees to take to the road for a week and more.[28]

The ritual repertoire of the elite was rounded out by astrology, divination, behavioral strictures dictated by taboos and omens, and ceremonies imported from the continent.[29] Sickness was often understood to result from curses or possession, and mediums regularly communicated with spirits. It was a matter of routine to purify oneself, one's house, and even the whole city of pollution caused by death, blood, misdeeds, and miscellaneous negative influences. Cults devoted to gods of pestilence and the ghosts of the unquiet dead flourished, as commoners and aristocrats alike sought to propitiate malevolent forces and turn them into benevolent deities.[30] In short, the range and frequency of ritual activity was considerable by any standard.

---

hallmarks of ritualizing among the Heian nobility (Hayami, *Heian kizoku shakai,* 69–145).

27. Okada, *Heian jidai no kokka,* 248–301, 325–92, 417–39; Mitsuhashi, *Heian jidai no shinkō,* 47–143. For visual representations of Heian festival processions, see *Nenjū gyōji emaki.*

28. On Mt. Kōya, see Drummond, "Negotiating Influence"; Lindsay, "Pilgrimage to the Sacred Traces"; and Londo, "The 11th Century Revival." For Kumano, see Moerman, *Localizing Paradise.*

29. See also Grapard, "Religious Practices," 547–64.

30. On spirit possession, see Meeks, "The Disappearing Medium"; for a discussion of literary representations of possession, see Bargen, *A Woman's Weapon.* On angry

For aristocrats, the measure of propriety in this crucial realm of activity was precedent, which is to say, traces. Although courtiers usually employed the word *rei* to refer to precedent, they used other locutions as well. In the same set of admonitions cited above, Morosuke instructed his descendants: "Do not undertake anything lightly. Always bear the actions of the sages in mind and do nothing for which there is no trace (*ato naki koto*)," that is, no precedent.[31] In their dedication to the standard of the past, Heian courtiers stood as heirs to continental norms, but they were also concerned with what their own forebears had done. From the ninth and tenth centuries onward, their primary sources of precedent were journals, or *nikki*, a literary genre fed by interest in protocol. It became a matter of duty for male members of both greater and lesser families to keep journals. As funds of information on protocol of all kinds, diaries became a vital form of cultural capital, preserved within, and sometimes traded between, lineage groups. Diarists considering choices in ceremonial and other matters sounded the common refrain, "We must look into precedent." In many cases, the verb used was *tazunu,* which was also routinely used to denote the process of seeking out the traces of gods and religious founder-figures. In terms of courtly protocol, the work of seeking out precedents involved sifting through diaries and annals and consulting with experts. Over time, specialists in ceremonial produced concordances and manuals, and these became a literary genre and source of authority in their own right.

Not surprisingly, concern with traces—or precedent—could breed conservative anxiety. When a diarist commented on somebody else's action, "There is no precedent," it was a decided criticism. In fact, the phrase "there is no precedent" (*furei,* alternatively read *rei arazu*) came to mean "ill," or "sickness." Surely this was no accident. When faced with departures from established protocol, most courtiers seem to have felt rather queasy. By the same token, they could be creative in terms of which precedents they cited and how they interpreted them; furthermore, a variation on an established theme could become a new precedent.

---

spirits, see, for instance, McMullin, "On Placating the Gods"; Plutschow, *Chaos and Cosmos,* 203–16; and Shibata, *Goryō shinkō.*

31. *Kujō ushōjō yuikai* (*NST,* 8:119, 297; for an alternative translation, see Sansom, *History of Japan,* 1:182).

Style played an important role in hallowing exempla and in mediating innovation. The élan with which one elaborated on established norms was widely remarked in ceremonial, as it was in poetry. Often, the two came together. For instance, Michinaga, famous as the regent extraordinaire, was renowned not only for his political acumen, but also for his sense of style. The historical tale *Ōkagami* (Great mirror) introduces a paean to Michinaga's poetic talents with a description of a pilgrimage during which he composed several creditable poems. On this occasion, Michinaga was accompanying his grandson, the fourteen-year-old Emperor Go-Ichijō (1008–36, r. 1016–36), to the Kasuga Shrine:

> For example, there was the Imperial visit to Kasuga Shrine, a custom inaugurated in the reign of Emperor Ichijō. Since Emperor Ichijō's precedent was considered inviolable, our present sovereign made the journey in spite of his youth, with Senior Grand Empress Shōshi accompanying him in his litter. To call the spectacle brilliant would be trite. Above all, what can I say about the bearing and appearance of Michinaga, the Emperor's grandfather, as he rode in the Imperial train? It might have been disappointing if he had looked anything like an ordinary man. The crowds of country-folk along the way must have been spellbound. Even sophisticated city dwellers, dazzled by a resplendence like that of Wheel-Turning Monarchs, found themselves, in perfectly natural confusion, raising their hands to their foreheads as though gazing on a buddha.[32]

In the course of following precedent with his grandson, said the narrator, Michinaga cut such a splendid figure that he appeared to be a *cakravartin*, or even a buddha. Fujiwara no Shōshi (alt. Akiko, a.k.a. Jōtōmon'in, 988–1074), who was Michinaga's daughter and Go-Ichijō's mother, composed a verse that cast the pilgrimage as a process of "seeking out the traces of an old imperial journey."[33] Together with her father, Shōshi was represented as expressing her conservatism in the most up-to-date and elegant way possible. The ability to combine

32. *Ōkagami,* "Michinaga" (*SNKBZ,* 34:314–15); translation from Helen McCullough, *Ōkagami,* 191.

33. *Ōkagami,* "Michinaga" (*SNKBZ,* 34:316); translation from Helen McCullough, *Ōkagami,* 192.

propriety with verve was one of Michinaga's great strengths: as the *Ōkagami* shows, he made the enactment of established norms a matter of fascination.

Ritual Regimes

Truly eminent men and women (and those who hoped to become truly eminent) developed repertoires of ritual practice in which piety and political interest, sincerity and calculation came together. In order to analyze these patterns, I refer to them as ritual regimes. Like their political counterparts, ritual regimes operated on a symbolic level by expressing their masters' authority, and on an instrumental level by enacting their mastery. They were coercive, for they compelled the participation of clients, family members, and other groups, but they were also attractive to their masters' peers and rivals. In this respect, they invited both emulation and competition. Successful ritual, including pilgrimage, generated status and authority, and thus affected the networks through which power flowed.[34]

Ritual regimes were often extremely complex; they can, however, be fruitfully analyzed in terms of a tripartite structure made up of signature sites, rites, and texts.[35] By using the term "signature," I mean to highlight the personal and inalienable qualities of each of these components; like legal signatures, they instantiated their masters' authority. The most successful regimes included two distinct but related constellations, one metropolitan and one remote. For the purposes of this book, it is important to attend to the spatial distribution of ritual and political activity in order to foster recognition of connections between what might otherwise appear as unrelated practices. The metropolitan constellation of a ritual regime very consistently included a grand, semi-private Buddhist temple, where a deluxe manuscript of an

34. See also Blair, "Rites and Rule."

35. For an example of a different approach, which strives for comprehensive scope, see Uejima's treatment of Michinaga in *Nihon chūsei shakai,* 147–89.

authoritative scripture—usually a full copy of the Buddhist canon—was installed, and where a gorgeous, large-scale, regularly scheduled rite was performed. The remote constellation tended to be anchored in a distinctive pilgrimage destination where *kami* worship played a central role, and where Buddhist theology took on a localized, non-normative cast. There, the signature texts were generally sutra manuscripts that pilgrims personally copied by hand or specially commissioned. The signature rites tended to focus on those texts; examples include sutra readings, sutra burial, and dedicatory offerings.

Because it is schematic, this morphology reduces the multiplicity of elite ritual activity to several components, but in compensation it offers an interpretive reward. The concept of ritual regimes provides a focused way to think through a complex range of historical data, as well as connections between textual practice, ritual performance, and spatial location. It helps to explain ritual and political change at the same time that it accounts for stability. Once an individual had created a particular regime, it became a template for other members of his or her family, and when he or she died, the old signatures passed to the next generation as a form of patrimony, often becoming loci for group identity. Thus, the great houses developed clusters of ritual regimes that endured over time. By the same token, those houses and their individual members were constantly competing with their rivals, seeking to differentiate themselves through ritual innovation. The art historian Mimi Hall Yiengpruksawan has examined similar dynamics in a different social group in her incisive analysis of the Northern Fujiwaras' projects to legitimate and majestify themselves.[36] Clearly, these patterns were both extensive and pervasive.

Ritual regimes shared a number of characteristics that further clarify their operation. In brief, they were distinctive; they were proprietary and heritable; they depended upon precedent and demanded preservation; they compelled the participation and support of their master's associates and dependents; and they invited both emulation and competition. Before providing specific examples of these distinguishing traits, it will be useful to sketch out the basic structure of the

36. Yiengpruksawan, *Hiraizumi.*

regents' ritual regimes. Among these, Michinaga's was particularly influential, though it was by no means the first.[37]

In 1002, Michinaga inaugurated his signature rite, a spectacular set of thirty lectures, including debates, on the *Lotus Sūtra,* which lasted for either half or a full month. Michinaga was likely expanding upon a set of twenty-eight lectures held by his sister Senshi, who as dowager empress had supported him during the opening phases of his political career. Until his death in 1028, Michinaga showcased his ability to recruit and reward the most learned members of monastic society by sponsoring this rite every year, usually in the fifth lunar month at his Tsuchimikado mansion.[38] Right across the street, on a site that was technically located outside the capital, he established his signature site, Hōjōji, beginning in 1019. Earlier that year, he had taken the tonsure due to illness, and then, when he made a full recovery, he received the full precepts at Tōdaiji.[39] From then on, Michinaga remained very active and influential in the political sphere, but he needed a new site appropriate to his new station as a fully ordained cleric. He was also suffering from health problems, and he looked to the buddhas for help.[40] Thus, he made the project to build Hōjōji a priority. The temple began with an Amitābha Hall called the Muryōjuin, but quickly grew into a grand compound marked by stunning architecture and iconography.[41] In 1021, Michinaga sealed the temple's status by depositing his signature text there. This was the only printed canon in Japan at the time, an edition of the Song xylograph canon that the monk Chōnen (938–1016) had brought to Japan in 987. In Hōjōji, then, Michinaga installed the most authoritative and technically advanced set of Buddhist manu-

37. For a discussion of ritual programs sponsored by Michinaga's grandfather and great-aunt, see Blair, "Peak of Gold," 63–73.

38. Tanabe, "The Lotus Lectures," esp. 402–4. On the importance of doctrine in the construction of Michinaga's authority, see Uejima, *Nihon chūsei shakai,* 155–56.

39. *Shōyūki,* Kannin 3.3.21, 4.24 (5:128–29, 139); *Sakeiki,* Kannin 3.9.27–29 (*ZST,* 6:79–80).

40. Yiengpruksawan, "The Eyes of Michinaga."

41. *Eiga monogatari* 15–18, "Utagai" through "Tama no utena," offers an especially colorful representation of Hōjōji (*SNKBZ,* 32:299–325; translation in McCullough and McCullough, *A Tale of Flowering Fortunes,* 2:493–580). For Hōjōji's layout and history, see Shimizu, *Heian jidai bukkyō kenchikushi,* 42–68; and Sugiyama, *Inge kenchiku no kenkyū,* 375–439.

scripts available.[42] For the remote component of his ritual regime, Michinaga went to Kinpusen, following precedent set by his father, Kaneie. Although Michinaga completed only one of three planned Kinpusen pilgrimages, his enthusiasm and that of his descendants indicates that his 1007 journey was a great success. In a rite that came to be deeply associated with Kinpusen, Michinaga buried sutra manuscripts upon the peak. These were literally his signature texts, for he had written them out as he prepared for his pilgrimage.[43]

To be sure, Michinaga was active at other sites, sponsored other rites, and produced other texts, but these elements—Hōjōji and Kinpusen, the canon and holograph sutras, the *Lotus* lectures and sutra burial—anchored his ritual regime.[44] Indelibly associated with him, they functioned as his signatures. After his death, these spatial, ritual, and textual components passed to his family members, whence they became central to the social identity of the regents' house.

Fujiwara no Yorimichi (992–1074), Michinaga's son and heir, maintained Hōjōji along with other family temples, and continued to sponsor the thirty *Lotus* lectures. He also developed a regime of his own. Building on a vow made by his father, Yorimichi commissioned a deluxe manuscript copy of the canon, which artisans created for him using indigo paper and silver ink. He completed this project in 1034.[45] Nearly twenty years later, Yorimichi built a splendid temple just south of the capital in Uji. This was the Byōdōin, which still stands along the banks of the Uji River.[46] He then originated his own signature rite to celebrate his

42. For Michinaga's ownership of Chōnen's canon, see *Midō kanpakuki,* Kannin 2.1.15 (3:237); for its installation, see *Shōyūki,* Jian 1.8.1 (6:34). On Chōnen, see Henderson and Hurvitz, "The Buddha of Seiryōji"; Kamikawa, *Nihon chūsei bukkyō keisei,* 203–49; Kimiya, *Nissō sō Chōnen.*

43. For Kaneie, see chapter 1, note 49. For Michinaga's planned 998 pilgrimage, see the colophons collected in *KSS,* 235–36; for the 1007 pilgrimage, see chapters 4 and 5; for another planned pilgrimage in 1011, see *Midō kanpakuki,* Kankō 8.1.8, 3.9, 3.12 (2:88–96).

44. For other temples built by Michinaga, see, for instance, Sugiyama, *Inge kenchiku no kenkyū,* 440–51.

45. *Sakeiki,* Chōgen 1.11.4 and Chōgen 7.9.21–23 (*ZST,* 6:250, 369–70). For a fuller discussion, see Blair, "Peak of Gold," 89–97.

46. On the Byōdōin, see Akiyama, *Byōdōin taikan*; and Yiengpruksawan, "The Phoenix Hall at Uji."

manuscript canon: an annual Canon Assembly (*issaikyō-e*). This performing arts extravaganza was held every spring at the Byōdōin.[47] For the remote component of his ritual regime, Yorimichi followed his father's example very closely: he made pilgrimages to Kinpusen in 1007, 1014, and 1049, burying sutras upon the peak.[48]

Later members of the regents' patriline maintained the regimes of their forebears. Between 1068 and 1072, the regency fell to Yorimichi's brother, Norimichi (996–1075), in a brief deviation from direct patrilineal succession. It is unclear whether or not Norimichi ever went to Kinpusen. When he took office, Norimichi was already seventy-three years old, which would likely have made treks to the southern mountains difficult. The regency soon reverted to a father-son succession, however. Yorimichi's son Morozane (1042–1101), became regent in 1075, followed by his son, Moromichi, in 1094. By this time, the regents' house had become increasingly dependent upon alliances with other great families, and the mood of its ritualizing shifted from innovation to preservation. In the capital, Morozane and his wife, Minamoto no Reishi (alt. Yoshiko, d. 1114), did build buddha halls in their Kyōgokudono compound; however, that complex does not appear to have been particularly elaborate, nor to have been associated with a specific rite or text. Meanwhile, Morozane and Moromichi maintained Hōjōji and the Byōdōin, and continued to sponsor the Thirty *Lotus* Lectures and the Canon Assembly. It is unclear whether or not Morozane, whose diary is not extant, went to Kinpusen, but Moromichi went twice, consulting with his father and following precedents laid down by Michinaga (see chapters 4 and 5).

The regents, then, elaborated an interlocking, intergenerational series of ritual regimes. In order to gain a better sense of how these operated, how they interacted, and why they were politically significant, we need to consider representative examples in closer detail. Here we return to the list of distinguishing traits outlined earlier, namely that ritual regimes were (1) distinctive, (2) proprietary and heritable,

47. Saitō Toshihiko, "Issaikyō to geinō."

48. *Midō kanpakuki,* Kankō 4.15.17 and 8.11 (1:222, 229, 329); *Shōyūki, mokuroku,* Chōwa 3.7.9 and 7.21 (10:35); *Fusō ryakki,* Eishō 4.7.1 (*SZKT,* 12:291).

(3) rooted in precedent and preservation, (4) deeply compelling, and (5) characterized by dynamics of emulation and competition.

(1) To operate successfully, elements in a ritual regime had to be distinctive signatures, capable of differentiating their master from his or her competitors. For instance, when Michinaga built Hōjōji, he drew on architectural precedent set by his grandfather, Tadahira, at his signature metropolitan site, Hosshōji (not to be confused with Shirakawa's homophonous temple). He also emulated his great-aunt Onshi (Yasuko, 885–954), who had dedicated a canon at Hosshōji.[49] At the same time, Michinaga also made distinctive choices of his own. In Hōjōji's Amitābha Hall, for example, he installed a stunning set of nine *jōroku* (approximately eight-foot) Amitābha triads. In the Śākyamuni Hall, he installed 101 images of the historical buddha—a central *jōroku* icon and 100 more life-sized images. Both arrays were unprecedented, setting new standards for multiplication and expansion in Buddhist iconography.[50] Meanwhile, with his Thirty *Lotus* Lectures, Michinaga expanded upon his sister's twenty-eight lectures, which in turn drew on an earlier custom of sponsoring a series of eight lectures on the same scripture. Michinaga's new rite was spectacular—and conspicuously expensive.[51]

Though Michinaga followed the precedent of Kinpusen pilgrimage set by his father, Kaneie, in 969, his choice of destination for the remote component of his ritual regime was dramatic. Even among longer pilgrimages, the journey to Kinpusen was exceptional. During the preparatory "long abstentions," pilgrims refrained from engaging in sex, eating meat, or drinking alcohol for three months. Because the journey required them to walk most of the way to the mountain, pilgrims were away from home for roughly two weeks, a remarkably long absence for men at the center of government. Through these vivid turns into ascetic, ritualized behavior, Michinaga set himself and his lineage apart.

49. On Tadahira's Hosshōji, Hōjōji, and Tendai advancement there, see Hiraoka, *Nihon jiinshi no kenkyū,* 581–99. On Onshi and Tadahira, see Blair, "Peak of Gold," 63–73.

50. See Yiengpruksawan, "The Eyes of Michinaga"; and Uejima, *Nihon chūsei shakai,* 167–88; see also note 41.

51. See Tanabe, "The Lotus Lectures," esp. discussions of ceremonial competition, expense, and Michinaga's innovations, 399–404.

(2) With the exception of remote pilgrimage sites, the master of a ritual regime exercised direct control over its components. Again, this was central to the quality of ritual regimes as inalienable signatures. A master owned his or her signature texts outright, and the metropolitan temple functioned less as a training ground for religious specialists than as a residence and ritual facility for its primary patron.[52] Pilgrimage sites, by contrast, were almost by definition open to a wide range of participants. There, masters of ritual regimes cast a site as theirs through repeated pilgrimages and spectacular patronage. Among the regents, the pattern was for the heir in each generation of the patriline to travel to Kinpusen between one and three times. Later, during the ascendancy of the retired emperors in the twelfth century, the royals traveled to Kumano more and more frequently.

Whether the elements of ritual regimes were legally or symbolically proprietary, they functioned as cultural capital and were fully heritable. As they passed down through great families, components in ritual regimes exhibited significant temporal endurance and stability. Yorimichi's provides an excellent example. In 1069, he began to hold the Canon Assembly at the Byōdōin; his descendants continued to sponsor this rite until the fourteenth century. On an annual basis, members of the regents' house gathered at this event to display their Buddhist devotion as they feted the canon with song and dance, incense and flowers, and recitations of sutras, vows, and verses.[53] This became an explicit element in the regents' patrimony: when a man assumed the headship of the Fujiwara family (and he was usually but not always appointed regent at the same time), he made a ceremonial visit to the Byōdōin. This was known as "the entry into Uji" (*Uji iri*).[54] Thus, the met-

52. Yamagishi, "Hosshōji no hyōka." Do note that signature temples did gradually accrue monastic populations. Tadahira's Hosshōji is a good example; for its growth and eventual transformation into a Zen temple, see Sugiyama, *Inge kenchiku no kenkyū*, 340–74.

53. For an extensive analysis of the components of the *issaikyō-e* and its role as a performing arts venue, see Saitō Toshihiko, "Issaikyō to geinō."

54. Fukuyama, *Jiin kenchiku no kenkyū*, 2:246. When Kujō Kanezane (1147–1209) became regent, for example, he viewed the Hōjōji treasures and then made a ceremonial inspection of the Byōdōin (*Gyokuyō*, Bunji 3.3.25 and 8.21 [3:346, 391–94]).

ropolitan portion of Yorimichi's ritual regime came to function as a palladium for his descendants.

(3) As their heritability suggests, ritual regimes depended on precedent and demanded preservation. Precisely because they were a form of cultural capital, regimes came with a charge upon their inheritors. To fulfill the duty of maintaining ritual custom was to uphold the family name and consequence, to keep alive the legacy of ancestors who had established the fortunes of the house. In this respect, ritual regimes were part of broader trace-based discourse and practice. As already mentioned, in the tenth century Morosuke had issued a ringing warning to his descendants: "Do nothing for which there is no trace." Six generations later, those descendants were still listening. In his 1090 pilgrimage to Kinpusen, for instance, Moromichi, the twilight regent, carefully copied Michinaga's Kinpusen diary onto the back of the scroll on which he was writing his own journal. Moromichi pored over other portions of Michinaga's diary as well, seeking out traces upon which to model his own activity. When he had trouble with his own plans, he wrote, "I will leave it to the Lord Novice's," that is, Michinaga's, "precedent."[55] In sum, the legitimizing power of ritual regimes was founded upon their capacity to reanimate the past in present practice.

(4) Just as they demanded preservation over time, in synchronic terms ritual regimes compelled the participation and support of their masters' associates and dependents. Participation in a ritual regime expressed relations of loyalty; depending on status differentials, that loyalty could shade into fealty or equality. Financial subsidies were a common means of participating in another's ritual regime; oftentimes, this involved a quid pro quo exchange. The subordinate party provided financial and other resources, and in return the superior party conferred appointments and emoluments.[56] This type of assistance could be dramatically physicalized. For instance, Michinaga turned the

55. For Moromichi copying Michinaga's diary, see *Go-Nijō Moromichiki,* Kanji 4.8.13, *uragaki* (2:6–9); for leaving it to Michinaga's precedent, see Kanji 4.7.27 (2:5).

56. See, for instance, Hurst, "Kugyō and Zuryō"; relations between elite pilgrims and provincial governors are also briefly discussed with respect to pilgrimage in Moerman, *Localizing Paradise,* 151–52, 164–65.

construction of Hōjōji into a vivid demonstration of his ability to command the service and resources of the entire court, and by extension, of all Japan. Throughout the building process, he extracted labor, natural resources, and financial support from his clients; more strikingly, he occasionally prevailed upon courtiers to participate physically in building the temple. During the first phase of construction, one observer, Minamoto no Tsuneyori (985–1039), wrote that senior aristocrats, lower-ranking courtiers, and members of the Office of Monastic Affairs worked alongside male and female menials, "carrying dirt and hauling timber."[57] Later on, Michinaga had nobles provide stones for the foundations of the temple's Lecture and Yakushi Halls; according to contemporary observers, nobles even helped to pull them through the streets.[58] This was a vivid performance of lordship: physical labor was not part of courtiers' behavioral repertoire, and yet Michinaga could compel it through his emergent ritual regime.

Attendance was a less dramatic, but no less important, mode of participation. In the eyes of court society, a ritual's success was measured not solely by the achievement of its stated aims (for example, safe childbirth or the posthumous well-being of a family member). Rites needed to succeed socially, as well. Therefore, a clear index of the status of a man or a woman—and by extension, his or her ritual regime—was the ability to attract a large audience. Over the course of the Heian period, the ritual calendar grew ever busier, and courtiers found it physically impossible to attend all the rites sponsored by the court, their patrons, family members, and colleagues. As a result, some ritualizers were faced with the embarrassment of having sponsored an underattended spectacle, a rite that had failed socially.[59]

(5) Ritual regimes invited emulation and competition. Their masters occupied lofty and therefore enviable social positions; in order to become like them, it followed that one ought to act like them. These men and women were arbiters of ritual fashion who made social, aesthetic appeals to taste with their ritual activities. Style was always important. Although correct action was grounded in precedent, the creativ-

57. *Sakeiki,* Kannin 4.2.12 and 2.15 (*ZST,* 6:88–89).
58. *Shōyūki,* Jian 1.2.29 and Jian 3.6.8, 11 (6:16, 171–72).
59. Sango, "Halo of Golden Light," 112–60.

ity and flair with which a patron elaborated upon established norms contributed significantly to the visibility and staying power of his or her ritual system.

The ritual regimes model, characterized by these five traits, contributes to the present study of Kinpusen by situating the mountain in relation to other sites and genres of activity. At the same time that aristocrats viewed Kinpusen as remote and wild, they traveled from the capital to the mountain in order to extend the reach of their own political and cultural order. In their hands, the diverse processes of copying texts, building halls, and making journeys formed complementary programs of religious practice. Although the nexus of site, rite and text seen in ritual regimes could certainly be used to build authority, it could also subtend political competition. That is precisely what we see with the ritual regime of Shirakawa, the first of the great retired emperors.

Shirakawa, the Insei, *and the Shift to Kumano*

Although the institution of the regency—and Fujiwara control of it—continued to structure political life, with the growth of the *insei* circa 1100, the center of political gravity shifted from the regents to the retired emperors. It is now generally recognized that rather than being tyrants, as prewar historians often claimed, retired emperors participated in relationships of interdependence with other members of Heian society.[60] Like the regents before them, they derived much of their influence from their patronage networks, and more particularly from their control of appointments. By conferring or denying status, Shirakawa and his successors were able to compel loyalty and financial support from a range of aristocrats and bureaucrats. Some historians have emphasized the importance of the wealthy class of provincial governors (*zuryō*) to the growth of the *insei*, for these men were especially important in underwriting the lavish lifestyles and religious projects of the retired emperors. Others have called attention to the retired

60. Hurst, *Insei*.

emperors' close retainers (*in no kinshin*), men and women of comparatively low rank who achieved great influence in backstage politics on the basis of their personal relationships with royals.[61] Although the retired emperors' household agencies (*in no chō*) are no longer believed to have been the primary source of *insei* political might, they did provide retired emperors with administrative capabilities and loyal staffs.[62] Like the regents, the retired emperors were also able to appropriate the Council of State's administrative apparatus, which lent them further legitimacy and authority.[63]

Although the beginning of the *insei* period is often dated to 1086, when Shirakawa abdicated in favor of his young son, Horikawa (1079–1107, r. 1086–1107), it was at the turn of the century that a crucial shift occurred in the rapprochement between the retired emperor, the regents, and the throne. Moromichi, who had been serving as regent, died at age thirty-eight in 1099; two years later, his father, Morozane, died as well.[64] At the time, Tadazane, Moromichi's heir, was only twenty-four years old. Callow and unprotected, he was of an age with the reigning emperor. By contrast, Retired Emperor Shirakawa had three decades of political experience, half as reigning and half as retired emperor. With his son on the throne and no one to force his hand, he declined to appoint Tadazane regent until 1105, creating the first formal gap in the regency in a century. In the 1120s, Shirakawa began to exercise decisive control of official appointments; it was no accident that he also revoked Tadazane's right to review palace documents (*nairan*) in 1120. That Shirakawa was later able to push Tadazane out of the political arena entirely stands as a vivid index of the relativization of the regents' position.[65]

61. For *zuryō,* see note 56; and Hayashiya, *Kodai kokka no kaitai*; for *in no kinshin,* see Maki, *In no kinshin*; for a discussion of both groups, see Motoki, *Inseiki seijishi kenkyū,* 117–66.

62. Suzuki Shigeo, *Kodai monjo*; Hashimoto Yoshihiko, *Heian kizoku shakai,* 3–33, 98–113.

63. Ihara, *Nihon chūsei no kokusei,* 145–232; Mikawa, *Insei no kenkyū,* 41–105.

64. For 1099–1101 as a watershed in the attenuation of the regency, see Motoki, *Inseiki seijishi kenkyū,* 102–3.

65. Hurst, *Insei,* 147–49 and 155–56, though note that the year in which Shirakawa rescinded Tadazane's rights to inspect palace documents was not 1122, but 1120 (Hōan 1); cf. *Chūyūki,* Hōan 1.11.12 (*ZST,* 13:259).

During the crucial period between 1086, when he abdicated, and 1120, when he dramatically curtailed the regents' rights, Shirakawa used ritual to present himself as the equal, and then the superior, of the regents. Under Morozane and Moromichi, the regents entered a stage of political and ritual stasis; meanwhile, Shirakawa began to create a new ritual regime anchored at Hosshōji, literally the Temple of Dharma Triumphant. Shirakawa started construction on this temple in 1075 while he was still on the throne, and he inaugurated his signature rite there in 1078. This was the Mahāyāna Assembly (*daijō-e*), which quickly became an annual event, though it originated as a celebration for the completion of the initial phase of a manuscript canon Shirakawa was sponsoring.[66] When that canon, written in gold ink on indigo paper, was finally completed in 1110, Shirakawa deposited it, predictably enough, in Hosshōji.[67]

Throughout this early phase, Shirakawa emulated, even cooperated with, the regents. He built his temple on land given to him by Morozane, using an architectural plan derived from Michinaga's Hōjōji.[68] When he produced his canon, he used the regents' as his master copy, requesting or commandeering texts as necessary.[69] And when he created the Mahāyāna Assembly to fete his great body of scripture, he implicitly referred to Yorimichi's annual Canon Assembly. At the same time, a competitive impulse informed Shirakawa's agenda, growing stronger as time wore on. Hosshōji's architecture and siting alluded to the royal palace, implying that it was the greatest of all places. The temple's Golden Hall bore striking architectural similarities to the Royal Audience Hall (*daigokuden*). The western gate, which served as the main entrance to the temple, lay at the far end of Second Avenue, due east of the palace complex's southern gate. Both gates, the palace's and Hosshōji's, stood a monumental two stories tall. Stylistic superlatives did not stop there. Nine stories in height, Hosshōji's pagoda was a technological

66. *Fusō ryakki,* Jōryaku 2.10.3 (*SZKT,* 12:320); *Hyakurenshō, SZKT,* 11:36. This project is discussed in Kamikawa, "Issaikyō to chūsei no bukkyō," 11, 12.

67. *Denryaku,* Ten'ei 1.2.28–29, 3.11, 3.23, 5.11 (3:76, 79, 81, 89).

68. Shimizu, *Heian jidai bukkyō kenchikushi,* 91–104; Hiraoka, *Nihon jiinshi no kenkyū,* 601–26; and Uejima, *Nihon chūsei shakai,* 209–14, 464–96.

69. *Go-Nijō Moromichiki,* Eichō 1.4.5 (3:184); *Denryaku,* Kōwa 3.7.29 and 10.18 (1:61, 78).

wonder. By far the tallest building in the capital, it was visible across the cityscape, a monument to Shirakawa's authority.[70]

Shirakawa strove to give further expression to his supremacy with his texts. When he finished his canon, he made much of the fact that it had been lettered in golden ink upon indigo paper. Foreshadowing the *Hōbutsushū*'s celebration of gold as a kingly medium, in his dedicatory prayer Shirakawa exclaimed:

> Should one desire to fix the precious teachings of the Venerable Śākya, there is nothing like copying texts. Should one wish to transmit them until the advent of the Merciful One [Maitreya], nothing is better than writing. In heaven there are five phases; at the center is gold. On earth there are seven treasures; first among them is gold. You may rub gold 100 times, but you will not alter its character; you may hoard it forever, but it will not tarnish. Though the merits of copying are many, it is rare to write in gold. Though the way of writing is broad, golden letters are the most excellent. Thus I have used indigo paper and golden ink, and copied the sacred teachings during my reign.[71]

Shirakawa was declaring that his signature text was the best, implying that it surpassed the regents' manuscript canon, sponsored by Yorimichi and written in mere silver.

Not surprisingly, competition with the regents shaped the remote component of Shirakawa's ritual regime as well. Soon after his abdication in 1086, Shirakawa undertook a number of early pilgrimages. This was a phase of exploration, during which he seems to have been concerned primarily with examining his options and matching the regents. During an emperor's reign, custom limited him to visits to major shrines with well-established ties to the court, such as Kamo, Kasuga, and Iwashimizu. Once Shirakawa retired, however, he was free to range more widely. In 1088 and 1091 he went to Mt. Kōya, and in 1090 he visited Kumano for the first time.[72] Then, in 1092, he gathered up his retainers

70. Tomishima, "Inseiki ni okeru Hosshōji," and "Shirakawa: inseiki 'ōke.'" Shirakawa also appropriated royal rites at Hosshōji (see Yamagishi, *Chūsei jiin no sōdan,* 55–93).

71. *Gōtotoku nagon ganmonshū* 1.12, dated Tennin 3.5.11 (140–41).

72. For the 1088 Mt. Kōya pilgrimage, see *Fusō ryakki,* Kanji 2.2.22–3.1 (*SZKT,* 12:328–30); and *Chūyūki,* 2.22 (1:187–88). For the 1091 pilgrimage, the most detailed

and headed to Kinpusen, scrupulously following a ritual script created by the regents.[73] Shirakawa may have been looking to the example of Retired Emperor Uda, who was said to have gone to Kinpusen in 900 and 905, but no clear patterns emerged at this stage in his career as a pilgrim.[74] It was only as his political influence was swelling during the second decade of the twelfth century that Shirakawa definitively established Kumano as the remote component of his ritual regime. Beginning in 1116, nearly twenty-five years after his first visit, Shirakawa traveled to Kumano seven more times. From then on, it became the most important pilgrimage destination of the *insei.*

Royalizing mythology enhanced Kumano's political significance at precisely the time the retired emperors were leading the *insei* pilgrimage boom there. Ise, which enshrined Amaterasu, the sun goddess known as the ancestor of the royal house, might have seemed attractive as a kingly site, but early Heian laws stipulated that only the reigning monarch held the right to make offerings there. Furthermore, throughout the Heian period a lack of precedent barred the emperor from physically visiting the Ise Shrine.[75] In this context, Kumano was construed as a viable, royal alternative. The question of whether or not the deities of Kumano and Ise are one and the same was one of the central points taken up in *Chōkan kanmon* (Opinions from the Chōkan era), a set of legal briefs written between 1163 and 1164. Although experts rendered opinions on both sides of the question, the controversy indicates that at least some *insei*-period thinkers viewed Kumano as an analogue of Ise because the gods enshrined there were effectively the same.

---

source is *Chūyūki,* Kanji 5.2.17, 23, and 27 (1:74). For the 1090 Kumano pilgrimage, the most detailed source is again *Chūyūki,* Kanji 4.1.16, 1.22, and 2.26 (1:49–52).

73. Information on Shirakawa's abstentions appears in *Chūyūki,* Kanji 6.4.28–7.2 (1:131–39), and *Go-Nijō Moromichiki,* Kanji 4.28–30 (2:247–48). For the pilgrimage itself, see *Fusō ryakki,* Kanji 6.7.2 and 13 (*SZKT,* 12:332); *Chūyūki,* 7.2–7.17, 7.26 (1:139–43, 146); *Gōtotoku nagon ganmonshū* 2.1, dated Kanji 2.7.13 but emended to Kanji 6.7.13 (247–57); "*Gōki* fragment."

74. For Uda, see *Nihon kiryaku,* Shōtai 3, tenth month and Engi 5, ninth month (*SZKT,* 11:6, 10).

75. On restricted rights at Ise, see, for instance, Mori, "Ancient and Classical Japan," 56. On the lack of precedent for royal pilgrimage to Ise, see Okada, *Heian jidai no kokka,* 386, 392n24.

As a complement to its royal attraction, Kumano had the added benefit of approximating many of Kinpusen's qualities while remaining almost entirely free of the regents' traces. With the exception of Moromichi, who appears to have visited Kumano as a young man in 1080, the regents had little, if any, contact with this site during the eleventh century.[76] Located in the same mountainous region, it, like Kinpusen, was home to combinatory deities known as *gongen*; it also boasted flexible theology, along with access to heaven, hell, and the realms of the dead. It was even, perhaps in imitation of Kinpusen, said to have flown from China or India to Japan. As D. Max Moerman has shown, the retired emperors capitalized fully on Kumano's potential, enacting their sovereignty in ever-more-splendid processions to the far southern reaches of the Kii Peninsula.[77]

Shirakawa's ritual regime and his choice of Kumano as his signature pilgrimage site were an unqualified success. Retired Emperor Toba (1103–56, r. 1107–23), Shirakawa's grandson, visited Kumano twenty-one times (an average of once every nineteen months). Retired Emperor Go-Shirakawa is said to have gone thirty-four times (an average of once a year), and Retired Emperor Go-Toba, twenty-eight times (an average of once every ten months).[78] In the capital, Shirakawa's male successors Horikawa, Toba, Sutoku (1119–64, r. 1123–41), and Konoe (1139–55, r. 1141–55), together with Fujiwara no Shōshi (alt. Tamako, Taikenmon'in, 1101–45), who was his foster daughter and Toba's empress, built five more temples adjacent to Hosshōji. These came to be known as the "six triumphal temples" (*rokushōji*) because, in imitation of Shirakawa's, each of them had the character "victory" (*shō*) in its name.[79] Similarly, the retired emperors and imperial ladies continued to produce manuscript copies

76. For Moromichi's pilgrimage, see *Suisaki,* Jōryaku 4.11.22, 11.26, 12.26 (*ZST,* 8:137–40). Note that here Moromichi is referred to twice by his post, Major Captain of the Left; however, the entry for 11.26 contains an error in which he is referred to as Major Captain of the Right.

77. Moerman, *Localizing Paradise,* esp. 139–80.

78. These averages are courtesy of Mikawa, *Shirakawa hōō,* 182. For a caveat on the count for Go-Shirakawa, see Matsumoto, "Go-Shirakawa-in no shinkō sekai," 116.

79. For classic treatments of the significance and design of these temples, see Hiraoka, *Nihon jiinshi no kenkyū,* 626–75; and Shimizu, *Heian jidai bukkyō kenchikushi,* 104–19.

of the canon in golden ink; in several cases, they deposited these in Hosshōji, which thus became their collective scriptural treasury.[80] Meanwhile, they expressed their sovereignty in new, grandiose rites. Toba and Go-Shirakawa, for example, routinely sponsored thousandfold offerings, a ritual form Shirakawa had come to favor starting around 1110. These spectacular occasions required the participation of one thousand monks, who recited from one thousand manuscripts of a particular scripture.[81] In the realm of architecture, too, the retired emperors embraced monumental scale: Toba and Go-Shirakawa enshrined magnificent sets of one thousand images in their signature buddha halls, the Tokuchōjuin and Rengeōin.[82]

Imposing grandeur notwithstanding, even the retired emperors' ritual regimes were subject to contestation and change. As I have shown elsewhere, when the military noble Taira no Kiyomori (1118–81) managed to break into the high aristocracy, he developed a ritual regime of his own, creating a base from which he mounted a serious challenge to the retired emperors' hegemony. As it had been with other regimes, spatial politics was at work in Kiyomori's choices. Turning westward, away from the southern mountains and the capital, he focused on Itsukushima, an island shrine in Aki Province, and Fukuhara, a settlement on the shore of the Inland Sea near the mouth of the Yodo River. Although Kiyomori's ritual and political regimes ultimately foundered, his departure from well-trodden paths represented a bold effort to reimagine ritual and political spatiality. At the same time, his innovations were rooted in earlier patterns for the use of real-and-imagined space.[83]

Viewed in the *longue durée* of Heian-period ritual practice, pilgrimage to Kinpusen thus represents one phase in changing configurations of rites and rule. Accordingly, it should be understood not as a unique iteration of narrow concerns, nor as the attribute of a unique

80. Toba dedicated a second golden canon at Hosshōji in 1134 (*Chūyūki,* Chōshō 3.2.17 [*ZST,* 7:77–81]; *Chōshūki,* same date [*ZST,* 17:181–86]). Fujiwara no Tokushi (alt. Nariko, a.k.a. Bifukumon'in, 1117–60) dedicated yet another in 1150 (*Taiki,* Kyūan 6.10.2 [2:42]; *Honchō seiki,* same date [*SZKT,* 9:729–30]).

81. Kan, "Inseiki ni okeru butsuji."

82. Uno, "Rengeōin: midō to sentaibutsu."

83. Blair, "Rites and Rule."

site, but rather as an example of broader patterns of strategic, politically invested place-making and devotion.

Conclusion

Kinpusen's rise and eventual fall as an elite pilgrimage destination were linked to the culture of the capital and its shifting flows of power. In this respect, it is important to note that the practices analyzed here as ritual regimes intersected with the political groupings that Kuroda Toshio referred to as power blocs. Kuroda argued that power blocs, associated either with the court, religious institutions, or warrior houses, were distinguished by independent administrations through which the head of the bloc could issue direct orders to all its component members.[84] Any bloc was founded upon control of estates, clientage networks, and administrative structures. As a means for consolidating social bases among other members of the aristocratic elite, ritual regimes supported the formation of the power blocs over which the regent and the retired emperor presided. High-ranking courtiers displayed allegiance by participating in a patron's grand rites, while low-ranking nobles did the same by underwriting temple-building and canon-copying projects for their benefactors. Furthermore, a signature temple tended to remain associated with its founding patron, and by extension, his or her power bloc, instead of developing into a fully independent center. At the same time that ritual regimes contributed to the internal growth of courtly power blocs, they also became grounds for external interactions, both positive and negative. The potential for symbiotic relationships between courtly and religious power blocs is illustrated by Shirakawa's Mahāyāna Assembly or Michinaga's *Lotus* Lectures. When monks, most notably men from the power-bloc temples Enryakuji and Onjōji, served at these rites, they were rendered eligible for court-conferred honors and promotions. These rites thus provided the regents

84. Kuroda, "Chūsei kokka to tennō" (in *Kuroda Toshio chosakushū,* 1:3–46), esp. 12–15 for characteristics of power blocs, and 21 for the *insei* as a period of coalescence.

and retired emperors a way to strengthen their relationships with powerful temples. By contrast, ritual regimes also sometimes became sources of friction. In an example analyzed in the third part of this book, Kōfukuji men took such umbrage at Shirakawa's involvement with Kinpusen that they launched a campaign to force the mountain into their own power bloc. In this case, activities associated with a ritual regime provoked a religious power bloc into violence.[85]

By cementing ties between members of the ruling elite and religious sites, ritual regimes played an important role in spatial imagination and practice. Cultured men and women already nurtured long-standing concerns with remote locations for aesthetic and economic reasons. Famous place-names were bound to the conventions of poetry, a key medium for communication among the literate classes.[86] More prosaically, the provinces were sources for craft products, natural resources, labor, and income. When powerful men and women who otherwise would not, or even could not, leave the capital began to place their own, politically significant imprimatur on the landscape by undertaking long pilgrimages to signature destinations, they began to transform the way members of the elite experienced and imagined space. In engaging with Kinpusen, the regents and the retired emperors capitalized upon the condensation of site, rite, and text that characterized ritual regimes more broadly. During their pilgrimages, they used the notion of traces to conceptualize writing and walking, place and text, and the past and the divine, thereby implying that these varied domains shared an underlying commonality. Both trace-based discourse and ritual regimes appear to have been powerful precisely because they were integrative enterprises. In this respect, they suited the regents', and later the retired emperors', position at the top of the sociopolitical hierarchy. As lords, these men worked to bring their subjects together;

85. Japanese researchers have emphasized the regents', and especially the retired emperors', use of ritual as a means to compete with and control powerful religious institutions (see, for instance, Mikawa, *Insei no kenkyū*, 107–31; Hiraoka, *Nihon jiinshi no kenkyū,* esp. 600–675; and Uejima, *Nihon chūsei shakai,* 442–51).

86. On the literary convention of "pillow words" (*utamakura*), among which toponyms are particularly common, see Kamens, *Utamakura, Allusion, and Intertextuality.*

as ritualizers, they sought to bring the wide world into harmonious unity.

Part 2 of this book focuses on pilgrims' engagement with traces and with real space, first along the route leading to the mountain, and then at Kinpusen itself. Texts created by Michinaga, Moromichi, Shirakawa, and their contemporaries testify to the ways in which the "real" Kinpusen, which had been so assiduously built up in imagination, redounded upon practice, and how, in turn, these men sought to reconfigure the real-and-imagined mountain to suit their own purposes.

PART II

The Real Peak

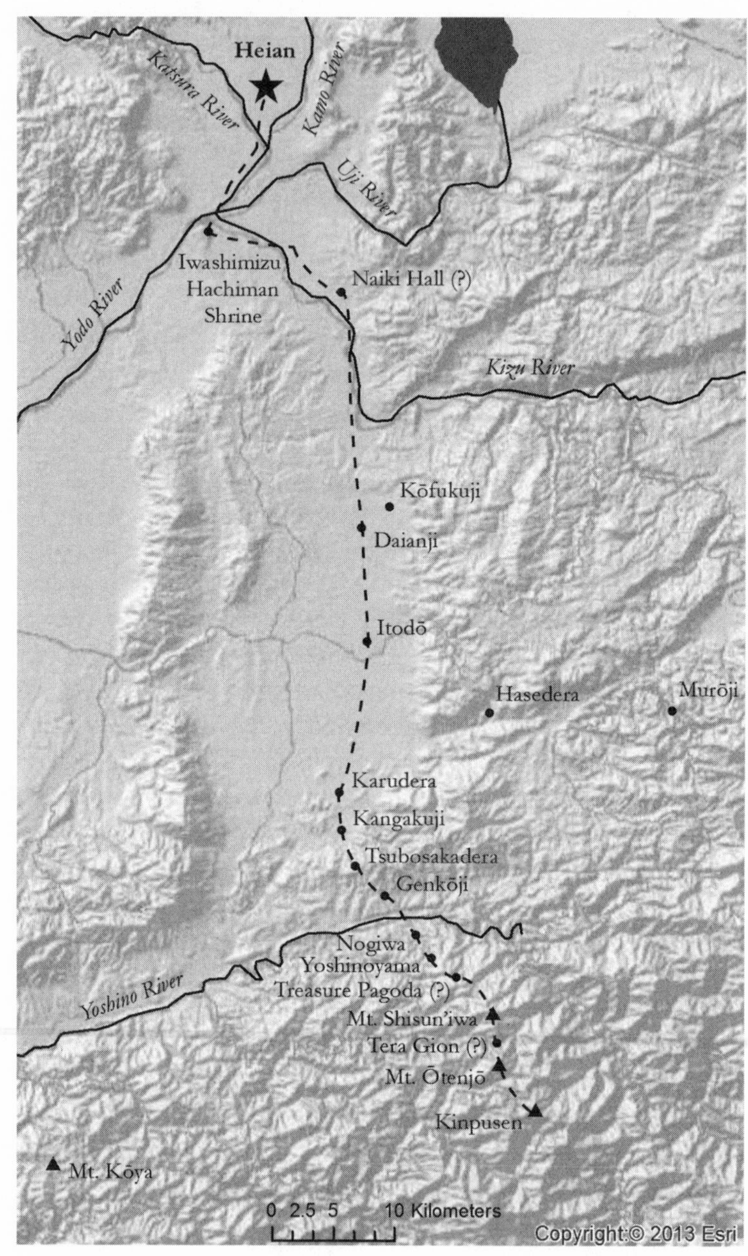

MAP 2 The route to Kinpusen. Map by Theresa Quill, Indiana University Bloomington.

CHAPTER FOUR

The Trail

> The traces of Śākyamuni do not rest on Gṛdhrakūṭa, the Soaring Peak of the Eagles. The traces of the one who perceives the world continue among the wonderful peaks upon our shores. When we inquire into the reason for this, it is simply due to the character of the land.
>
> —*Kōya goshuin engi* (Kōya *engi* with handprints)[1]

From generation to generation, the Fujiwara regents figured Kinpusen as their signature site with both their walking feet and writing hands. They followed a well-established trail to the mountain, described their pilgrimages in their journals, and buried holograph sutra manuscripts at the peak. Texts they wrote are among the most important sources we have for pilgrimage to Kinpusen, or indeed, Heian-period pilgrimage in general. Based on an analysis of the diaries and prayers of Fujiwara no Michinaga and his great-grandson Moromichi, this and the following chapter present a tightly focused account of the regents' pilgrimage activities—what they did, where they did it, and how they represented it.[2]

Although Michinaga and Moromichi respectively epitomize the glory and the twilight of the Fujiwara regency, the similarity of their ritual protocols testifies to a decided conservatism in religious practice. This orthopraxy can fruitfully be understood in terms of "trace-ism" (*atoshugi*). By coining this term, I hope to bring into focus a range of concerns—with precedent, texts, trails, and the divine—that found

1. *Kōya goshuin engi* (427).

2. Most Japanese-language research has focused on Michinaga (see, for instance, Saitō Tōru, "Fujiwara no Michinaga," which includes a research review). For an annotated French translation of the relevant portion of Michinaga's journal, see Hérail, *Notes journalières,* 2:179–88. On Moromichi's pilgrimage, see Satō Kenji, "Fujiwara no Morozane, Moromichi," 234–37; and Moerman, "Archaeology of Anxiety," 264–66.

conceptual integration in the notion of traces. Fujiwara no Morosuke, as discussed in the previous chapter, had employed the word "trace" to mean "precedent" in the tenth century. His descendants used the journals of their forefathers to learn how to make the pilgrimage to Kinpusen. In turn, they expected that their own offspring would quite literally follow in their footsteps. This was fitting enough: the word for footprints was (and is) "foot-traces" (*ashiato, sokuseki*). The practice of sutra burial at Kinpusen was also linked to traces that took the forms of manuscripts, relics, and gods, as we shall see in chapter 5; here, I examine the role of precedent in structuring pilgrimage.

The regents' representations of their journeys were also inflected by what I call spatial soteriology. On the one hand, protocol demanded that nearly identical rites be performed at a series of stations between the capital and the peak. This phase of the pilgrims' ritualizing downplayed geographic differentiation. By contrast, once the regents had reached the southern mountains, they attended to particularity: to all appearances, they interpreted specific locations at and around Kinpusen as stages along the bodhisattva path. Taken together, the ritual erasure of variation along the lowland route and the interpretation of the mountain landscape in terms of spiritual progress suggest that the regents were participating in a broader trend toward the spatialization of Buddhist soteriological paradigms. Over the course of the Heian period, pilgrims and specialized religious practitioners formed the conviction that they could ritually become buddhas by making their way through a sacred landscape to a place of enlightenment. Kinpusen was just such a place—simultaneously Gṛdhrakūṭa, a portal to Tuṣita Heaven, and the abode of Zaō, a deity who was at once Śākyamuni and Maitreya. It was also very much a real mountain, where pilgrims could go in order to stand, however briefly, in the presence of the *kami* and in the footprints—the traces—of the buddhas.

Journals, or Hand-Traces

The way to Kinpusen was at once textual and territorial. Like other tenth-century aristocrats, Michinaga and Moromichi took to heart the expectation that noblemen ought to diarize every day. *Ritsuryō* government officers had kept journals, and though many early daily records are now lost, they were key sources for the official histories compiled between 720 and 901. By the mid-900s, courtiers were honing their knowledge of precedent and producing ceremonial manuals by compiling journal extracts. Journals thus came to be treated as a form of literary patrimony to be handed down within noble families. Aristocrats also lent, copied, and transferred them in strategic exchanges of cultural capital.[3] Within the five generations of patrilineal succession from Kaneie to Moromichi, only the journals kept by Michinaga and Moromichi have survived until the present day; these are respectively known as *Midō kanpakuki* (The record of the chapel regent) and *Go-Nijō Moromichiki* (The record of Moromichi of Second Avenue). Although neither is complete, partial holographs and Heian-period copies of both survive, having been passed down through the Fujiwara family and into the Yōmei Bunko, the library of the Konoe branch of the regents' house.[4]

Moromichi's reading, writing, and copying practices show that he used family journals as traces of a past to be remembered and reenacted. A memorial eulogy composed after his death declares, "When he had time free from his duties, he loved to study and never tired of it."[5] His diarizing was part of his learning: while his early journal entries were very brief, as Moromichi came into his majority and assumed

3. For example, Moromichi's diary passed to his son Tadazane (*Denryaku,* Kōwa 3.8.11 [1:63]). Later, Tadazane gave the diary to his younger son, Yorinaga (1120–56), whom he notoriously preferred; however, he did eventually arrange for his elder son, the regent Tadamichi (1097–1164), to receive it (*Taiki,* Kyūan 7.1.3 [*ZST,* 24:53]).

4. Michinaga's *Midō kanpakuki* covers the years 995 to 1021. The most important manuscripts, which are owned by the Yōmei Bunko, are a fourteen-scroll manuscript in Michinaga's hand and a twelve-scroll copy, which may have been produced by Morozane or Moromichi. I have used the *Dai Nihon kokiroku* edition, which is based on the Yōmei Bunko manuscripts with additional reference to the five-volume, Edo-period Hiramatsu manuscript, owned by the Kyoto City Library. Moromichi's *Go-Nijō Moromichiki* covers most of the fifteen-year period from 1084 to 1099. The most authoritative manuscripts are a one-scroll holograph and a twenty-nine-scroll, Heian-period copy, both held by the Yōmei Bunko. The longer manuscript includes variants (*bekki*) for some dates, indicating that there were at least two early recensions of the diary. Again, I have used the *Dai Nihon kokiroku* edition, which is based on the Yōmei Bunko manuscripts with emendations from the six-volume Yōyakuin manuscript.

5. *Honchō seiki,* Kōwa 1.6.28 (*SZKT,* 9:307). On Moromichi's relationships with Ōe no Masafusa, who was one of his teachers, see Kimoto, *Heianchō kanjin,* 107–18.

more political responsibility, he took increasingly careful and extensive note of court protocol. From his own testimony, we also know that he sought to consult and borrow others' diaries as he studied precedent and example. As Moromichi's father prepared him to take on the regent's aegis, he conferred a number of diaries upon him.[6] Furthermore, when Moromichi was planning his second trip to Kinpusen in 1090, his father sent him the *Midō kanpakuki* and discussed with him the examples Michinaga had set back in 1007.[7]

When we read Michinaga and Moromichi's journals together, it becomes clear that they are closely related. Moromichi was so determined to follow Michinaga's precedent that he copied Michinaga's pilgrimage entries from 1007 onto the back of the paper on which he wrote his description of his own journey in 1090.[8] As mentioned in chapter 3, an examination of both itineraries shows that Moromichi painstakingly retraced not only his great-grandfather's writing, but also his footsteps, even timing his trip so that he would arrive at the same sites on nearly the same dates as Michinaga had eight decades earlier. The regents were thus engaged in an ongoing, intertextual call-and-answer, by turns seeking out and leaving traces. This habit, which I propose we conceptualize in terms of trace-ism, was institutionalized in ritual regimes, which emphasized both the articulation of signatures and participation in shared protocols.

Preparation for the Journey

Pilgrimage to Kinpusen required an extensive purification regimen called *sōjin* or *sōji,* which was related to continental practices and canonical Buddhist prescriptions. Now pronounced *shōjin,* this term

6. Between 1090 and 1092 Morozane lent or gave Moromichi copies of Michinaga's *Midō kanpakuki,* Morosuke's *Kyūreki,* Tadahira's *Teishinkōki,* Yukinari's *Gonki,* and Emperor Daigo's *Daigo tennō gyoki* (*Go-Nijō Moromichiki,* Kanji 4.7.14, 11.12, 12.8; Kanji 5.1.5; Kanji 6.9.2, 9.13 [2:3, 27, 39, 69, 285, 288]). For further discussion of Moromichi's use of journals to study precedent, see Kimoto, "Go-Nijō Moromichi no gishikikan."

7. *Go-Nijō Moromichiki,* Kanji 4.6.29, 7.2 and 7.14 (1:317, 2:2–3).

8. *Go-Nijō Moromichiki,* Kanji 4.8.13, *uragaki* (2:6–9).

originated as a translation of the Sanskrit *vīrya,* or effort, one of the ten perfections cultivated by bodhisattvas as they work to save other beings. In Japan, *sōjin* had come to refer to specific ritual abstentions from meat, spicy food, and sex, as well as avoidance of mourning and contact pollution.[9] In this respect, Heian *sōjin* rules resembled older, continental *zhai* (J. *sai*) abstentions, which had different valences in Daoist and Buddhist contexts.[10] The Kinpusen regimen was also known as the "long abstentions," a term used in Buddhist scripture to refer to fasts prescribed for devout laypeople during the first, fifth, and ninth months.[11] Actual practice in Japan differed significantly from canonical prescriptions, however. Aristocrats set the dates for their *sōjin* not by the lunar calendar, but according to divinations performed by yin-yang masters. Ideally, the regimen lasted for one hundred days, and although the actual duration tended toward eighty-odd days, it was still much longer than a conventional fast.[12] In fact, the Kinpusen

9. As far as I know, the only clear evidence for sexual abstentions comes from the *Shishi liutie* passage quoted as an epigraph to the introduction of this book. Two prayers give evidence for abstentions from oily, spicy foods and meat: Moromichi's prayer, dated Kanji 2.7.27 (*KSS,* 329–32; also published in *Heian ibun,* supp. doc. 280 [addenda vol., 63–64]); and Shirakawa's prayer, dated Kanji 2.7.13 but emended to Kanji 6.7.13, *Gōtotokunagon ganmonshū* 2.1 (247–57). Regarding mourning and pollution, note that during his 1007 abstentions, Michinaga sent proxies to memorial services for his family members; when he contracted a contact pollution in 1011 due to a dog giving birth, he ended up having to cancel his pilgrimage (*Midō kanpakuki,* Kankō 4.7.2, Kankō 8.1.21, 3.2, 3.9, 3.11 [1:225, 328; 2:89, 95–96]).

10. In 2010, Sylvie Hureau, Steven Bokencamp, and Robert Campany presented papers at the national meeting of the Association for Asian Studies in Philadelphia, showcasing the diversity of *zhai.* The panel, no. 97, was titled "Zhai: The Meanings of Periodic Abstinence in Early Medieval China."

11. Forte and May, "Chōsai"; Hureau, "Buddhist Rituals," 1120–26. Note that both these articles attend far more to canonical prescriptions than to historical descriptions of abstention regimens.

12. Heian-period sources repeatedly refer to the Kinpusen *sōjin* as lasting for one hundred days. See, for example, *Gōtotoku nagon ganmonshū* 6.18, dated Ōtoku 2, sixth month (859). We have historical data on four sets of Kinpusen abstentions. In 1007, Michinaga's lasted for eighty-two days, inclusive of his round-trip pilgrimage; in 1088 and 1090, Moromichi's lasted for eighty-seven and eighty-four days respectively. In 1092, Shirakawa's lasted for seventy-seven days See *Midō kanpakuki,* Kankō 4.i5.17–8.14 [1:222–30]; *Go-Nijō Moromichiki,* Kanji 2.5.4–8.2 and Kanji 4.5.18–8.13 [1:200–203, 1:313–2:6]; and *Chūyūki,* Kanji 6.4.30–7.17 [1:131–43].

preparations were of unparalleled scale and difficulty; by contrast, pilgrimage to Kumano required only seven days of *sōjin* prior to departure.[13]

Given the descriptive, rather than explanatory, conventions of the *nikki* genre, it is not surprising that accounts of *sōjin* were laconic. Nonetheless, the regents were clearly interested in detail. Moromichi began his 1090 citations of his great-grandfather's journal with Michinaga's entry for the first day of his abstentions, thereby signaling that *sōjin* marked the beginning of the pilgrimage process. In reading the journal, we hear two voices, for Moromichi quoted Michinaga directly, while eliding some portions of the original text.

> Regarding the protocol for pilgrimage to Kinpusen, the Lord Novice's diary says:
>
> Kankō 4, intercalary fifth month, seventeenth day: At the hour of the snake [9:00–11:00 a.m.] we went to the place of *sōjin* abstentions (Takamasa's house in Muromachi). First we went out to the East River to do a *harae* purification. The people in seclusion with me did this, too. At the hour of the horse [11:00 a.m.–1:00 p.m.], I went to court, and at the hour of the dog [7:00–9:00 p.m.], I withdrew.[14]

As this entry shows, abstentions began with a change of residence, such that pilgrims-to-be underwent a spatial separation from their families. Although this did not entail social isolation, it did support the ritualization and purification of pilgrims' bodies. Michinaga moved into a mansion owned by his client Minamoto no Takamasa (n.d.). Takamasa was in service to one of Michinaga's daughters, Shōshi, who was empress consort at the time. Similarly, in 1088, Moromichi moved into a residence owned by Fujiwara no Arisada (1043–94), a low-ranking noble and provincial governor. In other cases, aristocrats constructed

13. For Kumano, see, for example, *Chūyūki*, Kanji 4.1.16–22 (1:49–50), on Shirakawa's 1090 pilgrimage.

14. *Go-Nijō Moromichiki*, Kanji 4.8.13, *uragaki* (2:6–7); cf. *Midō kanpakuki*, Kankō 4.i5.17 (1:222). The small font indicates interlineal text.

dedicated residences to be used for *sōjin* protocols.[15] This habit has survived into the present: even today, men and women engaging in purifications differentiate themselves socially by adopting separate residences or cooking their food at separate hearths.[16]

For the duration of *sōjin, harae* purification rites played a central role in maintaining pilgrims' purity, so much so that sometimes several would be held in a single day. These rites were not unique to the *sōjin* regimen, for they were part of the normal round of aristocratic life. On a small scale, they cleansed individuals of negative residues from missteps and accidents or from failure to meet a ritual obligation.[17] On a larger scale, the court sponsored a great *harae* at the end of the sixth and twelfth months to purify the capital (and thus, symbolically, the entire country) of malevolent spirits and the lingering traces of any transgressions. These rites were also combinatory in character. Conventionally, *harae* are associated with Shintō and traced back to the ritual formula *Ōnakatomi harae kotoba* (The Ōnakatomi words of purification), one of the ancient prayers (*norito*) collected in the early eighth-century *Kojiki*.[18] Nonetheless, both the classical text and the associated rituals drew heavily on Daoist prototypes, and the regents relied upon yin-yang masters to perform their purifications. Notably, *harae* also entered the Buddhist ritual canon during the Heian period.[19]

Harae protocols often required pilgrims to move around the capital, thereby rendering *sōjin* a spatial, as well as ritual, engagement with the local landscape. Many, but not all, of Michinaga and Moromichi's

15. *Go-Nijō Moromichiki,* Kanji 2.5.4 (1:200). In 1024, for instance, Fujiwara no Sanesuke mentioned *sōjin* quarters that Fujiwara no Ietsune (992–1058) and Fujiwara no Hironari (977–1028) had built especially for their Kinpusen pilgrimage (*Shōyūki,* Manju 1.3.2 [7:15]).

16. For example, see the description in Earhart, *A Religious Study,* 91–92.

17. Mitsuhashi, *Heian jidai no shinkō,* 288–301.

18. For textual recensions of the classical Ōharae formula, see Miyachi, Yamamoto, and Kōno, *Ōharai kotoba.*

19. See, for instance, Shigeta, *Onmyōji to kizoku shakai,* 48–54; and *Go-Nijō Moromichiki,* Kanji 2.5.4, Kanji 4.5.18, 7.1 (1:200, 313, 2:2). For esoteric Buddhism and *harae,* see Teeuwen and van der Veere, *Nakatomi Harae Kunge*; and, for example, *Asabashō, T. zuzō* 3190 (94:168c2–174a22).

harae took place at the Kamo (or East) River.[20] When he made plans to go to Kinpusen in 1011, Michinaga noted that he undertook a program of *harae* at "the seven places:" the Kamo River; the "Crying Waterfall" (Narutaki); the Mimito River; Matsugasaki; the Ōi River; the East River; and the waterfall at Hannyaji.[21] These resonated numerically with "purifications at the seven rapids" (*nanase no harae*), which were routinely held at points along the Kamo River to purify the person of the emperor. In addition to evincing spatial variation, pilgrims' *harae* also took different forms. Moromichi noted that following *harae* on the first day of the month, he "drew the rope," by which he likely meant that the officiating yin-yang master passed a hoop of plaited straw or rushes over his body.[22] *Harae* could also involve the transfer of bodily ills onto paper dolls, which could then be thrown into a body of water to be washed away.[23] All of these methods are still used in purifications today.

Even though pilgrims were sufficiently concerned with purity that they moved into alternative residences, observed special behavioral rules, and regularly performed *harae,* they did not withdraw from society per se. Pilgrimage was profoundly social: everyone knew when an eminent pilgrim-to-be had entered *sōjin* and who was attending him. In 1007, Michinaga listed a retinue of sixteen lesser courtiers, including his son and heir, Yorimichi, who undertook *sōjin* with him; most of these men also accompanied him to the mountain.[24] In addition to retinues of courtiers, the regents recruited a ritual staff of eminent monks who would preside over grand rites at the summit. In effect, this meant that elite pilgrims brought metropolitan ritual and doctrinal

20. For salt and hot water, see *Midō kanpakuki,* Kankō 4.8.2 (1:227, 327). For the "East River," see, for instance, *Midō kanpakuki,* Kankō 8.3.1, 2, and 5 (2:95).

21. *Midō kanpakuki,* Kankō 8.2.16–26 (2:93–94). As pointed out in the annotated edition of Michinaga's diary, there is some overlap here with the list of seven sites for *harae* given in the encyclopedia *Shūgaishō* (Yamanaka, *Midō kanpakuki zenchūshaku: Kankō 8,* 27–28).

22. *Go-Nijō Moromichiki,* Kanji 4.6.1 and 7.1 (1: 313, 2:2).

23. See, for instance, passages in *Asabashō, T. zuzō* 3190 (94:170b18–25; 172a16–19).

24. *Midō kanpakuki,* Kankō 4.i5.17 (1:222). Moromichi did not copy this passage out, which indicates that what attracted his attention was usable precedent, not detail per se.

culture into the mountains with them.[25] This lent the undertaking a pronounced political valence, as discussed in chapter 3.

Moromichi signaled that he understood his 1090 pilgrimage as a matter of consequence to the state by making a pointed series of offerings to shrines during his *sōjin*. In person, he traveled to the Gion, Yoshida, Kamo, Hirano, Kitano, and Inari shrines, all of which were located near the capital in Yamashiro Province. Slightly farther afield, he also sent offerings via proxy to Matsuno'o, Ōharano, and Umemiya, as well as to Iwashimizu Hachiman and Kasuga. Each of these institutions had been recognized as one of the Twenty-Two Shrines. In fact, the only institution located in Yamashiro and included in the Twenty-Two Shrines that he did not propitiate was Kibune. Moromichi, then, systematically availed himself of the protection of the gods of the state, mantling himself and his journey with liturgical and political authority.

At the same time that the regents sought the blessings of the *kami* and engaged in Daoist-inflected purifications, they also engaged with the word of the Buddha. Moromichi, for instance, commissioned private readings of the *Great Perfection of Wisdom Sūtra* and lectures on the *Lotus Sūtra* and the *Benevolent Kings Sūtra* during his abstentions in 1090. When he got to Kinpusen, he offered copies of the same scriptures.[26] Because sutra copying was thought to generate merit only if the scribe were pure, *sōjin* was a perfect opportunity to copy the scriptures pilgrims would bury at the peak. Michinaga commented in his diary that during his *sōjin* for his planned pilgrimage in 1011, he was copying sutras

25. See chapter 6 for political and administrative outcomes associated with this habit. In 1007, Michinaga's train included Jōchō (935–1015) and Fukō (966–1035), monks who were affiliated with Kōfukuji, Kakuun (953–1007) and Eju (970–1026) from Enryakuji; and Myōson (971–1063) and Jōki (975–1033) from Onjōji (*Midō kanpakuki,* Kankō 4.8.11, *uragaki* [1:229, 329]). The composition of Moromichi's monastic retinues is not very clear, but his 1090 train included Saijin (1029–1095), a Fujiwara by birth and a Kōfukuji administrator (*Go-Nijō Moromichiki,* Kanji 4.8.10, *uragaki* [2:6]; *Kōfukuji bettō shidai* [*DNBZ,* 124:11]).

26. *Go-Nijō Moromichiki,* Kanji 4.6.9; 7.19, *uragaki*; 8.10, *uragaki* (1:315; 2:4, 6). It is not clear whether Moromichi offered the *Benevolent Kings Sūtra* at Kinpusen in 1090, but he certainly did in 1088, as shown by his prayer on that occasion (see note 9). For the scriptures themselves, see *Da bore boluomiduo jing* (*Great Perfection of Wisdom Sūtra;* J. *Dai hannya haramitta kyō*), *T.* 220 (5:1–7:1110); *Miaofa lianhua jing, T.* 262 (9:1–62); *Foshuo renwang bore boluomi jing* (*Benevolent Kings Sūtra;* J. *Bussetsu ninnō hannya haramitsu kyō*), *T.* 245 (8:825–34).

in golden ink. Similarly, Moromichi noted in the colophon to one of the sutra scrolls he buried in 1088 (since excavated) that he had copied it during his abstentions.[27]

After months of discipline, purifications, and sutra copying, the regents finally set out. They did so physically marked, for they donned "pure robes" (*jōe*), which were probably made of unbleached, hempen cloth. Sei Shōnagon, who so vividly imagined the experience of a woman left behind by her pilgrim-lover (see chapter 1), deplored the aesthetics of this custom when she wrote that "even very exalted people dress in extremely shabby clothing" to go to the mountain. The use of "pure robes" was so ingrained that when Fujiwara no Nobutaka (d. 1001), Murasaki Shikibu's husband, went to Kinpusen in fine and colorful attire, everyone was scandalized. As Sei (or perhaps a later interpolator, for the authenticity of this passage has been called into question) wrote: "Men who were on their way home, as well as those who were on pilgrimage at the time, all thought it wonderfully strange, and said that since days of old no one dressed like that had ever been seen on the mountain."[28] According to this account, it was rumored that Nobutaka's appointment as Governor of Chikuzen soon afterward showed that the mountain pantheon approved of his sartorial daring.

Whether or not the gods liked fancy clothes, the reactions of Nobutaka's contemporaries confirm that precedent set the threshold for pilgrims' behavior and expectations, before, during, and after their pilgrimages. Although there are hardly any extant journal entries for Moromichi's 1088 *sōjin*, his entries for 1090 show that he repeatedly looked to his great-grandfather's journal for guidance on matters ranging from which shrines he ought to visit, to appropriate robes for the monks, to the proper form for mountaintop rites.[29] And as he set out from the capital, Moromichi walked carefully in Michinaga's footsteps.

27. *Midō kanpakuki*, Kankō 8.1.20, 1.28 and 2.29 (2:89, 90, 94). Colophon from a fragment of Moromichi's 1088 *Lotus Sūtra* (*KSS*, 238–39). On scribal purity, see Lowe, "The Discipline of Writing."

28. *Makura no sōshi* 114 (*SNKBT*, 25:153–54; for an alternative translation, see McKinney, *The Pillow Book*, 119).

29. *Go-Nijō Moromichiki*, Kanji 4.6.29, 7.2, 7.14, 27 (1:317, 2:2–3, 5).

On the Road

Michinaga's journal entry for the second day of the eighth month of 1007 provides the most detailed extant account of a departure for Kinpusen. That Moromichi copied this entry indicates that the protocol was a matter of ongoing interest eight decades after the fact. Michinaga and his fellow pilgrims set out between one and three in the morning, a time astrologers and diviners had found to be most auspicious. "As we left the gate," wrote Michinaga, "they sprinkled our party with salt and hot water." The pilgrims then processed southward along Suzaku Avenue and performed another *harae* before leaving the city.[30] Boarding boats south of the capital on the Kamo River, they floated through the confluence with the Katsura River, to where the Uji and Kizu join the Kamo and become the Yodo River (see map 2). Rather than continuing downstream, the pilgrims disembarked, arriving at the Iwashimizu Hachiman Shrine around noon.

Iwashimizu was familiar to Michinaga and other elite pilgrims as an important shrine in receipt of court patronage. On this occasion, Michinaga wrote, "we presented streamers, offertory verses, and thirty lengths of Shinano cloth." This set of offerings formed a template: at each religious institution Michinaga visited along the way to Kinpusen, he made identical offerings, except that he differentiated between *kami* and buddhas. To *kami* like Hachiman, he presented streamers (*hei, nusa*) made of paper or cloth. To buddhas and bodhisattvas, he presented light by underwriting the cost of lamp oil. This was the most expensive element in the customary sixfold set of Buddhist offerings: flowers, powdered incense, solid incense, water, food, and light. At Iwashimizu and all subsequent stations, Michinaga also presented offertory verses (*fuju*). Formalized as letters of gift (*fujumon*), these functioned as itemizations of gifts presented in the course of a dedicatory

30. *Midō kanpakuki,* Kanji 4.8.2 (1:227, 328); cf. *Gō-Nijō Moromichiki,* Kanji 4.8.13, *uragaki* (2:7). After they reached the Suzaku thoroughfare via Second Avenue and before they had departed from the Rajōmon at the southern end of Suzaku, they "worshiped and did a *harae* below the bridge." As Francine Hérail has noted, the identity and location of this bridge are open questions (Hérail, *Notes journalières,* 2:179–80n3).

liturgy. The last element in his donation, hempen Shinano cloth, doubled as currency in the Heian economy. In sum, at Iwashimizu, Michinaga inaugurated a series of gifts—in-kind offerings, formal itemizations, and currency—with which he marked his way to the mountain.

On the same day, Michinaga wrote, "We left the shrine, crossed the ford heading east, and lodged at a place called Naiki Hall."[31] Inns only developed in relation to much later growth in the economy and transport. Since there were no dedicated lodgings for travelers, elite Heian-period pilgrims often stayed in temples or shrines, or, if the governor of the province where they traveled numbered among their clients, they might require him to build temporary lodgings (*kariya*) for them. Judging from its name, the Naiki Hall was a small Buddhist temple, though its location is unclear. The following day, the pilgrims moved south of the Kizu River and began to travel into the Nara Basin (see map 2).

Judging from their rate of travel, members of Michinaga's party, and very likely all pilgrims to Kinpusen, walked the entire way from Iwashimizu to the peak. This physical display of sincerity and effort was exceptional, for noblemen were accustomed to travel by carriage and horseback; indeed, they rode part of the way on their return.[32] At first, the terrain was comparatively flat and easy, as pilgrims made their way through the Nara Basin, but even then they did not travel quickly. The route was punctuated by ritual protocols, and pilgrims brought with them a significant cargo of gifts, scriptures, and other supplies. Once they had left the Naiki Hall and turned south, Michinaga's party spent three nights traversing the Nara Basin, traveling between 7.5 and 18 kilometers per day.

On their second night on the road, Michinaga's party stayed at Daianji, one of the most venerable temples in the old Heijō capital. Fukō, a member of Michinaga's monastic retinue, was Daianji's current steward and thus "rendered services" to the pilgrims at the temple.[33] The following day, the company traveled a scant 7.5 kilometers south to

31. Here I have followed Hérail's suggestion on emending the text (Hérail, *Notes journalières*, 2:179–80n5).

32. *Midō kanpakuki*, Kankō 4.8.13 (1:230, 330); *Go-Nijō Moromichiki*, Kanji 4.8.13 (2:6).

33. *Midō kanpakuki*, Kankō 4.8.3 (1:227, 328).

what is now the city of Tenri, presumably via the long-established Middle Road (Nakatsu michi), which ran north-south through the Nara Basin. Their lodging, the Itodō, seems to have been a small temple also known as Myōkanji, which is said to have been built over a well. Although the hall was destroyed during the government-mandated campaign to separate Buddhism and Shintō during the Meiji period, traces of it remain in the form of a regency-period statue preserved by the Idodō community in the city of Tenri.[34] The following day, the pilgrims traveled about ten kilometers farther south to Karudera, which was located along the Lower Road (Shimotsu michi) in what is now the city of Kashihara (see map 2). Karudera, which appears to have dated back to the seventh century, is no longer extant, but it lends its name to the Ōgaru neighborhood in Kashihara.[35]

To all appearances, Michinaga took no special interest in any of these temples. He kept his journal entries brief, and at each stop presented "lamps, offertory verses, and thirty lengths of Shinano cloth." This was the Buddhist variation on the theme sounded at Iwashimizu. The donative protocol for the route thus had an objective, equalizing cast: temples and shrines would be recognized without being differentiated. The tenor of the journey changed, however, as the pilgrims left Karudera on the sixth day of the month.

After their route took them past the old capitals of Asuka and Fujiwara, Michinaga and his retinue entered the Ryūmon Mountains, which separate the Nara Basin from Yoshino and the southern mountains. Their first stop was Tsubosakadera, known as a mountain temple and center for the worship of Avalokiteśvara. There, Michinaga again presented "lamps, offertory verses and thirty lengths of Shinano cloth."[36] The pilgrimage party spent three days in the Ryūmon area, indicating that the spatial transition from the basin to the mountains was quite significant. At Tsubosakadera, Michinaga had a chance to look out

34. *Midō kanpakuki,* Kankō 4.8.4 (1:228, 329); Tenrishi Shi Hensan Iinkai, *Kaitei Tenrishi shi,* 1:782, 2:532; *Nihon rekishi chimei taikei,* 30:725–26.

35. *Midō kanpakuki,* Kankō 4.8.5 (1:228, 329); *Nihon rekishi chimei taikei,* 30:336; Kashiharashi Shi Henshū Iinkai, *Kashiharashi shi,* 87–88.

36. *Midō kanpakuki,* Kankō 4.8.6 (1:228, 329); on Tsubosakadera's history, see Tsuji Hidenori, *Narachō sangaku jiin no kenkyū,* 41–76.

over the site of the old capitals and the Nara Basin: the temple's vistas recall the trope of "surveying the realm" discussed in chapter 3. As he had processed past ancient temples and the seats of former kings, Michinaga had used his own movement to make implicit claims of sovereignty; now he paused to look back.[37]

Even though old southbound transportation routes crossed the ridge just above Tsubosakadera, when Michinaga left the temple on the seventh day of the month, instead of heading south, he retraced his steps approximately 3.5 kilometers back down the Takatori River valley to pay a visit to another temple, Kangakuji. Initially founded under the name Kojimadera in the eighth century, this temple had ties to religious practitioners who frequented Yoshino and Kinpusen.[38] In Michinaga's day, a well-known Kōfukuji cleric named Shinkō (alt. Shingō, 934–1004) had moved there, founded a cloister, and reshaped the temple into a center for esoteric and exoteric studies in doctrine and ritual. When Michinaga had met Shinkō in the capital, he had invited the monk to his residence, taking "great pleasure" in his visit and giving him gifts.[39] Shinkō had died several years earlier; by interrupting his southward progress, Michinaga may well have been paying his respects. And yet he treated Kangakuji in exactly the same way he had treated other temples on his itinerary, presenting lights, offertory verses, and thirty lengths of Shinano cloth.

From Kangakuji, Michinaga resumed his southward journey, up and over the Ryūmon Mountains. It is possible that his party crossed through Ashihara Pass, which is about 1.5 kilometers west of Tsubosakadera, but the direct route would have taken them back up Mt. Takatori, past Tsubosakadera, and through Tsubosaka Pass, at an elevation of 359 meters. From there, they would have headed south, following the Ōyodo drainage down the southern slope of Mt. Takatori to a site called

37. The dynamics here are similar to those discussed in Geertz, "Centers, Kings, and Charisma."

38. *Midō kanpakuki,* Kankō 4.8.7 (1:228, 329). Tsuji Hidenori credits the *ubasoku* Hōon (d. 795), who was active in the Yoshino area, with founding Kojimadera (Tsuji, *Narachō sangaku jiin,* 197–234, 252–57).

39. For Michinaga's relationship with Shinkō, see Hamada, "Fujiwara no Michinaga," 145; and *Midō kanpakuki,* Kankō 1.1.8, 1.11, 5.19 (1:65, 66, 89, 297, 309).

Taguchi, where there was a sizeable settlement in early modern times. From Taguchi, the way descends slightly and then traverses the lower flank of the mountain, running east. At present, this area is home to residential neighborhoods, sawmills, and plantation forest, affording occasional views across the Yoshino River valley to Yoshino.

It was probably afternoon by the time Michinaga reached a temple that he called Genkōji, a 9.5-kilometer walk over the mountain from Kangakujii via the Ōyodo road.[40] Through its long history, this temple has gone by many names, including Hisodera. As mentioned in chapter 1, during the eighth and ninth centuries, it had been a popular retreat for such well-respected clerics as the Gangōji scholiast Gomyō and the immigrant *vinaya* expert Daoxuan. Here, Michinaga was revisiting the legendary history of Japanese Buddhism, for a family of narratives dating from the eighth through twelfth centuries asserted that Hisodera housed the first Buddhist images to be sculpted on Japanese soil. It was said that a miraculous camphor log had been found drifting off the Izumi coast in the 500s, and that, with royal permission, sculptors had used the wood to fashion buddha images, which shone with light. Later on, it was said, these images were moved to Yoshino in order to protect them from the depredations of Mononobe no Moriya (d. 587), the infamous anti-Buddhist partisan of classical narrative. As a result of the telling and retelling of this story, Hisodera, the temple where the miraculous images were supposed to be enshrined, enjoyed a reputation as a foundational Buddhist site.[41] Despite Genkōji's significance in legend and history, Michinaga accorded it no special patronage: once again he presented lights, offertory verses, and thirty lengths of Shinano cloth.

From Genkōji, the pilgrims pressed on to make their lodgings for the night of the seventh at Nogiwa, south of the Yoshino River.[42] Given

40. *Midō kanpakuki,* Kankō 4.8.7 (1:228, 329). On old transportation routes, see Ōyodochō Shi Henshū Iinkai, *Ōyodochō shi,* 632–33.

41. *Nihon shoki,* Kinmei 14.5.7 (*SNKBZ,* 3:420–21); *Nihon ryōiki* 1.5 (*SNKBT,* 30:13–17, 206–8); *Fusō ryakki,* Suiko 3, spring and fourth month (*SNKT,* 12:39); *Konjaku monogatarishū* 11.23 (*SNKBT,* 35:66–67). See also Como, *Weaving and Binding,* 68–69.

42. It is clear that Nogiwa was located south of the river because Michinaga stayed there before fording the Yoshino on his return (*Midō kanpakuki,* Kankō 4.8.12 [1:229–30, 330]).

that after he left Nogiwa, "the edge of the meadows," Michinaga would lunch in the Yoshinoyama area, this site may have been located closer to the river, near the contemporary Yoshino train station. There, at an elevation of roughly two hundred meters, the land begins to rise up from the river valley. When the pilgrims arrived at Nogiwa, they had already traveled thirteen kilometers, gained and then lost several hundred meters of elevation, and forded the Yoshino River. Even in Michinaga's day there was a buddha hall in Nogiwa, for his party once again presented lamps, letters of offering, and Shinano cloth. The hall must have been small, however: it received only ten lengths of cloth in contrast to the thirty given to Tsubosakadera, Kangakuji, and Genkōji. Of his surroundings, Michinaga wrote only: "Eighth: It rained all day. [We stayed] in our lodging."[43] Thus, the weather compelled the pilgrims to spend a good deal of time in what were likely cramped quarters.

On the ninth it continued to rain periodically, but the pilgrims set out again, now climbing steeply into the mountains. First, they would have arrived at Yoshinoyama, where the elevation is roughly 350 meters. Since at least the Middle Ages, this area has provided winter housing to religious practitioners who spend the summers at the peak of Kinpusen or at sites deeper in the mountains. Today, a huge hall enshrining Zaō dominates Yoshinoyama, but a large-scale structure was probably not built in the area until the twelfth or thirteenth century.[44] In his journal, Michinaga mentioned only three particular sites, suggesting that the area was lightly developed in his day. "Ninth," he wrote, "It rained from time to time. We lodged at Tera Gion. We had lunch at the Treasure Pagoda. At both temples we presented offertory verses and lights." The "Treasure Pagoda" was almost certainly located in the upper reaches of Yoshinoyama, perhaps in Aizen, the area around the contemporary Kinpu Jinja. On his return, Michinaga mentioned that he

43. *Midō kanpakuki,* Kankō 4.8.8 (1:228, 329).

44. Working from later sources, Shudō Yoshiki surmises that a large hall stood in Yoshinoyama by circa 1100. Given that Moromichi did not mention such a hall in his 1090 diary, I suspect that the structure may have been erected later, but as Shudō points out, the *Kinpusen sōsōki* claims that many rituals set in the Zaō Hall began in the twelfth century (Shudō, *Kinpusenji shi,* 64–67).

visited the pagoda again, as well as Iwakura, an area that he found particularly beautiful.[45]

The location of Tera Gion (or Gion) is more difficult to ascertain, but it was probably situated between Yoshinoyama and Kinpusen. Colophons for a copy of the *Great Perfection of Wisdom Sūtra* dating to 1113 mention Gozu Tennō, the god enshrined in the Gion shrine in the capital, as a member of Kinpusen's pantheon, and in later centuries he was indeed enshrined in the Yoshinoyama area. Nonetheless, since Tera Gion was Michinaga's last lodging before he reached the peak of Kinpusen around noon the following day, it is likely that it was located considerably farther south.[46] Although it is possible to walk from Aizen, on the outskirts of Yoshinoyama, to Kinpusen in one day, Michinaga's pace had so far been leisurely, and he is not likely to have traveled faster over the increasingly difficult terrain. Moreover, time and water would both have been significant limiting factors, and the way through the mountains was and is dangerous. Mists rise suddenly in the Ōmine Range, heavy rains and slides are common, the slopes are treacherous, and the mountains are home to potentially aggressive bear and boar.[47] Michinaga would have been wise to travel during the day, and since it was late September in the solar calendar, he had approximately twelve hours of daylight to do so.

Michinaga's party would have needed water for their camp. Although rainfall in the Ōmine Range is exceptionally high, water tends to drain away, only emerging as springs and streams lower on the slopes. Water sources are scarce along the pilgrimage trail, which follows the ridgelines. At present, a mountain hut known as Ashizuri is located just

45. On the Aizen area, which is located near the contemporary Kinpu Jinja, see Shudō, *Kinpusenji shi,* 517–23; and Miyake, *Ōmine shugendō no kenkyū,* 360. That Michinaga was served food at both the Treasure Pagoda and Iwakura indicates that these sites were not one and the same (*Midō kanpakuki,* Kankō 4.8.12 [1:229, 330]).

46. For the sutra colophons, which appear on manuscripts held by the Ryūmon Bunko, see *KSS,* 239. For the Gozu Shrine circa 1300, see *Kinpusen sōsōki* (*SS,* 3:365; *KSS,* 48); and *Kinpusen himitsuden* (*KSS,* 33–34, 43); as well as Shudō, *Kinpusenji shi,* 502–4.

47. The trail grows more remote and challenging south of Kinpusen, but even the northern part can be deadly. For example, between Yoshino and Goban Pass in 2006, I saw notices asking hikers to watch for any sign of a solo male hiker who had disappeared in the area when he was en route to Kinpusen the preceding year.

FIGURE 4.1 View south from Mt. Shisun'iwa. Photograph courtesy of the author, 2006.

south of the peak of Mt. Shisun'iwa (1,236 m) (fig. 4.1, map 2), and is served by rain cisterns. A second, Nizō Hut, is located just north of the ascent to Mt. Ōtenjō (1,439 m), with present-day access to a stream. There is also a dependable stream on the eastern side-slope of the same mountain. As Hamada Takashi has pointed out, a sixteenth-century list of stations given in the *Ryōbu mondō hishō* (Secret digest of questions and answers about the two peaks) locates another site, known as Ima Gion, near the Nizō Hut, and a "Tera Kumi," literally "temple pump," south of Ōtenjō, probably near Goban Pass.[48] On balance, then, local topography and toponyms suggest that Michinaga camped either at the northern or southern foot of Mt. Ōtenjō.

From the northern side of Mt. Ōtenjō, the pilgrims would have walked for perhaps five hours to reach the peak of Kinpusen; if they set out around daybreak, they would have been able to arrive by noon. Michinaga wrote: "Tenth: Rain fell from time to time. We arrived at the

48. Hamada, "Fujiwara no Michinaga," 147.

FIGURE 4.2.1 Seasonal lodges at the summit of Kinpusen. Photograph courtesy of Bill Blair, 2006.

quarters of Konshō near the divine presence. At the hour of the horse [11:00 a.m.–1:00 p.m.] we bathed; a *harae* purification." As the incumbent steward (*bettō*) at the mountain, Konshō (d. 1018) was in charge of Kinpusen's monastic administration. Lineage charts identify him as a Dharma-heir of Shinkō, the Hossō and Shingon expert who had resided at Kangakuji, and with whom Michinaga had been so impressed.[49] Thus, Michinaga had a loose personal connection to Konshō, and by extension, the mountain's hierarchy. Along the northern approach to the summit at Higashi no Nozoki (View to the East), seasonal lodgings now stand on shelves in the rock (see figs. 4.2.1 and 4.2.2). Konshō's dwelling was probably located in the same area, looking out over the steep valley.

49. Michinaga explicitly referred to Konshō as *bettō* (*Midō kanpakuki,* Kankō 4.8.11, *uragaki* [1:229, 329]; Kannin 1.10.20 [3:122]). For more on the mountain's hierarchy, see chapters 5 and 6. On Konshō's lineage, see *Shingon denbō kanjō shishi sōshō kechimyaku,* cited in *Dai Nihon shiryō,* 2.15:64. See also Oishio, "Kojimadera Shinkō," 46.

FIGURE 4.2.2 View from the seasonal lodges at the summit of Kinpusen. Photograph courtesy of Bill Blair, 2006.

Although winters at Kinpusen are hard, cold, and dangerous, from the late spring through the early fall, an entire community of Heian monks took up residence near the summit. They stayed in quarters large enough to receive aristocratic pilgrimage parties, and Michinaga mentioned a bathhouse at the peak. The bath was probably of the steam rather than immersion type, and Moromichi commented in 1088 that the water was as "cold as ice," indicating that the facilities were not luxurious.[50] Nonetheless, that there was a bathhouse at all testifies to the stability and organization of the local community. Because there are no water sources on Kinpusen itself, residents would have had to rely on rainwater, wells, and the spring at Ozasa (1,650 m), a secondary religious site some two kilometers east-southeast of the peak along the ridge.

A couple of hundred meters up the trail from the seasonal lodgings, Zaō was enshrined as a "divine presence" in a hall upon the peak. A Zaō Hall still stands there today (fig. 4.3), and archaeological remains

50. *Go-Nijō Moromichiki,* Kanji 2.7.25, *uragaki* (1:202).

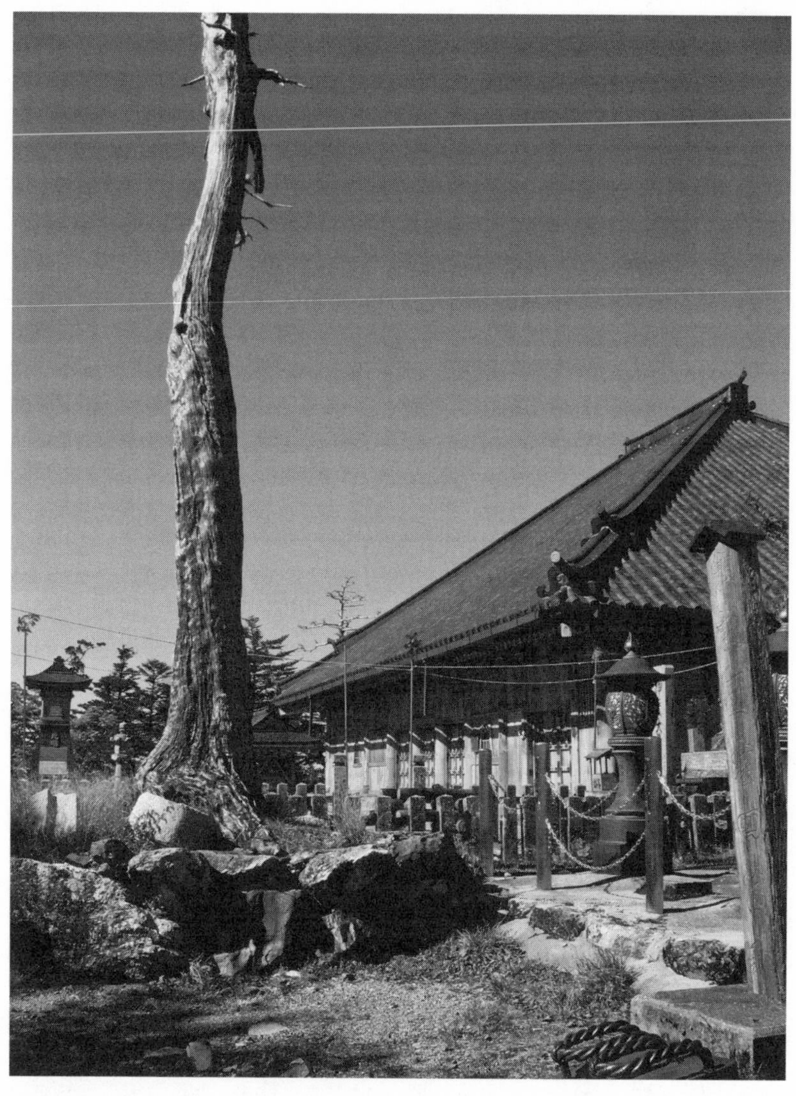

FIGURE 4.3 The mountaintop Zaō Hall. Photograph courtesy of Bill Blair, 2006.

confirm that by the Heian period there was a structure at this site. Over the years, however, the hall has been rebuilt many times, having repeatedly fallen victim to wind, rain, and fire.[51] After nine full days of travel, nearly all of it on foot, Michinaga and his party had arrived.

As we have seen, in his journal Michinaga noted his offerings at every stop along the way to Kinpusen. At Iwashimizu, Daianji, Itodō, Karudera, Tsubosakadera, Kangakuji, Genkōji, Nogiwa, the Treasure Pagoda, and Tera Gion, he made nearly identical offerings: he presented either streamers or lights, offertory verses, and lengths of hempen cloth. The journey thus had a recurrent donative theme, performed to the beat of personal exertion (walking) in an ascetic mode (regulated by *sōjin* rules). In sensory terms, Michinaga's gifts were visual, aural, and tactile. Their formal consistency and even spatial distribution emphasized the status of these sites as equal parts in an integrated path. Not coincidentally, the figure of the path (Skt. *mārga;* J. *michi, dō*) pervades Buddhist discourse and came to be a sustaining metaphor in medieval Japanese arts and letters.[52] Moromichi began to apply this metaphor to Kinpusen, contributing to the ongoing development of a landscape that was both physically real and richly imagined.

Mountain Trail as Bodhisattva Path

Spatial interpretations of soteriology became a hallmark of later practice in the Ōmine Range. The mandalization of landscape, by far the most celebrated spatio-ritual schema to be applied to the mountains, can be traced back to the *insei* period; however, it must be noted that it is documented only from the twelfth century onward. There is no evidence that the regents viewed the mountains as mandala. They do, however, seem to have conceived of the path to Kinpusen as a way to enlightenment. For the most part, the soteriological significance of the

51. Sugaya, Maezono, and Saitō, "Ōminesanji hakkutsu chōsa." Note that today the Zaō Hall in Yoshinoyama is the devotional core of the temple Kinpusenji, whereas the Zaō Hall at the summit of Kinpusen is separately incorporated as Ōminesanji, which is run jointly by temples in Yoshinoyama and Dorogawa.

52. See, for instance, Pinnington, "Models of the Way," and *Traces in the Way.*

landscape remains inchoate in their texts, but it does surface in Moromichi's journal. Accordingly, here we turn from Michinaga's account of the lowland trail to Moromichi's more detailed comments on his arrival at Kinpusen.

As he approached the summit on both his pilgrimages, Moromichi made much of scaling a crag that stands less than a kilometer north of the peak (fig. 4.4). Today this is known as Kanekake (Hanging Bell), but Moromichi called it Kanikake or Kagikake (Hanging Key). In 1090, he described his encounter with this crag by writing on both the front and the obverse (*uragaki*) of the scroll on which he wrote his journal entries:

> Eighth: Cloudy skies. We set out from Gion at the hour of the tiger [3:00–5:00 a.m.]. After a while it rained while we were on the road, but there was no thunder. Below the Hanging Key we rested a bit, and the rain stopped. Our party climbed Key Mountain, but when we came up below the Key, which stuck out like a beak, the others looked up to heaven and their faces blanched. Resolutely mindful of Zaō, I gripped the mountain rock with my hands and feet, and gradually climbed up.
>
> [*Uragaki*:] We came to the Gate of Equal Awakening, and laid out round seats. We bowed down three times. Before long, we arrived. I was exceedingly glad and told this to the esoteric master Kōsan. I shed tears like rain. Afterward, we prostrated ourselves once. When we had finished our devotions, we went to the bathhouse. The resident monks said that by the hour of the sheep [1:00–3:00 p.m.], we would not be able to see the sun.[53] They gave us water for the bath. When we finished our *harae* purification, we rested at the steward's. At Tenjō Peak we had put on straw raincoats, but we took the raincoats off below the Key.[54]

Like Michinaga, Moromichi lodged at a site known as Gion, continued past Mt. Ōtenjō, and arrived at Kinpusen, where he stayed in the steward's quarters near the peak. Kōsan, Moromichi's interlocutor, was seniormost in orders at Kinpusen, and his career is discussed further in chapters 6 and 7. Here it is important to note that he, like Konshō, maintained a close relationship with the regents.

53. It is unclear why the sun would not have been visible, but it may have been that mists were rising.

54. *Go-Nijō Moromichiki,* Kanji 4.8.8 (2:5–6). See also entries for Kanji 2.7.25 (1:202), discussed at the end of chapter 1.

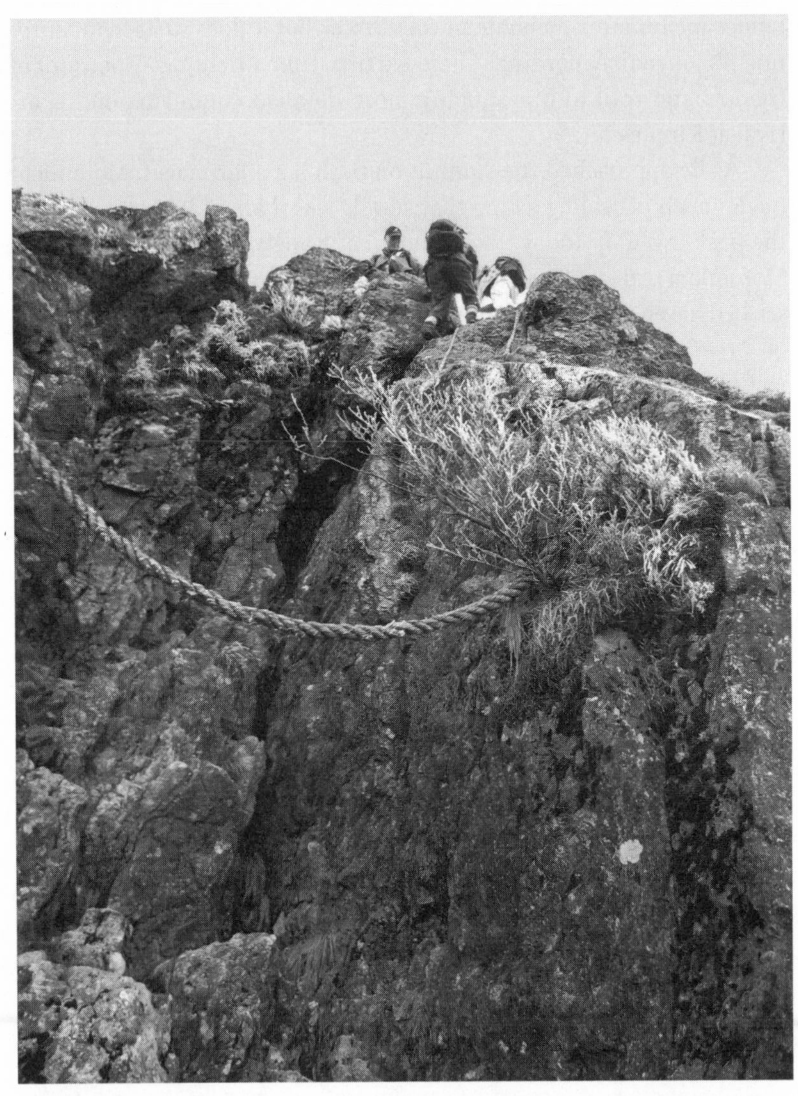

FIGURE 4.4 Kanekake Crag. Photograph courtesy of Andrew Reichman, 2005. "Eighth: Cloudy skies. We set out from Gion at the hour of the tiger [3:00–5:00 a.m.]. After a while it rained while we were on the road, but there was no thunder. Below the Hanging Key we rested a bit, and the rain stopped. Our party climbed Key Mountain, but when we came up below the Key, which stuck out like a beak, the others looked up to heaven and their faces blanched. Resolutely mindful of Zaō, I gripped the mountain rock with my hands and feet, and gradually climbed up."

Moromichi's rain of tears upon his arrival at the summit is remarkable and thus deserves attention. Whereas similar expressions of emotion recurred so often in tale literature and poetry that they became cliché, *nikki* are usually an emotionally dry genre that tends toward the laconic. Especially for contemporary readers, the terseness of most passages in the regents' accounts may minimize the effort it cost them to reach Kinpusen; however, this was the longest, most physically intense journey of their lives. They had never been farther from the capital, and other mountains they climbed were only half so high.[55] By weeping at the summit and then writing about it, Moromichi was responding to, and then reinscribing, the affective landscape examined in chapter 1.

With all his exertion, Moromichi seems to have felt himself to be doing the work of a bodhisattva. By his day, at least one gate in the mountains gave material expression to an interpretive outlook correlating the bodhisattva path to the mountain trail, and, by extension, physical to spiritual progress. The equal awakening that gives its name to the gate (Tōgakumon) where Moromichi's party made obeisance represents a stage in Mahāyāna practice at which a bodhisattva's awakening is virtually equal to the buddhas'.[56] Moromichi's ritualization of his arrival at this physical site suggests that he saw the gate as a locative instantiation of spiritual attainment. A Gate of Equal Awakening still marks the way to the peak today, testifying to the mountain's ongoing status as a physical, local manifestation of the realm of enlightenment. By the late eleventh century, if not much earlier, there also seems to have been a Gate of Generating the Aspiration for Enlightenment (Hosshinmon) in Yoshinoyama.[57] At some point, a Gate of Pure Mind (Jōshinmon) was erected at Dorotsuji, a small saddle on the

55. The elevations for Mt. Kōya and Mt. Hiei, for instance, are approximately 850 meters, compared to 1,719 meters for Kinpusen.

56. "Equal" or "virtual" enlightenment (*tōgaku*) was given different valences in Pure Land, Tendai, and Kegon materials, but was consistently used to refer to a stage toward the end of the bodhisattva path. It retained this general sense in vernacular materials (see, for instance, *Konjaku monogatarishū* 12.34 [*SNKBT,* 35:171], in which a mysterious old man tells the holy man Shōkū [d. 1007], "You are illuminated by the light of the *Lotus*. You must have attained equal enlightenment").

57. This gate is mentioned in passing in the Nichizō narrative discussed in chapter 2 (*Fusō ryakki,* Tengyō 4 [*SZKT,* 12:219]).

northern approach to the peak. Doctrinal formulations of the bodhisattva path vary significantly, but the popular *Mahāyāna Awakening of Faith* brings together "pure mind" and "aspiration for enlightenment" in a concise summation: "Those who have realized the aspiration for enlightenment—from those at the stage of pure mind up to the bodhisattva's ultimate stage—what condition do they realize? That which is called suchness."[58]

Whether or not Moromichi passed through a series of material gates representing stages on the bodhisattva path is unclear, but he did frame his *sōjin* regimen in terms of bodhisattva practice. Addressing Zaō in his 1088 prayer, Moromichi wrote:

> During the first half of the month of summer rains, I, your disciple, uprooted the brambles from my heart, making myself truly sincere. First, I desisted from fatty and pungent foods, and then I steadily generated a faithful aspiration for enlightenment. So readily that one may say the clock has passed three marks, I will have kept the abstention precepts for ten sets of ten days.[59]

Carried to its logical conclusion, Moromichi's figuration of *sōjin* as the aspiration with which bodhisattva practice begins implied that the end of the path (the mountaintop) constituted enlightenment.

Moromichi hinted that this was in fact the case. Both he and Michinaga reported that they performed *harae* when they reached the peak. In 1007, Michinaga had written of his purification using a two-character term that can be pronounced either *gejō* or *harae* (解除).[60] This was predictable enough, for the regents preferred this usage to the single-character *harae* (祓), which is standard today. In his 1088 journal, however, Moromichi described his mountaintop ablutions not as *gejō*, but as *gedatsu* (解脱), which uses the same character for "*ge*." *Gedatsu* is the Japanese translation of the Sanskrit term *vimokṣa*, a

58. *Dasheng qixin lun* (*Mahāyāna Awakening of Faith;* J. *Daijō kishin ron*), *T.* 1666 (32:581a26–28; for an alternative translation, see Hakeda, *The Awakening of Faith,* 87).

59. See note 9. Although Moromichi may not have authored this text, he did write it out in manuscript form.

60. For pronunciation, see Kanchi'in ms. of *Ruijū myōgishō* 3:6 (recto) (32:271).

synonym for *nirvāṇa*.[61] The only holograph manuscript of Moromichi's diary begins with entries from 1093 (Kanji 7), well after he completed his pilgrimage; therefore, we cannot know whether the graphic choice was Moromichi's or a copyist's, or whether it was a pun or a mistake. And yet as wordplay, intentional or otherwise, it is suggestive: Moromichi's lustrations ritually liberated him. By extension, the peak became his seat of enlightenment.[62]

Moromichi's emergent vision of the mountainscape as a realm of awakening was not an isolated case of spatial soteriology. As time wore on, the rhetorical and ritual figuration of the mountain trails as the bodhisattva path became more explicit. For instance, the *Kumano sansho gongen Kinpusen kongō Zaō gokibun* (The Record of the three Kumano *gongen* and Vajra Zaō of Kinpusen), a brief, *engi*-style text that was probably composed in the late twelfth or early thirteenth century, emplaces not only the stages of the bodhisattva's progress but also the Mahāyāna perfections at Kinpusen:

> Between the Gate of Equal Awakening and the Gate of Wondrous Awakening, there are the sacred sites of the ten stages, there are the peaks of the six perfections. Through Gṛdhrakūṭa and Daṇḍaka, they manifest the two gates of the provisional and the true. Those who practice in the spring become a buddha in a moment, with the rank of equal awakening in the ten stages. Those who practice in the fall display three incalculable eons and one hundred great eons of practice. That is, five nines or forty-five years.[63]

According to the *Gokibun,* by walking the mountains one can physically perform the bodhisattva's stages and perfections. The text makes it clear that this is a spatialization of temporality, in which eons of practice condense into a lifetime (forty-five years) by materializing within a walkable territory. It bears noting that this specific formulation is not narrowly orthodox. Conventional scriptural formulae maintain that a

61. *Go-Nijō Moromichiki,* Kanji 2.7.25, *uragaki* (1:202).

62. The oldest manuscript including this passage is the "Old Copy," which bears a colophon dating to Ninpei 1 (1151).

63. *Kumano sansho gongen Kinpusen kongō Zaō gokibun* (76–77).

practitioner completes the ten stages *before* arriving at equal and then wondrous awakening. Furthermore, forty-five years (or even 5,945 years in an alternate and less tenable reading) is by any measure a tremendous reduction of even one traditionally reckoned eon. As noted in chapter 2, doctrinal canons did not rule Zaō's domain; in this respect, the spatialization of soteriology is another example of the non-normative, adaptive qualities of the Kinpusen cult.

By supporting the translation of religious practice from a temporal to a spatial idiom, Kinpusen's mountainscape offered a potent opportunity to elite pilgrims in that spatial soteriology made even brief stints of mountain practice worthwhile. Social norms might prevent aristocratic devotees from embarking upon lives of permanent ascetic reclusion, but pilgrimage allowed laymen to become temporary holy men, as argued in chapter 1. The same ritual compression that made temporally limited practice effective also increased the importance of every gesture along the pilgrimage trail. In this respect, spatial soteriology reinforced the importance of precedent as a guide for right action. Thus, when the regents sought out the traces of their forefathers, they not only turned toward the heart of political orthodoxy but also undertook soteriologically effective action.

Conclusion

Michinaga and Moromichi's textual trail has continued to shape the ways their readers—both their own descendants and contemporary researchers—have interacted with the physical terrain. Conversely, their journal entries evince territorial qualities, for reading about a pilgrimage encourages imaginary participation in the journey.[64] For us as readers, as much as for the regents themselves, the real and imagined qualities of place recursively influence each other as we seek the traces of past pilgrims in the physical landscape and project the landscape

64. In their territorial aspect, these journal entries bear strong similarities to the Tibetan pilgrimage guidebooks that Toni Huber has analyzed as "textual maps" (Huber, *The Cult of Pure Crystal Mountain,* 58–77).

into their texts. It is this mutuality of the territorial and the textual, the historical and the physical, that has made Kinpusen meaningful as a cultural landscape.

Text and place interfused in other figurations of the pilgrimage trail as the path to enlightenment, as well. In the years following Moromichi's death, spatial transpositions of the Buddhist path onto specific territories grew stronger and more explicit. For example, during his 1109 pilgrimage to Kumano, the courtier and diarist Fujiwara no Munetada (1062–1141) wrote: "Over the course of many days, I have left the capital far behind, climbed remote peaks, peered into deep valleys, trod steep banks, and passed along seaside beaches. Austerity and tribulation: it is like living, and it is like dying. Is this not truly to walk the hard road of life-and-death, and arrive at the far shore of enlightenment?"[65] Eschewing the conventional metaphor that figures *saṃsāra* as a sea, Munetada portrayed it as the way through the mountains, complete with blisters and sore legs.

Representations of Kinpusen—or Kumano—as a realm of enlightenment should not lead us to conclude that mountains were lands of abstraction or quiet contemplation for aristocratic pilgrims. Rather, completion of the well-traced path marked the beginning of a spate of intense ritual activity. At the Peak of Gold the regents sponsored magnificent rites, capitalizing upon the power of traces to forge relationships with the gods and to generate benefits, including salvation, for themselves and their families. It is to those ritual practices that we now turn.

65. *Chūyūki,* Tennin 2.10.26 (*ZST,* 11:448).

CHAPTER FIVE

Offerings and Interments

> Painstakingly, with unshakeable sincerity, [I copied sutras with ink like] drops of dew falling from my hands. I put them in a bronze box and buried them on the Peak of Gold.
>
> —Fujiwara no Moromichi, prayer written out and buried (since excavated) at Kinpusen[1]

Once the regents had reached the mountaintop, which they had imagined as a realm of enlightenment, they initiated a complex ritual performance, through which they acted upon Kinpusen's real space. First they made a preliminary set of offerings to lesser members of the local pantheon, and then they presided over a pair of complementary rites. The first was large scale, above ground, and public—an offering of hundreds of scrolls of sutras for the protection of the state and the regents' house. The second was small scale, subterranean, and private—a burial of single copies of a few sutras, linked to personal prayers and individual salvation. These rites resonated with the localizing ethos of Kinpusen's theology in that they combined mainstream customs with nonnormative practices. They also involved activities that were at the heart of Kinpusen's cult and ritual regimes more generally: the textualization of place and the emplacement of text. The regents' choices thus influenced not only the physical and social aspects of Kinpusen's space, but also the ways in which the mountain was, and could be, imagined.

Although the grandest mountaintop rite was held to dedicate scriptures that were to be preserved above ground, presumably in a sutra repository, it is the regents' sutra burials that have drawn the attention of modern scholars. Numerous objects, some of them quite spectacular,

1. Moromichi's prayer, dated Kanji 2.7.27 (*KSS,* 331; also published in *Heian ibun,* supp. doc. 280 [addenda vol., 63–64]).

have been excavated from Kinpusen in the course of early-modern construction projects and twentieth-century archaeological digs. Among these are fragments of Michinaga's and Moromichi's sutra manuscripts, Michinaga's 1007 sutra tube (fig. 5.1), and a portion of Moromichi's 1088 prayer.[2] Sutra burial, an unusual practice in the broader context of East Asian Buddhism (see chapter 2), took root in Japan during the tenth and eleventh centuries, precisely when the regents were forming the habit of going to Kinpusen. Although it is possible that sutra burial was pioneered in Kyūshū or elsewhere in the archipelago, Michinaga's interment of fifteen scrolls at Kinpusen is the earliest firmly datable instance of the practice in Japan. Because of its novelty, sutra burial was attractive as a signature rite. By offering a way to preserve fragments of the past while binding text to place, it also fit seamlessly with other elements in the regents' ritual regimes and precedent-based political culture.

As argued in the previous chapter, we can speak of a certain trace-ism on the part of the regents and other members of the Heian elite. In coming to the peak, they were following in the steps of their forefathers. They were treading ground where En no Gyōja had set down his "traces of the practice of the Way," and where Zaō had erupted from the earth in order to "unfurl his traces upon the peak." There they buried holograph sutra manuscripts, which Michinaga referred to as "traces of his own hands." By copying out Buddhist sutras, pilgrims created textual, physical doubles for themselves, which, like the unfurling traces of buddhas or bodhisattvas, were meant to remain in situ. By emplacing their textual doubles within Zaō's realm, pilgrims sought a perpetual intimacy with the buddha of the past, the buddha of the future, and the *gongen* of the present.

Although sutra burial was certainly a devotional practice, we also need to appreciate that it was suffused with political significance. Moromichi sounded this theme when he addressed Zaō in his 1088 prayer:

> Happily, I, your disciple, have been born into a house of great fortune. I have risen quickly to the rank of the three ministers. I simply make the ancient deeds of my ancestors my hope; I simply make the achievements of

2. Illustrations of Michinaga and Moromichi's sutra fragments, Moromichi's prayer, and many other artifacts from Kinpusen can be found in Kyoto Kokuritsu Hakubutsukan, *Fujiwara no Michinaga*; Ōsaka Shiritsu Bijutsukan, *Inori no michi*; and Ishida and Yajima, *Kinpusen kyōzuka.*

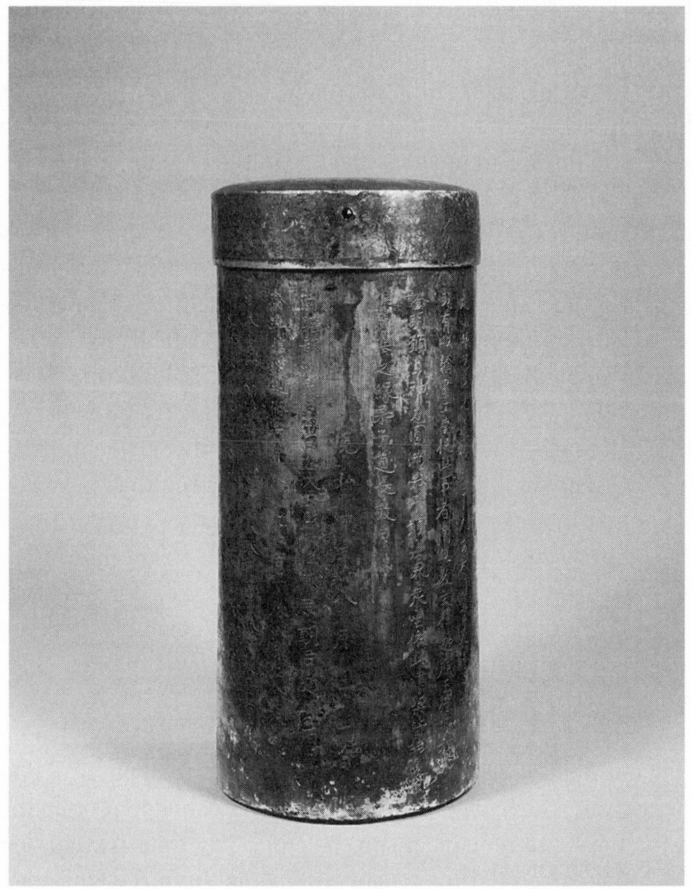

FIGURE 5.1 Fujiwara no Michinaga's gilt bronze sutra tube, excavated from Kinpusen, 1007. 35.8 x 15.7 cm. Photograph by Morimura Kinji, courtesy of Nara National Museum. Reproduced by permission of Kinpu Jinja.

> my descendants my prayer. The success of my house is like the Han [Emperor Mingdi's] dream of the sun suspended on high. The pillars [of state] pass down their traces, as the Duke of Zhou's breezes fan us from afar.[3]

Moromichi's "pillars of state" were his own ancestors, whose traces included not only political success but also funds of precedent in ceremo-

3. See note 1. Further citations to this source are elided.

nial and governance, assiduously passed down through their journals. By maintaining their heritage, Moromichi felt that he was able to recall, even reembody, the greatness of Chinese statesmen from the distant past.

No matter what form traces took—texts, gods, or exempla—the regents were convinced that they could outlast time. In this respect, Moromichi's preoccupations with his ancestors and descendants pointed to his conviction that familial success was defined by temporal endurance. On the one hand, Moromichi modeled his mountaintop rites, like his *sōjin* regimen and his pilgrimage route, on his great-grandfather's example; on the other, he hoped that the manuscripts he buried would endure for millennia. In the following discussion, I consider Michinaga's and Moromichi's activities as multiple iterations of a single, shared protocol, which the regents themselves assumed would remain constant from generation to generation. This protocol fell into three basic phases: preliminary votive observances; an offering (*kuyō*), which resembled state rites and was conducted on a grand scale; and the comparatively private rite of sutra burial. We will consider these in order of their performance.

Preliminary Rites

When the regents arose on the day following their arrival at Kinpusen, they took a purifying bath and walked up to the summit, where they spent the day putting their convictions about the mountain into practice through liturgical discourse and material gifts. First, they made offerings to deities who participated in the rapprochement between *kami* worship and Buddhist practice. These were Komori, Kinpusen's water and fertility goddess; the Thirty-Eight, Zaō's idiosyncratic retinue; and the Dharma protectors, who guard against malevolent influences. These local deities all received offerings, namely streamers, appropriate for *kami,* but they were also understood to be Buddhists who relished the sutra literature. Thus, the regents gave them scriptures. Whereas Michinaga presented his textual gifts in the second phase of his ritualizing, Moromichi offered them during his initial observances at the shrines.

The regents described their first set of offerings as follows. Because Moromichi's journal entries for 1088 are exceedingly brief, here I quote from his 1090 account. To make parallels and divergences readily understandable, I have rendered quoted passages side by side.

Michinaga, 1007, eighth month
Eleventh day:
Early in the morning we went to the bathhouse and bathed with ten ladles of water in a purification. Before we set up the things [for Zaō], we went to the three Komori deities. We presented gold, silver, five-colored silken streamers, paper streamers, and also paper and rice. The same for the Dharma protectors. We went to the Thirty-Eight, and did the same, offering streamers. Chōnin, one of the five masters, presented them, and we gave him a robe.[4]

Moromichi, 1090, eighth month
Tenth day:
Kiko interdiction.[5] Clear skies. We bathed with water at the hour of the dragon [7:00–9:00 a.m.]. When we had finished, we donned formal attire and went to the bright deities of the Small Temple [=Komori]. We brought gold, silver, and streamers, and bowed down three times. When we had finished, Kōsan presented these [offerings], and said the prayers. (Two people took five-colored streamers and paper streamers, and set them up.) We held a dedicatory offering for three scrolls of the *Heart Sūtra* and six scrolls of the *Guiding Principle Section.* The officiant was Kōsan. To the Dharma protectors, we brought gold and silver, [bowing down] three times. When we finished, we went to the Thirty-Eight and the Small Temple [=Komori], and our observances were like this.[6]

The details in these accounts indicate that the rites for local deities featured local personnel, distinguishing them from subsequent rites. Chōnin (n.d.), who assisted Michinaga, was one of the five masters

4. *Midō kanpakuki,* Kankō 4.8.11 (1:229, 329). Further citations are elided; readers are referred to subsequent entries in the same source.

5. On *kiko* days, one was barred from embarking on journeys, returning home, changing residences, getting married, etc.

6. *Go-Nijō Moromichiki,* Kanji 4.8.10 (2:6). Further citations are elided; readers are referred to subsequent entries in the same source.

(*goshi*) in charge of everyday temple affairs at Kinpusen. Kōsan, who presided over Moromichi's offerings, held the rank of esoteric master (*ajari*) and was Kinpusen's senior monk, though he did not hold an administrative post at the time.

In chronicling Michinaga's triumphs, the *Eiga monogatari,* which was written later in the Heian period, claimed that he attributed the conception and birth of his grandson Emperor Go-Ichijō to the blessings of Kinpusen's deities.[7] Ever since, it has been widely assumed that Michinaga traveled to Kinpusen to pray that his daughters would give birth to imperial princes. There are, however, serious issues with this hypothesis.[8] In his extant journal entries, sutra colophons, and sutra-tube inscription, Michinaga made no mention of reproductive concerns; moreover, in 998, when he first laid plans to go to Kinpusen, his daughters were still unmarried and very young. That said, both Michinaga and Moromichi addressed themselves to Komori, who was connected with fertility, and Michinaga even wrote the goddess's name with characters meaning "protector of children." Furthermore, during the eleventh century Kinpusen did develop a reputation as a source for reproductive blessings and protection. For instance, in 1026, to ensure that one of his daughters, Empress Consort Ishi (a.k.a. Takeko, 999–1036), would safely deliver her child, Michinaga commissioned daily sutra readings during the last four months of her pregnancy. These rites were carried out at Kinpusen, Mt. Hiei, and Michinaga's signature temple, Hōjōji.[9] Similarly, at the end of the eleventh century, the reigning emperor and empress consort, Horikawa and Princess Tokushi (alt. Atsuko, 1060–1114), who had no children, each copied one scroll of the two-scroll *Benevolent Kings Sūtra.* Regarding their aims, Horikawa privately confided to Fujiwara no Munetada, "What we pray for in our hearts is just to continue our line." In the fall, they sent their sutra, along with one thousand more copies of the same text, to Kinpusen.[10]

7. *Eiga monogatari* 8, "Hatsuhana" (*SNKBZ,* 31:387–88; translation in McCullough and McCullough, *A Tale of Flowering Fortunes,* 1:265).

8. For critiques of the fertility hypothesis, see, for instance, Hosaka, *Kyōzuka ronkō,* 21–22; and Saitō Tōru, "Fujiwara no Michinaga."

9. *Sakeiki,* Manju 3.8.17 (*ZST,* 6:185). Note that in this case, Michinaga explicitly royalized the connection to Kinpusen: whereas the cloth to pay for the Hiei and Hōjōji recitations came from his own stores, the cloth for Kinpusen was sent from the palace.

10. *Chūyūki,* Jōtoku 1.4.21 and 8.16 (3:206, 216).

As these activities show, sutra manuscripts were a key medium for ensuring that the gods and buddhas responded to one's prayers. In part, this mediation rested on the familiar mechanics of merit and karma. Among the numerous manuscripts that members of the Heian elite dedicated at Kinpusen, only a few fragments survive. Nonetheless, it is clear that there, as at other sites, donors routinely composed their colophons using such phrases as, "With the merit from copying this sutra, I pray that such-and-such may happen."[11] By and large, copyist-donors could expect that that merit was boundless. The *Lotus Sūtra,* which played such an important role in the Kinpusen cult, famously promises immense benefits to those who copy and promulgate it. In one among many similar formulations, Śākyamuni explains in the "Medicine King Chapter" that "even the wisdom of a buddha" cannot comprehend how much merit one generates by having someone else write out the *Lotus.*[12] At Kinpusen, pilgrims offered merit-making copies of sutras to a pantheon whose members they understood to be good Buddhists, even bodhisattvas: by sowing textual seeds in these "fields of merit," they were compounding the benefits of their copying projects. For instance, in 1088, Moromichi closed his prayer for his sutra burial with this praise for the mountain pantheon: "Your merit is fathomless; your benefits are boundless. Respectfully I address myself." In this respect, the regents used their sutras to inscribe themselves within a recursive circle of benefits.

As the next phase of their ritualizing shows, the regents' motivations were neither narrow nor venal. Rather, their votive offerings display what Wendi Adamek, paraphrasing Marcel Mauss, has characterized as the "intermingling of self interest, collective interest, and disinterest" bound up in the giving of a gift.[13] In their own eyes, the regents were acting for the entire world, and doing so at great expense. To produce the scriptures they offered to the local pantheon, they had to pay for paper, brushes, spindles, and ink. They had to hire paper-polishers and trimmers, copyists and proofreaders. In addition, ritual norms demanded that workers observe *sōjin*-style abstentions for the duration of their labors, lest any impurity compromise the power of the texts they were reproducing.[14]

11. *KSS,* colophon nos. 3–7, 11–12 and 16 (235–39).
12. *Miaofa lianhua jing, T.* 262 (9:54b20–21).
13. Adamek, "The Impossibility of the Given," 142.
14. Lowe, "The Discipline of Writing."

Finally, the finished manuscripts had to be physically transported, presumably by porters who had also followed the *sōjin* rules for pilgrimage. Relying upon the real and imagined aspects of Kinpusen's spatiality, the regents trusted that the gesture of emplacing the manuscripts at Kinpusen would yield a "great good root" of merit.

The Offering Rite

In terms of scale, spectacle, and expense, the ensuing offering at the Zaō Hall marked the height of the regents' ritualizing at the peak. The liturgical structure, intended beneficiaries, and content of the sutras to be dedicated all shed light on the rite's significance as a public observance tied to metropolitan, state-recognized norms. By the same token, the number of manuscripts offered shows that this was the grandest, most expensive segment of the mountaintop protocol.

Although Moromichi made only the barest mention of the rites he conducted in the Zaō Hall in 1088 and 1090, Michinaga was more forthcoming:

Michinaga, 1007 (entry for 8.11, continued)	Moromichi, 1090 (entry for 8.10, continued)
Next we came into the divine presence. We presented twenty hanks of silk floss and ten parasols. We offered lamps. We dedicated sutras: one hundred copies of the *Lotus Sūtra* and [blank space] of the *Benevolent Kings Sūtra* for the Thirty-Eight; also, eight scrolls of the *Guiding Principle Section* for Emperor [Ichijō], Retired Emperor Reizei, Empress Consort [Shōshi], and Crown Prince [Okisada]; and 110 scrolls of the *Heart Sūtra* for the Eight Great Dragon Kings. We invited seven monks plus one	We came into the divine presence and held a dedicatory offering for the sutras.

> hundred monks. When the dedicatory offering was finished, we gave one damask robe to the lecturer and one to the prayer reciter, and one plain robe to each of the five other monks.

Moromichi's brief journal entry may be supplemented with his 1088 prayer, in which he wrote: "Sincerely I besought several tens of monks and invited them to make offerings for several hundred scrolls of sutras. The incense and flowers scatter and fly away, as if in a tempest at the bodhi tree. They chant the Sanskrit verses loudly: it is like the full moon—how can one add to its glory?"

These accounts, whether laconic or poetic, show that the offering in the Zaō Hall was governed by the same norms as a large-scale rite such as would be held at the palace, a great monastery, or the regents' signature temples. The ritual components were oriented around a reading and exegesis of scripture, with a full set of seven officiants presiding: a lecturer, reader, prayer reciter, prostrations master, cantor, flower strewer, and hall master. Even if we take Michinaga's "one hundred" monks to be a figurative exaggeration, both he and Moromichi obviously sought to recruit a large cast of supporting ritualists, some of whom may have hailed from other temples. More importantly, a hierarchy in personnel reinforced the rite's quality as an orthodox event suited to metropolitan norms. As Michinaga and Moromichi indicated in subsequent journal passages, the roles of the seven officiants were filled by monks who had accompanied them from the capital (see below). This choice in staffing constituted an intervention in the mountain's social space, for it subordinated the mountain monks to men who had come from the capital.

As if to emphasize his own stature as a grand patron, Michinaga carefully itemized his gifts to his liturgical staff on the back of the paper on which he wrote the journal entry cited above:

> [*Uragaki*] Eleventh: We gave the hundred monks one short length of silk each, and one monastic over-robe each. Before [the hour of] the sheep [1:00 p.m.–3:00 p.m.], we sent sets of monastic robes and

> tortoiseshell-patterned monastic over-robes to the seven officiants. In addition, there were overnight robes. One was for the monk who presented the lamps. As for gifts to the seven officiants and the hundred monks, we gave two bales of rice and three lengths of Shinano cloth to each of them. We provided one hundred sheets of offertory verses. To the monks of the entire temple, we offered one hundred bales of rice.

With his gifts, Michinaga exemplified the perfection of generosity, the cardinal virtue of the Buddhist layman, at the same time that he imprinted the mountain with his influence. The actual volume of a bale (*koku*) varied by time and place, but Michinaga likely gave enough grain to feed about three hundred men for a year.[15] Moreover, his numerous gifts of textiles could be used in kind or as currency. That he presented offertory verses, which could pledge as well as itemize support, suggests that he also provided ongoing funding to Kinpusen's monastic community. This kind of lavish and sustained patronage was the primary means for making a remote pilgrimage destination into a signature site. The mountain monks would remember Michinaga as they wore robes and ate food he had given them: inasmuch as his gifts recalled his presence, they were traces, too. Thus Michinaga ensured that he would continue to be imagined within the real space of Kinpusen.

The time-honored tradition of state protection (*chingo kokka*) gave a public cast to the regents' grand offerings. When Michinaga gave one hundred-odd copies of the *Lotus* and the *Heart Sūtra,* staple Mahāyāna classics, to the Thirty-Eight and the Eight Dragon Kings, he solicited the benevolent protection of powerful but parochial deities on behalf of the political center.[16] At the same time, he dedicated two copies each of the *Guiding Principle Section* to benefit the royal family, the state

15. As Charlotte von Verschuer notes, the premodern diet depended on other grains and beans, as well. For her discussion of the eighth-century diet, which she treats as a baseline, and caloric intake, see *Le riz,* 285–87, 369.

16. For the sutras, see *Bore boluomiduo xin jing* (*Heart Sūtra*; J. *Hannya haramitta shingyō*), *T.* 251 (8:848); *Miaofa lianhua jing, T.* 262 (9:1–62); *Foshuo renwang bore boluomi jing, T.* 245 (8:825–34).

personified.[17] Importantly, the royals were also Michinaga's family: Emperor Ichijō was his nephew, Empress Consort Shōshi was his daughter, and Crown Prince Okisada (976–1017), who later ruled as Emperor Sanjō, another nephew. As is well known, the political success of the regents' house rested in part upon its close blood relationships with the royals. In safeguarding the state, Michinaga was also protecting his own interests.

Moromichi did not describe his offerings in his journal, but his 1088 prayer indicates that his agenda paralleled that of his great-grandfather. Because the first part of the manuscript is torn, the opening passages are lost; however, the extant text begins with an itemization of dedicated (not buried) sutras. Moromichi allocated comparatively more scriptures to his nuclear family, but he also listed his offerings in order of the social consequence of the beneficiaries, which meant that the royals took precedence. Judging from the overall pattern, Moromichi almost certainly began with a dedication of multiple copies of the *Benevolent Kings Sūtra* and the *Vajra Longevity Sūtra* for the benefit of the reigning emperor, Horikawa, and his empress consort, Tokushi.[18] Next, for Retired Emperor Shirakawa, his deceased empress consort, Minamoto no Kenshi (alt. Katako, 1057–84), their three daughters, and one of Shirakawa's daughters by another consort, Moromichi allocated one copy each of the *Benevolent Kings Sūtra.* Lastly, he dedicated copies of the *Lotus, Benevolent Kings,* and *Vajra Longevity Sūtra* for his own family, scaling the number of copies to the social status of the intended beneficiary. To his father, the regent, he apportioned respectively ten, five, and one hundred copies of these scriptures. For his mother and his wife, whose status was lower because they were women, he dedicated five, five, and one hundred copies. For his eleven-year-old son, Moromichi dedicated three copies of the *Benevolent Kings* and one hundred copies of the *Vajra Longevity Sūtra.* Because this boy, the future

17. By the *"Guiding Principle Section"* (*Rishubun*), Michinaga probably meant the 578th division in the *Da bore boluomiduo jing, T.* 220 (7:986–91), which constitutes one of several East Asian translations of the *Perfection of Wisdom in 150 Verses.* Moromichi used the same text in his 1090 gifts to the local gods (see note 6).

18. *Jingang shouming tuoluoni jing* (*Vajra Longevity Sūtra*; J. *Kongō jumyō darani kyō*), *T.* 1134b (20:577–78).

regent Tadazane, was the juniormost member of the family, his was the smallest scriptural portion. By the same token, Moromichi likely expected that when Tadazane came of age he would come to Kinpusen to dedicate a full complement of his own sutras.

The reproduction and dedication of sutras was as much a hermeneutic effort as it was material and liturgical, for the regents chose their scriptures based on their content.[19] Given the complexity of the offerings, a restatement of which sutras were offered where and for whom is in order. To minor members of the local pantheon, Michinaga offered the *Lotus* and *Benevolent Kings Sūtra*, and Moromichi presented the *Heart Sūtra* and *Guiding Principle Section.* (As noted earlier, Michinaga presented these texts as part of his grand *kuyō,* whereas Moromichi presented them during his preliminary worship at the deities' shrines.) During the main offering rite in the Zaō Hall, Michinaga dedicated copies of the *Guiding Principle Section* on behalf of the royals, whereas Moromichi offered the *Lotus, Benevolent Kings,* and *Vajra Longevity Sūtra.*

Beyond its importance at Kinpusen, the popularity of the *Lotus Sūtra* among both ordained Buddhists and laypeople can hardly be overstated.[20] The *Lotus*, which casts itself as a comprehensive expression of the Mahāyāna, is the primary text of the Tendai school, but has been much beloved by monastics regardless of their sectarian background. During the Heian period, it served as the anchor for penance, *samādhi,* and esoteric rites. For lay aristocrats, its most important application was in privately sponsored, multiday lecture assemblies, which were staples in the ritual calendar; Michinaga, for instance, had made the Thirty *Lotus* Lectures his signature rite (see chapter 3). Meanwhile, nobles and commoners regularly reproduced the *Lotus* in sutra-copying projects, in part because the scripture famously promises myriad blessings to those who copy and revere it. Accordingly, patrons used

19. On devotional and other uses of scripture in which meaning does not take pride of place, see Campany, "Notes on Devotional and Symbolic Uses"; Eubanks, *Miracles of Book and Body*; Levering, "Scripture and Its Reception"; and Rambelli, *Buddhist Materiality,* 88–128.

20. For the importance of this scripture, see Tanabe and Tanabe, *The Lotus Sutra in Japanese Culture.* For the scripture itself, see *Miaofa lianhua jing, T.* 262 (9:1–62).

it to pray for aims ranging from good rebirth to cures for present ills. Their interest was not limited to the scripture's instrumental powers, however; for instance, they alluded to its teachings in their poetry and prose.[21] The *Lotus Sūtra,* in short, was so authoritative that it could be applied to almost any devotional context. It was also particularly well suited to Kinpusen because, as noted in chapter 2, Zaō had a personal fondness for it.

Whereas the *Lotus Sūtra* was a core text for religious practice in general, the *Benevolent Kings Sūtra* was a pillar of state religion across East Asia.[22] From their youth, Japanese aristocrats were schooled in the ritual and rhetoric of this scripture, which was recited in semi-annual *Benevolent Kings* Assemblies at court. Moromichi, for instance, routinely attended these rites and took careful notes on their correct performance. He also took an interest in the relevant doctrine: during his Kinpusen *sōjin,* he had the Vinaya Master Enshin (d. 1100) lecture on this scripture.[23] In giving the *Benevolent Kings Sūtra* to Kinpusen's deities, the regents capitalized upon the scripture's ties to kingship to strengthen their own authority.

Among the shortest sutras in the perfection of wisdom corpus, the *Heart Sūtra* and the *Guiding Principle Section* were both well-known elements in the aristocratic textual repertoire. The *Heart,* perhaps the most popular of all Mahāyāna sutras, summarizes the doctrine of emptiness, includes a powerful apotropaic *dhāraṇī,* and has been recited by Buddhists of all stripes for roughly two millennia.[24] Heian aristocrats commonly included it in sutra-copying projects because it is short (and therefore easy to copy), yet powerful. In writing that they offered the

21. Yamada, "Poetry and Meaning"; Morrell, "The *Shinkokinshū,*" and "The Buddhist Poetry"; Kamens, "Dragon–Girl, Maidenflower"; LaFleur, *The Karma of Words,* 80–106.

22. For Amoghavajra's use of the scripture to appeal to Chinese emperors, see Orzech, *Politics and Transcendent Wisdom.* For the sutra itself, see *Foshuo renwang bore boluomi jing, T.* 245 (8:825–34).

23. In 1093, for instance, Moromichi helped orchestrate the spring *Benevolent Kings* Assembly and then attended a once-per-reign version of the rite several months later (*Go-Nijō Moromichiki,* Kanji 7.3.8–25, 5.26 [3:26–33, 76–77]). For lectures during his Kinpusen preparations, see ibid., Kanji 4.6.9 (1:315).

24. See note 16.

Guiding Principle Section at the mountain, Michinaga and Moromichi were probably referring to the tenth division (corresponding to the 578th fascicle or scroll) of Xuanzang's monumental translation of the *Great Perfection of Wisdom Sūtra.*[25] For the regents, the *Guiding Principle Section* seems to have functioned as a condensation of the *Great Perfection of Wisdom Sūtra,* copies and readings of which Moromichi offered to the gods of Kinpusen on several other occasions.[26]

As its name suggests, the short *Vajra Longevity Sūtra* gained popularity due its promise of long life. In a telling departure from Michinaga's example, Moromichi relied upon it in a wide range of situations. Certainly, it suited his aims at Kinpusen: again and again in his prayer, he repeated the phrase "increase their good fortune and augment their longevity" (*zōchō fukuju*). But the sutra also had a broader significance. Its narrative action centers on the buddha Mahāvairocana's (J. Dainichi) transmission of a *dhāraṇī.* Mahāvairocana describes this formula in the following terms:

> If there should be men and women of good birth who maintain and recite this a thousand times three times a day, then even though causes and conditions from past and present misdeeds should make their lives brief and cut short their lifespan, because they maintain this mantra, their faith will be pure. Their karmic obstacles will disappear, and their lifespans will increase. If they practice and perform this *samādhi,* then after their present lives, they will not be reborn to a mother and father.[27]

25. See note 17. For more on Xuanzang's translation, see Watanabe, *Daihannya to Rishubun no subete,* 279–545. It is also possible, though much less likely given the regents' reference to a "section," that they were referring to Amoghavajra's version of the *Perfection of Wisdom in 150 Verses, Dale jingang bukong zhenshi sanmoye jing,* also known as *Liqu jing* (*Guiding Principle Sūtra*; J. *Dairaku kongō shinjitsu sammaya kyō,* or *Rishukyō*), *T.* 243 (8:784–86), which has played the role of esoteric classic in the Shingon school.

26. For the scripture, see *Da bore boluomiduo jing, T.* 220 (5:1–7:1110). During his Kinpusen *sōjin* in 1090, Moromichi commissioned a lecture on this text (*Go-Nijō Moromichiki,* Kanji 4.7.19 [2:4]). After his return, he began copying it once again (ibid., Kanji 4.11.22 [2:34]). He commissioned further readings of the same sutra in later years, dedicating at least two to Kinpusen (ibid., Kanji 6.9.29, Kanji 7.6.27 [2:291, 3:84]).

27. *Jingang shouming tuoluoni jing, T.* 1134b (20:577c18–22).

Like other Mahāyāna texts, especially those of an esoteric bent, this sutra opens up a loophole in karmic causality, providing escape from *saṃsāra* and speedy access to enlightenment. In addition to its brevity and promised benefits, the sutra's emphasis on repetition helps to explain Moromichi's choice to dedicate it in batches of one hundred.

In fact, the regents presented all of these sutras in multiple copies, with the result that they offered scrolls by the hundreds. Including the sutras that he earmarked for lesser deities, in 1007 Michinaga dedicated at least 219 discrete sutra manuscripts, which amounted to at least 920 scrolls in total. In 1088, Moromichi dedicated at least 599 sutra manuscripts, inclusive of the texts he offered at the subsidiary shrines and the Zaō Hall: these added up to at least 793 scrolls. In 1090, Moromichi dedicated yet another set of sutras, although the full content of that collection is unclear.[28] Measuring with scrolls as the basic unit, in a single pilgrimage to Kinpusen a regent deposited a volume of texts equivalent to between one-seventh and one-fifth of the entire Buddhist canon. In light of this emphasis on volume, it is important to note that in 1096, during the twilight of the regency, Moromichi, his father, and his son helped to ensure that a full copy of the canon was indeed installed at the mountain.[29] Scale mattered: the more sutras, the more merit, the closer the karmic tie, and the more visible the patronage.

By bringing texts to Kinpusen, the regents impressed their mark upon the mountain. As Heian-period narratives show, Japanese Buddhists were firmly convinced that sutra manuscripts could and did exert ongoing effects on their surroundings and their sponsors.[30] Once emplaced, Michinaga and Moromichi's texts became material traces of the regents' devotion and hopes, and embodiments of their merit. Kinpusen had been said to store gold; now it was literally a textual treasury, filled from the regents' stores.

28. Unfortunately, no prayer is extant for Moromichi's 1090 pilgrimage. His diary mentions six copies of the *Guiding Principle Section* and three copies of the *Heart Sūtra*, apparently dedicated at the Komori Shrine, as well as a *Great Perfection of Wisdom Sūtra*, which he buried (*Go-Nijō Moromichiki,* Kanji 4.8.10 [2:6]).

29. For the 1096 canon, see chapter 7.

30. Eubanks, *Miracles of Book and Body.*

Sutra Burial

In the next phase of their protocol, the regents switched registers, moving from large to small scale, from public to private aims, and from normative to non-normative rites. They also began to engage more explicitly with the corporeal quality of scripture when they buried sutras at the Zaō Hall (see fig. 4.3). Whereas their journals provide useful information about their dedicatory offerings, their votive texts give much greater detail about sutra burial, the third phase in their ritual observances. In Michinaga's case, the relevant text comes from an inscription on the gilt bronze tube that he used as a sutra container (see fig. 5.1); in Moromichi's, from his dedicatory prayer. Michinaga's inscription begins:

> In the eighth month, in the autumn of Kankō 4, I took up copies of the *Sūtra of the Lotus of the Wonderful Dharma* (eight scrolls); the *Sūtra of Measureless Meaning* and *Sūtra on Contemplating Samantabhadra* (one scroll each); the *Amitābha Sūtra* (one scroll); the *Sūtra of [Maitreya's] Ascent, Sūtra of [Maitreya's] Descent,* and *Sūtra of [Maitreya's] Buddhahood* (one scroll each); and the *Heart Sūtra* (one scroll). I put them, fifteen scrolls in all, into a bronze tube, and buried them at the Peak of Gold. Above them I erected a gilded bronze lantern, and offered an eternal flame.[31]

In his journal, Michinaga specified that he had copied these fifteen scrolls in his own hand.

Similarly, Moromichi wrote in his 1088 prayer that "with unshakeable sincerity" he had copied and then buried "the *Sūtra of the Lotus of*

31. *KSS,* 236–37. For canonical citations for the *Heart* and *Lotus Sūtra,* see note 16. References for the other scriptures are as follows: *Wuliang yi jing* (*Sūtra of Measureless Meaning;* J. *Muryōgi kyō*), *T.* 276 (9:383–89); *Foshuo guan Puxian pusa xingfa jing* (*Sūtra on the Method for Contemplating the Practices of the Bodhisattva Samantabhadra;* J. *Kan Fugen bosatsu gyōhō kyō*), *T.* 277 (9:389–94); *Foshuo Emituo jing* (*Amitābha Sūtra;* J. *Amida kyō*), *T.* 366 (12:346–48); *Foshuo guan Mile pusa shangsheng duoshuaitian jing* (*Sūtra on Contemplating the Bodhisattva Maitreya's Ascent and Rebirth into Tuṣita Heaven;* J. *Bussetsu kan Miroku bosatsu jōshō Tosotsuten kyō*), *T.* 452 (14:418–20); *Foshuo Mile xiasheng jing, T.* 453 (14:421–23); *Foshuo Mile da chengfo jing, T.* 456 (14:428–34). The small font indicates interlineal text.

the Wonderful Dharma in golden ink (eight scrolls); and the *Sūtra of Measureless Meaning, Sūtra on Contemplating Samantabhadra, Heart Sūtra,* and *Vajra Longevity Sūtra* (one scroll each)." Moromichi used the *Vajra Longevity Sūtra* in lieu of the Maitreyan scriptures, but otherwise he followed his great-grandfather's precedent very closely: both men buried single copies of the *Lotus Sūtra,* plus the scriptures understood to introduce and conclude it (the *Sūtra of Measureless Meaning* and *Sūtra on Contemplating Samantabhadra*), and the *Heart Sūtra* in bronze containers. Because of their status as Mahāyāna classics with great protective powers, these scriptures were popular choices in other sutra burials as well, but they were not the only options. In 1090, for instance, Moromichi buried a copy of the huge, six-hundred-scroll *Great Perfection of Wisdom Sūtra* at Kinpusen.[32] This, the longest scripture in the perfection of wisdom corpus, and indeed in the entire canon, represented an overwhelming commitment to the Dharma. It also seems to have had a particular significance for Moromichi. Even after he returned to the capital, he used the *Great Perfection of Wisdom Sūtra* in his devotions, commissioning readings dedicated to Kinpusen.[33]

Several factors distinguished the texts the regents buried from those they had offered with the expectation that they would be preserved above ground. The texts to be interred were holographs, they were single copies, and they were produced using deluxe materials according to stringent ritual protocols.

Whereas aristocrats often commissioned votive sutras from professional scribes, it was customary to bury only sutras that one had copied out oneself. The lengthy *Great Perfection of Wisdom Sūtra* may have been an exception, but Moromichi almost certainly participated in the reproduction of that text as well, perhaps by writing out the titles. The reason for the emphasis on personal copying seems to have been that copyists maintained a physical connection with their manuscripts. As Charlotte Eubanks has shown, sutras could and did function as bodies with their own agency, inclined toward symbiosis with their human copyists, reciters, and memorizers. In dreams and visions recorded in Heian narratives, scriptural texts sometimes incarnated in

32. *Go-Nijō Moromichiki,* Kanji 4.8.10, *uragaki* (2:6).

33. See note 26.

human form, interacting with those who had copied or protected them. Conversely, human bodies could be textualized. In one of several stories set in the Ōmine Range and featuring sutra reciters whose incorruptible tongues continued to speak scripture long after death, an itinerant holy man en route to Kumano discovered a fully articulated skeleton chanting the *Lotus Sūtra.* According to one recension, this auditory experience was so affecting that, like text, it was "carved" into the holy man's bones.[34] By extension, the process of writing out a sutra not only produced a manuscript that had bodily characteristics, but also wrote the text onto and into the copyist's own body. Thus, in Eubanks's words, "the body, the mind, and the page" operated as "metaphorically intertwined locations for the inscription of sacred Buddhist text."[35] For the regents, this meant that they and their texts interpenetrated.

The one-to-one mutuality between copyist and manuscript helps to explain the fact that unlike offered sutras, buried sutras were singular. In offering one copy of each scripture, the point seems to have been less to pile up merit and symbolic capital than to create a textual body-double that could be emplaced for perpetuity within the real space of the mountain itself. This made for a striking numeric difference in the textual components of the mountaintop rites. For instance, in contrast to the 219 manuscripts in 920 scrolls that Michinaga dedicated in his *kuyō,* he buried only eight manuscripts in fifteen scrolls.

Ritual rules mediated the link between buried texts and living patrons. As mentioned in the previous chapter, the regents copied their sutras during their preparatory *sōjin* regimens. The colophon from one of the scrolls of the *Lotus Sūtra* Moromichi buried in 1088, which has since been excavated and is now in the collection of the Kyoto National Museum, reads, in part: "Copied while maintaining the precepts during *sōjin*. Among the six roots, the root of my ears is pure."[36] Such statements indicate that the body of the copyist contracted a karmic tie

34. Eubanks, *Miracles of Book and Body,* 159; *Hokke genki* 1.11 (*NST,* 7:519, 628n13.4). Note that "bones" appears in one of the manuscripts, but "spirit" in another. The *NST* editors used the latter.

35. Eubanks, *Miracles of Text and Body,* 133.

36. *KSS,* colophon 16 (238–39).

with the text he or she was producing, further suggesting that the writing process could purify and heal the copyist's body.

Not surprisingly, the regents took great care over the physical qualities of their buried texts. Moromichi noted that the scriptures he dedicated in the second phase of his ritual observances were rendered in black ink; by contrast, he wrote the texts he buried in golden ink on indigo paper. Michinaga's excavated manuscripts are of the same style. Chrysographs (manuscripts written in golden ink) had long numbered among the most aesthetically authoritative texts produced by the royalty and nobility. They were also very expensive due to the use of precious materials and labor-intensive dyeing techniques.[37] The regents thus complemented the ethos of monumentality and multiplicity that had dominated their *kuyō* with the jewel-box splendor of indigo-and-gold scriptures, created to be hidden in the earth.

It was only appropriate that the holograph sutras should be consecrated prior to being interred, and the regents apparently sponsored an offering rite to do so. Most likely, this was appended to the earlier *kuyō*, for the same monks officiated; however, the rite seems to have been held on a smaller scale. In 1090, for instance, a staff of thirty monks supported the officiants for the consecration of Moromichi's buried sutras, whereas a set of one hundred had served Michinaga in dedicating his above-ground manuscripts in 1007. The regents described this process as follows. Once again, due to the brevity of Moromichi's 1088 journal entries, I cite his entries from 1090.

Michinaga, 1007 (entry for 8.11, continued)	Moromichi, 1090 (entry for 8.10, continued)
Also, we had the same seven monks of the Way present the single copy of the *Lotus Sūtra* in golden ink that I had copied in a prior year, as well as the three scrolls of the Maitreya sutras, the *Amitābha Sūtra*, and the *Heart Sūtra* that I copied this time.	[*Uragaki*:] When [the offering for the other sutras] was complete, we made a dedicatory offering for the *Great Perfection of Wisdom Sūtra*. The ritual master was Minor Right Reverend (*shōsōzu*) Saijin. Seven monks plus thirty resident monks [officiated].

37. Tanabe, *Art of the Lotus Sūtra*, 35–36, 78–80.

The lecturer was Major Right Reverend (*daisōzu*) Kakuun, the prayer reciter was Major Right Reverend Jōchō, the reader was Dharma Bridge Fukō, the cantor was Eju, the prostrations master was Myōson, the flower strewer was Jōki, and the hall master was Unchō. We gave them all gifts.

As for the aforementioned sutras, we set up a gilt bronze lantern before the divine presence, buried [the sutras] underneath it, and offered a perpetual flame. Today and every day I will sponsor offertory verses.

[*Annotation in red ink*:] The protocol for going into the divine presence.

We performed three sets of one hundred bows. When we had finished, we installed the *Great Perfection of Wisdom Sūtra* in a cabinet. When we had finished, we bowed three times, and buried it before the seat of the divine presence. When we had finished, we bowed three times. Then, at the great rock that brought forth Zaō, we bowed three times.

Given the brevity of the descriptions, it seems that the burial process itself was quite straightforward, a supposition borne out by Ōe no Masafusa's description of Shirakawa's 1092 sutra burial, which is discussed in the next chapter. Excavations indicate that, prior to burial, sutras were often placed in metal tubes, which were then inserted into stone or clay jars, which were then placed in chambers lined with charcoal and stones. There seems to have been some variation in the material logistics of burial at Kinpusen, however. The tube that Michinaga used in 1007 provides one example of an interior container (see fig. 5.1), but sutra boxes have also been found at the peak. In 1090, Moromichi actually placed his scriptures in a cabinet (*zushi*), presumably because the *Great Perfection of Wisdom* was so voluminous that it would not fit into a smaller container.[38] Once the burial was complete, some pilgrims sought to ensure the symbolic visibility of their texts. Michinaga, for instance, erected a lantern for which he provided an endowment to provide oil for an eternal flame. The subsequent popularity of sutra burial at Kinpusen

38. This is the only instance I know of in which such a large container was used in a sutra burial. Though Moromichi is quite explicit in saying that he buried (*uzumu*) a cabinet, no such container has been recovered during excavations at Kinpusen.

testifies to just how compelling this gesture was: buried sutras might be hidden, but they were still known.

Even as Michinaga was casting himself as a great donor to be remembered by posterity, he worked to ensure that other members of his family could participate in the mountaintop rites. He noted that his sixteen-year-old heir, Yorimichi, who accompanied him to Kinpusen, dedicated his own sutras, using a rite of the same grand, seven-officiant scale. Michinaga's wife, Minamoto no Rinshi (alt. Tomoko, 964–1053), who had not come, also dedicated her own sutras, presumably with Michinaga or Yorimichi acting as her proxy. Whether Rinshi and Yorimichi buried sutras is unclear; regardless, the fact that they consecrated manuscripts underlines the concerns for family cohesion and continuance that pervaded the regents' devotions. Rinshi's sutra dedication also shows that the physical ban on women did not prevent them from participating, albeit by proxy, in religious activity at the mountain.

Moromichi, too, may have overseen sutra burial rites on behalf of his spouse. Among the sutras he listed in his 1088 prayer, he noted two sets under the heading "in fulfillment of vows made by my wife." One set, lettered in black ink, matched the texts he dedicated for other family members, and was likely offered during the *kuyō* in the Zaō Hall. The second had been written out in gold, which suggests that it, like his own golden-ink sutras, was buried. The texts in question included the *Guiding Principle Section,* the *Heart Sūtra,* and the *Sūtra on Avalokiteśvara* (the twenty-fifth chapter of the *Lotus Sūtra,* treated as an independent scripture). These were standard choices, but there were also two indigenous Chinese scriptures from the fringes of the Buddhist canon. One, the *Sūtra on the Spell of the Eight Yangs of Heaven and Earth,* is a polemic against directional and five phases divination that promises its readers, copyists, and devotees protection from all kinds of difficulties. Most strikingly, it asserts that copying or reading it is equivalent to copying or reading the entire canon.[39] This suited the regents' preoccupations with comprehensive scale. The other scripture, the *Sūtra on the Universal Ambrosia Dhāraṇī with Eight Names,* records a *dhāraṇī* that prevents

39. *Foshuo tiandi bayang shenzhu jing* (*Sūtra on the Spell of Eight Yangs of Heaven and Earth*; J. *Bussetsu tenchi hachiyō shinju kyō*), *T.* 2897 (85:1422–25; for statements on the equivalence of the *dhāraṇi* and the full canon, see 1425a8–10).

anyone who hears it from falling into the realms of hell or hungry ghosts. It further ensures their rebirth into Tuṣita Heaven, whence they will be able to descend to this world with the future buddha, Maitreya.[40] Given its content, this text appears to have provided an alternative to the better-known Maitreyan sutras favored by Michinaga or the *Vajra Longevity Sūtra* favored by Moromichi.

Not only were these scriptures distinctive in form and content but they also served a different purpose. Whereas Moromichi had tendered prayers for the longevity of the royals and his other family members, regarding these texts he wrote, apparently in the voice of his wife: "Although in age I am in my prime, in body I am childless. I am bitter about this, and my prayers and thoughts are of nothing else." Moromichi himself had several children, and his heir, Tadazane, had been born to his principal wife, Fujiwara no Zenshi (alt. Matako, 1060–1150). Most likely the woman involved in the Kinpusen sutra-copying project was his second wife, the daughter of Fujiwara no Nobunaga (n.d.), who had no children.[41] In light of the specificity of the wish and the golden ink used for these sutra manuscripts, it seems most likely that she copied the scriptures out herself and then had Moromichi bury them on her behalf at the peak. Her prayers show that fertility was indeed one of the concerns aired at Kinpusen, and that women participated personally and materially in the mountain's cult.

Traces

Once the regents had overseen rites sponsored by other members of their family and interred their own holographs, they headed home without any further ado. If they had no reason to linger, we may ask,

40. *Baming pumi tuoluoni jing* (*Sūtra on the Universal Ambrosia Dhāraṇī with Eight Names*; J. *Hachimyō fumitsu darani kyō*), *T.* 1365 (21:883–84; for statements on hell, see 884a2–7).

41. The name of this woman is unclear; Satō Kenji identifies her as Shinshi (alt. Nobuko), while Kimoto Yoshinobu identifies her as Gishi (alt. Noriko) (see Satō, "Fujiwara no Moromichi, Morozane," 232, 236; and Kimoto, "Kanpaku Go-Nijō Moromichi," 91–92).

then why was it so important for them to carry out these rites themselves? Why could they not have dedicated their sutras in the capital and then sent them off to the mountain by proxy? The answer is to be found in the notion of traces, the corporeality of texts, and the scriptural resonances of sutra burial.

The trace-ism so evident in Kinpusen's pantheon and the regents' political culture also surfaced in their textual practices. Like other Heian writers, the regents were wont to construe the act of writing as a process of trace-making, and written words as traces.[42] For instance, Fujiwara no Morosuke, who had directed his descendants to "do nothing for which there is no trace," also advised them on how to spend their time: "In the morning, read the Chinese classics. Then study hand-traces (*shuseki*). Thereafter amusements are permitted."[43] The term "hand-traces" connoted good calligraphy; accordingly, in Michinga's day the greatest calligraphers were hailed as the "three traces" (*sanseki*) to distinguish them from the "the three brushes" (*sanpitsu*) of the early Heian period.[44] In his sutra-tube inscription, Michinaga characterized his holograph manuscripts in similar terms:

> Ah! I generate the aspiration for enlightenment; I repent of my innumerable misdeeds. I harbor the resolve of a minister; I magnify the infinity of the southern mountains. I bury the relics of the Dharma body; I revere the compassion of Śākyamuni. I treasure the traces of my devoted hands; I depend upon the dragon deities' protection. The root of my vow is already firm; my hopes are already fulfilled.

42. For examples of the term "trace" being used to refer to writing, see *Midō kanpakuki,* Kankō 1.8.23, Kankō 1.i9.12, and Kankō 2.1.8 (1:104, 110, 127). *The Tale of Genji* provides another example, in which Murasaki Shikibu has the emperor praise Genji's calligraphy and painting by exclaiming, "You seem to eclipse the traces of the talented ink-painters of the past" (*Genji monogatari*, "E awase" [*SNKBT,* 20:183; for an alternative translation, see Royall Tyler, *The Tale of Genji,* 2:329]).

43. *Kujō ushōjō yuikai* (*NST,* 8:117, 296; for an alternative translation, see Sansom, *A History of Japan,* 1:81).

44. The Three Brushes were Kūkai, Emperor Saga (786–842, r. 809–23), and Tachibana no Hayanari (d. 842); the Three Traces were Ono no Michikaze (894–966), Fujiwara no Sukemasa (944–98), and Fujiwara no Yukinari (972–1027).

As the literary, parallel prose of his inscription makes clear, Michinaga viewed his manuscripts both as his own physical traces and as "relics of the Dharma body" (*hosshin no shari*).[45] The meaning, or better, the meanings, of the term "Dharma body" (Skt. *dharmakāya*, C. *fashen*, J. *hosshin*) have long been subject to diverse interpretations, but in East Asia, Buddhists have sometimes been of the opinion that the *dharmakāya* is a hypostasized, singular, and ineffable body in which all buddhas participate. Kūkai, for instance, maintained that the buddha Mahāvairocana *is* the Dharma body, a cosmic, scriptural being whose textual activity animates the universe.[46]

Michinaga's own understanding probably derived from *Lotus*-centered Tendai doctrine, in which he took a strong interest. He had studied the *Commentary on the Lotus Sūtra,* in which the patriarchs Zhiyi and Guanding declare, "bones are the relics of the living body, but sutras-scrolls are the relics of the Dharma body."[47] It is possible to read this statement in light of the standard view in the early to middle Mahāyāna as reconstructed by Paul Harrison, namely, that the term *dharmakāya* refers collectively to the Buddhist teachings, and is better understood as a doctrinal corpus than as a metaphysical body.[48] At the same time, the Tendai position took the physical nuances of the term quite seriously. The *Lotus Sūtra,* which was both the object and inspiration for Zhiyi and Guanding's hermeneutics, is famous for asserting that the sutra—and by extension, its manuscripts—actually embodies the buddha(s). In the "Preachers of the Dharma Chapter," the *Lotus* states that anywhere there is a copy of the sutra, "there is the whole body of the thus-come one."[49] The "Apparition of the Jeweled Stupa Chapter" represents the buddha Prabhūtaratna in exactly the

45. For an analysis emphasizing this point, see Hosaka, *Kyōzuka ronkō,* 9–54.

46. On the meaning of the term *dharmakāya* in the early to middle Mahāyāna, see Harrison, "Is the *Dharma-kāya*?" For a treatment that focuses on buddha-body theory as elaborated in the Tibetan literature, see Makransky, *Buddhahood Embodied.* For Kūkai's position, see Abé, *The Weaving of Mantra,* 286–88.

47. *Miaofa lianhua jing wenju, T.* 1718 (34:110c2–3). In this passage, the commentary claims to cite from a "*Shilun,*" which I have been unable to identify. For Michinaga's study of the commentary, see *Midō kanpakuki,* Kankō 1.7.8 (1:99).

48. Harrison, "Is the *Dharma-kāya*?"

49. *Miaofa lianhua jing, T.* 262 (8:31b26–29).

same terms. At the same time that he is the "whole body of the thus-come one," Prabhūtaratna is clearly a relic: he died eons ago and appears inside a stupa, that is, a reliquary.[50] Equally clearly, he is deeply textual, for according to the scripture, it is only the preaching of the *Lotus Sūtra* that can call him forth through time and space. With its phrasing, then, the sutra implies that buddha, text, and relic interfuse, merging theoretical categories and physical embodiments.

Devotional customs across Asia show that Buddhist conceptualizations of texts as relics were in no way unique to Japan, much less to the Kinpusen cult. As Daniel Boucher has shown, the classical verse summary of the doctrine of dependent origination was routinely inscribed upon or inserted into stupa structures in medieval India. As a number of art historians have noted, in China, texts, like relics, were often buried below or enshrined within pagodas.[51] Similar practices obtained in Japan, where copyists were prone to use visual cues to represent text as relic. Copyists working in the "one stupa per character" (*ichiji hōtō*) style, for instance, inscribed each character of a sutra within a stupa, such that the manuscript itself became a reliquary for its words.

Manuscripts thus functioned as pivots, material locations where buddha and copyist, trace and text could fuse into a relic-like object capable of remaining present through time in a particular site. As previously mentioned, Charlotte Eubanks has argued that a copyist (or a reciter) participated in a physical, symbiotic relationship with the scriptures that s/he reproduced. In producing textual doubles of their own bodies in the form of "traces of their hands," pilgrim-copyists recalled the "Appearance of the Jeweled Stupa Chapter," where Śākyamuni's myriad manifestations, literally his "partial bodies" (J. *bunshin*), gather before Prabhūtaratna's stupa. In other words, at the same time that pilgrims were creating a "whole body of the thus come one" by copying out the *Lotus* and other sutras, they were also creating textual manifestations that functioned as their own "partial bodies."

50. *Miaofa lianhua jing, T.* 262 (8:32c8; see also 32c15, 32c18, 33b29).

51. Boucher, "The *Pratītyasamutpādagāthā* and Its Role"; Shen, "Realizing the Buddha's *Dharma* Body"; Tsiang, "Embodiments of Buddhist Texts," 59–60 and 372nn30–34. Cf. Strong, *Relics of the Buddha*, 8–10.

Zaō, too, operated as a pivot, and his traits clarify how sutra burial could be used to negotiate time. As discussed in chapter 2, Zaō was known as a provisional manifestation of both Śākyamuni and Maitreya. The regents explicitly called on all three of his personae, past, present, and future. In 1088, Moromichi wrote in the prayer he copied out to bury with his sutras: "I go forward in consideration of Śākyamuni's precious teaching of the single vehicle; I go back to form a karmic tie with the three future assemblies of the Merciful One." He added: "I revere the miraculous powers of Vajra Zaō."[52] According to his own testimony, then, Moromichi was supremely confident in the ability of sutra burial to bind him to the Dharma of the buddha of the past, to assure him of a place in the audience of the buddha of the future, and to secure the blessings of Zaō in the present.

Modern interpreters have tended to assume that patrons who engaged in sutra burial were anxious to preserve the Buddhist teachings because they were convinced that the Dharma had attenuated after the death of the historical buddha, entering an age of precipitous decline (*mappō*); according to some calculations, this decline was to begin in 1052.[53] As Moromichi's prayer shows, the regents certainly did wish to meet Maitreya. It is also true that *mappō* anxieties did motivate sutra burial at other sites, but it does not follow that the regents buried sutras because they were convinced that the Dharma was fading away (see chapter 2). Equipped as they were with relics and traces, Michinaga and Moromichi were sure of their ability to maintain contact with the buddhas and the Dharma. Their journals and votive texts are almost entirely free of *mappō* eschatology, and when they did speak of "the latter ages," as often as not they adopted a positive tone. One of Moromichi's rare references to the end of the Dharma is illustrative: reflecting upon a dream in which he had encountered Kōbō Daishi's (that is, Kūkai's) place of practice while traveling in

52. This portion of Moromichi's prayer is also discussed in the conclusion to chapter 2.

53. The *locus classicus* for the *mappō* thesis is Ishida and Yajima, *Kinpusen kyōzuka ibutsu*.

the southern mountains, he remarked, "Despite the end of the Dharma, wondrous effects (*reigen*) are no different."[54]

Rather than *mappō* anxiety, resonances between text, body, and relic, and between Śākyamuni, Maitreya, and Zaō shaped the regents' rationale for sutra burial. In his 1007 inscription, Michinaga specified his goals for the scriptures he buried. He began, "As for the *Lotus Sūtra,* it is to repay the kindness of Lord Śākyamuni, to meet Maitreya directly, to draw near to Zaō, and to bring me to enlightenment." He continued, "As for the *Amitābha Sūtra,* it is for my final hours, that my body and mind shall not be distracted, that I may be mindful of Lord Amitābha, and that I may be reborn in the Realm of Bliss." He then looked even farther ahead: "As for the Maitreya sutras," that is, the *Sūtra of Maitreya's Ascent,* the *Sūtra of Maitreya's Descent,* and the *Sūtra of Maitreya's Buddhahood,* "they are to clear away my misdeeds from ninety billion eons of birth-and-death, that I may realize unproduced forbearance and meet the Merciful Lord when he comes to this world." Michinaga then went on to amplify his hopes for a future encounter with Maitreya, adding, "Reverently, I vow that when the Merciful Lord becomes a buddha, I will return from the Realm of Bliss to the buddha's place, in order to listen to the Dharma Flower Assembly and receive a prediction that I will become a buddha." Michinaga thus saw Amitābha's Pure Land not as a final destination from which he would pass out of the cycle of rebirth, but rather as a station on his way back to Kinpusen to meet Maitreya. Furthermore, Michinaga's (and Zaō's) own scriptural preferences seeped into his rhetoric. Although Maitreya is usually expected to teach at the threefold Dragon Flower Assemblies, Michinaga wrote of "Dharma Flower," that is, *Lotus,* Assemblies, a slippage that hints that he expected Maitreya to preach the *Lotus Sūtra* at Kinpusen. Michinaga concluded this passage in his inscription with a forceful declaration: "The scrolls of the sutras that I bury in this place will naturally spring forth and cause the assembled throngs to perform good works."

54. *Go-Nijō Moromichiki,* Kōwa 1.3.22, *uragaki* (3:268). According to word searches conducted using the *Kokiroku furutekisuto deitabeisu,* Moromichi used the term *mappō* twice and the synonym *matsudai* seven times in his journal. The extant colophons for sutras buried by the regents at Kinpusen do not mention the end of the Dharma (see *KSS,* colophons 3–6, 16 [235–39]).

In his expectation that his manuscripts would emerge from the ground far in the future, Michinaga echoed tropes of textual eruption associated with Śākyamuni, Zaō, and Maitreya. It was when Śākyamuni preached the *Lotus Sūtra* that Prabhūtaratna emerged from the earth as a textual relic-buddha. Zaō, who loves the *Lotus,* likewise sprang from the earth (see chapter 2). Similarly, Maitreyan narratives predict that Buddhist texts will metaphorically spring forth when the future buddha arrives. According to the *Sūtra of Maitreya's Buddhahood,* which Michinaga buried at Kinpusen, before Maitreya preaches the Dharma, he will travel to Wolf Trace Mountain and open the living rock. There, Mahākāśyapa, one of Śākyamuni's disciples who long ago secreted himself within the mountain, will emerge from a deep meditative trance and give Maitreya Śākyamuni's robe, which he has been safeguarding for thousands of years. Mahākāśyapa will then fly up into the air, work wonders, and expound "the scriptures in the twelve divisions," that is, the entire canon. When he completes his recitation, he will burst into flames, thereby spontaneously cremating himself. The assembled disciples will then install his relics in a stupa atop the mountain.[55] In light of Mahākāśyapa's recitation of the full corpus of the teachings and Japanese convictions that reciters shared a physical identity with their scriptures, the relics installed at Wolf Trace Mountain could be fairly understood to be, like Michinaga's buried sutras, traces of the Dharma body.

Canonical narrative and commentary did not deliver a logical *summa* on the relationships between relics, traces, bodies, texts, and manuscripts, but they did provide representational resources to elite pilgrims. In developing their own standards for sutra burial, the regents drew on canonical tropes, as well as Kinpusen's narrative theology. When Michinaga wrote that his manuscripts would emerge from the mountain at Maitreya's coming, his statement resonated with scriptural portrayals of Mahākāśyapa and Prabhūtaratna, as well as with tales of Zaō. At the same time, his characterization of his sutras as his own hand-traces gestured toward the culture of precedent exemplified by his ancestor Morosuke's rules and general preoccupations with deities' manifestations in partial bodies and unfurling traces.

55. *Foshuo Mile da chengfo jing, T.* 456 (14:433b11–434a2).

Conclusion

The regents' interaction with the real space of Kinpusen was deeply conditioned by ritual custom and theological imagination. Pilgrims carefully distinguished Kinpusen, the site for their sutra burials, as a space apart. Through the *sōjin* regimens discussed in the previous chapter, they distanced themselves from their families and associates while they prepared for the journey. When they set out, they wore undyed clothing devoid of the conventional signs of status and rank, and when they arrived at the mountain they were as far as they had ever been from home. Thus, for the duration of their journey to and from the Peak of Gold, the regents inhabited paradigmatically liminal conditions. Classical Turnerian models of pilgrimage, with their emphasis on rites of passage as theorized by Arnold van Gennep, would suggest that these efforts served to transform the regents ritually, so that upon their return they could take on new, more authoritative roles within established social structures. The regents did remake themselves by temporarily leaving home, appropriating the charismatic personae of holy men, and returning with enhanced status as righteous rulers. And yet their departure from the bounds of everyday life, followed by their reintegration into society, does not account for their entire ritual agenda.

The regents' trace-ism, and specifically their use of the term "traces" in the context of sutra burial, points to their engagement in a broader integrative enterprise. Temporally, sutra burial promised to link the past, present, and future. Materially, it offered pilgrims a chance to generate textual bodies of their own that shared in the corporeality of the buddhas. Spatially, it provided them with an enduring tie to Kinpusen, its buddhas, and its gods. The interment of scripture was all the more compelling because, being directed at the trace deity Zaō, it resonated with *honji suijaku* discourse. At the same time, it mimicked dynamics of textual storage and emergence found in canonical narratives, while complementing established rites of manuscript reproduction. Finally, because manuscripts were construed as hand-traces and because prior example was a determining factor in ritual practice, sutra burial connected to the all-important domain of precedent. For all of these reasons, the interment of scripture was particularly attractive: it condensed a range of concerns into a single action, producing a rich and satisfying array of meanings.

At the same time that sutra burial exemplifies trace-ism, it also testifies to the ability of laypeople to develop new practices to suit their own interests and agendas. The regents used traces—in this case, material, textual presences—to act upon place and to trump time. In the course of their ritual regimes, they produced sites in the capital that were proper to themselves; they also went to Kinpusen to place textual embodiments of themselves within the mountain. In doing so, they made Kinpusen the corollary of their metropolitan domain, reworking the mountain's place in the larger real-and-imagined landscape.[56] They also anticipated that their descendants would commemorate them by following their example, and that the mountain community would honor them in perennial rites that they themselves had endowed. These gestures meant that even in cases when a particular regent made only one pilgrimage to the Peak of Gold, his rites of textualization and emplacement ensured that he would "be there" in perpetuity. By extension, his intimacy with Zaō and the local gods safeguarded his personal well-being and the political position of his line far into the future. One index of the effectiveness of these practices was their popularity. Like other aspects of their ritual regimes, the examples the regents set at Kinpusen were so compelling that other pilgrims took them as models for their own conduct. The best-documented and politically most significant case of this type of emulation, namely, Retired Emperor Shirakawa's pilgrimage to Kinpusen in 1092, is taken up in the next chapter.

56. Abe Yasurō has explicitly correlated regency-period sutra burial to *insei*-period projects to copy the canon and emplace it at sacred sites like Kumano, Iwashimizu, and Mt. Fuji (Abe, *Chūsei Nihon no shūkyō tekusuto,* 174–98).

CHAPTER SIX

Personnel and Politics

> Ah! The strange heights and fantastic boulders, the switchbacks leading up the long slope to the summit! Even a small step is hard to bear. The sacred shrines of the gods of heaven and earth are in the deep recesses among the thunderclouds and streams, among the dragons and the valleys. We are greatly overawed, and it is easy to go astray.
>
> —Retired Emperor Shirakawa, prayer for his Kinpusen pilgrimage; text by Ōe no Masafusa[1]

Shirakawa's activities during his 1092 pilgrimage brought spatial and political change to Kinpusen. Inasmuch as the retired emperor focused on bringing the mountain into his own ambit, his encounter with its real-and-imagined space exemplifies the dynamics of emulation and competition that characterized ritual regimes more generally. It also typifies some of the basic power relations from which he derived his political influence. Shirakawa sought to match the regents' ritual protocols and thereby overwrite their symbolic claims to the Peak of Gold. By conferring emoluments and appointments upon mountain monks, he maneuvered Kinpusen's hierarchs into becoming his, and not the regents', clients. Furthermore, inasmuch as members of Shirakawa's pilgrimage party maintained a range of clientage relationships with him, their participation underscores the coercive, political nature of ritual action.

By endowing a cloister and new monastic positions at the mountain, Shirakawa contributed to Kinpusen's local institutional development in a way that fostered the growth of new interest groups with

1. *Gōtotoku nagon ganmonshū* 2.1, dated Kanji 2.7.13, but emended to Kanji 6.7.13 (249).

strong ties to the retired emperors. His activities also exacerbated friction between Kinpusen and Kōfukuji, typifying the polarization of institutional relationships that characterized the *insei* period more generally. Having originated as a Fujiwara family temple in the Nara Basin, Kōfukuji became a formidable power bloc during the eleventh and twelfth centuries, subjugating other religious institutions across the province of Yamato and accruing an immense portfolio of estates. By 1092, Kōfukuji's partisans had already set their sights on Kinpusen and were asserting that they held the right to direct its affairs. In response, the mountain monks insisted that they would retain their independence at all costs. When the retired emperor came to Kinpusen, the resident monks asked him to support their position, and he indicated his willingness to assist. By involving himself with Kinpusen's administration, Shirakawa signaled that he might hamper any outside effort to exercise control over the mountain. As we shall see in chapter 7, this proved to be a motivating factor in armed conflicts that erupted between Kinpusen and Kōfukuji in 1093 and 1094.

In this chapter, I focus primarily upon a firsthand account of the 1092 pilgrimage recorded in a journal fragment, which I discovered in the archives of the Imperial Household Agency and the Historiographical Institute at the University of Tokyo. As I have shown elsewhere, this account almost certainly constitutes an extended citation from the *Gōki* (Ōe's record), the diary, now dispersed, of the noted courtier and man of letters Ōe no Masafusa.[2] Masafusa accompanied Shirakawa to Kinpusen in 1092 and composed a prayer on the retired emperor's behalf for the occasion; this text is now preserved in the *Gōtotoku nagon ganmonshū* (Collection of prayers by the Ōe governor-counselor). The journal fragment includes the most detailed extant description of rites held at the summit. It also contains a record of a conversation between the retired emperor and Kinpusen's senior monk, an esoteric master named Kōsan. This conversation sheds light on the mountain's position vis-à-vis Kōfukuji in the early 1090s; it also shows that during his mountain rites, Shirakawa's attention was drawn to issues of personnel and their political implications.

2. "*Gōki* fragment"; Blair, "Shinshutsu '*Gōki* itsubun' shōkai," and "Mountain and Plain." Cf. *Gōki* for fragments identified and collected by Kimoto Yoshinobu.

It is important to note that Shirakawa's 1092 pilgrimage did not constitute his first engagement with the physical and social space of Kinpusen. Aware of the mountain's reputation and popularity among the nobility—that is, its imagined space—Shirakawa began to reshape its administration and built environment through the strategic use of patronage while he was still on the throne. In 1080, he held, but almost certainly did not attend, a dedication for a facility he had sponsored in the Yoshinoyama area. This was known as the Treasure Pagoda.[3] In all probability, it was an enlargement or reconstruction of a cloister that had been in place since the early eleventh century. Michinaga wrote that he had stopped at the Treasure Pagoda on his way to and from Kinpusen in 1007; similarly, according to the *Fusō ryakki,* Shirakawa fell ill "at the Treasure Pagoda at the bottom of the mountain," that is, in Yoshinoyama, on his way to Kinpusen in 1092.[4] What little we know of the history of the Treasure Pagoda indicates that Shirakawa meant it to be a center for his own influence. An account of an 1134 dispute among Kinpusen monks indicates that at some point, Shirakawa made Kōsan the director (*shikkō*) of the pagoda and deeded over the Ogura estate to provide revenue for ritual supplies. In addition, he endowed positions for six "offering monks" (*gusō*) at the pagoda, designating Kōsan chief among them. Although Shirakawa retained the right to appoint subsequent directors, after his death the succession fell to the monks themselves. In 1134, no fewer than five men laid claim to the position, suggesting that it was a source of considerable influence. The fact that the litigants approached Retired Emperor Toba to resolve the dispute also demonstrates that the pagoda was viewed as a vow temple (*goganji*) where administrative rights remained a royal prerogative.[5]

In sum, both before and after his pilgrimage, Shirakawa worked to exert influence over Kinpusen. In his own way, he was perfectly aware

3. *Sōgō bunin,* entry for Jōryaku 4 (*DNBZ,* 123:203). Note that Shudō Yoshiki's treatment of this facility, though cogent, relies heavily on later sources (Shudō, *Kinpusenji shi,* 59, 506–8, 711).

4. *Midō kanpakuki,* Kankō 4.8.9, 12 (1:228–29, 329–30); *Fusō ryakki,* Kanji 6.7.13 (*SZKT,* 12:332).

5. *Chōshūki,* Chōshō 3.5.6 (*ZST,* 17:198–200).

of what European and North American spatial theorists have been arguing since the 1970s, namely, that the places we inhabit are as social and political as they are physical. It was Kinpusen's imagined space, particularly its reputation as a source of blessings and its close association with the regents, that brought Shirakawa to Kinpusen. Once there, the retired emperor sought to alter the real circumstances of the mountain by playing upon the interconnections between social space, physical space, and ritual performance—by making appointments, building temples, burying sutras, and making offerings.

Ritualizing the Mountaintop

During the rites he sponsored at the summit, Shirakawa carefully elaborated upon precedent set by the regents, creating an authoritative position for himself through ritual performance. Having mantled himself in orthopraxy, he sought to exert control over the administrative affairs of Kinpusen, countering the influence of both the regents and Kōfukuji. Nearly every aspect of his encounter with Kinpusen was mediated by ritual; therefore, in this discussion, I follow Masafusa's lead in attending closely to Shirakawa's ceremonial protocols.

Shirakawa's 1092 rites were the first large-scale offering to be made by an eminent pilgrim at Kinpusen since the mountaintop Zaō Hall had been damaged by a typhoon in 1091. The structure had been rebuilt by the Izumo governor Takashina no Shigenaka (1069–1120), who had close ties to the regents. When the pilgrimage party arrived, reconstruction was almost complete.[6] As both ritual managers and participants, Masafusa and other members of Shirakawa's entourage set about fitting the new hall with signs of their master's largesse, literally covering the ritual space with offerings they had brought from the capital.[7]

6. For damage to the hall in 1091, see *Go-Nijō Moromichiki,* Kanji 5.8.16–17 (2:168); cf. *Fusō ryakki,* which less reliably attributes the damage to an earthquake, Kanji 5.8.7 (*SZKT,* 12:332). For Shigenaka's reconstruction, see *Chūyūki,* Kanji 7.9.22 (1:235).

7. "*Gōki* fragment." Subsequent references to the same text are elided in the following discussion.

The built environment was divided between residents and visitors, a distinction that mapped onto the difference between Zaō and his supplicants. The hall was structurally divided into two precincts, a Primary Hall (*shōdō*) and a Worship Hall (*raidō*), with a connecting aisle (*yukiainoma*) running between.[8] The Primary Hall, which Masafusa also referred to as the Treasure Hall (*hōden*), was Zaō's sphere. At its core was a chancel (*moya*) three bays wide and two bays deep, with plank walls on three sides. Although Masafusa did not comment on the contents of thtis "place of presence" (*gozaisho*), it likely housed one or more images of Zaō that were customarily kept hidden from view. Such secret images (*hibutsu*) were common in premodern times and continue to be so today.[9] Devotees had, however, "set up many wooden images" of Zaō on an altar of pounded earth in front of the hall, along with "tiers of unfinished wooden shelves" upon which lamps could be arranged for offerings of light.

To the south of the Primary Hall, the Worship Hall customarily housed a raised altar of pounded earth and had a fence running along its northern perimeter. According to Masafusa, "no one except resident monks" was allowed to pass beyond this barrier; however, neither the altar nor the fence had been rebuilt at the time of Shirakawa's visit. As its name suggests, the Worship Hall was where pilgrims were expected to carry out their devotions; accordingly, Shirakawa's attendants prepared seats there for the retired emperor, his monastic retinue, and Kinpusen's monastic leaders. These were oriented according to a hierarchical spatial schema in which the highest-ranking members of the party enjoyed the greatest proximity to Zaō. As the primary patron, Shirakawa sat in a screened seat in the northern aisle (*hisashi*) of the Worship Hall, directly opposite the place of presence. Toward the rear, seats were laid out for the highest-ranking members of Shirakawa's retinue. His monastic attendants, all of whom were members of the Office of Monastic Affairs, sat in the center. Kinpusen's hierarchs had lower-

8. On the basis of Yamagishi Tsuneto's criticisms, I have revised the interpretation of the mountain architecture that I advanced in Blair, "Peak of Gold," and "Mountain and Plain." For more on the structural and ritual relations between buddha halls and worship halls, see Yamagishi, *Chūsei jiin shakai to butsudō*, 79–142.

9. For hidden images, see Rambelli, "Secret Buddhas."

ranking seats on the left (that is, on Zaō's right), though only one, Kyōshō, took the seat allotted to him. At the other end of the same row, on Zaō's left, sat the senior nobles in Shirakawa's entourage, with other courtiers placed in the back. The southwest corner of the building had been curtained off and dedicated to a supplementary ritual of constant prostrations (*fudan raihai*) carried out by a single monk on Shirakawa's behalf.

Though he was barred from physically occupying Zaō's domain, Shirakawa demonstrated symbolically that this was his place and his god. Drawing on gifts from his own clients, he provided the curtains and cords hanging in the Primary Hall's chancel, as well as twenty sutra desks, low ritual platforms (*raiban*), and special mats used for seats. His brocades decked the steps of the daises, while his canopies and cloth hung from the ceilings and walls. The sutras that he would dedicate were laid out upon desks before the seats of the primary officiants and other participating monks. He literally brought all of this to light by making an offering of three hundred lamps, placed in 150 vessels decorated with flowers.[10]

Shirakawa performed his rites in three distinct phases, the first of which was a large-scale dedicatory offering (*kuyō*). Both the ritual form of the dedication and the offerings themselves indicate that Shirakawa was consciously overwriting the regents' protocols. Like Michinaga, he invited "one hundred monks" to participate and had a member of the Office for Monastic Affairs preside as the lecturer. By way of contrast, he added an icon to his gifts. This was "a polychrome, life-sized image of Zaō." By positioning it at the center of the southern aisle in the Primary Hall, directly opposite Shirakawa's seat, the ritual staff aligned the retired emperor, his image of Zaō, and Zaō's hidden presence in the curtained chancel. This physical symmetry emphasized the icon's quality as a visible trace of Zaō and Shirakawa, both of whom remained screened from view.

Like the regents, Shirakawa brought one set of manuscripts to bury, and a second, larger set to dedicate. The sutras to be buried, which Shirakawa had copied out himself in golden ink, lay on a desk before the lecturer. In content, they exactly matched those used by Moromichi in

10. The lamps had to be arranged in the *yukiainoma* due to spatial constraints.

1088. The sutras to be dedicated were distributed across the desks for the hundred monks who were to assist the seven primary officiants. These scriptures comprised a set of the fivefold Mahāyāna sutras—the *Great Perfection of Wisdom, Flower Ornament, Mahāparinirvāṇa, Great Collection,* and *Lotus Sūtra*—executed in golden ink, and one hundred copies of the *Lotus Sūtra,* presumably written in black ink.[11] In part, this scriptural corpus replicated elements from the metropolitan component of Shirakawa's ritual regime: when he had inaugurated his signature rite, the Hosshōji Mahāyāna Assembly, in 1078, he had done so with a set of the fivefold Mahāyāna sutras written in golden ink.[12] At the same time, Shirakawa's use of multiple copies of the *Lotus Sūtra* recalled, but departed from, the regents' use of multiple copies of the *Benevolent Kings Sūtra.* Together, these choices ensured that Shirakawa would leave more scriptures at the mountain than the regents, and that his texts would be distinctive. By my count, he dedicated 1,568 scrolls, considerably more than either Michinaga or Moromichi had managed to provide.

The dedicatory offering was a modular rite, made up of discrete components with conventional scripts and managed by Shirakawa's lay retinue. Preparations for the first segment, an offering of light, were overseen by one of Shirakawa's chamberlains, Minamoto no Akikuni (n.d.), with the assistance of youths in the service of the mountain's most eminent monks. Once all the participants and audience members had taken their seats, Kōsan, Kinpusen's respected elder monk, presided over the dedication of the lamps. The next ritual segment focused on the dedication of the Zaō icon and was staffed jointly by monks in

11. The *Gōki* fragment mentions the fivefold Mahāyāna sutras and "other" sutras; the *Fusō ryakki* mentions one hundred copies of the *Lotus Sūtra* and a set of the fivefold Mahāyāna sutras in golden ink (*Fusō ryakki,* Kanji 6.7.13 [*SZKT,* 12:332]). Both sources also refer to a set of holograph sutras that Shirakawa copied in golden ink; these texts were buried (see the ensuing discussion in this chapter). For the scriptures, see *Da bore boluomiduo jing, T.* 220 (5:1–7:1110); *Da fangguang fo huayan jing* (*Flower Ornament Sūtra;* J. *Daihōkō butsu kegongyō*), *T.* 278 (9:395–788); *Da banniepan jing* (*Mahāparirvāṇa Sūtra;* J. *Dai hatsunehangyō*), *T.* 274 (12:365–603); *Da fangdeng daji jing* (*Great Collection Sūtra,* J. *Daihōdō daijikkyō*), *T.* 397 (13:1–407); *Miaofa lianhua jing, T.* 262 (9:1–62).

12. *Fusō ryakki,* Jōryaku 2.10.3 (*SZKT,* 12:320); cf. chapter 3.

Shirakawa's retinue and Kinpusen's residents. The Onjōji monk Ryūmyō (1019–1104), who served as lecturer, had accompanied Shirakawa from the capital, whereas the reader, Jōsen (n.d.), appears to have been a mountain monk. These men recited an invocation (*keibyaku*) to the *kami* and buddhas from their daises on the southern aisle of the Primary Hall, and then proceeded to the connecting aisle, where they sat facing Shirakawa's Zaō icon in order to consecrate it. After chanting two verses, all the officiants circumambulated the chancel in the Primary Hall, strewing flowers as they walked. Here the scale of Shirakawa's rite overwhelmed that of the mountain architecture: the space was so crowded that it took an inordinate amount of time for all the monks to complete their circuits. Though inconvenient, the traffic jam emphasized the ability of the retired emperor to provide a surfeit of offerings.

Following a set of liturgical segments in the connecting aisle, including hymns and recitations of verse and scripture, the officiants dedicated the sutras. The lecturer performed a second invocation (*hyōbyaku*) and then read out a dedicatory prayer, along with letters of gift (*okuribumi*) promising financial support. The dedicatory prayer used in this portion of the rite likely corresponds to the "Prayer for the Retired Emperor's Pilgrimage to Kinpusen" attributed to Masafusa and preserved in the *Gōtotoku nagon ganmonshū*.[13]

In response, the participating monks chanted the titles of the sutras that Shirakawa was dedicating, and then a litany of buddhas' names and epithets. After a teaching on the titles of the sutras, a consecration for the *kami*, and an invitation to the *kami* and buddhas, the lecturer began to expound upon the sutras (*shakkyō*). When he was done, the assembled monks made a sixfold offering (water, flowers, food, light, and two kinds of incense), and distributed merit generated by the rite to all beings. The lecturer descended from his dais, and a set of closing verses was recited.

13. As the "*Gōki* fragment" shows, two prayers, one copied out by Shirakawa and one copied out by Masafusa, were used in the mountaintop rites. Shirakawa's holograph was almost certainly buried alongside his holograph sutras. Given that the prayer preserved in *Gōtotoku nagon ganmonshū* is general in tone, is attributed to Masafusa, and does not list the scriptures Shirakawa interred, it was likely used for the *kuyō*, but not for the sutra burial. See note 1.

With the dedication complete, Shirakawa's retainers again took center stage, dispensing robes, bolts of cloth, and pledges of rice to the primary and auxiliary officiants. Like the regents, Shirakawa engaged in conspicuous giving. He passed out bolts upon bolts of silk, committed to support hundreds of monks during their summer retreat, and promised to fund an endowment for a set of ten monks, plus "other monks." Shun'en (n.d.), a Kinpusen resident, ceremonially read out offertory verses itemizing these pledges so that the gods, buddhas, and audience members would all understand the extent of the retired emperor's largesse. In the prayer preserved in the *Gōtotoku nagon ganmonshū*, Shirakawa took the opportunity to comment publicly on the significance of these gifts: "Thereby we increase the illustrious authority of Zaō and enhance the brilliance of Kinpu, the Peak of Gold."[14] He was also, of course, magnifying his own role as primary benefactor to the mountain community.

Following the *kuyō*, the rites moved into a new phase, in which the mountain monks became the primary agents. Before beginning a set of one hundred prostrations, Shirakawa instructed Masafusa to "inquire into the protocols and conduct the other rites." The primary "other rite" was a *Guiding Principle samādhi* (*rishu zanmai*), in which a ritual master conducted an esoteric altar rite while a chorus of monks chanted the *Guiding Principle Sūtra*. This East Asian recension of the *Perfection of Wisdom Sūtra in 150 Verses* tends to be closely related to esoteric interpretation and practice, especially in the Japanese Shingon traditions.[15] Masafusa declined to describe this portion of the observances, only remarking: "Matters such as the ritual protocol are related to esotericism. I will not record them at all." Given Masafusa's deep interest in ritual matters, his reticence is striking. In his eyes, the offering was an exoteric rite, and the *rishu zanmai* its esoteric supplement.

The *kuyō* and the *rishu zanmai* thus created a classic exoteric-esoteric (*kenmitsu*) pair characterized by a division of labor. Whereas

14. *Gōtotoku nagon ganmonshū* 2.1 (249).

15. As noted in chapter 5, although there are numerous translations of this text, the version most used in Japan is *Dale jingang bukong zhenshi sanmoye jing*, better known by its abbreviated title, *Liqu jing*, *T.* 243 (8:784–86). This text is favored by the Shingon school; on its reception and exegesis, see Astley-Kristensen, *The Rishukyō*.

Masafusa and other members of Shirakawa's retinue, both lay and monastic, had played prominent roles in the *kuyō*, the *rishu zanmai* was carried out exclusively by mountain monks. The integration of a rite with esoteric content and a local staff may have grown out of Shirakawa's experience at Mt. Kōya several years earlier. Neither Michinaga nor Moromichi sponsored a *rishu zanmai* at Kinpusen, but during Shirakawa's 1088 pilgrimage to Mt. Kōya, the retired emperor had sponsored a *rishu zanmai* after "monks and laymen together made offerings of robes."[16] The structural similarity of the Kōya and Kinpusen rites was matched by their personnel: the monk Ryūmyō attended Shirakawa on both occasions and presided over both observances. Far from being isolated occurrences, pilgrimages to the southern mountains were embedded in larger patterns of practice, a point emphasized with the ritual regimes model in chapter 3 of this book. In this case, protocols may have been imported from another pilgrimage destination.

In order to reconfigure the ritual space of the Zaō Hall in preparation for the *rishu zanmai*, Masafusa directed the monks to put away the "god's treasures (*shinbō*)." Kōsan seated himself on a low ritual platform to read a prayer (*jugan*), while other monks prepared an esoteric altar in the Primary Hall's southern aisle, directly in front of the chancel. This was the same spot that had been occupied by Shirakawa's Zaō icon during the earlier offering; now the ritualists set a vajra-wheel on each corner of the altar, arranged a low ritual platform before it, a table holding a drum to the right, and a table bearing wands and water to the left.

While these preparations were under way, Kōsan ministered to the retired emperor, who had finished his prostrations. After presenting Shirakawa with mountain rhododendron blossoms, Kōsan gave him a cup of perfumed water. Much earlier, Kōsan had "put that perfumed water into a bottle, set it in front of a buddha image," presumably an icon of Zaō, "and prayed over it for several months." Shirakawa drank some of this tonic, a gesture that signified not only the sanctification of his person from the inside out but also his linkage to the *rishu zanmai*, during which the officiant would sprinkle consecrating water with a wand. Meanwhile, outside the hall near the gate (*torii*) at the shrine for the Thirty-Eight, a procession of twenty cantors formed. Led by Shun'en,

16. *Fusō ryakki*, Kanji 2.2.20, passage narrating events for 2.27 (*SZKT*, 12:329–30).

whom the mountain monks had elected to serve as ritual master, these men marched into the Primary Hall. Despite all the attention Masafusa devoted to preparations for the *rishu zanmai,* we do not know how the rite proceeded. Not only did Masafusa refrain from describing it due to its "esoteric" nature, but he also did not witness it.

While other "people were still doing prostrations, and were all in attendance in the Worship Hall," Masafusa went outside to bury the retired emperor's sutras. He appears to have done so alone, unaided by any monastic officiant and without his patron's oversight. Masafusa prepared a large hole "in the court, facing the buddha," south of the Worship Hall. "The site," he commented, "was three or four *jō* square. They say it is the traces of En no Gyōja's practice of the Way. People have buried many sutras in this place. At a depth of about two or three [feet], we dug up many old boxes and so on." One of the most notable elements in Masafusa's account of the sutra burial is his reference to En no Gyōja, for it provides very early evidence that En was revered as a founder-figure at the peak. It also, of course, testifies to the pervasiveness of trace-based discourse. Just as clearly, En's were not the only traces to mark the peak. Masafusa's testimony that the ground was already full of texts in 1092 is borne out by modern archaeological excavations, which have yielded significant numbers of Heian-period artifacts from the summit of Kinpusen.[17]

Occasionally referring to Shirakawa in the third person, Masafusa continued:

> The sutras in the royal hand (the *Lotus Sūtra* in eight scrolls, plus the opening and closing sutras in two scrolls, the *Heart Sūtra,* [*Vajra*] *Longevity Sūtra,* and *Amitābha Sūtra*) were on indigo paper. They had vajra-and-flower spindles (embossed), painted frontis pieces, Chinese cords, wrappers with Chinese brocade edges, and a box. (We added a prayer that the emperor had written out on indigo paper in golden ink, and we added a cover sheet). We put it inside a gilt bronze box (square). It was embossed (with seven letters) and had a lock. (As for the lock, although he had provided it, there was a discussion, and we did not use it.) Then we buried it in the hole. (He did not inspect it.

17. Sugaya, Maezono, and Saitō, "Ōminesanji hakkutsu chōsa"; Nara Sangaku Iseki Kenkyūkai, *Ōmine sangaku shinkō iseki*; Ishida and Yajima, *Kinpusen kyōzuka ibutsu.*

> Why?) We buried it in the place the Master of the Empress Consort's Household had indicated. We put a stone on top as a sign.[18]

When the retired emperor finally emerged from the Worship Hall, he performed seven prostrations facing the buried manuscripts and the Zaō Hall. He then departed promptly for the monastic residences "without viewing the famous sites," though according to Masafusa, he had earlier planned to do so. After a meal and another round of gift-giving, the pilgrimage party departed for the capital.

Shirakawa's mountaintop rites formed a carefully constructed, totalizing whole that elaborated on precedent in important ways. The retired emperor integrated esoteric with exoteric modes of worship; he combined metropolitan and local personnel; and he juxtaposed a *kuyō* with state-protecting overtones with the private rite of sutra burial. He also enjoyed freedom in terms of how he participated. Shirakawa apparently did not feel that the process of scriptural interment required his presence or close attention, and he truncated his stay at the peak in order to expedite his homeward journey. Furthermore, Masafusa's record shows that during the lecture, which was the formal centerpiece of the offering rite, Shirakawa drew Kōsan and Masafusa into a complex discussion of how he could best institutionalize his ties to the mountain by rewarding its monks. This indicates that while Shirakawa was determined to fulfill the canons of pious practice, what absorbed his attention during his pilgrimage was the issue of personnel, and beyond that, the complex flows of power that could make, or break, his own position.

Interacting with the Mountain Monks

In approaching his pilgrimage to Kinpusen as an opportunity to elicit allegiance by bestowing appointments in return for service, Shirakawa enacted a strategy that characterized his *insei* more generally. His political influence depended in part upon clientage networks, and ritual

18. The small font indicates interlineal text.

occasions provided high-profile forums for the maintenance and expression of social relationships. Like other rulers before him, Shirakawa was also eager to capitalize on the ability of mountain practitioners to supply protection and blessings.

The administrative history of Kinpusen is difficult to reconstruct due to scarce documentation, but it is possible to sketch out the institutional structures upon which Shirakawa sought to make his mark. A pagoda in the Kinpusen-Yoshino area burned in 970, indicating that a fair degree of development must have occurred in the area by that time. In 1007, Michinaga referred to the site Iwakura as a "temple" (*tera*) near the Treasure Pagoda in Yoshinoyama, and in 1080, the courtier Minamoto no Toshifusa (1035–1121) wrote of a cloister called the Yakushiin.[19] Thus, by the late eleventh century, the Kinpusen-Yoshino area appears to have been home to a stable religious community. The key figure in the local organization was the steward (*bettō*), analogous to the variously titled abbots at other temples, such as the *chōja* at Tōji or *chōri* at Onjōji. Scattered historical references indicate that although elite pilgrims might develop close relationships with Kinpusen's stewards, these men were not members of the high monastic elite. In general, they did not hold appointments to the Office for Monastic Affairs, and they appear only rarely in the documentary record.[20] Below the *bettō*, a standard administrative hierarchy was in place: Masafusa referred to "the three officers (*sangō*) and five masters (*goshi*) below the steward." In addition, Kinpusen occasionally had an overseer, or *kengyō*. Although outsiders were apt to confuse the *bettō* and the *kengyō*, it appears that the *bettō* was traditionally a member of the mountain community, whereas the title of *kengyō* was granted to monks from other temples whom the court appointed to oversee Kinpusen's affairs. Masafusa's record indicates that in 1092 a monk named Eshin (alt. Kaishin, 1007–94) was in office as steward, a certain Kan'on (n.d.) was one of the

19. *Nihon kiryaku,* Tenroku 1.9.8 (*SZKT,* 11:117); *Midō kanpakuki,* Kankō 4.8.12 (1:229, 330); *Suisaki,* Jōryaku 4.5.4 (*ZST,* 8:97).

20. See Royall Tyler, "Kōfukuji and the Mountains," 178–86; and Miyake Hitoshi, *Shugendō soshiki no kenkyū,* 117, for lists of men said to have been appointed stewards and overseers. Note, however, that these lists largely rely on later sources and should be approached with a degree of caution.

three officers, and Kyōshō was another. Kōsan spoke with moral authority as an esoteric master and elder, but he held no formal office. There appears to have been no overseer.

Despite its surface unity, Kinpusen's community was split into factions. *Sōgō bunin* (Appointments to the Office for Monastic Affairs) reports that both Eshin and Kyōshō had been trained at Kōfukuji. These monks may have resided at Kinpusen sometimes, but they were active elsewhere, as well.[21] Kōsan led the opposing camp of permanent residents (*jūjōsō*), acting as their spokesman both during Shirakawa's visit and later altercations with Kōfukuji. As we shall see, Kōsan's faction wished to wrest administrative control of Kinpusen from the hands of Kōfukuji monks.

Although Shirakawa had previously promoted the Kōfukuji-trained Eshin to honorary rank, during his 1092 pilgrimage he took a particular interest in Kōsan and expressed his willingness to support Kinpusen's independence. During the lecture portion of the dedicatory *kuyō*, Shirakawa drew Kōsan and Masafusa into a conversation that revolved around three points: the promotion of Kōsan and Kyōshō to honorific monastic ranks; the appointment of three esoteric masters at the mountain; and control of appointments to the office of Kinpusen's stewardship. This discussion illuminates the complex relationship between Shirakawa, the mountain monks, and Kōfukuji. It also shows that Shirakawa used the time and space of his offering rite to pursue, and to ritualize, his own political agendas. Here I translate Masafusa's record of the discussion with extensive commentary.

Having noted that the lecturer had just begun his doctrinal exposition, Masafusa wrote, "Meanwhile, the retired emperor summoned me and said, 'You must inquire into the matter of Kōsan.'" At issue was Shirakawa's plan to promote Kōsan to one of three court-conferred honorific monastic ranks; in ascending order, these were Dharma Bridge (*hokkyō*), Dharma Eye (*hōgen*), and Dharma Seal (*hōin*). There was a long history for such promotions. Michinaga had granted the Kinpusen

21. *Sōgō bunin,* entries for Enkyū 3 and Jōryaku 4 (*DNBZ,* 123:196, 203). These entries report that Eshin was active at Enshūji, which, having been founded by Emperor Go-Sanjō (1034–73), maintained close ties to the royals. On Enshūji, see Hiraoka, *Nihon jiinshi no kenkyū,* 557–81.

steward Konshō the rank of Dharma Bridge in 1017 in recognition of "the efficacy of his prayers over the years," and when Shirakawa went to Kumano in 1090, he rewarded the Kumano steward Chōkai (1037–1122) with the same rank.[22] The retired emperor had arrived at Kinpusen with the intention of doing the same for Kōsan. "Item," he declared: "we shall appoint him to the rank of Dharma Bridge." There was, however, a problem: "On the other hand, one opinion is that we should promote him to Dharma Eye, as he has not wanted to become Dharma Bridge." Kōsan, in other words, had been hoping for a direct promotion to a higher rank. Historically, that type of fast-track promotion had been reserved for aristocratic monks. "This is a thorny matter," Shirakawa continued. "Men who have gone forth" from lay life "may not use their original family names. Nonetheless, in terms of precedent, men who have been appointed straight to Dharma Eye have been the sons of princes or ministers." Kōsan's lack of exalted lineage made it virtually impossible to expedite his rise: "There are no other precedents for such appointments at all." This put the retired emperor in a difficult position. "I may wish to appoint him Dharma Bridge," he said, "but that is not what he hopes for. I may wish to refrain from meddling, but that would cause trouble with this mountain. How would that be?" Shirakawa's comments show that despite an ongoing trend toward the use of monastic rank and office as rewards conferred by powerful patrons, there were still rules to be observed.

Shirakawa expressed the second point on his agenda as follows: "Item: we shall install three esoteric masters (*ajari*). However, one opinion is that there is a problem regarding who might be able to send the letter" of nomination. There was already a tradition of esoteric masters being active at Kinpusen, and both Moromichi and Shirakawa had referred to Kōsan as an *ajari*.[23] In installing a new set of esoteric masters, Shirakawa meant to do something more conspicuous: he wanted to establish a group of men who would embody his favor and become conduits for his influence at the mountain. Over the course of the eleventh

22. *Midō kanpakuki,* Kannin 1.10.20 (3:122); *Chūyūki,* Kanji 4.2.26 (1:52).

23. Earlier in the Heian period, the court is reputed to have appointed and supported *ajari* at the "seven high mountains," which included Kinpusen (see chapter 1, note 37).

century, the duties associated with the position of esoteric master had come to center on prayers for state-protection and the well-being of the emperor.[24] For Shirakawa, then, these were politically significant positions that could bring him direct personal benefit, as well as local influence.

Although royals had been sponsoring esoteric masters for decades, in Kinpusen's case the nomination process raised political difficulties due to the mountain's vexed relationship with Kōfukuji. Protocol demanded that an influential Tendai or Shingon temple submit a letter to the Council of State to nominate candidates for the position of *ajari*, whereupon the Council would hand down an official appointment. As Shirakawa put it, "Kōfukuji belongs to an exoteric school (*kenshū*). While Kōsan is alive, he could send the letter, but who knows what might happen later on?" Shirakawa implicitly recognized that Kōfukuji had been exerting control over Kinpusen's affairs, but for him this was much less a problem than the temple's stereotyped reputation as an exoteric institution. Even though its monks could and did engage in esoteric studies, Kōfukuji was clearly not seen as a viable sponsor for *ajari*. To cope with the need for inarguably esoteric sponsorship, a member of Shirakawa's monastic retinue had suggested an alternative during an earlier discussion. According to Shirakawa, "Ryūmyō said, 'This mountain was opened to practice by the Most Reverend (*sōjō*) Shōbō. Perhaps a Ninnaji man could send the letter.' " Early biographies of Shōbō, a famous ninth-century Shingon patriarch, assert that he spent time in the Yoshino-Kinpusen area (later he came to be revered as a founder of Shugendō).[25] Accordingly, Ryūmyō was suggesting that monks from the Shingon temple Ninnaji, which had been founded by one of Shōbō's Dharma heirs, might justifiably claim a connection with Kinpusen. Although Ryūmyō's comments show that Shōbō was already accepted as one of Kinpusen's early proponents, the mountain monks were not

24. Okano, *Heian jidai no kokka*, 303–24.

25. For biographies, see *Shōbō sōjō den* (*ZGR*, 8.2:720), for which a date of 937 is generally accepted; cf. the version of *Daigoji engi* collected in *Dai Nihon bukkyō zensho* (*DNBZ*, 117:249). For Shōbō's received status as a founder in Shugendō, see Sekiguchi, *Shugendō kyōdan seiritsushi*, 25–62.

eager to invite another influential temple into their affairs. Shirakawa again wondered, "How would that be?" and then turned his attention to long-standing hostilities between Kōfukuji and Kinpusen.

The mountain monks had asked Shirakawa to help them free the stewardship from the influence of Kōfukuji. "Item," the retired emperor noted, "an appeal has been made that the senior resident monk should be appointed steward." The problem was that, "Through claims that the steward should be appointed on the basis of Kōfukuji's nomination (*kyo*)," the right of appointment "has been seized by that temple and its clansmen," the Fujiwara. In other words, Kōfukuji had been asserting—or, from Kinpusen's point of view, usurping—the right to appoint stewards. "Therefore, it would also be difficult to hand down a royal decree. How would that be?" For Shirakawa, the most obvious option was to issue a decree appointing a steward, but that would inevitably meet with opposition from Kōfukuji, and perhaps the regents as well.

The historical record offers no evidence that the regents issued directives appointing Kinpusen stewards during the eleventh century; nonetheless, their rights and responsibilities at Kōfukuji were such that they may well have taken a hand in previous nominations. Michinaga and Moromichi had brought Kōfukuji hierarchs, including that temple's stewards, along on their own pilgrimages to Kinpusen.[26] Thus, by taking steps to return Kinpusen's stewardship to the control of the mountain's resident monks, Shirakawa would be ranging himself against Eshin, Kōfukuji, and by extension, the regents.

Shirakawa had now laid out his major points: he wished to promote Kōsan, he intended to establish three esoteric masters at the mountain, and he was concerned about how best to do so. He was also intrigued by the possibility of supporting Kinpusen's bid for self-governance, which might provide an opportunity to block Kōfukuji-Fujiwara influence at the mountain. Kōsan now had a chance to talk back.

26. At the time of their attendance upon Michinaga, Jōchō and Fukō were incumbent and future Kōfukuji stewards; Saijin, who accompanied Moromichi, was supernumerary steward (*Midō kanpakuki,* Kankō 4.8.11, *uragaki* [1:229, 329]; *Go-Nijō Moromichiki,* Kanji 4.8.10, *uragaki* [2:6]).

According to Masafusa, who was acting as interlocutor, "Kōsan said, 'It was not my hope to be Dharma Bridge, but I said that because I was upset about not being promoted to Dharma Eye. It is difficult to avoid a discussion of doubts about what I said, but I will simply obey the royal decision.' " Whether Kōsan was being honest or simply capitulating, he strove to focus the discussion upon what he saw as a much more important issue. He continued, "As for the esoteric masters, if you dedicate them to Zaō, then it would not do for a man from another temple to send the letter" of nomination. For Kōsan, the prospect of outside administrative influence was unacceptable; he wanted Kinpusen to be run by and for Kinpusen's residents. Apparently, someone else had suggested that Tōji, another powerful Shingon temple, might submit the nomination, but Kōsan rejected that notion out of hand. "Why should we obey Tōji in this matter?" he asked. Royal patronage or no, if the esoteric masters were going to compromise Kinpusen's autonomy, then Kōsan would rather not have them: "If this," namely, the nomination process, "is a problem," he said, "you need not dedicate them at all."

Kōsan proceeded to expand upon Kinpusen's right to independence. "The issue of making a permanent resident the steward is of great concern to this mountain," he said. "Basically, the stewardship at this temple dates back to the pilgrimage of the Kanpyō Emperor," Uda, who is said to have made pilgrimages to Kinpusen in the early 900s after he had abdicated.[27] "At that time," Kōsan explained, the court "appointed only resident monks." Kōfukuji (here referred to by its older name, Yamashinadera) had overturned this custom by capitalizing on hierarchical lineage relationships: "After several reigns had passed, the Yamashina steward Shinki and monks from our mountain had a teacher-student relationship. Therefore, [Kōfukuji] has nominated and appointed members of his line willy-nilly." It is next to impossible either to verify or refute Kōsan's claims, but the Dharma-heirs of Shinki (927–1000), who rose to the top of the Office of Monastic Affairs and served as steward at Kōfukuji, did have connections to Kinpusen. Jōchō and Fukō, who, as mentioned above, attended Michinaga on his 1007 pilgrimage to Kinpusen, were Shinki's students and

27. *Nihon kiryaku,* Shōtai 3, tenth month, and Engi 5, ninth month (*SZKT,* 11:6, 10).

Kōfukuji stewards.[28] Eshin, the incumbent Kinpusen steward at the time of Shirakawa's 1092 pilgrimage, had trained at Kōfukuji, apparently under Rinkai (951–1025), another Kōfukuji steward and one of Shinki's disciples.[29]

According to Kōsan, opposition to the influence of Kōfukuji had led to serious disruptions. "When we have had disputes with that temple," he said, "the regents have made repeated declarations." Although historical evidence of earlier conflict with Kōfukuji is scant, Kōsan's statements are corroborated by a journal entry written by Fujiwara no Tamefusa (1049–1115), a close associate of the regent Morozane. Tamefusa reported that in 1085 members of the Kōfukuji *sangha* mustered soldiers from the temple's estates in preparation for a march on Kinpusen. The attack, however, was averted by the repeated dispatch of directives from the head of the Fujiwara family.[30] With this type of dispute in mind, Kōsan voiced his adamant opposition to Kōfukuji's drive to make Kinpusen into a branch temple: "Nevertheless, we have long insisted that we will not obey the decisions of Yamashinadera." Kinpusen's monks were quite willing to use force of arms to maintain their independence. "In particular," Kōsan said, "disputes about the steward have turned into riots. While the mountain monks are enjoying the arts of war and preparing their weapons, it seems as though Zaō's Buddhist teachings will be extinguished." Though Kōsan lamented the prospect of violence, he distanced himself from the sentiment that conflict destroys the Dharma by stating that he was speaking as a representative, not as an individual: "This is just what is said at our mountain, not what I say for myself." Thus, Kōsan ended by hinting that force of arms might, in fact, have a role to play in protecting Kinpusen.

28. *Kōfukuji bettō shidai* (*DNBZ,* 124:8–9). The same text states that En'en (990–1060), one of Fukō's disciples, served as Kinpusen overseer circa 1049 (*DNBZ,* 124:10–11); however, this appointment is not otherwise substantiated.

29. On Eshin's tie to Rinkai, see *Yuima kōji kengaku ryūgi shidai,* entry for Enkyū 2 (scroll 2). On Rinkai's tie to Shinki, see the Kankō 3 entry in the Shōkōkan manuscript of *Sōgō bunin,* cited in Hirabayashi and Koike, *Gojūonbiki sōgō bunin,* 334; see also *Kōfukuji bettō shidai* (*DNBZ,* 124:8–9).

30. *Tamefusa kyōki,* Ōtoku 2.8.26, Kyōto Daigaku Sōgō Hakubutsukan ms. This entry is more readily available as an extract in *Shiryō sōran,* the full text of which is available through *Dai Nihon shiryō deitabeisu.*

Shirakawa responded point by point to Kōsan's comments. "In turn," Masafusa wrote, "the royal reply was, 'Regarding your promotion to Dharma Bridge, I am very pleased that you have said that you will obey my decision.' " Shirakawa pointedly remarked that the promotion was less an expression of gratitude to Kōsan than of devotion to the mountain as a whole. "In this," he said, "I am entirely devoted to your mountain as a temple. If I were to slog through deep mud to come to this mountain, but not reward the one venerable monk who strives in his practice, it would cause me deep regret." In fact, when Shirakawa returned to the capital, he promptly arranged for Kōsan to be appointed Dharma Bridge.[31]

Shirakawa was also determined to have his esoteric masters, no matter how vexed the nomination process might be. "Regarding the *ajari*," he continued, "we will have your temple submit the letter nominating them. Afterward, we will have the Council of State send it to Tōji. How would that be?" Determined to press forward regardless of inter-institutional rivalries, Shirakawa brushed aside Kōsan's resistance to involving another temple; he also made it clear that he intended to tap the authority of the Council of State and a powerful Shingon temple to expedite the process.

Shirakawa then outlined a plan to return the mountain's governance to the hands of the resident monks, but without making any promises of success: "Regarding the stewardship, one opinion is this. Eshin, the present steward, has said that if we promote Kyōshō," his disciple, "to Dharma Bridge as a reward for his service today, then he would certainly step down from the office of steward." Eshin's resignation would make it possible to appoint a resident monk steward, just as the Kinpusen monks wanted. Even so, "If that is what happens, then we will surely have to tell the Kōfukuji office to nominate Kōsan. If that temple does not comply, then it would not be within our power" to insist on the appointment. In other words, Shirakawa was perfectly aware

31. In his journal, Fujiwara no Munetada wrote, "Later I heard of the rewards: Kōsan was promoted to Dharma Bridge (he is the seniormost long-term resident at Kinpusen). Kyōshō too was promoted in the same way (the steward and Dharma Eye Eshin forwent a reward in his favor). Three *ajari* have also been awarded" to the mountain (*Chūyūki,* Kanji 6.7.17 [1:143]).

that he could not appoint a steward on his own, nor could he force Kōfukuji to carry out his wishes. For that matter, he could not compel Eshin, either: "If Eshin does not resign, then we would have to remonstrate with him to make him cede to Kōsan. And yet, if he were determined not to resign, once again, it would not be within our power" to compel him. Shirakawa was also willing to bring the regents into the discussion, for he commented, "We should also remonstrate with the head" of the Fujiwara family in order to convince him "that Kinpusen must not become Yamashinadera's branch temple. And yet, if there is a standoff, it is not within our power" to resolve it.[32]

This was power-bloc politics, where negotiation was the only real option. If Shirakawa were to press the issue of Kōsan's appointment or Kinpusen's independence, he risked provoking Kōfukuji, whose men might run riot. If that happened, then the only sure outcome would be that the situation would deteriorate. Kinpusen's position was constrained, too: its monks wished Shirakawa to back their claims to independence because they needed an ally, but his support would almost certainly come at the cost of his involvement in their affairs. With the future of the stewardship still unresolved, the conversation ended, and the participants' attention returned to the ritual action continuing around them.

In reporting on Shirakawa's discussion with Kōsan, which was embedded within the space and time of the grand offering rite, Masafusa testified to the accommodating qualities of ritual. The predictable, rule-bound *kuyō* created a place for a wide range of activities. For instance, Masafusa commented that some members of Shirakawa's retinue went out during the rite to see the "famous sights." Although this might potentially be read as an expression of lack of interest or even dissent, the ritual sponsor himself was spending the same time reflecting on how best to manipulate social and institutional relationships. Meanwhile, the lecturer was expounding the Dharma. For Shirakawa, this was both expedient and appropriate. The rite was effective by vir-

32. Shirakawa indicated his intention to remonstrate with "the *chōja*." In an earlier essay (Blair, "Mountain and Plain"), I interpreted this term as a reference to the abbot of Tōji. After having discussed this passage with several Japanese researchers, I am now of the opinion that it more likely points to the head of the Fujiwara family.

tue of its proper performance, and the lecture, perhaps its quietest and lengthiest component, gave him the opportunity to further his agenda as sponsor. The collocation and simultaneity of Shirakawa's two projects, to worship Zaō and to influence his men, show just how close the bonds were between rights and rites. The use of ritual to create and strengthen social bonds in fact pervaded the pilgrimage process as a whole. To better understand the social ramifications of Shirakawa's pilgrimage to Kinpusen, we need to examine his retinue, for its members embodied key facets of the social structure of the *insei.*

Shirakawa's Retinue

Shirakawa's preoccupations with appointments, emoluments, and promotions were integral not only to his pilgrimage but also to his *insei.* Immediately after Shirakawa's death, Fujiwara no Munetada wrote: "He gave rein to his own predilections and was unconstrained by law when he made appointments and promotions. Present or past, there never was the like." Shirakawa was indeed swayed by his passions. Later in his life, for instance, he adopted Fujiwara no Shōshi, who had been the foster daughter of one of his consorts. When Shōshi reached pubescence, Shirakawa scandalized onlookers by making her his sexual partner; Heian-period norms cast this as a case of incest. As Munetada indicated, Shirakawa's partiality also manifested itself directly in the realm of public affairs: "He was biased when he made rewards and punishments, and he was extreme in love and hate." This made for an obvious gap between "the impoverished and the wealthy." As a result, "the hearts of the people, lofty and lowly, have been uneasy."[33] That Shirakawa was quixotic and willful did not mean that the personal relationships characterizing his rule, his life, and his religiosity did not follow patterns, however. For his 1092 pilgrimage, the retired emperor mobilized the same networks of people—royals, high aristocrats, dependent clients, and

33. For Munetada's comments, see *Chūyūki,* Daiji 4.7.7 (*ZST,* 14:65–66). On Shōshi, see Tsunoda, *Taikenmon'in Shōshi no shōgai.*

eminent monks—as he did for more obviously political purposes in the capital.

In his bid to reconfigure Kinpusen's real-and-imagined space, Shirakawa had his daughter Princess Teishi (alt. Yasuko, a.k.a. Ikuhōmon'in, 1076–96), act as his ritual proxy in the capital while he brought his *insei* into the mountains in the form of his retinue. At the time, Teishi held the title of Dowager Empress in recognition of her honorary status as foster mother to her brother, reigning Emperor Horikawa. This influential young woman was already habituated into the patterns of pilgrimage, for she routinely accompanied her father on visits to religious sites near the capital.[34] Even though she herself did not, and according to the gender rules discussed in chapter 1, could not, go to Kinpusen, Teishi participated in *sōjin* abstentions with Shirakawa as he prepared for his trip in the fourth month of 1092.[35] Whether she planned to go all the way to Kinpusen, to travel as far as Yoshino, or to stay in the capital is unclear, but in the fifth month, her *sōjin* was called off. She had fallen ill and diviners diagnosed the problem as an "impurity" (*fujō*).[36] Teishi, however, treated this as a setback, not a disqualification. Once Shirakawa and his attendants had departed for the south in the seventh month, she mirrored her father's practice in the capital. The pilgrimage party was scheduled to arrive at Kinpusen between the eleventh and thirteenth day of the month; at that time, Teishi moved to the palace, where members of the court engaged in *sōjin* abstentions with her. Then, as Shirakawa turned toward home on the fourteenth, Teishi returned to her own residence.[37] By observing purity rules and moving about the capital, she mimetically enacted her father's pilgrimage, ensuring that the court would remain mindful of his activities.

Meanwhile, Shirakawa took a carefully selected entourage to Kinpusen. In his journal, Fujiwara no Munetada listed twenty of these men, each of whom was in some sense a client of Shirakawa. The largest

34. For example, Teishi had already made pilgrimages with her father to Nishidera in Hikone, as well as Kiyomizudera and Iwashimizu Hachimangū (*Chūyūki,* Kanji 3.12.22, Kanji 4.10.9 and 11.29 [1:46, 59, 62–63]).

35. *Chūyūki,* Kanji 6.4.28–30 (1:130–32).

36. *Chūyūki,* Kanji 6.5.23 (1:133).

37. *Chūyūki,* Kanji 6.7.13–17 (1:142–43).

subgroup was made up of six of the retired emperor's close retainers (*in no kinshin*), Fujiwara no Kinhira (n.d.), Fujiwara no Korenobu (n.d.), Fujiwara no Motoyori (1040–1122), Fujiwara no Akitaka (1072–1129), Minamoto no Akikuni, and Takashina no Tamekata (n.d). These were men with courtly connections but comparatively low social status, whom Shirakawa had favored with appointments to the Retired Emperor's Household Agency (*in no chō*) or Chamberlains' Office (*kurōdo dokoro*).[38] Over the course of their careers, *in no kinshin* could and did rise to influential positions, but in many cases they remained dependent upon (and loyal to) their patron. Fujiwara no Akitaka, who was instrumental in distributing gifts to the mountaintop monks, is an excellent example of this type. Akitaka's family had a tradition of service to the royal family, and he himself served the royals as a chamberlain for two decades, from 1087 to 1116.[39] As a result of his close ties to ruling and retired emperors, Akitaka's influence eventually grew so great that Munetada remarked that government matters hung upon a word from him, and the *Imakagami* (Mirror of the present) dubbed him the "after-hours viceroy" (*yoru no kanpaku*).[40] Toward the end of his life, Akitaka did finally enter the upper aristocracy, but when he went to Kinpusen in 1092, he was just twenty-one years old and only beginning to develop the intimacy with Shirakawa that would later become the basis for his own power. In sum, Akitaka came to Kinpusen as a callow administrator who was very much Shirakawa's man.

Shirakawa also drew his attendants from the opposite end of the aristocracy, men of high standing who found it useful to cooperate with him for the sake of mutual social and political benefit. Three members of Shirakawa's Kinpusen entourage, Minamoto no Morotada (1054–1114), Minamoto no Masazane, and Ōe no Masafusa, were men of this type. Senior nobles who had once served in Shirakawa's Chamberlains' Office, they had all risen due their own merits and family connections,

38. See, for instance, Maki, *In no kinshin*; Hashimoto Yoshihiko, *Heian kizoku shakai*, 3–33; and Kōno, *Heian makki seijishi kenkyū*, 269–82.

39. Maki, *In no kinshin*, 33–58; Wada Hisamatsu, *Kokushi kokubun no kenkyū*, 181–204, esp. 190–91.

40. *Chūyūki*, Daiji 4.1.15 (*ZST*, 14:14); *Imakagami*, "Suberagi no chū" (*SZKT*, 21.2:37). On Akitaka's career, see also *Kugyō bunin*, entry for Hōan 1 (*SZKT*, 54:386).

and had been appointed to posts on the Council of State.[41] That they were not members of the Fujiwara family also speaks to Shirakawa's interest in cultivating men who were not bound to the regents. Masazane epitomizes the qualities of Shirakawa's high-ranking allies. A member of the Murakami Genji lineage, he was the blood brother of Shirakawa's deceased empress consort, Kenshi; he was also the son of the current Minister of the Left, Minamoto no Akifusa (1037–94), and the nephew of the current Minister of the Right, Minamoto no Toshifusa. Later, when Shirakawa's *insei* gained strength and the regents' influence faltered, Masazane rose to become Palace Minister, Minister of the Right, and ultimately Minister of State. As a scion of a noble lineage, he could have expected an adequate career no matter what, but his own and his family's ties to the retired emperor ensured his spectacular success.[42]

Together with these laymen, Shirakawa also brought three eminent clerics with him to Kinpusen. All were distinguished members of the Office for Monastic Affairs: the Most Reverend Ninkaku (1045–1102), the Supernumerary Most Reverend Ryūmyō, and the Supernumerary Major Right Reverend Kan'i (1054–1101). Among them, Kan'i may have had the closest relationship with Shirakawa; his career also shows how dynamics of service in the monastic realm mirrored those in the lay world. Kan'i boasted a royal pedigree by blood and ordination: he was the son of Prince Atsusada (1014–61) and the disciple of Shōshin (1005–85), who had been Prince Moroakira in lay life. In 1081, Kan'i entered Shirakawa's service as a protector monk, and in the following years, Shirakawa appointed him steward of Enshūji, a temple that had been founded by Shirakawa's father. Following his appointment to the Office of Monastic Affairs, Kan'i accompanied Shirakawa to Mt. Kōya in 1088, and then attended the

41. Morotada and Masazane, both of whom were born to rank and consequence, were Major Counselors. Masafusa, who had risen from the literati stratum of the lower aristocracy, was Consultant and Major Controller of the Left. For these men's earlier positions as chamberlains, see *Shikiji bunin,* entry for Shirakawa-in (*GR,* 3:129–30); for their posts in 1092, see *Kugyō bunin,* entry for Kanji 6 (*SZKT,* 54:354–55).

42. For the Murakami Genji, see Sakamoto Shōzō, "Murakami Genji no seikaku."

retired emperor during his purificatory abstentions for his first pilgrimage to Kumano in 1090.[43]

Shirakawa had nurtured Kan'i's career, and in return, Kan'i advanced Shirakawa's agendas in the temples. A month before the journey to Kinpusen, Kan'i gave a Dharma transmission to Shirakawa's eighteen-year-old son Kakunen (later Kakugyō, 1075–1105) at Ninnaji.[44] Several days before the initiation, Shirakawa bypassed traditional monastic channels by appointing Kakunen directly to the rank of esoteric ritual master (*isshin ajari*). Later, the retired emperor designated Kakunen a Dharma prince (*hosshinnō, hōshinnō*), setting an influential precedent for monastic preferment based on bloodlines. Thus, by blood and collaboration, Kan'i contributed to the aristocratization of Buddhist institutions, which became a hallmark of the *insei* period.[45]

The last subgroup within Shirakawa's retinue comprised servants of much lower rank, including three attendants and two warriors whom Munetada did not even deign to mention by name; a personal body servant named Hata no Takemoto (n.d.); the Head of the Bureau of Medicines, Tanba no Tadayasu (1053–1106); and the Head of the Granary Bureau, Kamo no Mitsuhira (1071–1125). Like *in no kinshin,* these men depended on Shirakawa for their livelihoods, but they could never expect to rise to positions of eminence or power. Lastly, Shirakawa took a doctor and a yin-yang master with him in case he might require their services.[46]

At every level, then, Shirakawa's companions were men whom he had promoted or employed, or with whom he cooperated. Because they

43. For the Kumano pilgrimage, see *Chūyūki,* Kanji 4.1.16, 2.22, 2.26 (1:49–52); for Mt. Kōya, see *Fusō ryakki,* Kanji 2.2.22–3.1 (*SZKT,* 12:328–30). For biographical information on Kan'i, see the numerous sources compiled in the entry for his death in *Dai Nihon shiryō,* Kōwa 3.6.16 (3.5:984–92).

44. *Chūyūki,* Kanji 6.3.19–20 (1:118–119).

45. On the emergence of Dharma princes under Shirakawa, see for instance Yokoyama, "Shirakawa inseiki ni okeru hosshinnō." For now-classic treatments of the aristocraticization of Buddhism, see articles by Abe Yasurō and Okano Kōji in Hayami, *Inseiki no bukkyō.*

46. "*Gōki* fragment."

were socially indebted to him, they could be depended upon to support him. Nevertheless, Shirakawa's network of clients had not yet fully matured: Akitaka was still very young; the Murakami Genji had not yet reached their apogee, and Kan'i's disciple had not yet become Dharma prince. Similarly, neither Shirakawa's ritual regime nor his *insei* had reached full strength.

Although Kinpusen never became one of Shirakawa's signatures, the retired emperor's 1092 pilgrimage gives some indication of how activities associated with ritual regimes contributed to the growth of a power bloc. In the social field, pilgrimage provided Shirakawa an opportunity to forge relationships with new constituencies (in this case, Kinpusen's monks). The long period of *sōjin,* followed by the journey itself, was a means for strengthening bonds with his dependents and higher-ranking associates. Some of these men had ties to other power blocs: Ryūmyō, for instance, was affiliated with the influential Tendai temple Onjōji, and Masafusa had a long and close relationship with the regents. Pilgrimage bound them more closely to Shirakawa. Ritual regimes (and by extension, pilgrimage) also positioned members of the elite vis-à-vis other power blocs. By visiting Kinpusen, Shirakawa ranged himself over and against the regents, and also against Kōfukuji's partisans, who wished to bring Kinpusen under their own control.

Conclusion: From Pilgrimage to Patronage

It bears reiterating that for Shirakawa, piety and political exigency went hand in hand. There is no reason to suppose that the retired emperor was being disingenuous when he invoked Kinpusen's affective landscape to emphasize his own sincerity and devotion in the prayer he commissioned for his 1092 pilgrimage. In this text, with his "heart quickening at the breeze from the treasure chamber," where relics are installed at the base of a pagoda, Shirakawa declared that he was inspired by the Buddhist teachings. He maintained that throughout his journey, even on the mountain trails, he was at home in his own domain: "Is there anywhere that is not our home village? We walk, turning toward the unfathomable road. Treading the clouds from the caves and scaling the breezes from the peaks, we come to feel as free as the wind or the clouds in the deep sky. Appropriating the autumn moon, we draw the valley water. The response of water and moon occurs of itself."[47] Casting himself as a natural pilgrim, Shirakawa made allusions to Daoist-style roaming ("scaling the breezes") and Buddhist awakening ("the response of water and moon occurs of itself").

As the most eminent pilgrim to visit Kinpusen since Uda's storied visit(s) in the early 900s, Shirakawa also exerted visible effects upon the mountain's real space. He made the largest on-record series of honorary appointments to the mountain monks, and his cloister is the first in the area known to have been endowed by a royal or aristocrat. Although there is very little direct evidence for the institutional organization of Kinpusen during the remainder of the *insei* period, during the Kamakura and Muromachi periods, local monks saw the retired emperors, and Shirakawa in particular, as having initiated a period of intensive development that continued through the twelfth century. The *Kinpusen sōsōki*, a copy of which has been preserved in Yoshinoyama, was probably compiled circa 1300 as a local history by and for the Yoshino-Kinpusen community. In its detailed lists of annual rites and local institutions, this text dates the founding of most of the area's temples, shrines, and rites to the *insei* period.[48] In addition to crediting Shirakawa with the foundation of the Treasure Pagoda, which it associates with a temple called Sekizōji (Iwakuradera), the "fundamental hall of this mountain," the *Kinpusen sōsōki* maintains that in 1102 Shirakawa inaugurated annual lectures on the *Lotus* and the *Benevolent Kings Sūtra*, together with a long sequence (*chōjitsu*) of summertime offerings to Zaō at the peak.[49] It also claims that Retired Emperors Toba and Go-Shirakawa continued this trend by underwriting their own vow temples, establishing positions for esoteric masters, and

47. See note 1.

48. The oldest manuscript of the *Kinpusen sōsōki* probably dates to the Muromachi period and is held by Kinpusenji (see Shudō, *Kinpusenji shi*, 121–22; and Satō Torao, "Kinpusen no kenkyū"). Note that this text has widely been used to reconstruct the mountain's Heian history, an approach that overlooks its rhetorical and ideological dimensions.

49. *Kinpusen sōsōki* (*KSS*, 48; *SS*, 3:365). Note that the "*Gōki* fragment" mentions gifts to be made "for the three *Benevolent Kings* Lectures," while *Gōtotoku nagon ganmonshū* 2.1 refers to financial support for summer practice at the peak (249).

endowing a number of annual rites, such as readings of the *Great Perfection of Wisdom Sūtra*.[50] These assertions were surely filtered through later institutional wants and needs, but on balance, they seem plausible enough. Details in Masafusa's record, for instance, indicate that in 1092 Shirakawa did state his intent to provide support for monks on summer retreat and to subsidize lectures on the *Benevolent Kings Sūtra*.

Although the retired emperors were credited with underwriting a steep increase in monastic activity at the mountain, the historical record demonstrates that they led an equally sharp decrease in elite pilgrimage to Kinpusen. There is no reliable evidence that Shirakawa returned to the mountain after 1092 or that Retired Emperor Toba or Go-Shirakawa ever visited it at all.[51] Furthermore, with Moromichi's death in 1099, the regents' personal involvement with Kinpusen attenuated. Although Minamoto no Masazane returned to Kinpusen in 1106, when his cousin Shōkaku (1057–1129) performed an esoteric Dharma transmission there, evidence for aristocrats' physical presence at the mountain after that time is scant to nonexistent.[52] By contrast, Shirakawa and subsequent retired emperors undertook repeated journeys to Kumano from the 1110s onward. They also explored new sacred sites, both near and far. Go-Shirakawa, for instance, traveled to Itsukushima, and Go-Toba to Kasagi.[53] Thus, with the decline in the regents' influence and increased competition from other pilgrimage sites, Kinpusen lost its position as the destination of choice among the elite. Conflict with Kōfukuji also brought profound changes to the mountain.

50. *Kinpusen sōsōki* (*KSS*, 46–49; *SS*, 3:363–65).

51. The widely cited *Kumano gongen kongō Zaō hōden zōkō nikki*, which was probably composed in the late twelfth or early thirteenth century, claims that Shirakawa made three pilgrimages to Kinpusen; however, as Kawasaki Tsuyoshi has shown, the text includes so much fabrication that it cannot be considered a reliable report of historical events (Kawasaki, "*Kumano gongen kongō Zaō hōden zōkō nikki* to iu gisho").

52. Sources for Masazane's pilgrimage include *Gōtotoku nagon ganmonshū* 3.5, inferred date of Kashō 1.7.18 (425–30); a dedication for a bell, attributed to Ōe no Masafusa and dated to the seventh month of Chōji 3 (=Kashō 1), in *Honchō zoku monzui* 7 (*SZKT*, 29:116–17); and *Chūyūki*, Kashō 1.7.11 (6:193). On Shōkaku's participation in the Dharma transmission, see *Kinpusen kanjō nikki* (*KSS*, 51–54).

53. Blair, "Rites and Rule," 34; "Jōgen yonnen guchūreki," *uragaki*, 9.18, cited in *Dai Nihon shiryō*, 4.10:836.

Tensions between Kinpusen and Kōfukuji intensified after Shirakawa's visit, with violent conflict breaking out in 1093 and 1094. Although we do not know whether Shirakawa actually engineered Eshin's resignation from the stewardship in favor of Kōsan, he did add to the velocity of Kinpusen's transformation from an independent pilgrimage destination into a client institution subordinated to Kōfukuji. In this respect, Shirakawa helped to move the Peak of Gold into the emerging medieval order of power blocs and factionalism. This shift brought the golden age of elite pilgrimage to Kinpusen to an end while opening a new phase of ritual and institutional development at the mountain. This process, which began with Kinpusen's military defeat, is discussed in the third part of this book.

PART III

Changing Landscapes

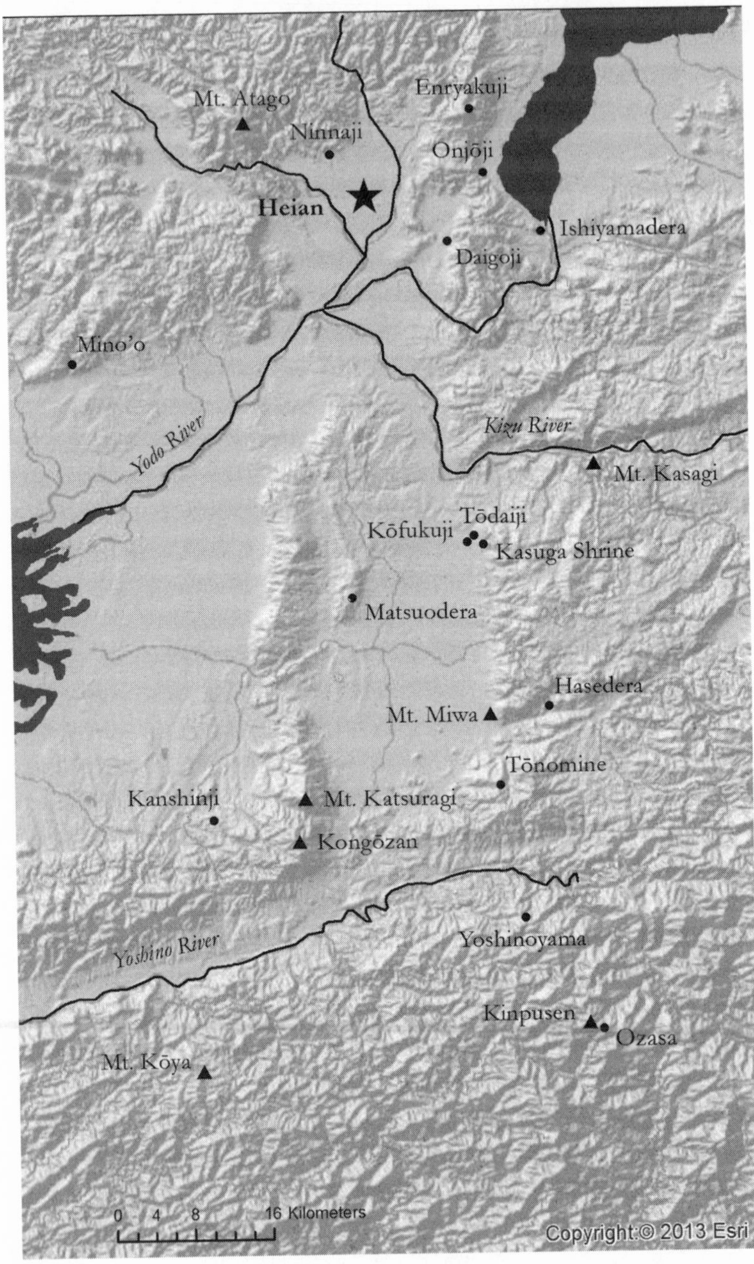

MAP 3 Kinpusen and religious institutions in the Nara Basin. Map by Theresa Quill, Indiana University, Bloomington.

CHAPTER SEVEN

The Fall of the Peak of Gold

> The Retired Emperor . . . asked [Minamoto] no Tameyoshi, "Many learned monks of [Kōfukuji] have died in this conflict with their branch temple. Why?"
>
> Tameyoshi replied: "The fortress of Kinpusen is not to be attacked rashly. In my view, one should press it cautiously."
>
> The retired Emperor objected: "But then, the besieged would kill many of the scholars in their sallies."
>
> "But the fortress would fall," answered Tameyoshi. "When they had exhausted all their resources, they would surrender."
>
> —*Kōfukuji ruki* (Kōfukuji's holdings)[1]

Part 3 of this book turns from microhistorical analyses of specific pilgrims' journeys to their after-effects. In the wake of the mid-Heian boom in elite pilgrimage to Kinpusen, the mountain's institutional circumstances underwent dramatic changes, which in turn fed into shifts in representational practice, taken up in chapter 8. In this chapter, the focus is on the ways in which conflict and growth reconfigured the physical, social, and ritual space of the mountain over the course of the *insei* period.

In the years following Retired Emperor Shirakawa's pilgrimage to Kinpusen, violent altercations with Kōfukuji wrenched the mountain into a political landscape dominated by power blocs and factionalism. Combining physical with ritual violence, Kōfukuji men marched on Kinpusen in 1093 and burned the mountaintop Zaō Hall. Aimed at truncating Kinpusen's cult by despoiling its most sacred site, this assault marked the beginning of a minor war. Kinpusen's defeat the following

1. *Kōfukuji ruki,* entry on the Dharma Bridge Chōen (d. 1150) (*DNBZ,* 123:23); translation from Royall Tyler, "Kōfukuji and the Mountains of Yamato," 183.

year set the tone for the twelfth century as a time of violence, but also growth, as the mountain's institutional subordination fed into processes of expansion, transforming the real-and-imagined Peak of Gold.

Changes at Kinpusen were part of a general trend during the *insei* period wherein influential temples and shrines developed into power blocs by amassing landholdings and extensive networks of client or "branch" institutions (*matsuji, massha*).[2] Status as a branch brought some benefits, primarily guarantees of tax-exempt status and protection from territorial incursions by other parties; however, it literally came at a price. Main temples or shrines extracted annual levies from their branches and often seized their administrative rights.[3] In some cases, as with Kinpusen, the creation of a main-branch relationship was fraught with violence. This chapter begins with the story of Kinpusen's defeat at the hands of Kōfukuji monks, and then scrutinizes Shirakawa's role in the conflict, Kōfukuji's motivations, and the regents' responses. It then examines a late-twelfth-century rapprochement that repositioned the mountain as part of a regional landscape and its men as members of the "*sangha* of the southern capital" (*nanto no shuto*), that is, as members of the religious establishment of the Nara Basin.

War with Kōfukuji

Early in the eighth month of 1093, Kōfukuji monks accused one of Retired Emperor Shirakawa's protégés, the Ōmi governor Takashina no Tameie (1038–1106), of encroaching upon estates that had been commended to the Kasuga Shrine. Kōfukuji's assertion of the right to defend Kasuga's property was part of a long-term effort to establish control over the shrine.[4] The charges against Tameie were dubious: the

2. For the formation of temple networks, see Adolphson, "Institutional Diversity."

3. For a classic case study of what branch status meant, see Yoneda, "Eizanjii no Kōfukuji matsujika."

4. Kōfukuji's control of Kasuga is discussed later in this chapter. For the campaign against Tameie, see *Go-Nijō Moromichiki,* Kanji 7.8.6–28 (3:92–101); and *Fusō ryakki,* Kanji 7.8.22 (*SZKT,* 12:334).

Crown had recently prohibited new land commendations, and the plaintiffs could furnish no proof that Kasuga actually held rights to the land in question.[5] Nonetheless, Kōfukuji partisans forced the issue, first by creating a disturbance in Nara, and then by launching noisy protests in the streets of the capital. Bearing a portable shrine (*mikoshi*) from Kasuga, they descended upon the Kangakuin, the regents' family academy and administrative office. This was a pointed gesture. The Kangakuin steward was in charge of Fujiwara communications with Kōfukuji, but with irate monks camped outside his door, it was painfully clear how vexed those communications had become.[6] Moved to act by all the commotion, the court summarily exiled Tameie to Tosa Province.[7]

A month and a half later, Kōfukuji men leveraged this incident to foment conflict with Kinpusen. Pointing out that men from the "seven great temples" of Nara had participated in the campaign against Tameie, Kōfukuji representatives sent a message to Moromichi complaining about lack of support from Kinpusen: "They did not attend us when we came up to the capital last month. Because of that we will now turn toward Kinpusen via Nogiwa."[8] Hoping to prevent conflict, Moromichi put the roads under guard, but to no avail. Rumors that a conflagration had engulfed Kinpusen reached the capital one week later. Moromichi suspected that the fire might have been the work of "more than forty members" of Kōfukuji's "unruly *sangha* who had holed up at the mountain."[9] (The term "*sangha*" was often used to refer to temple men who had taken up arms.) To his horror, Moromichi soon learned that the mountaintop Zaō Hall had indeed been destroyed; this prompted him to exclaim repeatedly that the incident was "of great moment for the realm."[10] Others shared his sense of foreboding. His father, the regent

5. *Go-Nijō Moromichiki,* Kanji 7.8.10, *uragaki* (3:93).

6. For the Kangakuin and Fujiwara oversight of Kōfukuji, see Kawabata, *Shōensei seiritsushi no kenkyū,* 324–66; Okano, *Heian jidai no kokka,* 105–33; and Takayama, *Chūsei Kōfukuji no monzeki,* 25–112. For the structure and function of such protests by religious institutions, see Adolphson, *The Gates of Power.*

7. *Go-Nijō Moromichiki,* Kanji 7.8.27–28 (3:100–1).

8. *Go-Nijō Moromichiki,* Kanji 7.9.14 (3:103); cf. *Fusō ryakki,* Kanji 7.8.26 (*SZKT,* 12:334).

9. *Go-Nijō Moromichiki,* Kanji 7.9.22 (3:104); cf. *Chūyūki,* same date (1:235).

10. *Go-Nijō Moromichiki,* Kanji 7.9.22–29 (3:104–6).

Morozane, submitted a formal letter of resignation to the throne, citing as cause recent riots by Kōfukuji and Enryakuji men. "Moreover," he added, "Kinpusen has gone up in flames; it has been reduced to ashes. Because of these events, I humbly resign the office of regent."[11]

The razing of the Zaō Hall clearly exercised a powerful effect on the regents and other members of the court. Its loss signified a radical change in a place that was theoretically supposed to remain constant and inviolable. As discussed in previous chapters, Kinpusen had long been construed as the dwelling of Maitreya and Śākyamuni, a place where lay pilgrims could, through ritualized physical progress, reach enlightenment. Thus, even in the context of growing violence between religious institutions, the desecration of the mountaintop, conceived as a site out-of-time sealed with the traces of the buddhas, caused considerable shock.

Although the court recognized that the situation was dire, it took no decisive action. Unlike a modern state, the Heian court held no Weberian "monopoly on the legitimate use of force."[12] Armed confrontations with monks were not to be taken lightly: not only did militias associated with temples pose a physical threat, but they also claimed the moral authority of the buddhas, bodhisattvas, and *kami*. For the regents in particular, it was deeply problematic to contemplate conflict with representatives of their ancestral temple, no matter how violent those representatives had become. Two weeks after the fire, the court finally sent a minor official to ascertain what had happened at Kinpusen. Upon his return, the Council of State settled down to make a determination. The question, however, was not whom to blame, but whether the court would sponsor repairs.[13]

At the end of the month, the court finally intervened, though in a way that was virtually guaranteed to cause even greater mayhem: it appointed the Kōfukuji monk Jōzen (d. 1095) overseer (*kengyō*) of Kinpu-

11. Letter of resignation quoted in *Chūyūki,* Kanji 7.10.10 (1:242); see also *Go-Nijō Moromichiki,* same date (3:110).

12. Weber, *The Theory of Social Organization,* 154.

13. *Go-Nijō Moromichiki,* Kanji 7.10.2 (3:108); *Chūyūki,* Kanji 7.10.15 (1:243).

sen.[14] This official recognition of the mountain's subordinate status vis-à-vis Kōfukuji signified a thorough rearrangement of Kinpusen's place in the political landscape. Jōzen was a member of a lateral branch of the regent's house that had fallen into the class of provincial governors. An accomplished scholiast and ritualist, he had been appointed Supernumerary Minor Right Reverend (*gōnshōsōzu*) in the Office for Monastic Affairs in 1092.[15] Kōfukuji's monastic community was doubtless pleased, but the monks at Kinpusen viewed the appointment as an insult and refused to accept Jōzen as their master. Consequently, less than a week after he had been named overseer, Kōfukuji men marched on Kinpusen again, and the two forces met in battle "at the bottom of the mountain."[16]

Deeply concerned, Morozane, whose resignation had not been accepted, asked Moromichi to send a messenger to Kōsan. The regents' sense of urgency must have been heightened by rumor, for Moromichi noted that although "people are saying that three thousand men have turned toward Yoshino, we have heard no report from Kōfukuji."[17] The crisis was even beginning to affect ceremonial in the capital. For instance, when a monastic examination debate held as part of the Hōjōji *Lotus* Lectures had to be cancelled, Fujiwara no Munetada commented, "the Kōfukuji monks have all been led to Kinpusen." The ritualized examination depended upon the participation of men from Kōfukuji, but "between the battles and the riots," there was no one left to staff it.[18]

Although the details of the ensuing conflict remain hazy, it is clear that Kinpusen suffered a serious defeat. In the third month of 1094, Kōfukuji submitted a communiqué to the court. According to Munetada, one of the secretary-controllers in service to the Council of State made the following announcement:

14. *Chūyūki,* Kanji 7.10.27 (1:246).

15. *Sōgō bunin,* entry for Kanji 6 (*DNBZ,* 123:218).

16. *Chūyūki,* Kanji 7.11.3 (1:246); *Go-Nijō Moromichiki,* Kanji 7.11.4 (3:119).

17. *Go-Nijō Moromichiki,* Kanji 7.11.8 (3:120).

18. *Chūyūki,* Kanji 7.12.2 (1:257). For the Hossō examination (*ryūgi*) at Hōjōji, see Uejima, *Nihon chūsei shakai,* 174.

> Just now the *sangha* of Kōfukuji has sent a letter. It says:
>
> "In order to inquire of the *sangha* of Kinpusen, we sallied forth on the first day of the month. With the Dharma Bridge Kōsan as their leader, the mountain *sangha* sent us a letter of apology. Therefore the monks of our temple were satisfied and returned home. Still, some wicked monks wanted to advance [on Kinpusen], even though our *sangha* [as a whole] did not agree."
>
> The root of this incident is that Kinpusen is a branch temple of Kōfukuji. Therefore the court (*kuge*) appointed a man from the august temple [=Kōfukuji], the Minor Right Reverend Jōzen, to be overseer of the august mountain. And yet the august mountain's *sangha* did not install Jōzen in office. Therefore, the monks of the august temple repeatedly departed thence, and twice engaged in great battles. As [Kinpusen's monks] were still not obeying their main temple, they submitted an apology at this time.[19]

War had already altered the real space of the peak and its surrounds, reducing the Zaō Hall to ashes and battering its caretakers. Now, Kōfukuji monks pressed for a full articulation of Kinpusen's new political position. In response, the court affirmed Kinpusen's status as a branch of "the august temple," officially reconceptualizing the mountain as part of Kōfukuji's growing sociospatial and political domain. Together, these events wrought an epochal shift in the real-and-imagined space of the mountain.

Why Attack Kinpusen?

The interreligious violence surrounding Kinpusen in the late eleventh century stemmed in large part from Kōfukuji's drive to establish hegemony over the province of Yamato. This long campaign reconfigured the regional landscape such that it came to center on Kōfukuji and the associated Kasuga Shrine. The foundations for this expansionism were religious, economic, and military.

19. *Chūyūki*, Kahō 1.3.6 (2:28–29).

In the sphere of doctrine and ritual, Kōfukuji monks gained authority through official preferment based on participation in state-recognized rites. Appointments to the prestigious Office of Monastic Affairs had long been predicated upon a set of qualifications that included service as lecturer at the *Vilmalakīrti* Assembly, which was held every year at Kōfukuji. By the mid-tenth century, the lectureship had come to be restricted to monks from Kōfukuji itself, or, much less often, Tōdaiji. By the time an alternative promotion schedule based on the patronage of the retired emperors opened up opportunities to monks from Tendai temples, Kōfukuji's institutional ascendancy was already secure.[20]

In the meantime, Kōfukuji's economic stature increased as its monks accrued substantial personal landholdings over the course of the eleventh century. These propertied clerics began to form "cloister houses" (*inge*), which facilitated the transmission of estates within particular Dharma lineages. By leveraging relationships of patronage or kinship with powerful nobles, especially members of the regents' house, the masters of well-endowed cloisters steadily increased their holdings. As a result, temples, which were tax-exempt, came to hold nearly all the land in Yamato, with Kōfukuji by far the greatest landlord. This rendered the provincial governor virtually powerless to collect revenue or conduct other matters of basic governance.[21]

At the same time that its men amassed property, Kōfukuji developed military strength. Men associated with religious institutions had begun to take up arms during the 900s in order to defend their burgeoning interests. As power blocs formed, competed with one another, and split into internal factions, conflict became endemic. Thus, as Mikael Adolphson has noted, whereas "occasional skirmishes" had been the norm during the tenth century, "large-scale confrontations" between religious complexes became increasingly frequent during the eleventh.[22] Kōfukuji men were infamous for fomenting riots, attacking

20. For monastic promotions and Kōfukuji's ascendancy, see Uejima, *Nihon chūsei shakai*, 426–29, 442–47.

21. Kawabata, *Shōensei seiritsushi no kenkyū*, 142–70, 283–323.

22. Adolphson, *Teeth and Claws of the Buddha*, 11. For Kōfukuji's involvement in protests and armed conflict, see also Adolphson, *The Gates of Power*.

other temples and shrines, and staging armed protests in the capital. When they worked their way into a fighting frenzy, they were said to swarm (*hōki*), as though they were angry bees. Using their religious, economic, and military might, Kōfukuji's partisans routinely mounted campaigns to take control of other temples and shrines in Yamato.

Given this drive to annex other religious institutions, an attack on Kinpusen may have been inevitable; nonetheless, Retired Emperor Shirakawa played the role of proximate cause for the wars of 1093 and 1094. In the previous two years, he had ranged himself against the regents and Kōfukuji on several occasions, creating a triangle of competitive, even hostile, relationships. Through spatial positioning, Shirakawa deployed his growing influence to reorient sites in Yamato traditionally associated with the regents toward himself. During his 1092 pilgrimage to Kinpusen, Shirakawa not only offered conspicuous patronage to what had long been the regents' signature site, but also raised the possibility that he would block Kōfukuji's interests by supporting Kinpusen's bid for independence. One year later, he did something very similar at Kasuga. This may have alarmed the regents, but more importantly, it alerted Kōfukuji to the fact that its hold on Kinpusen and Kasuga was not yet assured.

Since its founding as the Fujiwara family shrine, Kasuga had flourished alongside Kōfukuji. It was recognized as one of the Twenty-Two Shrines, which defined the home territory of the court and played an integral role in the rites and ideology of state protection. Early in their ascendancy, the Fujiwara regents had arranged for reigning emperors to make ceremonial visits to Kasuga, thereby creating a tradition that showcased the indispensability of their family to royal authority.[23] Shirakawa initiated a reversal. After making the requisite pilgrimage to Kasuga while he was on the throne, he visited the shrine again as retired emperor in 1093, seven-and-a-half months after he had gone to Kinpusen. By compelling the regent, Morozane, and his heir, Moromichi, to ride in his train, Shirakawa mimicked the protocol, and symbolically laid claim to the authority, of a reigning monarch. He also hinted that the regents were not only his ritual but also his political subordi-

23. See chapter 1, notes 43–45.

nates.[24] Furthermore, his actions suggested that he might compromise Kōfukuji's emergent authority over Kasuga by meddling in the shrine's affairs. Whereas in later centuries Shirakawa's pilgrimage was celebrated as a mark of royal favor, in 1093 it appears to have prompted Kōfukuji to insist on its claims to Kasuga with the Tameie protests mentioned above.[25] Significantly, Tameie himself was one of Shirakawa's protégés; accordingly, Kōfukuji's anti-Tameie campaign constituted an indirect attack on the retired emperor.

As the most authoritative site for *kami* worship in Yamato, Kasuga, which is located right next to Kōfukuji, was a prime target for Kōfukuji's expansionism. The Tameie protests should be seen as a watershed in the amalgamation of the temple and the shrine.[26] Although it later became standard practice for protesters to carry the *kami* with them in *sakaki* branches or palanquins, the Tameie protests represent the first documented case of Kōfukuji men bringing the Kasuga deities to the capital. In addition to staging this vivid performance of their ritual control of the Kasuga gods, Kōfukuji monks also seized the opportunity to articulate their position verbally. In a memorial submitted to the court, they declared: "The radiant deities of Kasuga protect Kōfukuji. Kōfukuji aids the radiant deities of Kasuga. One may say 'temple,' or one may say 'shrine,' but being of a single place, they are interchangeable. The worries of the shrine are the worries of the temple."[27] These assertions of shared identity and shared space culminated several decades later with the establishment of the Onmatsuri, a spectacular festival celebrating the Kasuga gods but controlled by Kōfukuji monks.[28]

Campaigns directed at other institutions, such as Hasedera and Tōnomine, indicate that men associated with Kōfukuji used a range of

24. *Go-Nijō Moromichiki,* Kanji 7.3.20 (3:30–31); *Chūyūki,* same date (1:209–11); *Fusō ryakki,* same date (*SZKT,* 12:333); *Gōki,* same date (315–26).

25. For a later, celebratory representation of the pilgrimage, see *Kasuga gongen genki e,* scroll 2, *dan* 1 (*ZNE,* 13:8–11).

26. Nagashima, "Kasugasha Kōfukuji no ittaika," 16; Motoki, *Inseiki seijishi kenkyū,* 251. For contemporary descriptions of the protests, see *Go-Nijō Moromichiki,* Kanji 7.8.6–28 (3:92–101); and *Fusō ryakki,* Kanji 7.8.22 (*SZKT,* 12:334).

27. Memorial quoted in *Fusō ryakki,* Kanji 7.8.22 (*SZKT,* 12:334).

28. Yasuda, *Chūsei no Kōfukuji,* 5–41; see also Grapard, *The Protocol of the Gods,* 157–67.

strategies, such as violence, administrative support, rhetoric, and ritual display, to create an integrated regional landscape dominated by their temple and coextensive with the province of Yamato.[29] In this context, Kinpusen became an obvious target. Whereas the regents' long tradition of patronage had not threatened Kōfukuji's designs on the mountain, Shirakawa, whose relationship with Kōfukuji was nothing if not vexed, was another matter. The close timing of his pilgrimages to Kinpusen and Kasuga, the Tameie affair, and the first Kōfukuji-Kinpusen war strongly suggest that it was Shirakawa's involvement that prompted Kōfukuji men to violent action. In order to forestall any increase in Shirakawa's influence at Kinpusen, Kōfukuji moved to consolidate its own position by annexing the mountain.

Rebuilding: The Regents and the 1096 Canon

The initial reaction to Kinpusen's defeat was complex. Although the court formally recognized Kōfukuji's claims to Kinpusen, it also sought to protect the mountain's integrity as a distinctive cultic site. To mend the rupture in the sacred landscape created by the razing of the Zaō Hall, the court moved to sponsor reconstruction. In historical terms, this represented an intermediate phase in the allocation of responsibility for Kinpusen's real space. The previous rebuilding effort, which repaired damage from a typhoon in 1091, had been sponsored by a provincial governor with strong ties to the regents. By contrast, a later, Kamakura-period reconstruction appears to have been underwritten by Kōfukuji.[30] By formally assuming the financial burden for reconstruction, the court indicated that Kinpusen was a site of public concern. Furthermore, as though to counter Kōfukuji's influence, when the new hall was completed in 1096, members of the Council of State, many

29. The case of Hasedera stands as an example of a supportive takeover (see Uejima, *Nihon chūsei shakai,* 529–74, esp. 533–36). By contrast, Kōfukuji's long campaign to exert control of Tōnomine was unremittingly violent (see Adolphson, *The Gates of Power,* 92–96, 144–45).

30. For the 1091 reconstruction, see *Chūyūki,* Kanji 7.9.22 (1:235). For reconstruction in the 1220s, see Shudō, *Kinpusenji shi,* 98.

of whom had been to Kinpusen themselves, agreed that the dedication should be the responsibility of the mountain's temple monks (*honzan no jike*) rather than the emperor and the court (*kuge*).[31]

While reconstruction was under way, residents of the capital participated in an initiative to secure Kinpusen's future while also broadening its base of support. This took the form of a cooperative canon-copying project.[32] Earlier in 1096, a holy man named Jiō (n.d.) had announced plans for a spectacular textual emplacement, described by Fujiwara no Munetada as a "great good work." "In the capital," Munetada wrote, "a multitude of people, both high and low, copied the entire canon in one day. There is a holy man who had a dream telling him to recruit people, and to have each of them copy" a portion of the canon in his or her own house. The participants were to hold dedicatory offerings on an individual basis and then send their scriptures to Jiō.[33] Although communal copying projects had been common in the Nara period and returned to popularity in the mid-twelfth century, there is no evidence that any cooperative canon had been produced in the hundred years preceding Jiō's.

Not surprisingly, the regents were involved in this ambitious project, as both participants and sponsors. Moromichi, who had succeeded his father as regent, volunteered to contribute a copy of the *Flower Ornament Sūtra* in sixty scrolls. He apparently hired scribes to copy the text of the sutra, but inscribed the outer titles himself, with the understanding that doing so would ensure that he would "not fall into the

31. *Go-Nijō Moromichiki,* Eichō 1.6.27 (3:204). Moromichi noted that the assembled nobles "inquired into whether or not there were sixty monks from the mountain (*honzan*)" available to perform the dedication. When Horiike Shunpō read this passage, he interpreted *honzan* as a reference to Kōfukuji (Horiike, *Nanto bukkyōshi no kenkyū,* 2:514). However, use of the term *honzan* to mean "main temple" (*honji*) is a later phenomenon; furthermore, it is clear from Munetada's diary that Kinpusen monks were in fact in charge of the dedication. See *Chūyūki,* Eichō 1.7.8 (3:73).

32. For this canon as a sign (and perhaps a cause) of the spread of Kinpusen's cult, see Horiike, *Nanto bukkyōshi no kenkyū,* 2:515. For Jiō's initiative as a complement to the regents' sutra burials, as well as its relation to other canon-copying projects, see Abe, *Chūsei nihon no shūkyō tekusuto,* 174–98, esp. 188–89; Blair, "Peak of Gold," 54–118.

33. *Chūyūki,* Eichō 1.3.18 (3:37–38).

hells of the four sins."[34] Merit was certainly an important concern, but the canon presented opportunities for conspicuous patronage, as well.

Jiō was in need of logistical support, and the regents stepped easily into the role of sponsors, pressing the most venerable elements of their ritual regime into service. According to Munetada, once all the component texts had been copied, Jiō took up residence at Hōjōji, Michinaga's old signature site. There the holy man vetted the new manuscripts against "the copies at that temple," presumably manuscripts from Michinaga's Song xylograph, or perhaps Yorimichi's silver-and-gold canon. These were the regents' signature texts.[35] Munetada wrote that when Jiō finished proofreading in 1098, "he sent the canon to Kinpusen" with the support of the regents: "The Great Lord," Fujiwara no Morozane, "and the Lord Captain of the Left," Fujiwara no Tadazane, "provided him with corvée workers and pure robes, and sent them off. The people of the capital have formed a great karmic tie for the city."[36] Thus, at the same time that the regents used their patrimony to seal Jiō's undertaking, they capitalized upon the project's broad participation to reconfirm the high ritual status of their signature pilgrimage destination. Through ritual, text, and karma, Kinpusen was now bound to the entire capital.

The regents' involvement in Jiō's project likely stemmed in part from dismay at Kinpusen's subjugation. Kōfukuji may have been their family temple, but the actions of its partisans often contravened the wishes—and exceeded the control—of the regents. Moromichi's journal entries, for instance, speak to his sense of divided loyalties. Soon after his first pilgrimage to Kinpusen in 1090, he had written, "In my heart, [I sense that] Kinpusen and Kasuga jointly protect me." Six years later, after the Zaō Hall had been burned and rebuilt, and after he had forwarded his copy of the *Flower Ornament Sūtra* to Jiō, he confessed, "I

34. *Go-Nijō Moromichiki,* Eichō 1.3.18 (3:179). For the scripture, see *Da fangguang fo huayan jing, T.* 278 (9:395–788).

35. Whether the Song canon was still at Hōjōji or whether it had burned when that temple went up in flames in 1058 is unclear. Regardless, there must still have been a complete canon at the temple, or at the very least a good set of catalogues and scriptures. In support of this surmise, it may be noted that in 1104, Tadazane described a canon dedicated at Sonshōji as having been "copied from the Hōjōji version" (*Denryaku,* Chōji 1.2.29 [1:298]).

36. *Chūyūki,* Jōtoku 2.3.21 (4:18).

dreamed that I saw the *kami* of the southern mountains, who said, 'My distress over the Kōfukuji affair is boundless. Therefore you see my divine radiance in the south.' "[37]

Reproached in his dreams by the gods, Moromichi proved to be the last dedicated proponent of Kinpusen within the regents' house. At the end of the century, his family sustained a series of blows, with Moromichi himself dying in 1099, and Morozane following him to the grave in 1101. Over the course of the ensuing century, Kinpusen did continue to be recognized as an important sacred site, but the involvement of members of the court shifted from pilgrimage and devotion to pro-forma administrative dealings. Meanwhile, it was the regents' rivals, not their descendants, who followed the new precedent of dispatching a canon to a signature pilgrimage site: the retired emperors took to sending canons to Kumano.[38]

Although Jiō's canon did reaffirm the cultic importance of Kinpusen to the capital and the ruling elite, it did not forestall the coming shift in aristocratic devotion toward Kumano, nor did it stem the mountain's reimagination as a satellite of "the southern capital" and its monastic populations. Under Kōfukuji's suzerainty, Kinpusen's connections to other religious institutions and networks increased, while its constituency burgeoned and transformed. These were gradual changes, however; first, the resident community's opposition to Kōfukuji had to be overcome.

Men of Yamato: Overseers, Violence, and Ritual

Kinpusen's institutional subordination and eventual integration into the Kōfukuji-dominated regional landscape unfolded in stages over the course of the twelfth century. During the first half of the 1110s, the mountain monks did their best to recover Kinpusen as an independent domain, using force of arms to contest Kōfukuji's suzerainty. With the

37. *Go-Nijō Moromichiki,* Kanji 4.10.22, Eichō 1.10.11, *uragaki* (2:18, 3:227).

38. Shirakawa dedicated a canon at Kumano in 1118; Toba did the same in 1153 (*Chūyūki,* Gen'ei 1.9.22, i9.22, and 10.7 [*ZST,* 13:76, 81, 84]; *Honchō seiki,* Ninpei 3.1.28 [*SZKT,* 9:847]).

failure of separatism, however, the two institutions entered a phase of comparative amity. In fact, by the late twelfth century, Kinpusen's partisans were participating in campaigns to bring other institutions in Yamato under Kōfukuji's control. In this respect, they too became agents in the reconfiguration of the province as a united, if restive, religious and political territory.

The shift from opposition to assimilation is illustrated by the figure of the Kinpusen overseer, who was the symbolic axis for Kinpusen-Kōfukuji relations during the twelfth century. Heian-period sources show that it was difficult for lay observers to distinguish between the office of steward (*bettō*), which had once been the prerogative of Kinpusen monks, and that of the overseer (*kengyō*), through which monks from other temples gained rights of supervision. For instance, when Tadazane, the regent at the time, and Munetada described an imbroglio between Kinpusen and Kōfukuji in 1114, one wrote that the issue was "the Kinpusen steward," while the other saw it as "the Kinpusen overseer."[39] By contrast, Kōfukuji's late-medieval chroniclers treated the stewardship as a stable index of Kōfukuji's lordship. Taken together, confusion on the part of Heian writers and certainty among later monastic historians indicates that the significance of the office changed over time.[40]

The careers of Jōzen and Shin'en (1153–1224), whose incumbencies bracket the twelfth century, speak to the gradual normalization of Kinpusen-Kōfukuji relations. Jōzen, the overseer whose appointment sparked battles in 1093 and 1094, represented the emergent medieval power-bloc order at Kōfukuji and its gradual spread through the tem-

39. *Denryaku,* Eikyū 2.3.29–30 (4:94); *Chūyūki,* Eikyū 2.3.30 (*ZST,* 12:286–87).

40. The late-twelfth-century *Yuima koji kengaku ryūgi shidai* does not note appointments to the office of Kinpusen overseer. By contrast, the loosely parallel *Sanne jōitsuki,* which was compiled in the sixteenth century after Kōfukuji had lost control of Kinpusen, provides the sole evidence for the incumbencies of several twelfth-century overseers. Similarly, *Kinpusen kengyō shidai,* an oft-cited list of men who are supposed to have served as overseers, dates to the fifteenth century or later and is colored by late-medieval interinstitutional rivalries. For representations of the overseership in the latter two sources, see Royall Tyler, "Kōfukuji and the Mountains," 177–87. Note that Tyler also covers much of the same material in an earlier article, "Kōfukuji and Shugendō."

ple's territory. A paradigmatic "learned cleric" (*gakuryo*), Jōzen belonged to a privileged class that was organizationally distinct from lower-ranking "hall monks" (*dōshū*). His preferment was subtended by his pedigree: although his family members were provincial governors, Jōzen was one of Michinaga's great-grandsons. Like other *gakuryo*, Jōzen earned appointment to the Office of Monastic Affairs through service at official rites, which required doctrinal erudition.[41] The documentary record also indicates that he was the founding father of the Gonjōin, one of the early cloister lineages at Kōfukuji: by the end of his life, Jōzen had accrued at least fifteen estates. These he bequeathed to one of his disciples, who consolidated them into a single, wealthy cloister.[42]

In all these respects, Jōzen inhabited an entirely different world from that of Kinpusen's permanent residents, whose rejection of him was so emphatic that we do not actually know whether, or how, he assumed office. At the time of his appointment, there is no evidence for cloister lineages at Kinpusen, and judging from the general absence of references to specific Kinpusen monks in the historical record, the mountain's residents did not hail from aristocratic families. Moreover, the few cases in which Kinpusen's residents did achieve official rank indicate that they could only hope to attain such preferment through service to an eminent pilgrim. They cultivated an interest in esoteric ritual, as the *Gōki* fragment discussed in the last chapter shows, and Kōsan, the man whom they recognized as their leader, was an esoteric master. Jōzen's appointment, then, amounted to a declaration that outsiders would govern Kinpusen, and that they would be selected based not on what the mountain monks valued most, namely esoteric training, seniority, and permanent residency, but rather on aristocratic connections, landholdings, and high monastic rank.

The career of Shin'en, who held the office of overseer around the year 1200, represents the maturation of patterns begun with Jōzen. The

41. *Sōgō bunin,* entry for Eihō 1 (*DNBZ,* 123:204).

42. Upon his death, Jōzen deeded his estates to one of his disciples, Eison (n.d., not to be confused with the more famous *vinaya* advocate); in turn, Eison consolidated these properties into a cloister that he renamed the Gonjōin (*Heian ibun* 2441, dated Hōen 7.2.25 [*komonjo hen,* 5:2049–53]).

son of the regent Fujiwara no Tadamichi and brother of the famous Enryakuji prelate Jien (1155–1225), Shin'en embodied the success of the regents' house in asserting control over Kōfukuji, an initiative that had begun when two of Moromichi's brothers had entered the temple and then assumed its stewardship.[43] Shin'en had entered Kōfukuji while still a boy. He acceded to the abbacy of Kōfukuji's most influential cloisters, taking control of the Ichijōin as an adolescent, and the Daijōin in his twenties.[44] At age twenty-nine, he was appointed steward of Kōfukuji, and while in office he played an important role in rebuilding the temples of Nara, which had been destroyed during the Genpei War. After he stepped down in 1189, he remained an influential presence in temple life. And yet, powerful as he was, he did not enjoy total immunity. In 1208, Shin'en's great nephew, the regent Konoe Iezane (1179–1242), removed him from the post of Kinpusen overseer, later appointing Jisson (1180–1236) in his place. Together with the exile of several Kinpusen monks, Shin'en's dismissal was meant as punishment for an incident in which men from Kinpusen had taken up an old Kōfukuji vendetta against the religious complex at Tōnomine, which was located in the Ryūmon Mountains north of the Yoshino River.[45]

This incident illustrates several important points. First, whereas Jōzen's 1093 appointment appears to have been made through the joint action of the emperor, regent, and Council of State, by the early 1200s, it was clearly the regent who held the right to appoint and dismiss Kinpusen overseers. Inasmuch as a direct administrative line ran from the regents through Kōfukuji to Kinpusen, the regents exercised more control over the mountain at the opening of the thirteenth century than when they had visited it regularly during the eleventh. It is also, however, important to recognize that the regents' own political position

43. Morozane's sons Kakushin (1065–1121) and Jinpan (1101–1174) held the office of Kōfukuji steward. According to a variant manuscript of *Sōgō bunin*, Kakushin was also made Kinpusen overseer in 1116, but other sources do not corroborate his appointment (Mitō Shōkōkan manuscript of *Sōgō bunin*, Eikyū 4.2.21, *uragaki*, cited in Hirabayashi and Koike, *Gojūonbiki sōgō bunin*, 50).

44. Yasuda, *Chūsei no Kōfukuji*, 93–119. For succession within the Ichijōin and Daijōin, see Takayama, *Chūsei Kōfukuji no monzeki*, 115–77, esp. the helpful chart on 125.

45. *Inokuma kanpakuki*, Jōgen 2.i4.25 and Jōgen 2.8.28 (4:202, 5:17).

had been relativized, first by the ascendancy of the retired emperors, and then by the founding of the military government in Kamakura. In fact, Iezane noted in his diary that he appointed Jisson based on instructions received from Retired Emperor Go-Toba.[46] Thus, the regents held the symbolic right to oversee Kinpusen's administration, but their actions were constrained by the wishes of other political figures.

Second, Shin'en's appointment and dismissal indicates that the office of Kinpusen overseer had become a perquisite of abbots of the Daijōin and Ichijōin. The abbacies of these *monzeki* cloisters were monopolized by Fujiwara monks with close ties to the regents, and had begun to dominate nearly all aspects of life at Kōfukuji.[47] Limitations on the pool of candidates meant that the locus of administrative control remained stable even when the overseer changed. For instance, Jisson, the appointee who replaced Shin'en in 1208, illustrates this fact: he was actually Shin'en's Dharma-heir, nephew, and successor at the Daijōin.

Lastly, in attacking Tōnomine, Kinpusen monks had adopted their main temple's agendas. Tōnomine's cult centered Fujiwara no Kamatari (614–69), ancestor to the entire Fujiwara family. A sculpted image of Kamatari was enshrined at Tōnomine and kept under close watch, for changes to its appearance were deemed important auguries. When such omens were reported, the regents held divinations to interpret their significance and then observed taboos in accord with the warnings, usually remaining closeted in their residences for a fixed period of time. Well aware of the regents' ties to Tōnomine, Kōfukuji's partisans had periodically attacked it since the 1080s in efforts to dissociate it from Enryakuji, which had succeeded in making it a branch institution during the early eleventh century.[48] Yet even in the context of regular violence at Tōnomine, the 1208 assault was particularly vicious. Led by a Kinpusen monk named Shunken (n.d.), the attackers destroyed the image of Kamatari. In ruining the material and symbolic center of

46. See previous note.

47. For *inge* and *monzeki,* see Nagashima, *Nara bunka no denryū,* 159–82; Yasuda, *Chūsei no Kōfukuji*; and Takayama, *Chūsei Kōfukuji no monzeki*. For divisions within the monastic population, see also Inaba, *Chūsei jiin no kenryoku,* 223–57.

48. See note 29.

Tōnomine's cult, Kinpusen men reenacted the destruction wrought upon their own mountaintop Zaō Hall in 1092. This time, however, they used violence to range themselves with, rather than against, Kōfukuji.

In sum, a political, economic, and ritual transformation had occurred at Kinpusen. During the twelfth century, at the same time that the overseership was growing more institutionalized, Kinpusen's men gained a reputation for violence by participating in protests, attacks on other temples, and disputes over estates. In this respect, together with Kōfukuji men, they came to occupy a new conceptual space, that of the "wicked monk" (*akusō*). Through a set of edicts known as the *Hōgen shinsei* (New rules for the Hōgen era), issued in 1156 and 1157, the government sought to curtail the economic and territorial expansionism of religious institutions. The article focusing on the misdeeds of "wicked monks" begins with a list of the worst offenders:

> Kōfukuji, Enryakuji, Onjōji, Kumano, Kinpusen.
>
> As for the above, prohibitions only pile up regarding the brutality of their wicked monks. Nonetheless, the three temples and two mountains, their summer monks, equinox monks, pilgrimage guides, and men from their estates either turn a profit through usury, calling it "an offering to the monks," or else steal public and private property, saying that it is "funds for the head of the assembly."[49]

By positioning the "two mountains" alongside Kōfukuji, Enryakuji, and Onjōji, all of which were paradigmatic power-bloc institutions, the court testified to the frequency and visibility of controversies in which Kinpusen and Kumano's partisans involved themselves. The language of the edict also suggests that Kinpusen's constituency had expanded to include nonmonastics (e.g., men from their estates) and seasonal practitioners (e.g., the summer and equinox monks) who did not reside permanently in Yoshinoyama or Kinpusen. According to the *Hōgen shinsei*, these groups engaged in usury and theft. Whether the funds ever made their way into the pockets of the resident community is

49. *Heian ibun* 2876, dated Hōgen 2.3.17 (*komonjo hen,* 6:2365). This version of the rules was promulgated by the Council of State; for an imperial decree, which was issued the previous year, see *Hyōhanki,* Hōgen 1.i9.18 (*ZST,* 19:139–40).

unclear, but other members of Kinpusen's constituency were engaged in efforts to generate income, as well.

Competition over estates and other property rights was endemic for the simple reason that wealth derived primarily from the control of land. Economic interests were thus ipso facto territorial. Like most any other shrine or temple, Kinpusen sought to consolidate and increase its landholdings during the twelfth century. Although some disputes proceeded through legal channels, others erupted into violence. For example, a dispute over lands in Yamato's Uji District was bound up in a series of battles between Kinpusen and Kōfukuji between 1145 and 1146. According to the *Honchō seiki* (Annals of our country), Minamoto Morotō (n.d.), who was active during the 1140s, initially commended fields he had inherited to Kōfukuji, but then, deeming the temple's levies too high, switched the commendation over to Kinpusen. Predictably, a dispute ensued, feeding into yet another armed conflict between Kinpusen and Kōfukuji.[50] As Royall Tyler has noted, Kinpusen's defeat in this series of battles seems to have brought the mountain more firmly under Kōfukuji's control, putting an end to armed conflict between the two institutions.[51] Yet even during the relative peace that ensued, wrangling over estates continued. In 1160, for instance, the Council of State ordered Kinpusen monks to desist from their efforts to take over the holdings of Eizanji, another of Kōfukuji's branch temples; some years later, Kasuga accused a Kinpusen monk of causing problems with shrine land.[52] Such disputes indicate that although Kinpusen was indeed one of Kōfukuji's branches, it was not necessarily on good terms with other such institutions.

The violence that reworked Yamato into Kōfukuji's sovereign, yet fractious, domain was paired with ritual. Distinct but complementary gestures of consolidation and outward procession can be observed in records of twelfth-century ritual events. The clearest example of consolidation followed upon Kinpusen's defeat in 1146, when Kasuga

50. *Honchō seiki,* Kyūan 2.4.25 (*SZKT,* 9:488).

51. Royall Tyler, "Kōfukuji and the Mountains," 182–83. For the battles, see *Taiki,* Ten'yō 2.6.28, 7.12, 7.26, and 9.13 (*ZST,* 23:155–57); *Honchō seiki,* Kyūan 1.7.18, and Kyūan 2.4.25 (*SZKT,* 9:461, 488).

52. *Heian ibun,* 2936, 2940, and 3458, respectively dated Hōgen 3.7.28, Hōgen 3.8.7, and Nin'an 3.38 (*komonjo hen,* 6:2418–19, 2422–24, and 7:2715–16).

priests enshrined the mountain's gods—the Thirty-Eight, Komori, Katte, and a mysterious deity identified as Chūsai Kongō—on the grounds of the Kasuga Shrine.[53] The precise location of the shrine was significant: Kinpusen's gods were installed next to the Wakamiya Shrine, which Kōfukuji monks had been instrumental in founding, and where they had very recently inaugurated the Onmatsuri festival to showcase the integration of Kōfukuji and Kasuga.[54] The 1146 enshrinement thus located Kinpusen's pantheon at the spatial and ritual heart of Kōfukuji's most important institutional alliance.

Having thus been situated within a regional Yamato pantheon, Kinpusen's gods were also processed outward in the company of Kasuga's deities. The most common vehicle for such displays were protests (*gōso*) staged in the course of a dispute in order to coerce the court into rendering a favorable judgment.[55] Though protests threatened the social and spatial order of the capital, they were also deeply ritualized. As Kujō Kanezane noted in his journal in 1173: "For the most part, it is customary for the *sangha* to plan to enter the capital when they are involved in a legal action. Sometimes they go to the palace gates, and sometimes they gather at our family's [offices, the Kangakuin]. This has ever been the precedent."[56] In the particular dispute described by Kanezane, Kōfukuji men, fresh from an attack on Tōnomine, bore the "sacred trees" and palanquins of the Kasuga gods toward the capital, bringing divine might to bear on their claims that Enryakuji had been violating the property rights of the "seven great temples" of Yamato. Significantly, "the *sangha* of Yoshino went along, being of one mind" with Kōfukuji's men.[57] According to the *Kōfukuji bettō shidai* (Roster of Kōfukuji stewards), the contingent from Kinpusen was led by the monk Shun'yū (n.d.) and was made up of "seven or eight officials and more than one thousand soldiers (*heishi*) from eighteen villages" in Kinpusen's domain. The Kinpu-

53. "Sanjū hassho no koto," entry dated Kyūan 2.10.23, included in "Kyūki shōshutsu" (*Kasugasha kiroku*, 3). I have been unable to determine what type of deity Chūsai Kongō may have been.

54. See note 28.

55. As Adolphson notes, the term *gōso* came into use in the Kamakura period, but has been generalized in historical research (Adolphson, *The Gates of Power*, 241).

56. *Gyokuyō*, Shōan 3.11.3 (1:328).

57. *Hyakurenshō*, Shōan 3.6.25–7.11, esp. the entry for 7.7 (*SZKT*, 12:88–89).

sen men were said to have arrayed the Thirty-Eight and Katte alongside the Kasuga deities in a public show of divine displeasure.[58] Given Katte's martial character, his presence would have made the performance especially ominous. The chroniclers may have exaggerated the details or the numbers of men involved, but their accounts indicate that Kinpusen's partisans had closed ranks with Kōfukuji's men.

Such assertions of shared territorial identity derived force not only from the threat of violence, but also from a spatial inversion. Instead of welcoming aristocrats who had traveled to their mountain fastness, Kinpusen's protesters now brought their gods to the capital to harry erstwhile devotees. Settled in their shrines, *kami* were a source for blessings, but their presence verged on the polluting in the capital, where they were horribly out of place. Members of the court and the populace at large were thus eager to keep portable shrines—and their bearers—out of the city, fearing that irate and misplaced gods might bring curses and misfortune.

In transforming Kinpusen into a part of Kōfukuji's regional domain in Yamato, ritual provided the foil to violence and administrative change. Enshrinements and protests sealed Kinpusen's defeat by integrating the mountain's divine and human partisans into Kōfukuji and Kasuga's constituency. With the institutionalization of the overseership as the prerogative of *monzeki* like Shin'en, Kinpusen men came under the oversight of powerful clerics who were at once Fujiwara scions and Kōfukuji hierarchs. The resulting community was not harmonious, but it was vertically integrated and powerful.

Conclusion

Although Kōsan had declared that Kinpusen would never submit to Kōfukuji's oversight, by the end of the twelfth century Kinpusen men were in fact seen as members of the "*sangha* of the southern capital." This shift in the identity of Kinpusen's partisans and the imagination of its spaces began when Shirakawa's involvement in Kinpusen affairs

58. *Kōfukuji bettō shidai*, entry on Kakuchin (1099–1175) (*DNBZ*, 124:22).

pushed already-polarized institutions into open conflict in 1093. Although the ensuing war did not last long, outbreaks of violence punctuated the next five decades, making it clear that Kinpusen's subordination to Kōfukuji was first and foremost a product of military coercion.

In isolation, the *insei*-period decline in elite pilgrimage discussed at the end of chapter 6 might have weakened Kinpusen's cult. As it happened, however, integration into Kōfukuji's domain expanded the mountain's devotional reach within monastic and quasi-monastic groups. In addition to the permanent residents and Kōfukuji-affiliated administrators who interacted with Retired Emperor Shirakawa in 1092, new members of Kinpusen's constituency can be glimpsed in the twelfth-century historical record. The text of the *Hōgen shinsei* shows that men from Kinpusen's estates were participating in protests, and that mobile, seasonal practitioners were recognized as members of the mountain's broader community. Judging from their epithets, the summer monks and equinox monks likely departed from the mountains after limited periods of seasonal practice; similarly, pilgrimage guides (*sendatsu*) engaged in work that by nature kept them on the move. These groups may have ranged quite widely; indeed, material evidence indicates that the worship of Zaō, who more than any other figure embodied Kinpusen's cult, spread at least as far as the Japan Sea during the twelfth century.[59]

This expansion only continued in the ensuing years. The *Kinpusen sōsōki,* which was likely compiled in the early 1300s, represents the religious communities of the Yoshino-Kinpusen area in terms of a complex array of religious positions. In order of appearance, the following groups appear in the text: hall monks (*dōshū*), resident monks (*jūryo*), offering monks (*gusō*), scholar monks (*gakuryo*), sutra maintainers from nearby provinces (*kingoku jikyōsha*), sutra maintainers from this mountain (*tōzan jikyōsha*), shrine monks (*shasō*), *miko,* shrine workers (*jinnin*), temple monks (*jisō*), last-day-of-the-year *yamabushi* (*misoka yamabushi*), flower-offering *yamabushi* (*hanaku yamabushi*), *yamabushi* leaving the mountains (*shutsubu yamabushi*), vajra-holder monks

59. For instance, the main icon in a set of wood Zaō images preserved at Sanbutsuji in contemporary Tottori Prefecture bears an inscription dating it to 1168 (see Ikawa, "Sanbutsuji Zaō gongen zō").

(*jikongōshu*), hall men (*dōke*), and *yamabushi* from the various provinces (*shokoku yamabushi*).[60] Even though nothing approaching this level of complexity is visible in Heian-period sources, some of these groups almost certainly had roots going back to the twelfth-century reconfiguration of Kinpusen.

In the context of growth and exchange during the twelfth and thirteenth centuries, members of Kinpusen's increasingly diverse constituency sought to articulate new positions for themselves. Hybrid texts known as *engi* testify to the ways in which religious identity and mountain territory were reframed in response to shifts in the mountain's political and institutional circumstances. Accordingly, the rhetorical strategies, spatial imaginary, and dissemination of *engi* are taken up in the next chapter as evidence for the ongoing reimagination of Kinpusen.

60. *Kinpusen sōsōki* (*KSS*, 46–48; *SS*, 3:363–66).

CHAPTER EIGHT

Engi and Interchange

> In the east are the high mountains of Ise, which the great goddess Amaterasu protects. In the west is Kongōzan, where Hōki bodhisattva preaches the Dharma to benefit living beings. In the south is Kinpusen, where the great provisional bodhisattva awaits the advent of the Merciful Lord. In the north is Mt. Ōmiwa, where the unfurling traces of the thus-come ones save the common people.
>
> —Description of the location of Tōnomine, attributed to Jōe (643–65) in *Shozan engi* and *Shoji konryū shidai* (On the founding of many temples)[1]

Kinpusen's defeat and subsequent integration into Kōfukuji's domain exerted considerable influence upon the mountain's religious culture from the twelfth century into the thirteenth, that is, during the latter half of the *insei*. During this time, which bridged the transition from the Heian to the Kamakura period, representations of religious practice in the Ōmine region as a distinctive, independent tradition found expression in origin narratives known as *engi*. As this chapter demonstrates, advocates of mountain practice used *engi* to express a distinctive set of concerns, which ultimately carried over into Shugendō during the late Kamakura and early Muromachi periods. In short, *engi*, and by inference, the communities that created and used them, were preoccupied with canonizing mountain rites, valorizing En no Gyōja as a founder-figure, codifying the mountain terrain, and asserting the religious authority of *yamabushi*. Mountain practitioners appear to have produced the component parts of many early Ōmine *engi* in reaction to bids by power-bloc temples to assert control over the

1. *Shozan engi* (*NST*, 7:130, 359); *Shoji konryū shidai*, entry on Tōnomine (178).

southern mountains. Not only did Kōfukuji secure the right to oversee Kinpusen's affairs, but during the twelfth and thirteenth centuries Onjōji also succeeded in monopolizing the office of Kumano overseer, as discussed in the epilogue to this book. Even though *engi* assertively frame the Ōmine region as a space for independent religious practice, it is important to recognize that men from power-bloc temples and associated networks were also involved in the production and dissemination of these texts. Therefore, it makes sense to treat *engi* as sites for and products of interaction among diverse constituencies.

In addition to Kōfukuji's suzerainty, discussed in chapter 7, religious ferment in Yamato shaped the context for the composition and circulation of *engi* about Kinpusen and the broader Ōmine region. Following the Genpei War, in which Taira forces had put the temples of Nara to the torch, local monastics set to work reconstructing their built environment and renovating their religious culture. Their activities are collectively known as the Nara revival. From the late twelfth through the thirteenth century, learned revivalists created congregational liturgies and undertook new exegetical projects, thereby contributing to the transformation of preaching and devotional practices. Others led fund-raising campaigns to support reconstruction and new building projects. Meanwhile, advocates of renewed emphasis on the *vinaya* led a widespread movement focused on observance of the precepts, and women once again began to take full ordination.[2] Increased interest in mountain sites and practices was also part of this religious efflorescence. Some revivalists engaged in mountain austerities, while others worked to create a regional mountainscape by developing and redeveloping sites in the low mountains ringing the Nara Basin. *Engi* served as a key medium for connecting and representing these sites as an integrated landscape wherein austerities and pilgrimage enabled practitioners to become buddhas in their present lives. In the following pages, I argue that the rhetorical strategies of early Ōmine *engi*, together with

2. The literature on the Nara revival is quite rich. See, for instance, Goodwin, *Alms and Vagabonds* on fund-raising; Ford, *Jōkei and Buddhist Devotion,* and Quinter, "Invoking the Mother," and "Creating Bodhisattvas" on devotion and liturgy; Glassman, *The Face of Jizō,* 44–106, on image and performance; and Meeks, *Hokkeji,* on women's ordination.

their concerns with ritual and group identity, not only belonged to residents of the mountains but were also products of interchange with lowland communities.

Constructing Authority

It is impossible to determine precisely when *engi* about Ōmine were first written down, but the earliest extant materials can be loosely dated to the *insei* period, provided that we understand the *insei* as extending until the new military government's decisive defeat of Retired Emperor Go-Toba in the 1221 Jōkyū Disturbance. At present, a dozen-odd such texts have been identified; here I treat these collectively as products of the twelfth and thirteenth centuries. Extant in only one manuscript each, many of these *engi* are known by provisional titles proposed by contemporary editors in the absence of original paratextual notations. In no case can the author(s) be clearly identified. Indeed, far from being original compositions, these texts, which bear deeply intertextual relationships to each other, appear to be iterations of a shared body of oral and written lore.

The communities that produced and used Ōmine *engi* clearly labored at what Eric Hobsbawm and Terence Ranger have referred to as the invention of tradition.[3] Projecting their own habits and dispositions into a venerable past, twelfth- and thirteenth-century readers, writers, and ritualists defined an authentic, independent tradition of religious practice in the southern mountains. To frame *engi* as sources for and symbols of authority, they employed a range of strategies, among which emphases on traces, transmission, lineage, and secrecy stand out.

In order to characterize *engi* as authoritative, their creators and transmitters presented them as repositories for traces, thereby engaging in "trace-ism," a term introduced earlier in this book to refer to preoccupations endemic to *engi* and to Heian culture in general. The rhetoric of *engi* was thus congruent with that of the regents and retired

3. Hobsbawm and Ranger, *The Invention of Tradition.*

emperors, who had been deeply concerned with the legitimating power of precedent on the one hand and the sacred traces of gods and founders on the other. In much the same way that courtiers had exclaimed that they would "seek out precedent" and "seek out traces," the creators of *engi* looked for signs of the divine and the past.[4] For instance, *Shozan engi,* which is extant in a single manuscript copied early in the thirteenth century, begins with the following lines: "On the mountains of great enlightenment, from the land where the Buddha was born. The provisional and the true: we have inquired into their traces and recorded this."[5] With this declaration, the compiler(s) cast their text as a compendium of traces, while also intimating that doctrinal truths (the provisional and true) would guide the way through a landscape permeated by awakening. Later in the same passage, they charged their readers, "You must seek out the traces of Zendō," an ancestral and perhaps mythical practitioner, "for they are precious."[6] Zendō's activities, presented in terms of sites he visited, recalled the foot-traced trails, hand-traced manuscripts, and sites sealed by heroic practitioners with which the regents had engaged. To seek out Zendō's traces meant not only to traverse the Ōmine Range but also to read about him in texts such as *Shozan engi.* Like the regents, *engi* readers and writers exploited the mutuality of walking and reading, convinced that both activities could bring the past into the present through the medium of traces.

Unlike the elite pilgrims of the mid-Heian period, the textual communities associated with Ōmine *engi* lodged explicit claims about the ritual use of their texts. Several accounts recursively cast *engi* as arbiters of legitimacy that should be ritually installed in a sacred precinct. One of six early Ōmine *engi* held by the Nagoya temple Shinpukuji, the *Kumano gongen kongō Zaō hōden zōkō nikki* (Journal of the founding of the treasure halls of the Kumano deities and Vajra Zaō), asserts that in 1070 men enshrined an *engi* at Hongū in Kumano: "they installed the

4. For the phrase "seek out precedent" (*rei o tazunu*), see, for instance, *Shōyūki,* Kankō 8.7.13 (2:182); and *Chūyūki,* Kanji 7.11.15 (1:249). The phrase "seek out traces" (*ato o tazunu*) was less common in elite lay discourse, but for a representative example, see chapter 3, notes 32–33.

5. *Shozan engi* (*NST,* 20:90, 342); cf. *Shōbodaisantō engi* (*SS,* 3:375).

6. *Shozan engi* (*NST,* 20:100, 346).

Ōmine engi in the fourth bay in the rear of the Shōjōden," the shrine for the deity Ketsumimiko. The text goes on to claim that when Retired Emperor Shirakawa arrived at Kumano twenty years later, he viewed this *Ōmine engi* and had his retainers read it to him. Furthermore, it attributes Shirakawa's 1092 Kinpusen pilgrimage to "karmic causes from the *Ōmine hon'engi* (Original Ōmine *engi*)," which he supposedly ordered read to him during his sojourn in the mountains.[7] As Kawasaki Tsuyoshi has shown, these claims are extremely dubious. The *Kumano gongen kongō Zaō hōden zōkō nikki* laced verifiable fact with rank invention in a textual confabulation calculated to represent *engi* as causes for royal pilgrimages and sacred objects in their own right.[8] It also characterized the audiences of *engi* as recipients of privileged knowledge and divine inspiration, while deftly appropriating temporal authority (elite pilgrims of the past) to verify its own claims. In texts like this, elite laymen continued to affect the imagined space of the mountains in the twelfth and thirteenth centuries, even though Kinpusen was no longer the focus of the regents' or retired emperors' devotions.

Rehearsals of lineages of transmission further enhanced the authority of *engi* and their textual communities. For example, according to the *Kumano sansho gongen Kinpusen kongō Zaō engi* (*Engi* of the three Kumano deities and Vajra Zaō of Kinpusen), another of the Shinpukuji texts, En no Gyōja and his mother each transmitted *engi* through a particular lineage. En's mother passed her *engi* down to the women of the Takagamo family, who transmitted it through four generations, and then transferred it to the women of a priestly family at Hongū's worship hall (*haiden*). After eight generations, these women transmitted the *engi* to four monastic figures (presumably, but not necessarily, male), after which it "was secreted in a bay behind the image of the

7. *Kumano gongen kongō Zaō hōden zōkō nikki* (8–10, 23–24). The other Shinpukuji texts are *Kumano sansho gongen Kinpusen kongō Zaō engi*; *Kumano sansho gongen Kinpusen kongō Zaō gokibun*; *Kumano sansho gongen Kinpu kongō Zaō kōka onkoto*; *Kumano sansho gongen ōji kenzoku kongō Zaō hon'i*; and *En no ubasoku no koto*. For an introduction to these texts, see Kawasaki, "*Kumano Kinpu Ōmine engishū* kaidai."

8. Kawasaki, "*Kumano gongen kongō Zaō hōden zōkō nikki* to iu gisho."

god (*mishōtai*) in the Shōjōden."[9] Although this narrative is unusual because it features a female line of descent, its ending is standard fare: an *engi* becomes the sacred property of a priestly group, proving that their transmission from a great founder-figure is indeed authentic.

Claims about the authority of *engi* went hand in hand with a rhetoric of secrecy. During the Middle Ages, literary lineages formed and split, and writers, interpreters, and transmitters of texts increasingly sought to limit access to, and thereby increase the prestige of, their literary capital.[10] Likewise, an ethos of exclusivity pervaded discussions of transmission in the *insei*-period Ōmine *engi*. The *Shozan engi* sounds a paradigmatic call to secrecy with a notation at the head of the manuscript that reads, "It is said that these *engi* must not be shown to laypeople."[11] Directions given in the *Kumano sansho gongen Kinpusen kongō Zaō engi* exemplify this concern and tie it to rites of transmission. After stipulating that initiates must be of a certain age, the text cautions:

> You may not transmit it inside your quarters. Put on a raincoat and a rain hat (*minokasa*) to transmit it. If you put on a raincoat and rain hat, you will see no demons (*daima*). If you do not put on a raincoat and rain hat, then you may not transmit it after all. If you do put on a raincoat and rain hat, then you may transmit it after all.[12]

The atmosphere here is not one of formal grandeur, but rather of furtive text swapping in the cold mountain air, with foul-weather gear as the only regalia. Notably, *minokasa* commonly appear in medieval literature as an attribute of outcasts and low-ranking religious figures. Some scholars have traced this association back to representations of

9. *Kumano sansho gongen Kinpusen kongō Zaō engi* (66–70). Dharma names are not explicitly gendered; however, none of those given in the text include the suffix *–ni,* commonly used for nuns.

10. For factionalism, privatization, and exclusivity as hallmarks of medieval poetry, see Huey, "Medievalization"; for secrecy in the transmission of literary knowledge, see Klein, *Allegories of Desire*. On secrecy in medieval religious culture, see Scheid and Teeuwen, *The Culture of Secrecy*.

11. *Shozan engi* (*NST,* 20:90, 342).

12. *Kumano sansho gongen Kinpusen kōngō Zaō engi* (51).

Susano'o, Amaterasu's volatile brother, who, according to classical myth, was cast out of the High Plain of Heaven.[13] Members of the *engi*'s community may thus have been representing themselves as social, as well as spatial, outsiders vis-à-vis the formal Dharma transmissions favored by established Buddhist lineages. In any event, the sense of threat here is striking. It is tempting to read the *daima* as demonized Kōfukuji hierarchs or other "civilized" interlopers, who, it was feared, might seize mountain practitioners' ritual patrimony, together with their administrative autonomy.

Rites of transmission and preservation took on a different valence as the creators of *engi* appropriated the gesture of interment, which had been so central to the observances of elite, eleventh-century pilgrims. In a famous litany of sites, the *Shozan engi* enumerates places in the mountains where sutras and other texts were supposedly buried or "installed" (*hōnō*).[14] In educating their audience in the proper treatment of *engi,* the creators of *Kumano sansho gongen Kinpusen kōngō Zaō engi* directed readers to keep two copies: one to be transmitted to others and one to be installed in a shrine. But, they cautioned, "when there are no people of capacity, you should send a memorial to the emperor and bury the *engi* in the earth. It will be a karmic cause for the emperor's protection."[15] With the trope of ritual installation, *engi* likened themselves to sutras, arrogating canonical status to themselves. Buried, they took on talismanic functions: like the *Benevolent Kings Sūtra* and other scriptures Michinaga and Moromichi had offered at Kinpusen, *engi* protected the state. Other passages claim that *engi* have been buried when no one is available to receive them.[16] These texts wait for the right audience, like Mahākāśyapa hidden within Wolf-Trace Mountain, or like Michinaga's Maitreyan scriptures buried at Kinpusen. *Engi* thus figured themselves as condensations of past practice that could be reactivated by rediscovery and reinterpretation. In the process, they laid the groundwork for future invention by ensuring

13. Bialock, "Outcasts, Emperorship," 258.

14. *Shozan engi* (*NST,* 20:91–102, 342–47).

15. *Kumano sansho gongen Kinpusen kōngō Zaō engi* (49). Note that the *engi* identifies this passage as a quotation from a text it calls *Gyōja no kibun*.

16. *Kumano sansho gongen Kinpusen kōngō Zaō engi* (65).

that creators of new texts could claim that they had in fact discovered ancient treasures.[17]

The valorization of *engi* as repositories for traces, signs of transmission, and secret treasures made them effective tools in crafting a distinctive religious identity for mountain practitioners. The emphasis on *engi* as a source of authority complemented two more investments that later became pivotal in Shugendō: the elevation of En no Gyōja as a founder, and the conviction that the mountains are uniquely effective sites for religious practice.

The Founding Hero and Spatial Soteriology

During the *insei* period, mountain practitioners laid claim to En no Gyōja in the same way that participants in scholastic traditions looked to their patriarchs as legitimating symbols. During his 1092 pilgrimage to Kinpusen, Masafusa had characterized the area in front of the mountaintop Zaō Hall as "En no Gyōja's traces of the Way," thereby providing definitive evidence that by the end of the twelfth century En had been accepted as one of Kinpusen's founders (see chapter 7). Soon thereafter, En was established as Zaō's theurge: the compilers of *Konjaku monogatarishū* commented that En had "brought forth" the "bodhisattva Zaō of Kinpusen."[18] In the ensuing hundred-odd years, *engi* mediated a dramatic expansion in En's roles in narrative and ritual.

Perhaps the most important aspect of En's persona was that he was not, properly speaking, a monk. Widely referred to in *engi* as an *ubasoku,* En lent his imprimatur to religious practitioners who lacked conventionally accepted credentials like full ordination or authorized Dharma transmissions. Building on stock elements in En's earlier biographies, such as his ability to compel gods or his sojourn among immortals in China, Ōmine *engi* elaborated substantially upon his career.

17. *Engi,* in this respect, are comparable to Tibetan gTer-ma (treasure) texts (see Gyatso, "The Logic of Legitimation"; and Aris, *Hidden Treasures and Secret Lives*).

18. *Konjaku monogatarishū* 11.3 (*SNKBT,* 35:17). This was *not* an element in En's earlier biographies.

Some claimed that he had undergone seven rebirths in Japan, over the course of which he literally grew in stature, eventually reaching nine feet in height. While practicing in the mountains, he was said to have encountered his own skeleton from one of these past lives. The skeleton held ritual implements (a vajra, a sword, and/or a bell). In laying hold of these, En performed an auto-transmission, passing symbols of ritual knowledge from himself to himself.[19] Other accounts vested him with divinely conferred authority. According to the *Mino'odera engi,* which likely dates to the mid-twelfth century and focuses on Mino'o, located at the northern limit of present-day Ōsaka (see map 3), En received an esoteric initiation (*kanjō*) from Nagārjuna (Ryūju bosatsu) and Benzaiten in a dream.[20] This direct conferral of esoteric Buddhist expertise bypassed monastic hierarchies, putting En on par with more conventionally learned patriarchs. At the limits of En's persona, other *engi* went so far as to identify him with Hōki, a bodhisattva who features in the eighty-fascicle translation of the *Flower Ornament Sūtra.* Combining spatial transposition with deification, a passage in the *Shozan engi* asserted, "Of old, this practitioner," namely En, "was a holy man of Yamato Province; now, he is the third immortal in the great country of Tang and Hōki bodhisattva of Vajra Mountain (Kongōzan)." In this case, Kongōzan figured simultaneously as Hōki's dwelling in the *Flower Ornament Sūtra* and the highest peak in the Katsuragi Range.[21]

With En in place as a founder figure, Ōmine *engi* framed an outlook in which overseers faded from view while otherwise obscure *yamabushi* came into focus. In contrast to their pronounced silence with respect to overseers from Kōfukuji or Onjōji, these *engi* often rehearsed lineages for both ritual and textual transmissions among mountain practitioners. Such lineages ranged in scope, sometimes reaching more than a hundred names.[22] Whatever their historical veracity, these lists

19. *Shozan engi* (*NST,* 20:131–34, 359–60); cf. *Daibodaisantō engi* (126–27). This episode was later adapted for visual representation in illustrated handscrolls (see images from *Taimadera engi* reproduced in Nara Kokuritsu Hakubutuskan, *Taimadera,* 45).

20. Kawasaki, "Reizan no jikū no saikōsaku."

21. *Shozan engi* (*NST,* 20:136, 362). On En, Hōki, and Katsuragi, see Kawasaki, "Inseiki ni okeru Yamato," 411–15, and "Nihonkoku 'Kongōzan' setsu."

22. See, for instance, *Kumano sansho gongen Kinpusen kongō Zaō engi* (58–64).

served to delimit an imagined community for whom particular sites came to symbolize acts of transmission. Jinzen, a small saddle in the mountains two days' walk south of Kinpusen, was especially important in this respect. *Kanjō* initiations were held there from the Kamakura period onward, making it an important site for lineage production.[23] According to the sixteenth section of *Shozan engi,* manuscripts of other *engi* featuring narratives on En's career were enshrined in a three-tiered cave at Jinzen. In the corner of the cave where (according to the *engi*) the *engi* were kept, "one draws near to a stone wall bearing the characteristic marks of the Gyōja's likeness (*miei*)." The term *miei* is commonly used to designate Buddhist patriarch portraits, which instantiate lineage visually and ritually. This particular image "was transferred onto the stone and left like a seal"; in other words, En's likeness from his nine-foot incarnation was fixed upon the wall of the cave as clearly as if it had been printed onto paper.[24] Both quasi-textual and physical, this trace was supposed to make En present for his followers as they worked to construct their own lines of ritual descent.

With his adoption as patriarch, En's range expanded geographically. Whereas early and mid-Heian narratives had connected him to Katsuragi and, to a lesser extent, Kinpusen, the *Kumano kyūki* (Ancient records of Kumano), which was copied in 1237 but likely first compiled in the late 1100s, had En embark upon a pilgrimage to Kumano along the route used by retired emperors. This account is echoed in *Shozan engi* and the Ninnaji version of *Kumano engi,* another composite text from the mid-1200s.[25] Meanwhile, En was appropriated at Mt. Kasagi in the northeastern corner of the Nara Basin, and as time wore on, he also became a founder at sites much farther afield, in Kantō, Tōhoku, Kyūshū, and Shikoku.[26]

23. *Jinzen kanjō hiki* and *Jinzen kanjō keifu.*

24. *Shozan engi* (*NST,* 7:132, 360); cf. *Shōbodaisantō engi* (*SS,* 3:370).

25. The *Kumano kyūki* remains unpublished. On this and the *Kumano engi,* see Kawasaki, *Ōmine no kuden, engi,* 20–24. For the latter text, see Kawasaki, "*Kumano engi*: kaidai, honkoku."

26. For Kasagi, see discussion below. For other locations, see *En no gyōja hongi,* which was likely compiled during the Muromachi period; for translations from and discussion of this text, see Earhart, "Shugendō, Traditions, and Influence," 201–5; and Miyake Hitoshi, *Shugendō soshiki no kenkyū,* 514–40.

While En lent an imagined, temporal depth to the emergent traditions of *yamabushi*, developments in what I have called spatial soteriology established a theoretical basis for ritual practice in the mountains. By the late eleventh century, elite pilgrims had already begun to conceive of Kinpusen, and then Kumano, as places of enlightenment, and of the route through the mountains as the bodhisattva path (see chapter 4). During the 1100s and 1200s, the creators of *engi* applied a more complex spatial schema to the Ōmine region, representing the mountains as esoteric Buddhist mandalas. The most famous example of this type of mandalization occurs in the first section of *Shozan engi*, with parallels in *Daibodaisantō engi*. This passage correlates 119 sites, referred to as "peaks" (*mine*), to deities in the Matrix Mandala, and another twenty-one to the Vajra Mandala.[27] In both cases, the *engi* represent only a portion of the mandala's deities, but the structure of the text makes the spatial schema quite clear. The first several peaks illustrate the overall tenor of the passage.

> The initial gate to the Matrix (on the left side and the right side):
>
> First, on the left side, the Peak of Nanba, the Unassailable Celestial. They say this mountain is called the first perfection, [namely, generosity]. They say the holy man Kaisen (n.d.) carried a sutra for a long time in Hōki Province and enshrined it here; it is the holy man's *Flower Ornament Sūtra*.
>
> Likewise, on the right side, the place of Taimenten, the Facing Celestial. A place where celestials gather. *The Treatise Explaining the Ten Stages* is enshrined here. Five copies of a sutra copied in accord with the Dharma were offered.
>
> The Peak of Nanda. The *Sūtra on the Contemplation of the Buddha of Measureless Life* is enshrined here. It was due to a revelation by Erin (n.d.), the envoy for Emperor Tenji (626–71; r. 668–71). The holy man Saien (n.d.) placed a *Lotus Sūtra* copied in accord with the Dharma here. There are four copies of another sutra. Kangyō (n.d.) dedicated these. The *Sūtra of Golden Light* is enshrined here. The novice Jōsai (n.d.) put one copy of the sutra into the spur at Kokawa. The holy man Jūsai (n.d.), a man of Mikawa Province, enshrined a sutra copied in accord with the Dharma here. In the tenth month of the sixth year of the Ninpei era,

27. *Shozan engi* (*NST*, 7:90–102, 342–47); *Daibodaisantō engi* (121–26). For more sustained discussions, see Miyake Hitoshi, *Ōmine shugendō no kenkyū*, 287–302; Grapard, "Flying Mountains"; and Roth, "Where Mountains Fly."

Kūkaku, the tonsured Retired Emperor [Toba], enshrined a sutra here that had been copied in accord with the Dharma in the capital.[28]

The list of peaks continues in the same vein for more than a hundred additional entries.

While the list mandalizes the mountains, the annotations embark on a complementary project to historicize and textualize them. Most of the geographic sites mentioned would be impossible to locate without additional knowledge, many of the deities play minor roles in the mandala, and the majority of the holy men are unheard of beyond the confines of the text. This emphasis on the obscure may point to the real, social contours of the community who created this part of *Shozan engi*; however, references to eminent men, such as Retired Emperor Toba or Erin, indicate that at root, the *engi* was engaged in a strategy of specification. The text insisted that it was not simply that hundreds of men had recognized the mountains as mandala, but rather that each of them, regardless of his status, had left particular traces as testimony. Capitalizing on the popularity of sutra burial, *engi* such as this one maintained that pilgrims both noble and humble had enshrined, emplaced, or buried scriptures throughout the Ōmine Range. Inasmuch as these textual emplacements cannot be verified (and many may in fact have been fabricated), *engi* played a crucial role in creating textual presence. Once a scripture was buried, whether in reality or imagination, it was hidden away, rendering the *engi* its only perceptible trace.

Mandalization, and by extension the textualization used to validate it, drew heavily on esoteric Buddhist theory. At the beginning of the Heian period, Kūkai had formally introduced esoteric Buddhism to Japan, teaching practitioners to participate in the enlightening activity

28. Sutras copied according to the Dharma (*nyohōkyō*) were produced according to stringent ritual prescriptions. The Ninpei era only lasted for four years (1151–54): there was no Ninpei 6. References for the scriptures are as follows. *Da fangguang fo huayan jing*, *T.* 278 (9:395–788); *Foshuo guan wulianshoufo jing* (*Sūtra on the Contemplation of the Buddha of Measureless Life*; J. *Bussetsu kan muryōjubutsu kyō*), *T.* 365 (12:340–46); *Shizhu piposha lun* (*Treatise Explaining the Ten Stages*; J. *Jūjū bisha ron*), *T.* 1521 (26:20–122); *Miaofa lianhua jing*, *T.* 262 (9:1–62); *Jinguangming zuishengwang jing*, *T.* 665 (16:403–56). Small type represents interlineal annotations.

of the buddhas by using mandala, *mudrā*, and mantra.[29] His phrase "becoming a buddha in this very body" (*sokushin jōbutsu*) referred to the instantaneous enlightenment available to esoteric adepts. To argue for the possibility of becoming a buddha here and now, Kūkai was wont to reinterpret statements about time in terms of the spatial order of mandala. For instance, the *Sūtra on Vairocana's Samādhi Rite for the Practice of the Yoga of the Vajra Summit,* a short ritual text used in Japan and traditionally attributed to Vajrabodhi (671–741), states that "after sixteen births," those who recite mantras assiduously "will attain complete awakening."[30] Kūkai maintained that instead of referring to the long process of being reborn sixteen times, this phrase actually "indicates the sixteen great bodhisattvas."[31] With this interpretive move, he departed from a conventional, literal, and temporal reading of scripture in favor of a hermeneutic emphasis on spatialization and embodiment. The sixteen great bodhisattvas, who are arrayed around the four wisdom buddhas in the Vajra Mandala, personify the virtues of the enlightenment of the cosmic buddha Mahāvairocana. In the mandala rites advocated by Kūkai, the practitioner travels ritually through the mandala, which is to say the cosmos. In passing through the bodhisattvas' places, Kūkai suggested, one shares in their wisdom, undergoing a mental and physical reconfiguration in order to become (like) them. Several lines further into his commentary, Kūkai noted, "You should understand that your own body becomes the adamantine Vajra Realm." The practitioner thus comes to embody the mandala's enlightened and enlightening order, thereby becoming a buddha in this very body. *Engi* sounded very similar themes, but in a vernacular, geographical idiom.

According to Ōmine *engi,* the fact that the mountains are mandalas makes religious practice there both expedient and effective. The *Kumano sansho gongen Kinpusen kongō Zaō engi* comments: "As for

29. Abé, *The Weaving of Mantra*; see also Hakeda, *Kūkai: Major Works.*

30. *Jingangding jing yuqie xiuxi piluzhena sanmodi fa* (*Vairocana's Samādhi Rite for the Practice of the Yoga of the Vajra Summit Sūtra*; J. *Kongōchōgyō yuga shujū birushana sanmaji hō*), *T.* 876 (18:331b8).

31. *Sokushin jōbutsugi* (506; for an alternative translation, see Hakeda, *Kūkai: Major Works,* 226; or Giebel and Todaro, *Shingon Texts,* 65).

Dainichi-dake, it is the Womb and the Vajra [Mandalas]. Because it is the ground of both realms, it is called Dainichi-dake, Mahāvairocana's Peak. Therefore it is the sacred ground where one becomes a buddha in this very body; it is a place to practice Mahāyāna repentance."[32] Because this particular peak, which is located just south of Jinzen, is the place of the cosmic buddha, it instantiates the entirety of the twofold mandala, allowing one who practices there to enter spatially into Mahāvairocana's enlightenment. In a subsequent passage, the same text explicitly refers to a ritual-cum-spatial compression of time: "three times," that is, three stints of practice in the mountains, "makes a first incalculable eon (*sōgi*), six times makes a second incalculable eon, and nine times makes a third incalculable eon."[33] In other words, practitioners who have made nine ritual pilgrimages through the Ōmine Range have completed the three incalculable eons of religious practice conventionally deemed necessary for one to become a buddha. Not only do the mountains provide a space of and for enlightenment according to the *engi*, but they also compress time.

The effects of this sort of advocacy were not limited to the space of the mountains. During the twelfth and thirteenth centuries, the southern mountains drew the attention of a growing range of religious practitioners. Among them were eminent clerics associated with Kōfukuji and the Nara revival. These men sought to incorporate the Ōmine Range into their own regional landscape.

Engi *and the Yamato Landscape*

During the Nara revival, clerics both eminent and obscure founded and reconstructed numerous temples in the mountains ringing the Nara Basin, thereby creating a new, real-and-imagined mountainscape. Saidaiji-affiliated *vinaya* practitioners are perhaps the best-known such renovators, but Kōfukuji hierarchs, including men who served as Kinpusen overseers, also turned their hands to (re)establishing

32. *Kumano sansho gongen Kinpusen kongō Zaō engi* (56–57).

33. Ibid. (58).

religious sites in the Yamato mountains.[34] In particular, the Katsuragi Range, which runs along the western edge of the Nara Basin, was targeted for Kōfukuji-led construction projects, as was Mt. Kasagi in the northeastern corner of Yamato. As a textual effect of institutional development, *engi* represented these areas as centers for dedicated mountain practice and then linked them via narrative and symbol to the Ōmine Range.

At 288 meters, by most measures Mt. Kasagi is more a hill than a mountain, but its accessibility made it all the more attractive to Yamato monks looking to augment their regimens with mountain practice. Like Kinpusen, Kasagi was associated with Maitreya: a monumental image of the bodhisattva had been carved into a cliff face there, clearly visible to approaching pilgrims.[35] Given that Michinaga visited the temple during his 1007 *sōjin* preparations, it is possible that Kasagidera already had some connection to Kinpusen by that time. In any event, Mt. Kasagi's circumstances changed dramatically in the context of the Nara revival.

Jōkei (1155–1213), an eminent Kōfukuji-trained monk, helped to recreate Kasagidera as a Kōfukuji-controlled mountain center beginning in the 1190s.[36] Famous for his doctrinal erudition and liturgical creativity, Jōkei moved from Kōfukuji to Kasagidera in 1192. Although this move is often seen as an intentional retreat from the distractions of life at a powerful temple, after arriving at Kasagi, Jōkei put significant effort into making his new home a bustling center in its own right. In fund-raising appeals targeting commoners and courtiers, he touted a wide range of practices, including *nenbutsu,* the contemplation of Maitreya, recitation of *dhāraṇī,* study of the *Lotus Sūtra,* and the worship of relics.[37] Importantly, devotion to Zaō was also part of this mix. In ded-

34. On Saidaiji, see Andreeva, "Saidaiji Monks"; and Miyake Hitoshi, *Shugendō soshiki no kenkyū,* 738–55. For a broad examination of Kōfukuji's involvement in mountain centers, see Royall Tyler, "Kōfukuji and the Mountains." For Kōfukuji-led projects, see Kawasaki, "Inseiki ni okeru Yamato."

35. *Midō kanpakuki,* Kanji 4.6.8 (1:222); Brock, "Awaiting Maitreya at Kasagi."

36. For this stage of Jōkei's career, see Ford, *Jōkei and Buddhist Devotion,* esp. 22–25; and Quinter, "Invoking the Mother." For Kasagi, see Goodwin, *Alms and Vagabonds,* 46–66.

37. Goodwin, *Alms and Vagabonds,* 51–56.

icating the Perfection of Wisdom Platform (Hannya dai), a six-story pagoda that defined the section of the temple where Jōkei lived, he wrote, "Making a vow, I entrust this precinct in perpetuity to the Great Ise Shrine, to the bodhisattva Hachiman, to the Great Kasuga Deity, and to Zaō of Kinpusen."[38] This roster of deities had a pronounced spatial cast: whereas Kasuga (and by extension Kōfukuji) represented the center of Yamato, Kasagi and Kinpusen marked the province's northern and southern limits. To the east, Jōkei connected the domain of his new home temple to the royal shrine at Ise, and to the north, to the Hachiman shrine at Iwashimizu, which also had strong royal associations. There is no known evidence that Jōkei himself traveled to Kinpusen, but he was certainly active in the boom in vernacular liturgy, intertemple networking, and pilgrimage that characterized the religious culture of the Nara revival.[39]

After its renovation by Jōkei and his companions, Mt. Kasagi was featured among the "many mountains" celebrated in *Shozan engi.* "Ichidai-no-mine engi" (*Engi* of Single-Lifetime Peak), the nineteenth section of the compilation, explicitly sought to establish Mt. Kasagi as an extension of the southern mountains.[40] The text's creators stated that Kinpusen instantiates the Vajra Mandala, and Kasagi the Susiddhi Mandala, which is often used in Tendai-inflected esotericism to complement the Vajra-and-Matrix set emphasized in Shingon.[41] After signaling that Kinpusen and Kasagi form an integrated, mandalized territory, the "Ichidai-no-mine engi" asserted that their mutual identity went all the way back to India and up to heaven. According to the *engi,* Kasagi, like Kinpusen, is in fact a corner of Gṛdhrakūṭa; furthermore, while "that Kinpusen is the inner mansion of Tuṣita Heaven; this Single-Lifetime Peak of Kasagi is the outer mansion of Tuṣita Heaven."[42] The

38. Dedication for the Hannya-dai at Kasagidera, attr. Jōkei, dated Kenkyū 6.11.19, in *Sanbutsujō shō* (98).

39. On mobility in the Nara revival, see, for instance, Chikamoto, "Bunji kara Kenkyū e"; Andreeva, "Saidaiji Monks"; and Glassman, *The Face of Jizō,* 84–92.

40. Chikamoto, "Kujōke-bon shoji engishū," esp. 36–38.

41. Though the text includes no explicit geographical analogue for the Matrix Mandala, the overall structure and content of the *Shozan engi* suggest that in this case the Matrix was meant to be identified with Kumano.

42. *Shozan engi* (*NST,* 20:136–38, 361–62).

message was quite clear: Kasagi, controlled by Kōfukuji and located at the northern end of the Nara Basin, was in fact coextensive with Kinpusen.

A familiar cast of characters further strengthened this imagined spatial linkage. In line with other passages in *Shozan engi*, "Ichidai-no-mine engi" represented En no Gyōja as a founder-figure. It also featured a detailed account of Nichizō, the holy man famous for having died and come back to life at Kinpusen (see chapter 1). According to "Ichidai-no-mine engi," "the renunciant Nichizō, resident of Tsubakidera at Kinpusen in the country of Japan" performed the "secret rites" of the threefold (Vajra, Matrix, and Susiddhi) mandalas for thirty-five days in a cave at Kasagi. When a celestial told him of a pool below the cave, Nichizō was so inspired that he peeled off his skin and inscribed the threefold mandala upon it. He then entered a dragon hole in "Ākāśagarbha's cavern." Arriving thence at Mahāvairocana's palace, Nichizō encountered celestial lads who informed him that he had reached the outer mansion of Tuṣita Heaven. Thereupon he installed his threefold mandala in the cavern heaven.

This brief, visionary account sounded themes familiar from the version of Nichizō's dream record preserved in the *Fusō ryakki*. As at Kinpusen, Nichizō performed mandala rites, passed through death (symbolized by peeling off his skin), and traveled through the mountain to a heavenly realm, where he had a revelatory encounter with a deity. By the time the *Shozan engi* was copied in the 1200s, Nichizō had become a stock character well known for his connections to Zaō, Kinpusen, mountain austerities, and travel to other realms.[43] His presence at Mt. Kasagi could only enhance that mountain's reputation, as well as its (and, by extension, Kōfukuji's) ties to the southern mountains.

Like Kasagi, the Katsuragi Range was targeted for development by Kōfukuji monks and adopted as one of the "many mountains" described in *Shozan engi*. By the late eighth century, Katsuragi had already become famous as the haunt of En no Gyōja. Although the institutional history of the area remains hazy, we know that *yamabushi* were active there by the mid-eleventh century, and that a project to construct a

43. For Nichizō in the Kamakura period, see, for instance, the portion of the Metropolitan Museum of Art *Kitano tenjin engi emaki* illustrated in fig. 2.2.

temple at Kongōzan (1,125 m), the southernmost peak in the range, was under way by the early thirteenth.[44] As Kawasaki Tsuyoshi has noted, the leader of this project was likely Gaen (1138–1223), a monk who served as Kōfukuji steward an unprecedented four times. Gaen was an intimate of Retired Emperor Go-Toba; not surprisingly, he also seems to have been close to Jōkei, who is the probable author of a prayer for a dedication of two halls at Kongōzan during the Kennin era (1201–4).[45] This prayer connected Kongōzan with Kōfukuji when it stated, "This shrine originally faced north, with the intent of protecting Hossō," the school of Buddhist thought for which Kōfukuji is best known, "and reinforcing the foundations of imperial rule." After explaining that when it was reconstructed, the hall had been reoriented toward the east (that is, toward Kōfukuji), the dedication echoed *engi* by identifying Hōki bodhisattva with En no Gyōja.[46] En was thus repurposed as a protector of Kōfukuji's domain.

Katsuragi, reenvisioned and redeveloped by Nara revivalists from Kōfukuji, featured alongside Kinpusen, Kumano, and Mt. Kasagi in *Shozan engi.* The text's thirteenth section, "Denbōrinsan" (Turning-the-Dharma-Wheel Mountain), applies a novel rubric to the Katsuragi Range, itemizing ninety-five sites in the mountains and presenting them as a territorial instantiation of scripture.[47] According to this passage, En no Gyōja imprinted the *Lotus Sūtra* in the earth when he traversed the Katsuragi Range: "As the *gyōja* walked and walked, beneath his feet were 69,384 characters," the traditional word-count for the sutra.[48] These textual-cum-bodily traces were said to be distributed, chapter by chapter, among stations (*shuku*) in the mountains. Afuridera, the first site in the "Denbōrinsan" litany, was home to "the Introductory Chapter in 4,082 characters." In turn, "the first station," also identified as Hachiman or Hato no Tomari, was defined by "the Chapter

44. For En no Gyōja, see chapter 1; for the mid-Heian, see *Shin sarugakuki* (*NST,* 8:147–48, 305).

45. Kawasaki, "Inseiki ni okeru Yamato," 411–16, and "Nihonkoku 'Kongōzan' setsu," 18–19.

46. Dedication for Kongōzanji, attr. Jōkei, n.d., in *Sanbutsujō shō* (95); cf. note 21.

47. *Shozan engi* (*NST,* 20:117–29, 353–58).

48. *Shozan engi* (*NST,* 20:117, 353).

on Skillful Means in 4,854 characters."[49] This spatio-textual schema has persisted down to the present day: twenty-eight *Lotus Sūtra* mounds, one for each chapter in the Kumārajīva translation, serve as stations for ritual observances in the mountains.[50]

At the same time that the localization of the *Lotus Sūtra* proved to be immensely compelling, it created a tension by setting the scripturalized Katsuragi Range apart from the mandalized terrains of Kinpusen, Kumano, and Kasagi. Efforts at mediating this disparity are apparent in claims that Katsuragi's sites doubled as the haunts of deities familiar from the Ōmine area. For instance, one "Denbōrinsan" passage maintains that "Stone Zaō Mountain" is located near Katsuragi's station fifty-one, where there are many dragon holes. Not only do the interlinear annotations stipulate that this site is associated with the "1,163 characters" of the "Dharma Masters Chapter" in the *Lotus Sūtra*, but they also inform the reader that this "is the place where Zaō will spring forth."[51] The *Shozan engi* thus assured its audiences that Katsuragi and Kinpusen were home to the same gods and the same founder-figures. By implication, their human communities overlapped as well.

The mountains imagined in *Shozan engi* did indeed form a real, interconnected mountainscape in the practice of historical individuals. The activities of Chōgen (1121–1206), best known for his work raising funds for the reconstruction of Nara temples in the wake of the Genpei War, are illustrative in this respect. Chōgen epitomized the peripatetic tendencies of many of his contemporaries. After beginning his career at Daigoji, he traveled to China and northeastern Japan. According to *Namu Amida butsu sazenshū* (Anthology of the good works of Namu Amida Butsu), an autobiography or biography written by Chōgen or his close associates, he undertook practice (*shugyō*) in Ōmine five times, beginning when he was nineteen years old, that is, around 1140.[52] Three times he undertook sutra-copying projects "deep

49. *Shozan engi* (*NST*, 20:117–18, 353).

50. On the religious landscape of the Katsuragi mountains, see Miyake Hitoshi, *Shugendō shisō no kenkyū*, 330–59.

51. *Shozan engi* (*NST*, 20:122, 355).

52. *Namu Amida butsu sazenshū*, 321.

in the mountains"; in addition, "twice he arranged for specialists in the *Lotus Sūtra* to recite the scripture a thousand times in the peaks. They began at Kumano and chanted 'they paid their respects and departed,' the [last] phrase [of the sutra], at Mitake," that is, at Kinpusen. The account goes on to add, "He also recited one thousand copies of the *Lotus Sūtra* at Katsuragi, twice."[53] In treating Chōgen's activities at Kumano, Kinpusen, and Katsuragi as complementary elements belonging to a single category, *Namu amida butsu sazenshū* affirmed connections asserted in *Shozan engi.* Importantly, inscriptional evidence shows that Chōgen took an interest in Kasagidera, too: he donated a bell to that temple in 1196.[54] In both imagination and practice, then, participants in the Nara revival were linking the southern mountains to Yamato's home ranges.

Manuscript Histories

The material careers of Ōmine *engi* show that networks extending into the lowlands were crucial to the production and preservation of these texts. Among known manuscripts, not one has been preserved in the mountains; instead, early Ōmine *engi* were archived at power-bloc temples, their branches, or regional centers. Several examples help to illustrate this point. The *Daibodaisantō engi,* a text that parallels portions of *Shozan engi,* has been preserved at Matsuodera (see map 3), which was a center for the Tōzan Shugendō network from the Muromachi into the Edo period (1603–1867). Given that the temple was one of Kōfukuji's branch-temples in the Middle Ages, it is not surprising that the *Daibodaisantō engi* contains a significant number of references to men associated with Kōfukuji.[55] Meanwhile, the Dharma princes who held the abbacies of Ninnaji, a powerful temple located slightly northwest

53. Ibid., 321. For the last phrase of the *Lotus Sūtra,* see *T.* 262 (9:62a29). John Rosenfield's translation overlooks the allusion to the text of the *Lotus* (Rosenfield, *Portraits of Chōgen,* 224).

54. Ford, *Jōkei and Buddhist Devotion,* 23.

55. For information on the manuscript, see *Shugendō shiryōshū,* 2:749–53. For Matsuodera, see Suzuki Shōei, *Shugen kyōdan,* esp. 237–67.

of the Heian capital (see map 3), also took an interest in the southern mountains. Shukaku (1150–1202), the son of Emperor Go-Shirakawa, collected ritual texts about Kumano; today, Ninnaji's archives include the *Kumano kyūki*, *Kumano engi*, and *Kinpusen hon'engi* (The original Kinpusen *engi*), all of which may be considered Ōmine *engi*.[56] Another important group of texts is held by the regional temple Shinpukuji, located in contemporary Nagoya. As a result of manuscript-collection projects spearheaded by the Shingon monk Nōshin (1291–1354), the temple accrued a substantial library that is extremely well preserved. Along with sacred works from the Shingon school, texts related to Ise Shintō, and Chinese classics, Shinpukuji monks collected *engi* about Kumano and Kinpusen during the fourteenth century.[57] As these examples show, *engi* were mobile texts. Whereas their content suggests that they were created in reaction to the subordination of the southern mountains, their manuscript histories demonstrate that they circulated in lowland, even metropolitan, contexts.

The clearest example of the dynamics of socio-spatial interchange in the dissemination of *engi* is, once again, the hybrid, composite *Shozan engi*. The final colophon in the single extant manuscript states that it was copied by Keisei (1189–1268), a man of broad energies and interests. Keisei traveled to China, founded his own temple in the mountains west of Kyoto, and was an avid collector of manuscripts. He maintained relationships with leading exponents of the Nara revival, copying texts held by Jōkei and writing to Myōe (1173–1232). He also participated in post-Genpei renovation efforts at Hōryūji and retained close ties with Onjōji through his ordination lineage.[58]

Keisei's ties to prominent monastics appear to have been matched by his connections to a powerful natal family. He was likely the son of the regent Fujiwara (Kujō) no Yoshitsune (1169–1206), and thus the older brother of Kujō Michiie (1193–1252), a regent in his own right and

56. See note 25. On the *Kinpusen hon'engi*, see *Shugendō shiryōshū*, 2:748–49.

57. For an introduction to Shinpukuji's history and illustrations of some of its manuscripts, see Nagoyashi Hakubutsukan and Shinpukuji Ōsu Bunko Chōsa Kenkyūkai, *Ōsu Kannon*. For the *engi*, see *Kumano Kinpu Ōmine engishū*.

58. Horiike, *Nanto bukkyōshi no kenkyū*, 2:182–97; Shiba and Tonami, "Keisei to Onjōji," and "Keisei *Kondō honbutsu shūjiki*; Chikamoto, "Nanto fukkō."

father to the fourth Kamakura shogun.[59] In fact, Michiie and Keisei were quite close: when Michiie took the tonsure, Keisei served as his preceptor, and when Michiie fell ill, Keisei wrote about him in *Hirasan kojin reitaku* (Oracles from an old man of Mt. Hira). Keisei's family relationships are further borne out by the fact that more than twenty manuscripts from his collection, including the *Shozan engi,* have been preserved in the archives of the Kujō house.[60] Importantly, several of Keisei's relatives on his father's side held the office of overseer of Kumano or Kinpusen. Ryōson (1189–1246), who was probably Keisei's half brother, was pivotal in solidifying Onjōji's monopoly on the office of Kumano overseer in the mid-1200s.[61] Furthermore, Shin'en and Jisson, who were likely Keisei's great-uncle and second cousin, served as Kinpusen overseers in the early 1200s (see chapter 7).

Thus, Keisei was copying the *Shozan engi* at roughly the same time that his blood relatives were asserting administrative control over the southern mountains and his monastic acquaintances were redeveloping Kasagi and Katsuragi. That a man with such strong connections to the Fujiwara regents, the Nara revival, and the overseers of Kinpusen and Kumano reproduced the best-known Ōmine *engi* testifies to the shared nature of representations of Kinpusen and its surrounding mountainscapes.

Conclusion

The Ōmine *engi* that came into circulation during the twelfth and thirteenth centuries evinced a set of distinctive concerns, namely, interest in En no Gyōja as a founder-figure, fully developed spatial soteriology, and assertions of *yamabushi* authority. With respect to Kinpusen, Kōfukuji's lordship and the Nara revival were key factors in structuring

59. For Keisei's biography, see Hashimoto Shinkichi, *Denki tenseki,* 152–90; Hirabayashi, "Keisei shōnin denkō hoi"; and Kobayashi, "Keisei." For Keisei's activities in Nara, see previous note; and Chikamoto, "Nanto fukkō."

60. *Fushimi no Miyake Kujōke kyūzō shoji engishū.*

61. Sakai, "Chūsei Onjōji no monzeki," 72–77.

the articulation and dissemination of these sensibilities. Whereas some mountain practitioners surely strove to limit, or even deny, the influence of power-bloc institutions over the southern mountains, administrative ties and religious ferment made physical and textual exchange easy, perhaps even unavoidable. *Engi* should thus be read as discursive effects of the institutional reconfiguration of Kinpusen and the Yamato landscape discussed in chapter 7.

The project to construct *engi* as sources of authority was so successful that these texts recursively influenced the real, institutional landscape. This made them objects of desire in both mountain and lowland contexts. In an intriguing case studied by Kawasaki Tsuyoshi, during the 1180s a certain Gyōshun (n.d.) used a text referred to as the *Ōmine engi* as evidence in a dispute with Kōfukuji about land in the Katsuragi district of Yamato. Although it is not clear which party emerged victorious, the duration of Gyōshun's case indicates that his claims were compelling enough to withstand any effort at summary dismissal. Not only did Gyōshun himself became well known as an *engi* owner, but his bid for independence also inspired the creation of other Ōmine *engi*. As Kawasaki has shown, the Ōmine *engi* held by Shinpukuji were created by writers who knew about Gyōshun's text(s). It was because members of the monastic establishment at Kōfukuji and other great lowland temples recognized the suasive and even talismanic powers of such *engi* that they turned their hands to producing and collecting them.[62]

At the same time that Ōmine *engi* were being circulated, religious practitioners were physically crossing back and forth between the mountains and lowland monasteries.[63] In some cases, these moves were seasonal shifts; in others, they were integrated into a peripatetic lifestyle. The famous *vinaya* advocate Eison (1201–90) does not appear to have had a hand in the circulation of Ōmine *engi*, but his career does show that leading exponents of the Nara revival continued to be involved with the Yoshino-Kinpusen area into the late Kamakura period. Eison wrote in his autobiography that he visited Kinpusen during his travels in 1272, conferring "the bodhisattva precepts on 1721 people at

62. Kawasaki, "Inseiki ni okeru Yamato," esp. 407–11, and "*Kumano Kinpu Ōmine engishū* kaidai," 221–24.

63. Ueda, *Shugen to nenbutsu*, esp. 99–111.

the Lecture Hall" and instituting abstention rules, such as prohibitions on the taking of life, in over fifty villages in Kinpusen's domain.[64] A well-known wood sculpture depicting Shōtoku Taishi, which dates to 1274 and is now enshrined in the Yoshinoyama Zaō Hall, was almost certainly created in conjunction with Eison's activities in the area.[65] This image's ongoing location in Zaō's home place serves as a reminder that interactions between Kinpusen and the Nara Basin were reciprocal, not one-sided. Revivalists like Chōgen might come to the mountains to practice austerities; by the same token, local residents also participated in trends like the *vinaya* revival, which began in lowland circles. The creation and preservation of extant *engi* were rooted in these exchanges, as was the emergence of Shugendō, a process that forms the subject of the epilogue to this book.

64. *Kongō busshi Eison kanshingaku shōki,* Bun'ei 9, third month (38). Judging from the scale of the rite and the fact that Eison was in his seventies, it seems likely that he was referring to a lecture hall at Yoshinoyama, not the peak of Kinpusen.

65. For a photographic reproduction, see, for instance, Ōsaka Shiritsu Bijutsukan, *Inori no michi,* pl. 268.

Epilogue

The Rise of Shugendō

Kinpusen, together with the Ōmine region as a whole, is often touted as the cradle of Shugendō. As a consequence, many interpreters have generated teleological accounts in which earlier practice at the mountain features as a form of proto-Shugendō. By contrast, the aim of this book has been to reposition events surrounding Kinpusen within the context of the more general religious and political history of the Heian period. Thus, my analysis has centered on how regency- and *insei*-period pilgrims engaged with Kinpusen and how the aftereffects of their actions further transformed the mountain. In order to address the ongoing influence of Shugendō on perceptions of Kinpusen's past, this book closes with a brief treatment of that movement's emergence and growth, as well as an assessment of its impact on current representational practices.

Although Shugendō maintained a consistent focus on ascetically inflected mountain pilgrimage, it evinced substantial variation as it spread across Japan from the Middle Ages into the early-modern period.[1] Shugendō is often traced back to the activities of Heian pilgrims and holy men, and yet historical research has shown that the earliest evidence for its conceptualization as an independent "Way" (*dō, michi*) dates to the late Kamakura period. Instead of viewing Shugendō as the

1. For a survey of regional organizations, see Miyake Hitoshi, *Shugendō soshiki no kenkyū*, 379–513.

natural culmination of old, Heian-period patterns, it makes better sense to approach it as an analogue of other Kamakura- and Muromachi-period phenomena, such as sectarian movements in *kami* worship, the Nara revival, or new Buddhist schools. This epilogue presents Shugendō as having had its matrix not in continuity but in rupture, and casts the upheavals endemic to the Middle Ages—the formation of power blocs, civil war, and socioeconomic change—as decisive influences on the movement's formation and development.

Under the influence of the Japanese field of folklore studies, modern research on Shugendō has emphasized cultural continuity rather than historical change. The two most prolific scholars of Shugendō, Gorai Shigeru and Miyake Hitoshi, have both characterized their object of study as a form of folk religion. Adopting a sedimentary model, they have presented the formation of Shugendō as a process of accretion. For Gorai, the nucleus of Shugendō was an "originary" (*genshi no*) form of Japanese religion, overlain by other strata, most notably esoteric Buddhism, which transformed even as they fused with folk practices.[2] Whereas Miyake's work has been more historical, his approach has been decidedly structuralist: in his theoretical writing, he has laid out Lévi-Straussian models of folk religion as a comprehensive system.[3] As Ian Reader has noted, the resulting view of folk religion, and of Shugendō in particular, is stable, even static, to such an extent that it forecloses the possibility of dynamism or adaptation.[4] It also minimizes the disruptive quality of much historical change.

Both Miyake and Gorai traced the origins of Shugendō to the activities of mostly anonymous holy men such as those discussed in chapter 1. Miyake has also treated the early Ōmine *engi* discussed in chapter 8 as evidence that Shugendō was already in place by the late Heian period.[5] In terms of establishing mountain practices as a discrete field of inquiry, this approach makes good sense, but it has two problematic

2. See, for instance, Gorai and Inoue, *Yama no shūkyō,* 77.

3. On the historical end of his oeuvre, see Miyake Hitoshi, *Shugendō soshiki no kenkyū,* and *Ōmine shugendō no kenkyū.*

4. Reader, "Review of Miyake Hitoshi, *Shūkyō minzokugaku,*" 438; see also Miyake Hitoshi, *Shūkyō minzokugaku,* and in English, *Shugendō: Essays.*

5. Miyake Hitoshi, *Ōmine shugendō no kenkyū,* 275–309.

consequences. First, it inherits, then reifies, a tendency found in the seminal work of Wakamori Tarō, who dignified Shugendō as a subject of academic study in the 1940s. In his classic 1943 monograph, *Shugendōshi kenkyū* (Research on the history of Shugendō), Wakamori valorized *yamabushi* as individual practitioners, but framed the institutionalization of Shugendō as a source of decadence and decline.[6] Second, in defining Shugendō by its site (the mountains), the folkloric approach fails to establish criteria for differentiating Shugendō from Buddhism writ large. Inasmuch as Buddhist adepts undertook religious practice in the mountains from at least the Nara period onward, this creates a serious interpretive problem.[7]

By contrast, among researchers trained in history there is a growing consensus that the existence of *yamabushi* during the Heian period was not equivalent to the existence of Shugendō, and that independent Shugendō organizations formed only in the Kamakura and Muromachi periods. Following this line of thought, I take Shugendō to be a religious movement (1) with its own organizational hierarchies, institutions, rites, and texts, and (2) recognized by both participants and observers as distinct from other modes of religious practice. Understood in this way as a discursive and organizational entity, Shugendō began to coalesce in the late thirteenth century, emerging, and then differentiating, from the integrated forms of exoteric and esoteric (*kenmitsu*) Buddhism that had long dominated religious life.

The central characteristic of medieval Shugendō groups was a focus on collective, seasonal rites of "entering the peaks" (*nyūbu, mineiri*).[8] These rites testify to a key factor in Shugendō identity and organization: many, if not most, *yamabushi* traveled to the mountains because they did not actually live there. It follows that members of a mountain's resident community, whether at Kinpusen or elsewhere, did not necessarily identify with or as *yamabushi* (though they certainly might).

6. For instance, Wakamori saw the economic activities of settled (as opposed to peripatetic) Muromachi-period *yamabushi* as a form of secularization (Wakamori, *Shugendōshi kenkyū,* 246–47).

7. For research history and definitional issues in Shugendō studies, see Sekimori, "Shugendō: Japanese Mountain Religion."

8. Sekiguchi, *Shugendō kyōdan seiritsushi,* 8.

Shugendō, like the shift toward sectarian rhetoric seen in *engi*, grew out of the interface between religious communities associated with the mountains and the heavily settled plains.

From Shugen to Shugendō

Shugendō became recognizable through discursive differentiation and social organization. These two phenomena loosely correspond to the imagined and real dimensions of spatiality, and should be understood as mutually constitutive. In the late Kamakura period, the growing coherence and visibility of *yamabushi* groups drove verbal articulation of mountain practice (*shugen*) as an independent "Way." In turn, conceptual understandings of Shugendō influenced physical practice. Here, I consider the history of the word "Shugendō" and its cognates, and then turn to an examination of the groups to which these terms referred.

Perhaps the most important words that have been taken to denote Shugendō, its practices, and practitioners are *yamabushi, geza* (now pronounced *genja*), and *shugen.* After Wakamori Tarō demonstrated that all three terms were in active use during the Heian period, it was long assumed that they were effectively synonyms with stable referents.[9] Closer examination has, however, revealed that considerable semantic change occurred during the Heian-Kamakura transition. As a consequence, the notion that these terms denoted a consistent tradition of mountain practice has also been called into question.

Prior to the emergence of Shugendō, *yamabushi* were a recognizable type of religious specialist; they were not, however, viewed as members of a specific school or affiliates of a particular institution. The *Shin sarugakuki* (Account of the new monkey music), a comic essay written by the famous literatus Fujiwara no Akihira, illuminates the underdetermined quality of *yamabushi* identity during the Heian period. In a sketch of Jirō, the second son of a fictitious patriarch named Uzaemon, Akihira presented "*yamabushi* practice" (*yamabushi shugyō*)

9. Wakamori, *Shugendōshi kenkyū,* esp. 54–87.

as a supplement to conventional monastic discipline and esoteric expertise. The sketch reads as follows:

> Jirō is a great thaumaturge, abstinent his entire life. He is a master of mantras (*shingonshi*) in whom the three activities of body, speech, and mind are united. His years of constant, dedicated practice increase; his days maintaining the precepts and engaging in purification regimens (*sōjin*) grow longer. Hanging high the mirrors of the two realms, he polishes the jewels of the individual deities. With his fivefold mantras, the clouds clear; with his contemplation of the three secrets, the moon shines bright.[10] The Sanskrit syllables roll gently from his tongue; in forming the *mudrā* for rites of empowerment, his fingers are supple. He is never tardy in his chanting or performance of the "nine expedient means." When he burns poppy seeds during his esoteric rites, there are signs verifying his ritual efficacy (*gen*).[11] He is an esoteric master of the fire rite and the offering to the deities, a disciple who has received initiation into the study of the esoteric teachings. Altogether, regarding the Way of mantras (*shingon no michi, shingondō*), he has plumbed its depths; regarding the merit of ascesis (*kugyō*), he stands out from the crowd. He has completed ten summer retreats and has recited sets of one hundred thousand mantras on several occasions. Passing through Ōmine and Katsuragi, he has walked the byways for years and years. Kumano, Mitake, Tateyama in Etchū, Hashiriyu in Izu, the Konpon Chūdō [at Mt. Hiei], Daisen in Hōki, august Mt. Fuji, Hakusan in Echizen, Kōya, Kokawa, Mino'o, and Katsuragawa: among these mountains, there is nowhere he has not competed in practice or entered contests of power. Among *yamabushi* practitioners (*yamabushi shugyōja*), of old there were En no Gyōja and Jōzō, but they were just one-*dhāraṇī* thaumaturges. Now Jirō, Uzaemon's son, is a living buddha, already perfect in both wisdom and practice.[12]

10. The "two realms," namely, the Matrix and Vajra Mandalas, are populated by numerous buddhas, bodhisattvas, and celestials. By contrast, "individual deities" (*besson*) are represented and worshiped independently, though they may also appear in the larger mandalas. The fivefold mantras (*gobu shingon*) correlate to the five buddhas at the core of the Vajra (and also the Matrix) Mandala. The three secrets of body, speech, and mind (form, sound, and principle) are engaged in the practices of *mudrā*, mantra, and mandala, and are central to Shingon ontology and epistemology.

11. The "nine expedient means" is a component in penance rites associated with the Matrix Mandala. Poppy seeds may be burned in esoteric fire rites (*goma*), which are often integrated into larger ritual forms.

12. *Shin sarugakuki* (*NST*, 8:147–48, 305).

In the first two-thirds of this passage, Akihira devoted his attention to what he called the "Way of *shingon*." Whether we take this as a reference to the practice of mantras in general or to the Shingon school in particular, Akihira was pointing to recognizably esoteric techniques that, coupled with strict adherence to monastic rules, allowed Jirō to become a buddha in the course of a single lifetime. Akihira maintained that Jirō's expertise in the activities of body, speech, and mind, that is, the recitation of mantras, the execution of *mudrā*, and the ritual use of mandalas ("the two realms"), was amplified by mastery of specific ritual components (the fire rite and offering to deities). Being broad, the "Way of *shingon*" included, but was by no means limited to, ascesis in the mountains.

Whereas the treatment of Jirō's ascesis in the last third of the sketch does testify to the geographic range and vitality of *yamabushi* during the mid-Heian period, it does not frame the mountains as bastions of a "Way of *shugen*." Rather, Mitake (i.e., Kinpusen) features alongside a host of other mountains as a site for Buddhist practice. Inasmuch as *yamabushi* activities like Jirō's fit into the inclusive Buddhist culture of the Heian period, they were comparable to Pure Land devotion. They constituted an appealing body of practice that was distinctive enough to warrant its own terms (e.g., *yamabushi*, *kugyō*), and yet was not defined by sectarian consciousness or independent ecclesiastical hierarchies. This is not to say that Heian-period *yamabushi* were not recognizable types; indeed, they were. Rather, like scholar monks, sutra-maintainers, and other specialists, they operated within the larger conceptual sphere of *kenmitsu* Buddhism.

In similar fashion, *shugen* and *geza* were fairly generic terms until their meanings began to shift during the late Heian period. Between the ninth century and the twelfth, *shugen* referred to miraculous powers generated by religious practice of many types, including, but not limited to, ascesis in the mountains. Subsequently, the term began to refer to practice itself, rather than its results. During the twelfth and thirteenth centuries, it increasingly connoted the mountains, such that, in the words of the historian Hasegawa Kenji, "*yamabushi* and *shugen* were clearly being taken as a set" by the late 1200s.[13] The word

13. Hasegawa, "Shugendōshi no mikata," 23.

geza followed a similar arc, first coming into use during the tenth century to refer to healers whose success was seen as a divine sign verifying their religious practice. Although *geza* often used esoteric Buddhist techniques in their healing rites, the methods through which they gained their powers in the first place were diverse.[14] Again, the connection to mountains developed only gradually: according to Tokunaga Seiko, during the second half of the twelfth century, *geza* were increasingly assumed to practice in the mountains; by the second half of the thirteenth, this association had become indelible.[15]

Building upon the discursive convergence of the terms *yamabushi, shugen,* and *geza* in the late 1200s, observers and participants began to characterize *shugen,* by then understood as ascetically inflected religious practice undertaken in the mountains, as an independent Way. They also explicitly distinguished it from *kenmitsu* Buddhism. The *Tengu zōshi* (Goblin scrolls), a set of handscrolls completed circa 1296, illustrates this change both verbally and visually. In the Onjōji scroll, which focuses on the history and culture of the eponymous temple, the narrator declares:

> Speaking of the teachings of our temple, they are Shingon, Tendai, Hossō, and Kusha. Should one inquire about other temples, one may find that some are exoteric (*ken*) without being esoteric (*mitsu*), while others are esoteric without being exoteric. Though sometimes they may advocate the study of both exotericism and esotericism (*kenmitsu*), they do not have the single Way of *shugen* (*shugen no ichidō*). Our temple is the only one to serve the court by combining these three.[16]

The *Tengu zōshi*'s rhetorical differentiation of *shugen* from *kenmitsu,* together with its characterization of *shugen* as a distinctive Way, appears to have originated from within the *kenmitsu* establishment. Haruko Wakabayashi has argued that the creators of the scrolls were monks from Onjōji, a paradigmatic power-bloc temple. She has also

14. Tokunaga, "Shugendō seiritsu."
15. Tokunaga, "Kumano sanzan kengyō," 91–92.
16. *Tengu zōshi,* Onjōji scroll, *dan* 1, lines 121–26 (*ZNE,* 26:36, 133); for alternative translation, see Wakabayashi, *The Seven Tengu Scrolls,* 129.

shown that this rhetoric prevailed in the public sphere and other genres: a 1319 petition submitted by Onjōji monks to the military government in Kamakura parallels this portion of the scrolls, and praises Onjōji for its combination of "the three Ways of exotericism, esotericism, and *shugen*."[17]

The embodiment of the notion that "our temple" combined esoteric and exoteric Buddhism with the "single Way of *shugen*" was the person of the Kumano overseer. As at Kinpusen, the Kumano overseership had become a means for influential members of a power-bloc institution to assert influence over a popular pilgrimage site. Onjōji monks had periodically served as Kumano overseers during the twelfth century, when the office had come into use as an honor conferred upon men who served as pilgrimage guides (*sendatsu*) to retired emperors or as healers to royal consorts. Although it is widely assumed that Retired Emperor Shirakawa appointed the Onjōji monk Zōyo (1032–1116) as the first Kumano overseer in 1090, that appointment is recorded only in later sources. In fact, the office appears to have developed slowly. It was only in the mid-1200s that Onjōji succeeded in monopolizing the overseership as a prerogative of the abbots of that temple's *monzeki* cloisters.[18]

The overseer might be a privileged member of a power-bloc institution, but the Way of *shugen* was conceived as an alternative path. Despite the Kumano overseer's high rank, the *Tengu zōshi* portrays him as decidedly unlike his counterparts in the more conventional *kenmitsu* elite. The scrolls depict him untonsured and garbed in the distinctive peaked cap and figured robes worn by *yamabushi* in other Kamakura-period paintings (see fig. E.1; compare to the representation of Nichizō as a *yamabushi* in fig. 2.2). In visual terms, then, "the single Way of *shugen*" was a Way for para-monastic *yamabushi* who differed in both appearance and practice from conventional Buddhist monks.

17. For the authorship of the scrolls, see Wakabayashi, *The Seven Tengu Scrolls,* 123–40. For the Onjōji petition, see ibid., 132–35 and 169–72; and *Kamakura ibun* 27012 (*komonjo hen* 35:117).

18. Sakai, "Chūsei Onjōji no monzeki"; Sakamoto Toshiyuki, *Kumano sanzan to Kumano bettō,* 25–27; Tokunaga, "Kumano sanzan kengyō," 76–83.

FIGURE E.1 Gathering of *tengu,* detail from *Tengu zōshi,* ca. 1296. Ink and colors on paper, 30.5 cm ht. Courtesy of Nezu Museum.

The scrolls further amplify the alterity of the overseer-as-*yamabushi* vis-à-vis the *kenmitsu* establishment by representing Shugendō as an analogue for other new religious movements. As part of an overall critique of the clerical community, the *Tengu zōshi* depicts monastics of all persuasions as goblins (*tengu*), decidedly inhuman, though not necessarily malevolent, creatures. A scroll owned by the Nezu Museum and known as "Miidera B" includes a scene in which a diverse group of monks, each of whom sports the bird beak of a *tengu,* recommit themselves to sincere religious practice. The monks are seated in a square, with their rank expressed by the relative height and position of their seats and with their identities noted in written labels. Apparently due to trimming, the label for the highest-ranking *tengu* is truncated, but the art historian Komatsu Shigemi reconstructs it as "the torchbearer of the Shingon school, the pillar of *kenmitsu.*" To the right of this lofty personage sits "the Tendai superior." The "Kegon maestro" and "Tarōbō, the monk of Mt. Atago," occupy the next-highest seats, facing each other on either side of the square. The remainder of the assembly is seated in a row. Beginning with the highest-ranking *tengu,* these are "the Zen master who has attained the Dharma; the chief Sanron scholar; the Hossō reverend; the overseer of the Three Mountains [of Kumano]; the scrupulous Vinaya master; and the Nenbutsu holy man."[19]

To all appearances, this scene was meant as a comprehensive representation of the Buddhist monastic community, though it must be noted that the inclusion of Tarōbō, a notorious *tengu* whose exploits were the stuff of popular legend, sharpens its quality as comic travesty. Here, members of newer movements characterized by their focus on specific modes of practice (*zen, shugen, ritsu, nenbutsu*), take their places alongside exponents of the great *kenmitsu* scholastic traditions (the Shingon, Tendai, Kegon, Hossō, and Sanron schools).[20] Although at other points the *Tengu zōshi* does sharply censure Ippen (1239–89), a *nenbutsu* advocate, and Jinen Koji (n.d.), a popular exponent of *zen*, this scene emphasizes inclusion by displaying a religious community that embraces both long-established and newer, alternative religious identities.[21]

The *Tengu zōshi* thus calls our attention to Shugendō's status as one of a number of movements that began to differentiate themselves from the *kenmitsu* establishment in the hundred-odd years following the Genpei War. Modern interpretive models identifying specific schools—Pure Land, Zen, and Lotus—as the most significant forms of a "new Kamakura Buddhism" (*Kamakura shin bukkyō*) have been amply critiqued.[22] At the same time, it is important to recognize that the thirteenth century did indeed see a broad religious efflorescence, in which proponents of Buddhism and *kami* worship advocated new doctrines and practices.[23] Shugendō was very much part of this religious ferment.

19. *Tengu zōshi,* Miidera B scroll, *dan* 1 (*ZNE,* 26:66–67, 140).

20. For types and ranks of *tengu,* see Wakabayashi, *The Seven Tengu Scrolls,* 144–51.

21. On censure of Ippen and Jinen, see Wakabayashi, *The Seven Tengu Scrolls,* 106–22.

22. See, for instance, Payne, *Re-Visioning "Kamakura" Buddhism;* Morrell, *Early Kamakura Buddhism.*

23. See, for instance, Bodiford, *Sōtō Zen,* esp. part 1; Glassman, *The Face of Jizō*; Teeuwen, *Watarai Shintō*; and Stone, *Original Enlightenment.*

From Yamabushi to Shugendō

In the "real" complement to the "imagined," discursive articulation of Shugendō, groups of *yamabushi* began to create their own organizations during the late Kamakura period. Organizations focused on the Ōmine Range clearly grew out of interactions among monks associated with *kenmitsu* power-bloc temples, the resident communities of mountain pilgrimage centers, and regional practitioners who visited the mountains on a temporary basis. Relations between the first two groups have been explored in chapters 7 and 8; here, it is worth emphasizing that neither Shugendō organizations nor earlier, ad hoc groups of *yamabushi* were coextensive with local religious communities in the mountains. An account of a Kamakura-period protest over land commendations illustrates the sort of divide that obtained between *yamabushi* and Kinpusen's resident monks. In 1234, the nobleman and poet Fujiwara no Sadaie (better known as Teika, 1162–1241) noted in his journal that forty or fifty *yamabushi* had gathered outside the gates of the regent, Kujō Norizane (1211–35). At first, the reasons for this protest were unclear, but it soon emerged that "children of Yamato" had commended contested lands to Kinpusen. In protest, their fathers, the *yamabushi,* had come up to Kyoto.[24] The incident passed without further remark from the ruling elite until two months later, when "several hundred *yamabushi* from various places gathered in the vicinity of Hōjōji, and then went in a group to the regent's house" to protest the land commendations. "Morning and night, they blew their conch trumpets, startling the senses of the populace. It was most unsettling."[25] Here *yamabushi* from Yamato, many of whom likely practiced in the Ōmine Range, positioned themselves over and against Kinpusen's local community. Clearly, the interests and allegiances of these two groups diverged. In a similar vein, the *Kinpusen sōsōki,* a text compiled circa 1300 and introduced at the end of chapter 7, asserts that *yamabushi* participated regularly in seasonal rites at Kinpusen, but does not portray

24. *Meigetsuki,* Bunryaku 1.7.27, 8.1 (3:420–21).
25. *Hyakurenshō,* Bunryaku 1.10.1 (*SZKT,* 11:177).

them as fulfilling significant roles in the year-round community at Yoshinoyama.

Rather than being mountain residents, the *yamabushi* who formed Shugendō organizations active in the southern mountains were affiliated primarily with Onjōji or Kōfukuji. Groups centered on these temples respectively came to be known as the Honzan and Tōzan. The Honzan, which was headquartered at Onjōji and encouraged practice at Kumano, was characterized by power-bloc control of pilgrimage networks and symbiotic relationships with temporal authorities. Here I provide a brief summary of its historical development before doing the same for the Tōzan, which was headquartered at Kōfukuji and focused on practice at Kinpusen.

By the mid-twelfth century, Kumano's local community had divided into two groups, "permanent residents" (*jōjū*), who were led by the Kumano steward (*bettō*), and "visiting monks" (*kyakusō*), who were in many cases *yamabushi* who came to the area on a seasonal basis.[26] The *kyakusō* organization about which we know the most was called the "long hall corps" (*nagatokoshū*), among whom mountain austerities, particularly winter seclusions and peak entries, were prerequisites for leadership positions. The *nagatokoshū* appears to have formed during the mid-to-late twelfth century under the influence of Kumano overseers who were also Onjōji monks.[27] When Onjōji established a monopoly on the Kumano overseership during the first half of the thirteenth century, the *nagatokoshū*, and perhaps other similar groups, would have provided a local base at Kumano. As the *Tengu zōshi* shows, the overseer personified ties between Onjōji and Kumano; similarly, he was seen to embody both high-ranking status at a power-bloc temple and *yamabushi* identity.

The office of Kumano overseer became the core of the Honzan, which developed into an imposing Shugendō organization during the

26. For a more detailed overview of the Kumano organization in English, see Moerman, *Localizing Paradise,* 18–21. On the stewards, see Sakamoto Toshiyuki, *Kumano sanzan to Kumano bettō,* esp. 23–68 and 283–324.

27. The key source on the *nagatokushū* is an early Muromachi-period text, the *Yamabushi chō* (*SS,* 3:385–400), which has been taken as a reliable account of the group's history. For the formation of the *nagatokushū,* see Tokunaga, "Kumano sanzan kengyō," 81–83.

fifteenth century. Control of pilgrimage networks was an important factor: from the Kamakura period onward, warriors and commoners began to travel to Kumano. As a consequence of the growing popularity of the pilgrimage, regional *sendatsu* formed relationships with local constituencies in areas ranging from the eastern provinces to the island of Shikoku.[28] During the early 1400s, the Kumano overseers, who were increasingly also the abbots of the Shōgoin, one of Onjōji's *monzeki* cloisters, succeeded in bringing pilgrimage specialists and networks under their own control. In doing so, they substantially increased their geographic reach. They also capitalized upon the erosion of the authority of the stewards, who had long been appointed from among Kumano's resident community, and seized rights of local management at the shrines. Around this time, the Ashikaga shoguns appear to have lent their support to the Kumano overseers; certainly, they backed reconstruction projects at Kumano.[29] In uniting control of local administration with regional pilgrimage networks, the overseers established an extended devotional community presided over by the Shōgoin and favored by the shoguns. This was Honzan Shugendō.

The developmental arc of Tōzan Shugendō, which was oriented around Kinpusen, was substantially different, and is best understood in the context of the Nara revival. Working within the Kōfukuji-controlled Yamato mountainscape examined in chapters 7 and 8, low-ranking hall monks (*dōshū*, alt. *dōshu*) from Kōfukuji and associated temples began making organized pilgrimages to Kinpusen during the late Kamakura period. Undertaken as "peak entries," these sojourns were explicitly tied to revivalist activities. Kōfukuji *dōshū* participated in the Classical Vinaya (*kogi ritsu*) movement, which was organizationally distinct from but thematically similar to the more famous Shingon

28. On the formation of Kumano *sendatsu* networks, see, for instance, Shinjō Mieko, *Honzan-ha shugen* and Miyake Hitoshi, *Kumano shugen,* 127–218.

29. On the overseers' takeover of *sendatsu* networks and *bettō* prerogatives, see Hasegawa, "Chūsei kōki ni okeru kenmitsu jisha" and "Chūsei Kumano ni okeru sendatsu shihai"; as well as Miyake Hitoshi, *Kumano shugen,* 264–306, esp. 288–93; and Shinjō Mieko, *Honzan-ha shugen,* 31–49. On the renovation of Kumano, see Kawasaki, "Muromachi zenki ni okeru Kumano sanzan."

Vinaya (*shingon ritsu*) revival spearheaded by Eison.[30] In order to participate in precept-conferral ceremonies and advance through the Classical Vinaya hierarchy, *dōshū* had to perform peak entries under the guidance of *sendatsu.*[31] The resulting network of seasonal mountain practitioners and their leaders grew into the Tōzan organization from the late thirteenth century onward, with Kōfūkuji as its central node.[32] Whereas the Kumano overseer, and by extension Onjōji hierarchs, had been integral to the formation of the Honzan organization, the Kinpusen overseer does not appear to have played much of a role in the Tōzan. Nonetheless, Tōzan participants did operate within his domain. Kōfukuji's branch temples featured prominently among the headquarters of Tōzan *sendatsu*, and as the organization grew more robust and independent, *dōshū* from Tōdaiji and other regional temples joined in.[33]

The conflict between the Northern and Southern Courts, which dominated the middle decades of the fourteenth century, dramatically affected the Yoshino-Kinpusen area, and by extension, the emergent Tōzan organization. After defeating the military regime in Kamakura and effecting the Kenmu Restoration, Emperor Go-Daigo (1288–1339, r. 1318–39) came into conflict with his erstwhile military supporter, Ashikaga Takauji (1305–58). In 1336, the emperor fled from the capital to Yoshinoyama, where his son had previously built a fortress. There, Go-Daigo presided over the Southern Court, in opposition to the Northern Court, which enjoyed the protection of Takauji's emergent Ashikaga shogunate in Kyoto. Military conflict between the two regimes continued for decades, until the Southern Court sued for peace in 1392.[34]

30. Kamiya, "Jūgo seiki kōhan Kōfukuji dōshū," esp. 43–44; on *dōshū,* see Adolphson, "The *Dōshu.*"

31. Tokunaga, "Shugendō Tōzan-ha," 43–45.

32. Ibid., esp. 45–46; Suzuki Shōei, *Shugen kyōdan,* 79–82.

33. On the participation of Tōdaiji *dōshū,* see Sekiguchi, *Shugendō kyōdan seiritsu-shi,* 97–128. On the formation and development of the Tōzan, see Suzuki Shōei, *Shugen kyōdan,* esp. 78–135.

34. For a treatment of this period from the perspective of local history, see Yoshinochō Shi Henshū Iinkai, *Yoshinochō shi,* 1:71–145. For an English-language account of Go-Daigo's career and his relationship with Takauji, see Goble, *Kenmu,* esp. 244–61.

Shugendō activity continued throughout the Southern Court's occupation of Yoshinoyama. In fact, while in Yoshino, Monkan (1278–1357), one of Go-Daigo's monastic advisors, mobilized local deities for the ritual defense of his patron and wrote *Kinpusen himitsuden,* a text now received as a Shugendō classic.[35] Following political reintegration under the Ashikaga during the Muromachi period, however, Shugendō activity centered on Kinpusen appears to have declined.[36] For the Ashikaga, Yoshino, and by extension Kinpusen, connoted insurgency. It is no surprise, then, that the shoguns favored Kumano and the Shōgoin-led Honzan. During the sixteenth century, endemic unrest further weakened the Tōzan and contributed to a decline in the participation of Kōfukuji affiliates. At the same time, however, men connected with the powerful Shingon complexes at Mt. Kōya, Negoroji, and Kokawadera became enthusiastic participants in Tōzan peak entries. This infusion of new *shugenja* helped prepare the way for the apotheosis of the Tōzan as an independent sect in the Edo period.[37]

In the context of state efforts to rationalize (and control) religious hierarchies, in 1613 the new Tokugawa shogunate mandated the reconfiguration of the Honzan and Tōzan networks as Shugendō sects (*ha*), governed respectively by *monzeki*: Onjōji's Shōgoin and Daigoji's Sanbōin.[38] This restructuring also entailed formal affiliation with the Tendai and Shingon schools, which in turn fed a lively sense of sectarian identity. Edo-period *shugenja* produced numerous ritual and doctrinal compendia, including Honzan-Tōzan polemics.[39] In both organizational and intellectual terms, the seventeenth and eighteenth centuries can rightly be seen as a time of growth and efflorescence for Shugendō.

The fortunes of Shugendō changed dramatically with the 1868 Meiji restoration, however. In promulgating new policies aimed at separating

35. Abe, *Chūsei Nihon no shūkyō tekusuto taikei,* 238–65, 462–65.

36. Miyake Hitoshi, *Shugendō soshiki no kenkyū,* 143.

37. Sekiguchi, *Shugendō kyōdan seiritsushi,* 129–75.

38. On the Tōzan, see Sekiguchi, *Shugendō kyōdan seiritsushi,* 211–52; Suzuki Shōei, *Shugen kyōdan,* 201–218; and Miyake Hitoshi, *Shugendō soshiki no kenkyū,* 722–37. On the Honzan, see Shinjō, *Honzan-ha shugen to Kumano sendatsu,* or for a briefer treatment, Miyake Hitoshi, *Shugendō soshiki no kenkyū,* 583–609.

39. Miyake Hitoshi, *Shugendō shisō no kenkyū,* 99–139, esp. 121–27.

Buddhism from Shintō, the government proscribed Shugendō, requiring *yamabushi* and their institutions to disband or fully amalgamate with the Shingon or Tendai schools of Buddhism. In addition to disruptions wrought by the dismantling of Shugendō as an independent religious movement, the edicts separating Buddhism and Shintō caused significant trauma at mountain sites.[40] At Kinpusen, enforcement resulted in the closure of a number of cloisters, the dispersion of cultic objects, particularly images of Zaō, and drastic changes to religious personnel, the local economy, and liturgical culture.[41] This is not to say that devotional traditions were utterly cut off. On the contrary, mountain practice persisted throughout the first half of the twentieth century, with lay confraternities (*kō*) playing an enlarged role.[42] Following the promulgation of the post-war constitution, the Tōzan and Honzan schools re-formed. Once more headed by the Sanbōin and Shōgoin, they continue to be vital organizations. Differences between contemporary Shugendō and the traditions and institutions to which it lays claim merit further research; nevertheless, the resilience of the Honzan and Tōzan testifies to the hold these organizations exercise on both the real and imaginary aspects of Shugendō today.

As this brief survey shows, the rise of power-bloc institutions, coupled with subsequent political upheaval and state intervention, exerted a formative influence upon Shugendō. Growing out of Kinpusen's military subjugation to Kōfukuji and the broader ferment of the Nara revival, Tōzan Shugendō emerged among low-ranking men from Kōfukuji, its branch temples, and neighboring institutions. Honzan Shugendō, by contrast, was more closely connected to the apex of Onjōji's power bloc through the person of the Kumano overseer and drew the patronage of medieval rulers. As indicated in chapter 7, the processes, often violent, through which power-bloc temples came to dominate mountain pilgrimage centers entailed far-reaching changes to local religious culture. Similarly, shifts in the reigning political order, from the regency to the *insei,* to successive military governments, to the constitutional

40. Sekimori, "Paper Fowl and Wooden Fish"; Miyake Hitoshi, *Shugendō soshiki no kenkyū,* 1016–23; Thal, *Rearranging the Landscape,* 127–219.

41. Blair, "Zaō Gongen," 20–33.

42. Miyake Hitoshi, *Shugendō soshiki no kenkyū,* 1023–35.

Meiji state, reconfigured not only religious policy but also the real-and-imagined spaces of the mountains, and by extension the activities undertaken there.

Heian Pilgrims and Shugendō Yamabushi

This book began with a discussion of the emergence of pilgrimage as an accepted devotional activity among the tenth-century nobility. In ending with organized Shugendō, I wish to call into question narratives in which Shugendō appears as a stable, enduring object of inquiry with strong ties to Heian pilgrimage practices. To assess the distance between aristocratic Heian pilgrimage and Shugendō practice, it is helpful to consider the most representative Shugendō rite, the peak entry. This group event brought together multiple participants, who might hail from a range of places, under the leadership of *sendatsu*.[43] Shugendō peak entries were indices of membership and status, for a *yamabushi*'s rank within his organization was tied to the number of entries he had completed. Peak entries were scheduled on a seasonal basis and varied in terms of itinerary and length. Based on the study of documents in the archive of Matsuodera (see map 3), a onetime branch temple of Kōfukuji and center for Tōzan Shugendō, Suzuki Shōei has summarized the structure of the Tōzan "Flower Offering Peak" (*hanaku no mine*) during the late-medieval to early-modern period as follows.

Having arrived on the last day of the fourth month at Dorogawa, a village at the western foot of Kinpusen, *sendatsu* and *yamabushi* participating in the Flower-Offering Peak spent a week in ritual seclusion. After climbing into the mountains, the men arrived first at the peak of Kinpusen and then established themselves approximately two kilometers south along the ridge at Ozasa (see map 3), where they would stay for several days. In addition to conducting flower offerings at various halls and shrines in the mountains, participants held a grand fire rite (*saitō goma*), a vajra offering (*kongō ku*), and a set of ten realms rites.

43. For a schematic treatment of peak entries, see Miyake Hitoshi, *Shugendō shisō no kenkyū*, 693–713.

This last observance was aimed at bringing participants to enlightenment by having them engage in a ritual series of ten "rebirths," in which they ascended through the realms of hell dwellers, hungry ghosts, and other ranks of beings, until they were ultimately "born" as bodhisattvas and then buddhas.[44]

Antecedents for several aspects of the Flower-Offering Peak (and by extension other peak entries) can indeed be found in the activities of Heian-period pilgrims. By taking large retinues with them into the mountains, the regents established pilgrimage as a group activity. Similarly, by commissioning men to guide their journeys to Kumano, the retired emperors helped to institutionalize the role of the *sendatsu*. Heian *sōjin* regimens served to purify pilgrims, as did the much shorter seclusion in Dorogawa. Furthermore, Heian pilgrims do appear to have engaged in the ritual enactment of awakening. As discussed in chapter 5, Fujiwara no Moromichi viewed Kinpusen as a place of enlightenment and implicitly framed his physical progress toward the peak as movement along a spiritual path. By the early twelfth century, Kumano pilgrims such as Fujiwara no Munetada were expressing similar conceptualizations of pilgrimage as a ritual means to achieve enlightenment. In this sense, regency- and *insei*-period practices did resonate with the ten realms rites.

These similarities notwithstanding, the Flower Offering Peak differed substantially from Heian precedent. Whereas Heian rites centered on the offering and burial of scriptural corpora, sutra manuscripts fade from view in the Shugendō peak entry. Furthermore, the focus on the Zaō Hall seen in the Heian materials gave way to an expanded space for communal Shugendō rites. Among these, the implicitly esoteric *saitō goma* and vajra offering might conceivably have operated as analogs to the *rishu zanmai* mentioned by Ōe no Masafusa in 1092; in form and personnel, however, they were quite different. References to ten realms rites, which Miyake has identified as the core element in peak entries, first occur in texts dating to the middle of the Muromachi period.[45] There is no direct evidence that Heian pilgrims

44. Suzuki Shōei, *Shugen kyōdan,* 108–10; on ten realms rites, see also Miyake Hitoshi, *Shugendō shisō no kenkyū,* 713–37.

45. Miyake Hitoshi, *Shugendō shisō no kenkyū,* 693, 718.

construed their journeys to Kinpusen as symbolic enactments of death and rebirth, or that they engaged in rites of (re)generation. In this respect, ten realms rites were a medieval innovation. Perhaps most importantly, the participants in these two types of pilgrimages were dramatically different. In the former case, lay members of the high aristocracy traveled to the mountains, bringing eminent monks in their train. In the latter, low-ranking members of religious communities banded together to set themselves apart as exponents of an independent Way of mountain practice.

Beyond their collocation, then, neither the practices nor the personae of elite, Heian-period pilgrims and proponents of fully developed Shugendō can be said to be the same. They differed significantly in form, style, and social structure. Aristocratic pilgrimage, which made Kinpusen such a prominent site within the broader religious landscape between the tenth and eleventh centuries, emerged out of the political and cultural shifts from the *ritsuryō* to the court-centered state. By contrast, the rise of Shugendō was predicated upon twelfth- and thirteenth-century phenomena, namely, the growth of power blocs, the administrative subordination of local religious organizations, and sustained exchange with lowland communities. It was only with these developments firmly in place that the Shugendō movement took shape.

Conclusion

In contemporary imagination, Shugendō often represents cultural continuity, and the Ōmine Range figures as a timeless landscape. In 2004, Kinpusen was included in a new UNESCO World Heritage site, "Sacred Mountains and Pilgrimage Routes in the Kii Mountain Range." Part of the rationale given for this designation was the area's "persistent and extraordinarily well-documented tradition of sacred mountains over the past 1,200 years."[46] World Heritage status has led to increased interest and tourism in the Ōmine area, though this has not necessarily

46. UNESCO, "Advisory Board Evaluation."

translated into better environmental and living conditions for local residents.[47] On an ongoing basis the heritage designation also affects representational trends that emphasize historical stability over rupture, and aesthetic value over conflict.

Museum exhibitions provide a popular, accessible venue in which the display of cohesive material culture supports the imagination of historical continuity. For instance, *Inori no michi* (Paths of prayer), a blockbuster exhibition commemorating the 2004 World Heritage designation, brought together some three hundred objects in diverse media with the intention of showcasing "treasures from Yoshino, Kumano, and Kōya."[48] Although the enclosure of these pieces within the space of the exhibit (and the pages of the catalogue) made their collocation appear unproblematic, it was in fact the result of complex negotiations. From the early-modern period up until the present day, excavation, commodification, and the emergence of the modern art market have dispersed objects once located at Kinpusen throughout Japan, and indeed, the entire world.[49] In re-collecting material objects and presenting them to public view as an integrated corpus, museological projects like this one manage cultural memory by promoting images of unity and stasis in the face of dispersal and change. The cover of the *Inori no michi* catalogue illustrates these representational preferences: it shows the hands of an icon in a digitally modified teaching *mudrā* against a backdrop of misty, forested mountains. Such lovely, romantic images send the message that Kinpusen's religious culture is archaic, constant, and preserved unchanged in situ.

Film and video provide a complementary venue for mediatized representations in which the ancient and the contemporary form an apparently seamless whole. Documentaries about the Ōmine region and Shugendō are now not only a domestic but also a global phenomenon. Recent multilingual videos released by Canadian and European academics couple imagery of mountain terrain near Kinpusen and Kumano with voice-overs of passages from the *Shozan engi*. These scenes are intercut with footage depicting the religious practices and everyday

47. McGuire, "What's at Stake?"
48. Ōsaka Shiritsu Bijutsukan, *Inori no michi*.
49. Blair, "Zaō Gongen."

life of contemporary *yamabushi.*[50] Thus, filmmakers have opted to use an eight-hundred-year-old *engi* to reimagine the real mountain landscape and current Shugendō practices. These sequences vividly connect contemporary space and ritual to the Heian- and Kamakura-period past.

Not surprisingly, similar processes are at work within the Japanese Shugendō community. In his 2008 book *Ōmine engi,* Zenitani Buhei, a practicing *yamabushi* educated in the field of agricultural science, set out to map sites mentioned in Heian texts onto Edo-period traditions and current Shugendō practices. This project was based on oblique claims that the landscape itself is a repository for the past, such that ancient traditions live on, and can therefore be recovered, in situ. This type of approach relies upon the same sort of functionality attributed to traces in the Ōmine *engi* discussed in chapter 8. By making the past present, they work to erase or elide historical change. Like the creators of *engi,* who faced administrative subordination and institutional upheaval, contemporary Shugendō practitioners look to the past for authentication in the face of the detraditionalization of many aspects of contemporary life.

In this book, my aim has been neither to frame Heian pilgrimage as a form of proto-Shugendō nor to represent it as a living relic that can be discovered in current practices and landscapes. Rather, I have sought to examine the processes through which Kinpusen became a site of concern for the literate and ruling elites during the Heian period, and how it later became part of a medieval landscape dominated by power blocs and characterized by religious ferment. Recursive interactions in which human activity shaped and was shaped by the local environment rendered Kinpusen a dynamic real-and-imagined place. A mountain made sacred by ritual and theological labor, it offered its devotees access to the future and the past, opportunities for creative ritualizing, and a dynamic, combinatory pantheon.

Regency noblemen first began to travel to Kinpusen to secure personal blessings, such as longevity, through forms of physical discipline remarkable for their duration and intensity. Imagining themselves as holy men, male aristocrats spent months engaging in regimens limiting

50. McGuire and Abela, *Shugendō Now*; Roth and Roth, *Where Mountains Fly.*

their diet and sexual activity, and requiring a constant round of purificatory rites. Shifting from conventional models of patronage-by-hire to a participatory mode of ritual action, they personally created deluxe manuscripts of Buddhist scriptures, writing out sutras in golden ink on indigo-dyed paper. They also prepared generous gifts of paper, rice, oil, and textiles. After donning "pure robes" of undyed cloth, they set off on foot to make the longest, most arduous journey of their lives. When they reached the mountains, they crossed into a gendered space demarcated by ritual cordons. The social and ritual exclusion of women from the mountain's real space served to deflect attention from differences among Kinpusen's male constituencies, thereby preserving the ritual cohesion of otherwise diverse groups: monastic residents, elite laymen, and religious itinerants.

Bound together by gender and bodily discipline, men at Kinpusen prostrated themselves before Zaō, a combinatory deity who embodied the characteristics of a dragon, an autochthonous *kami*, the buddha of the past, and the buddha of the future. By offering and interring manuscripts in Zaō's domain, devotees sought to secure an enduring connection with the god. At once material and karmic, this bond was mediated and made possible by place. In that pilgrimage to Kinpusen entailed sutra burial, it condensed site with text, while also tapping into discursive and ritual preoccupations that I have analyzed as "trace-ism." Traces were deemed capable of making both the past and the divine present at particular sites, and were more generally capable of mediating what otherwise appeared as categorical distinctions. Inasmuch as elite pilgrims construed their gods, manuscripts, footprints, and precedents as traces, their pilgrimages were exercises in integrating and emplacing traces of all these types at Kinpusen.

To highlight the political valences of pilgrimage, I have argued that elite laypeople's engagement with Kinpusen can fruitfully be understood as part of ritual regimes enacted by royals and high-ranking aristocrats. The political aspects of religious action had real consequences for both pilgrims and the sites with which they engaged. With respect to Kinpusen, in using pilgrimage to strengthen their political authority, the regents symbolically bound the mountain to their ascendancy. As the regents' political position was relativized around 1100, however, the retired emperors reconfigured the ritual landscape by turning toward

Kumano. Even more critically for Kinpusen, friction with Kōfukuji flared into war in the mid-1090s. As I argued in chapter 7, Retired Emperor Shirakawa's campaign to position himself ritually as the equal, and ultimately the better, of the regents, contributed to a worsening of relations between Kinpusen and Kōfukuji. By the end of the war, Kōfukuji had achieved lordship over Kinpusen. Soon thereafter, the regents' tradition of pilgrimage to the mountain was truncated by the death of Fujiwara no Moromichi, who proved to be the last great Kinpusen devotee among the regents.

As a result, Kinpusen entered the twelfth century transformed: no longer the regent's favored pilgrimage site, it was now one of Kōfukuji's clients. For Kinpusen, as for other temples and shrines, the 1100s, and the *insei* period more broadly, marked the beginning of the ascendancy of power-bloc institutions, together with increases in organizational factionalization, religious diversification, and militarization. As part of these changes, the religious culture of the southern mountains took on a new trajectory. Although lay patrons still exerted economic, and occasionally administrative, influence, they were no longer present in-person at the mountain. Instead, Kinpusen became a site for religious interchange among residents, monks from Nara temples, and itinerant religious specialists. Although *engi* rhetorically cast mountain practice as separate from ritual life in a conventional temple, in sociospatial terms these texts were actually hybrid compositions. The religious communities that produced, circulated, and preserved *engi* included well-connected monastics from temples near the city of Heian and the southern capital of Nara. When Shugendō organizations began to emerge circa 1300, they took up the same kinds of values and rhetoric seen in earlier *engi*. Thus, older representations of the mountains as mandala came to subtend new ritual enactments of enlightenment; descriptions of *yamabushi* lineages provided a fund of lore about ancestral transmissions; and ritual protocols became grounds for elaboration and adaptation.

The development of Shugendō organizations was as significant a transformation in the real-and-imagined space of the southern mountains as the boom in aristocratic pilgrimage had been in the eleventh century or the "medievalization" of Kinpusen and Kumano during the twelfth. Not only did Shugendō practitioners travel from Kōfukuji and

Onjōji to the Ōmine Range but they also formed networks, both regional and transregional in scope. By stimulating the formation of new institutional relationships and religious identities, such networks actually threatened established structures and hierarchies. What we would now recognize as class was an important part of this dynamic. With no hope of ever entering the upper echelons of their temple hierarchies, low-ranking members of religious communities, such as the *dōshū* who formed the backbone of the Tōzan organization, looked to mountain practice as a means to gain status and authority. This strategy met with enough success that by the mid-1300s high-ranking clerics at regional temples were seeking to prevent or limit the participation of the lower monastic classes in Shugendō. At Kanshinji, for instance (see map 3), lower-ranking monastics had to forswear any involvement in *yamabushi* activities. A temple oath from 1406 reads: "Regarding the Way of *yamabushi,* since the distant past, it has been firmly prohibited at this temple. Similarly, henceforth it is absolutely impermissible to propagate that Way, nor is it permissible to mix with those groups. . . . If anyone breaks [these rules], his traces shall be erased for all perpetuity."[51] For some Buddhist monastics, then, mountain practice posed such a threat that it merited ostracism by the temple community: *shugenja* would be punished for seeking out the traces of En no Gyōja by having their own traces erased from temple records and collective memory. Ōishi Masa'aki, who called attention to this backlash against Shugendō, interpreted such institutional proscriptions as an attempt on the part of elite clerics to maintain control of temple lands in the face of the growing influence of powerful local laymen. In Ōishi's view, by transforming into *yamabushi,* "lower-ranking monks (*gyōnin* and *zenshū*) descended from local gentry or powerful farmers" played a key role in the "popularization" (*minshūka*) of regional religious institutions.[52]

Whether or not we see Shugendō as a force for popularization or even democratization, the new affiliations it afforded clearly had the potential to fracture allegiances based on ordination and residence. Hasegawa Kenji has shown, for instance, that in the fifteenth century

51. *Kanshinji monjo* 489, dated Ōei 13.6.20. In *Dai Nihon komonjo, iewake,* 6:439. See also Ōishi, *Nihon chūsei shakai to jiin,* 382.

52. Ōishi, *Nihon chūsei shakai to jiin,* 386.

affiliation with the increasingly integrated Honzan network forced a radical "separation" (*bunri*) of *yamabushi* from their home temples.[53] By strengthening external relationships with local lay communities and weakening established religious institutions' internal social structures, Shugendō undercut the traditional supports for power-bloc hierarchies. Meanwhile, it presented one in a growing range of alternatives to *kenmitsu* orthodoxy. Much as Retired Emperor Shirakawa's engagement in what had been a hallowed tradition of elite pilgrimage to Kinpusen helped to unravel the very tradition upon which he had sought to capitalize, the power-bloc structures that had provided the matrix for Shugendō were subsequently undercut by the very growth of that movement.

In light of its spectacular costumes and rites, dramatic settings, and ongoing vitality, it is not surprising that Shugendō has so strongly colored modern writers' views of the history of religious activity in the Ōmine Range. In seeking to reconstruct and reassess the more distant past, however, I have sought to look past contemporary, early-modern and late-medieval *yamabushi* in order to "inquire into the traces" of Heian-period aristocrats and *engi* writers. I have also emphasized first the rise of aristocratic pilgrimage, then the institutional subordination of Kinpusen, and finally the rise of Shugendō as important historical phases in which the imagined and real dimensions of the mountain landscape changed dramatically. On the one hand, I hope that this attention to dynamism may serve as a foil to synchronic views of religious history as a matter of integrated tradition and comparative stasis. On the other hand, and I believe more importantly, it highlights the ongoing interdependence of human action and the sites where it occurs. Kinpusen, after all, has always been a constantly becoming—and therefore constantly changing—real-and-imagined place.

53. Hasegawa, "Chūsei kōki jiin chitsujo," esp. 49.

Bibliography

Premodern Sources, Including Compendia and Full-Text Databases

Baopuzi 抱朴子. By Ge Hong 葛洪. *Baopuzi nei pian jiao shi* 抱朴子内篇校釋. Edited by Wang Ming 王明. 2 vols. Beijing: Zhonghua shu ju, 1985.

Chōkan kanmon 長寛勘文. In *Yamanashiken shi, shiryō hen* 山梨県史, 資料編, 3:845–79. Kōfu: Yamanashi Nichinichi Shinbunsha, 2001.

Chōshūki 長秋記. By Minamoto no Morotoki 源師時. 2 vols. *ZST,* 16–17.

Chūyūki 中右記. By Fujiwara no Munetada 藤原宗忠. 7+ vols. *DNK.*[1]

Chūyūki 中右記. By Fujiwara no Munetada 藤原宗忠. 7 vols. *ZST,* 9–15.

Daibodaisantō engi 大菩提山等縁起. In *Shugendō shiryōshū* 修験道史料集, 2:121–32.

Daigoji engi 醍醐寺縁起. In *DNBZ,* 117:246–50.

Dai Nihon bukkyō zensho (*DNBZ*) 大日本仏教全書. Edited by Bussho Kankōkai 仏書刊行会. 151 vols. Tokyo: Busshō Kankōkai, 1912–22.

Dai Nihon kokiroku (*DNK*) 大日本古記録. Edited by Tōkyō Daigaku Shiryō Hensanjo 東京大学史料編纂所. Multiple vols. Tokyo: Iwanami Shoten, 1952–.

Dai Nihon komonjo, iewake monjo 大日本古文書, 家わけ文書. Edited by Tōkyō Daigaku Shiryō Hensanjo 東京大学史料編纂所. Multiple parts and vols. Tokyo: Tōkyō Daigaku, 1904–.

Dai Nihon shiryō 大日本史料. Edited by Tōkyō Daigaku Shiryō Hensanjo 東京大学史料編纂所. 16 parts, multiple vols. Tokyo: Tōkyō Daigaku, 1901–.

1. The *DNK* edition of the *Chūyūki* is more reliable and thus cited preferentially; however, it is not yet complete and is therefore supplemented by citations to the *ZST* edition.

Dai Nihon shiryō sōgō deitabeisu 大日本史料総合データベース. Edited by Tōkyō Daigaku Shiryō Hensanjo 東京大学史料編纂所. Tokyo: Tōkyō Daigaku Shiryō Hensanjo, 2001–. wwwap.hi.u-tokyo.ac.jp/ships/db.html.

Daishi ongyōjō shūki 大師御行状集記. By Kyōhan 経範. In *Kōbō Daishi den zenshū* 弘法大師伝全集, 1:150–86.

Daodejing 道德經. Attr. Laozi 老子. *A Concordance to the Laozi.* Edited by D. C. Lau et al. The ICS Ancient Chinese Texts Concordance Series, Philosophical Works, no. 24. Hong Kong: Commercial Press, 1996.

Dengyō daishi zenshū 伝教大師全集. Edited by Tendaishū Eizan Gakuin 天台宗叡山学院. 5 vols. Shiga: Hieizan Tosho Kankōjo, 1926–27.

Denryaku 殿暦. By Fujiwara no Tadazane 藤原忠実. 5 vols. *DNK.*

Eiga monogatari 栄華物語. Attr. Akazome Emon 赤染衛門. 3 vols. *SNKBZ,* 31–33.

Engi shiki 延喜式. *SZKT,* 26.

En no gyōja hongi 役行者本記. In *SS,* 3:245–57.

En no ubasoku no koto 役優婆塞事. In *Kumano Kinpu Ōmine engishū* 熊野金峯大峯縁起集, 99–125.

Fushimi no Miyake Kujōke kyūzō shoji engishū 伏見宮家九条家旧蔵諸寺縁起集. Edited by Kunaichō Shoryōbu 宮内庁書陵部. Tokyo: Meiji Shoin, 1970.

Fusō ryakki 扶桑略記. Conventionally attr. Kōen 皇円. *SZKT,* 12.

Genji monogatari 源氏物語. By Murasaki Shikibu 紫式部. 5 vols., plus indices. *SNKBT,* 19–23.

"*Gōki* fragment." Attr. Ōe no Masafusa 大江匡房. Untitled first entry in *Gyozōbutsu narabini shinpitsu mikyō kuyō buruiki* 御造仏並辰筆御経供養部類記. Fushimi no Miya kiroku monjo 伏見宮記録文書 manuscripts, 76, 64717.1.461. Kunaichō Shoryōbu, Tokyo.

"*Gōki* fragment." Attr. Ōe no Masafusa 大江匡房. "*Gōki* itsubun" 江記逸文. Edited by Heather Blair (Hezā Bureia ヘザー・ブレーア). *Setsuwa bungaku kenkyū* 説話文学研究 49 (2014): 10–15.

Go-Nijō Moromichiki 後二条師通記. By Fujiwara no Moromichi 藤原師通. 3 vols. *DNK.*

Gonki 権記. By Fujiwara no Yukinari 原行成. 2 vols. *ZST,* 4–5.

Gōtotoku nagon ganmonshū 江都督納言願文集. By Ōe no Masafusa 大江匡房. *Gōtotoku nagon ganmonshū chūkai* 江都督納言願文集注解. Edited by Yamasaki Makoto 山崎誠. Tokyo: Hanawa Shobō, 2010.

Gunsho ruijū 群書類従 (*GR*). Edited by Hanawa Hokinoichi 塙保己一. 19 vols. Tokyo: Keizai Zasshisha, 1893–94. Reprint, 1901.

Gyokuyō 玉葉. By Kujō Kanezane 九条兼実. 3 vols. Tokyo: Kokusho Kankōkai, 1906–7.

Heian ibun, kinseki-bun hen 平安遺文, 金石文編. Edited by Takeuchi Rizō 竹内理三. Tokyo: Tōkyōdō, 1965.

Heian ibun, komonjo hen 平安遺文, 古文書編. Edited by Takeuchi Rizō 竹内理三. 10 vols., plus indices and addenda. Tokyo: Tōkyōdō, 1964–65.

Hōbutsushū 宝物集. By Taira no Yasuyori 平康頼. *SNKBT,* 40.
Hokke genki 法華験記 (*Dai Nihonkoku Hokkekyō genki* 大日本国法華経験記). By Chingen 鎮源. In *Ōjōden, Hokke genki* 往生伝・法華験記, edited by Inoue Mitsusada 井上光貞 and Ōsone Shōsuke 大曽根章介. *NST,* 7:44–219, 510–69.
Honchō monzui 本朝文粋. *SNKBT,* 27.
Honchō seiki 本朝世紀. *SZKT,* 9.
Honchō shinsenden 本朝神仙伝. Attr. Ōe no Masafusa 大江匡房. In *Ōjōden, Hokke genki* 往生伝・法華験記, edited by Inoue Mitsusada 井上光貞 and Ōsone Shōsuke 大曽根章介. *NST,* 7:255–76, 580–86.
Honchō zoku monzui 本朝続文粋. *SZKT,* 29.2.
Hyakurenshō 百錬抄. *SZKT,* 11.
Hyōhanki (alt. *Heihanki*) 兵範記. By Taira no Nobunori 平信範. 4 vols. *ZST,* 18–21.

Imakagami 今鏡. *SZKT,* 21.2.
Inokuma kanpakuki 猪隈関白記. By Konoe Iezane 近衛家実. 6 vols. *DNK.*
Ippen shōnin eden 一遍上人絵伝. *NE,* 20.
Ishiyamadera engi 石山寺縁起. *NE,* 16.

Jikkinshō 十訓抄. *SNKBZ,* 51.
Jinzen kanjō hiki 深仙灌頂秘軌. In *SS,* 2:67.
Jinzen kanjō keifu 深仙灌頂系譜. In *SS,* 3:312–29.

Kagerō nikki 蜻蛉日記. By Fujiwara no Michitsuna's Mother 藤原道綱の母. *SNKBT,* 24.
Kaifūsō 懐風藻. *NKBT,* 69.
Kamakura ibun, komonjo hen 鎌倉遺文, 古文書編. Edited by Takeuchi Rizō 竹内理三. 42 vols., plus addenda. Tokyo: Tōkyōdō Shuppan, 1971–91.
Kasuga gongen genki e 春日権現験記絵. 2 vols. *ZNE,* 13–14.
Kasuga jinja monjo 春日神社文書. 3 vols. Edited by Kasuga Jinja Shamusho 春日神社社務所. Nara: Kasuga Jinja Shamusho, 1928–42.
Kasugasha kiroku 春日社記録. 3 vols. *ZST,* 47–49.
Kinpusen himitsuden 金峰山秘密伝. Kyōto Daigaku Shimada Bunko 京都大学島田文庫 ms. In *SS,* 1:437–70.
Kinpusen himitsuden 金峯山秘密伝. Shōgoin 聖護院 ms. In *KSS,* 13–44.
Kinpusen hon'engi 金峯山本縁起. In *Shugendō shiryōshū* 修験道史料集, 2:120–21.
Kinpusen kanjō nikki 金峯山灌頂日記. In *KSS,* 51–54.
Kinpusen kengyō shidai 金峰山検校次第. In *SS,* 3:360.
Kinpusen sōsōki 金峯山創草記. Kinpusenji 金峯山寺 ms. In *KSS,* 44–50.
Kinpusen sōsōki 金峰山創草記. Shōgoin 聖護院 ms. In *SS,* 3:361–68.
Kinpusen zakki 金峰山雑記. In *SS,* 1:471–79.
Kitano tenjin engi emaki 北野天神縁起絵巻. Metropolitan Museum of Art version. "Legends of the Kitano Shrine." www.metmuseum.org/content/interactives/kitanomaki/legends.html.
Kōbō Daishi den zenshū 弘法大師伝全集. Edited by Hase Hōshū 長谷宝秀. 10 vols. Kyoto: Rokudai Shinpōsha, 1935.

Kōbō Daishi zenshū 弘法大師全集. Edited by Mikkyō Bunka Kenkyūjo 密教文化研究所. 8 vols. Wakamaya Prefecture: Mikkyō Bunka Kenkyūjo, 1967.

Kōfukuji bettō shidai 興福寺別当次第. In *DNBZ*, 124:1–59.

Kōfukuji ruki 興福寺流記. In *DNBZ*, 123:1–28.

Kōfukuji ryaku nendaiki 興福寺略年代記. In *ZGR*, 29.2:107–205.

Kojiki 古事記. *SNKBZ*, 1.

Kokiroku furutekisuto deitabeisu 古記録フルテキストデータベース. Edited by Tōkyō Daigaku Shiryō Hensanjo 東京大学史料編纂所. Tokyo: Tōkyō Daigaku Shiryō Hensanjo. wwwap.hi.u-tokyo.ac.jp/ships/db.html.

Kokon chomonjū 古今著聞集. By Tachibana Narisue 橘成季. *NKBT*, 84.

Kongō busshi Eison kanshingaku shōki 金剛仏子叡尊感身学正記. In *Saidaiji Eison denki shūsei* 西大寺叡尊伝記集成, edited by Nara Kokuritsu Bunkazai Kenkyūjo 奈良国立文化財研究所, 1–63. Kyoto: Ōtani Shuppansha, 1956.

Konjaku monogatarishū 今昔物語集. 5 vols. *SNKBT*, 33–37.

Kōya goshuin engi 高野御手印縁起. In *Kōbō daishi zenshū* 弘法大師全集, 5:426–33.

Kuchizusami 口遊. By Minamoto no Tamenori 源為憲. In *ZGR*, 32.1:61–85.

Kugyō bunin 公卿補任. 5 vols., plus index. *SZKT*, 53–57.

Kujō ushōjō yuikai 九条右丞相遺誡. By Fujiwara no Morosuke 藤原師輔. In *Kodai seiji shakai shisō* 古代政治社会思想, edited by Yamagishi Tokuhei 山岸徳平, Takeuchi Rizō 竹内理三, Ienaga Saburō 家長三郎, and Ōsone Shōsuke 大曽根章介. *NST*, 8:115–22, 296–97.

Kumano gongen kongō Zaō hōden zōkō nikki 熊野権現金剛蔵王宝殿造功日記. In *Kumano Kinpu Ōmine engishū* 熊野金峯大峯縁起集, 3–27.

Kumano Kinpu Ōmine engishū 熊野金峯大峯縁起集, edited by Kokubungaku Kenkyū Shiryōkan 国文学研究資料館. Shinpukuji zenpon sōkan 真福寺善本叢刊, vol. 10. Kyoto: Rinsen Shoten, 1998.

Kumano sansho gongen Kinpusen kongō Zaō engi 熊野三所権現金峯山金剛蔵王縁起. In *Kumano Kinpu Ōmine engishū* 熊野金峯大峯縁起集, 29–70.

Kumano sansho gongen Kinpusen kongō Zaō gokibun 熊野三所権現金峯山金剛蔵王御記文. In *Kumano Kinpu Ōmine engishū* 熊野金峯大峯縁起集, 71–78.

Kumano sansho gongen Kinpu kongō Zaō kōka onkoto 熊野三所権現金峯金剛蔵王降下御事. In *Kumano Kinpu Ōmine engishū* 熊野金峯大峯縁起集, 79–87.

Kumano sansho gongen ōji kenzoku kongō Zaō hon'i 熊野三所権現王子眷属金剛蔵王本位. In *Kumano Kinpu Ōmine engishū* 熊野金峯大峯縁起集, 89–98.

Makura no sōshi 枕草子. By Sei Shōnagon 清少納言. *SNKBT*, 25.

Man'yōshū 万葉集. 4 vols., plus index. *SNKBT*, 1–4.

Meigetsuki 明月記. By Fujiwara no Sadaie (Teika) 藤原定家. Tokyo: Kokusho Kankōkai, 1970.

Midō kanpakuki 御堂関白記. By Fujiwara no Michinaga 藤原道長. 3 vols. *DNK*.

Montoku jitsuroku 文徳実録 (*Nihon Montoku tennō jitsuroku* 日本文徳天皇実録). *SZKT*, 3.

Namu Amida butsu sazenshū 南無阿弥陀仏作善集. Attr. Chōgen 重源 or his circle. In *Ōsaka Sayamashi shi, shiryō hen.* 大阪狭山市史, 史料編, edited by Ōsaka Sayamashi

Shi Hensan Iinkai 大阪狭山市史編さん委員会 and Ōsaka Sayama Shiritsu Gōshi Shiryōkan 大阪狭山市立郷土資料館, 2:317–23. Osaka: Ōsaka Sayamashi Yakusho, 1997.

Nenjū gyōji emaki 年中行事絵巻. *NE,* 8.

Nihon kiryaku 日本紀略. 2 vols. *SZKT,* 10–11.

Nihon koten bungaku taikei (*NKBT*) 日本古典文学大系. 100 vols. Tokyo: Iwanami Shoten, 1958–66.

Nihon no emaki (*NE*) 日本の絵巻. Edited by Komatsu Shigemi 小松茂美. 20 vols. Tokyo: Chūō Kōronsha, 1987–88.

Nihon ryōiki 日本霊異記 (*Nihonkoku genpō zen'aku ryōiki* 日本国現報善悪霊異記). By Keikai (alt. Kyōkai) 景戒. *SNKBT,* 30.

Nihon sandai jitsuroku 日本三代実録. *SZKT,* 4.

Nihon shisō taikei (*NST*) 日本思想大系. 46 vols. Tokyo: Iwanami Shoten, 1970–82.

Nihon shoki 日本書紀. 3 vols. *SNKBZ,* 2–4.

Ōkagami 大鏡. *SNKBZ,* 34.

Ōmine dōjō shōgon jizai gi 大峰道場荘厳自在儀. In *SS,* 1:61–65.

Rihōōki (alt. *Ribuōki*) 吏部王記. By Prince Shigeakira 重明親王. *Shiryō henshū* 史料纂集, 39. Tokyo: Zoku Gunsho Ruijū Kanseikai, 1980.

Ruijū myōgishō 類聚名義抄. *Ruijū myōgishō, Kanchi'in-bon* 類聚名義抄, 観智院本. 3 vols. Tenri toshokan zenpon sōsho, washo no bu 天理図書館善本叢書, 和書の部, 32–34. Tokyo: Yagi Shoten, 1976.

Ryōbu mondō hishō 両峯問答秘鈔. In *SS,* 2:591–619.

Ryōi sōjō e'in giki 霊異相承慧印儀軌. In *SS,* 1:71–88.

Ryōjin hishō 梁塵秘抄. By Go-Shirakawa 後白河. *SNKBT,* 56.

Ryō no gige 令義解. *SZKT,* 22.

Sakeiki 左経記. By Minamoto no Tsuneyori 源経頼. *ZST,* 6.

Sanbōe 三宝絵 (*Sanbōe kotoba* 三宝絵詞). By Minamoto no Tamenori 源為憲. *SNKBT,* 31.

Sanbutsujō shō 讃仏乗抄. Collated by Sōshō 宗性. In *Kōkan bijutsushi shiryō, jiin hen* 校刊美術史料, 寺院編, edited by Fujita Tsuneyo 藤田経世, 3:71–106. Tokyo: Chūō Kōron Bijutsu Shuppan, 1976.

Sangō shiiki 三教指帰. By Kūkai 空海. *NKBT,* 71.

Sankaiki 山槐記. By Nakayama (Fujiwara) Tadachika 中山忠親. 3 vols. *ZST,* 26–28.

Sanne jōitsuki 三会定一記. In *DNBZ,* 123:289–431.

SAT Daizōkyō Database. http://21dzk.l.u-tokyo.ac.jp/SAT/index.html.

Scripta Sinica Database. http://hanchi.ihp.sinica.edu.tw/ihp/hanji.htm.

Seireishū (alt. *Shōryōshū*) 性霊集 (*Henjō hokki seireishū* 遍昭発起性霊集). By Kūkai 空海. *NKBT,* 71.

Senzai wakashū. 千載和歌集. *SNKBT,* 10.

Shakke kanpanki 釈家官班記. In *GR,* 15:41–60.

Shasekishū 砂石集. By Mujū Ichien 無住一円. *SNKBZ,* 52.

Shikiji bunin 職事補任. In *GR,* 3:109–99.

Shingishiki 新儀式. In *GR,* 5:35–78.

Shin Nihon koten bungaku taikei (*SNKBT*) 新日本古典文学大系. 100 vols., plus indices. Tokyo: Iwanami Shoten, 1989–2005.

Shinpen Nihon koten bungaku zenshū (*SNKBZ*) 新編日本古典文学全集. 88 vols. Tokyo: Shōgakkan, 1994–2002.

Shin sarugakuki 新猿楽記. By Fujwara no Akihira 藤原明衡. In *Kodai seiji shakai shisō* 古代政治社会思想, edited by Yamagishi Tokuhei 山岸徳平, Takeuchi Rizō 竹内理三, Ienaga Saburō 家長三郎, and Ōsone Shōsuke 大曽根章介. *NST*, 8:133–52, 301–7.

Shintei zōho kokushi taikei 新訂増補国史大系. Edited by Kuroita Katsumi 黒板勝美. 60 vols. Tokyo: Yoshikawa Kōbunkan, 1929–64.

Shintō taikei, jinja hen 神道大系, 神社編. Edited by Shintō Taikei Hensankai 神道大系編纂会. 52 vols. Tokyo: Shintō Taikei Hensankai, 1973–94.

Shishi liutie 釋氏六帖. By Yichu 義楚. *Giso rokujō* 義楚六帖. Koten sōkan 古典叢刊, vol. 2. Kyoto: Hōyū Shoten, 1979.

Shōbodaisantō engi 証菩提山等縁起. In *SS*, 3:369–77.

Shōbō sōjō den 聖宝僧正伝. By Ki no Yoshihito 紀淑人. In *ZGR*, 8.2:719–22.

Shoji konryū shidai 諸寺建立次第. In *Kōkan bijutsushi shiryō, jiin hen* 校刊美術史料, 寺院編, edited by Fujita Tsuneyo 藤田経世, 1:163–82. Tokyo: Chūō Kōronsha, 1976.

Shoku nihongi 続日本紀. *SZKT*, 2.

Shoku nihon kōki 続日本後紀. *SZKT*, 3.

Shōyūki 小右記. By Fujiwara no Sanesuke 藤原実資. 11 vols. *DNK*.

Shozan engi 諸山縁起. In *Jisha engi* 寺社縁起, edited by Sakurai Tokutarō 桜井徳太郎, Hagiwara Tatsuo 萩原龍夫, and Miyata Noboru 宮田登. *NST*, 20:89–139, 342–63.

Shugendō shiryōshū 修験道史料集. Edited by Gorai Shigeru 五来重. 2 vols. Sangaku shūkyōshi kenkyū sōsho 山岳宗教史研究叢書, vols. 18–19. Tokyo: Meicho Shuppan, 1983–84.

Shugendō shōso (*SS*) 修験道章疏. 3 vols. Edited by Nihon Daizōkyō Hensankai 日本大藏経編纂会. Tokyo: Kokusho Kankōkai, 1916–19. Reprint, 2000.

Sōgō bunin 僧綱補任. In *DNBZ*, 123:61–288.

Sokushin jōbutsugi 即身成仏義. In *Kōbō Daishi zenshū* 弘法大師全集, 1:506–20.

Sōniryō 僧尼令. In *Ritsuryō* 律令, edited by Inoue Mitsusada 井上光貞, Seki Akira 関晃, Tsuchida Naoshige 土田直鎮, and Aoki Kazuo 青木和夫. *NST*, 3:216–23.

Suisaki 水左記. By Minamoto no Toshifusa 源俊房. *ZST*, 8.

Taiki 台記. By Fujiwara no Yorinaga 藤原頼長. 3 vols. *ZST*, 23–25.

Taishō shinshū daizōkyō 大正新修大蔵経 (*T.*). Edited by Takakusu Junjirō 高楠順次郎 and Watanabe Kaigyoku 渡邊海旭. 85 vols. Tokyo: Taishō Issaikyō Kankōkai, 1924–32.

Taishō shinshū daizōkyō zuzō 大正新修大蔵経図像. Edited by Takakusu Junjirō 高楠順次郎 and Ono Genmyō 小野玄妙. 14 vols. Tokyo: Daizō Shuppan, 1932–34.

Tamakisan gongen engi 玉置山権現縁起. In *Shugendō shiryōshū* 修験道史料集, 2:148–55.

Tamefusa kyōki 為房卿記. By Fujiwara no Tamefusa 藤原為房. *Dai Nihon shiryō sōgō deitabeisu* 大日本史料総合データベース. Edited by Tōkyō Daigaku Shiryō Hensanjo 東京大学史料編纂所. Tokyo: Tōkyō Daigaku Shiryō Hensanjo, 2001–. wwwap.hi.u-tokyo.ac.jp/ships/db.html.

Tamefusa kyōki 為房卿記. By Fujiwara no Tamefusa 藤原為房. Kyōto Daigaku Sōgō Hakubutsukan 京都大学総合博物館 ms. Unpublished.
Tengu zōshi 天狗草紙. *ZNE,* 26.

Uji shūi monogatari 宇治拾遺物語. *SNKBT,* 42.

Yamabushi chō 山伏帳. In *SS,* 3:385–400.
Yuima kōji kengaku ryūgi shidai 維摩講師研学竪義次第. Two scrolls plus bound addendum. Tokyo: Kunaichō Shoryōbu, 1973.

Zhuangzi 莊子. *A Concordance to Chuang-Tzu.* Harvard-Yenching Institute Sinological Index Series Supplement, no. 20. Cambridge: Harvard University Press, 1956.
Zōho shiryō taisei (*ZST*) 増補史料大成. Edited by Zōho Shiryō Taisei Kankōkai 増補史料大成刊行会. 48 vols. Kyoto: Rinsen Shoten, 1965.
Zoku gunsho ruijū (*ZGR*) 続群書類従. Edited by Zoku gunsho ruijū kanseikai 続群書類従完成会. 37 vols. Tokyo: Zoku Gunsho Ruijū Kanseikai, 1923–72.
Zoku nihon no emaki (*ZNE*) 続日本の絵巻. Edited by Komatsu Shigemi 小松茂美. 27 vols. Tokyo: Chūō Kōronsha, 1990–93.

Secondary Sources, Including Reference Works

Abé, Ryūichi. *The Weaving of Mantra: Kūkai and the Construction of Esoteric Buddhist Discourse.* New York: Columbia University Press, 1999.
Abe Yasurō 阿部泰郎. *Chūsei Nihon no shūkyō tekusuto taikei* 中世日本の宗教テクスト体系. Nagoya: Nagoya Daigaku Shuppankai, 2013.
Adamek, Wendi L. "The Impossibility of the Given: Representations of Merit and Emptiness in Medieval Chinese Buddhism." *History of Religions* 45, no. 2 (2005): 135–80.
Adolphson, Mikael S. "The *Dōshu*: Clerics at Work in Early Medieval Japanese Monasteries." *Monumenta Nipponica* 67, no. 2 (2012): 263–82.
———. *The Gates of Power: Monks, Courtiers, and Warriors in Premodern Japan.* Honolulu: University of Hawai'i Press, 2000.
———. "Institutional Diversity and Religious Affiliation." In Adolphson, Kamens, and Matsumoto, *Heian Japan: Centers and Peripheries,* 213–44.
———. *The Teeth and Claws of the Buddha: Monastic Warriors and* Sōhei *in Japanese History.* Honolulu: University of Hawai'i Press, 2007.
Adolphson, Mikael, Edward Kamens, and Stacie Matsumoto, eds. *Heian Japan: Centers and Peripheries.* Honolulu: University of Hawai'i Press, 2007.
Akiyama Terukazu 秋山光和 et al., eds. *Byōdōin taikan* 平等院大観. 3 vols. Tokyo: Iwanami Shoten, 1987–92.
Ambros, Barbara. *Emplacing a Pilgrimage: The Ōyama Cult and Regional Religion in Early Modern Japan.* Cambridge: Harvard University Asia Center, 2008.

———. "Liminal Journeys: Pilgrimages of Noblewomen in Mid-Heian Japan." *Japanese Journal of Religious Studies* 24, nos. 3–4 (1997): 301–45.

Andreeva, Anna. "Saidaiji Monks and Esoteric Kami Worship at Ise and Miwa." *Japanese Journal of Religious Studies* 33, no. 2 (2006): 349–77.

Aris, Michael. *Hidden Treasures and Secret Lives: A Study of Pemalingpa (1450–1521) and the Sixth Dalai Lama (1683–1706)*. New York: Kegan Paul International, 1989.

Arntzen, Sonja, trans. *The Kagerō Diary: A Woman's Autobiographical Text from Tenth-Century Japan.* Ann Arbor: Center for Japanese Studies, University of Michigan, 1997.

Assman, Jan. *Religion and Cultural Memory: Ten Studies.* Translated by Rodney Livingstone. Stanford: Stanford University Press, 2006.

Astley-Kristensen, Ian. *The Rishukyō: The Sino-Japanese Tantric Prajńāpāramitā in 150 Verses (Amoghavajra's Version)*. Buddhica Britannica, Series Continua 3. Tring, U.K.: Institute of Buddhist Studies, 1991.

Averbuch, Irit. "Dancing the Doctrine: *Honji Suijaku* Thought in *Kagura* Performances." In *Buddhas and Kami: Honji Suijaku as a Combinatory Paradigm,* edited by Mark Teeuwen and Fabio Rambelli, 313–32. New York: RoutledgeCurzon, 2003.

Bargen, Doris G. *A Woman's Weapon: Spirit Possession in the Tale of Genji.* Honolulu: University of Hawai'i Press, 1997.

Basso, Keith H. *Wisdom Sits in Places: Landscape and Language among the Western Apache.* Albuquerque: University of New Mexico Press, 1996.

Bhabha, Homi K. *The Location of Culture.* New York: Routledge Classics, 2004.

Bialock, David T. *Eccentric Spaces, Hidden Histories: Narrative, Ritual, and Royal Authority from the "Chronicles of Japan" to the "Tale of the Heike."* Stanford: Stanford University Press, 2007.

———. "Outcasts, Emperorship, and Dragon Cults in *The Tale of the Heike.*" *Cahiers d'Extrême-Asie* 13 (2002): 227–310.

Birnbaum, Raoul. "Light in the Wutai Mountains." In Kapstein, *The Presence of Light: Divine Radiance in Religious Experience*, 195–226.

———. *Studies on the Mysteries of Mañjuśrī: A Group of East Asian Maṇḍalas and Their Traditional Symbolism.* Boulder, CO: Society for the Study of Chinese Religions, 1983.

Blair, Heather. "Mountain and Plain: Kinpusen and Kōfukuji in the Early Middle Ages." In *Nara, Nanto bukkyō no dentō to kakushin* 奈良・南都仏教の伝統と革新, edited by Samuel C. Morse and Nemoto Seiji 根本誠二, 1–39. Tokyo: Bensei Shuppansha, 2010.

———. "Peak of Gold: Trace, Place, and Religion in Heian Japan." Ph.D. diss., Harvard University, 2008.

———. "Rites and Rule: Kiyomori at Itsukushima and Fukuhara." *Harvard Journal of Asiatic Studies* 73, no. 1 (2013): 1–42.

——— (Hezā Bureia ヘザー・ブレーア). "Shinshutsu '*Gōki* itsubun' shōkai—Shirakawa-in no Kanji roku-nen Mitake mōde o megutte" 新出「江記逸文」紹介—白河院の寛治六年金峯詣をめぐって. *Setsuwa bungaku kenkyū* 説話文学研究 49 (2014): 1–9.

———. "Zaō Gongen: From Mountain Icon to National Treasure." *Monumenta Nipponica* 66, no. 1 (2011): 1–47.

Bock, Felicia G. *Classical Learning and Taoist Practices in Early Japan: With a Translation of Books XVI and XX of the Engi-shiki*. Tempe: Center for Asian Studies, Arizona State University, 1985.

———, trans. *Engi-Shiki: Procedures of the Engi Era*. 2 vols. Tokyo: Sophia University, 1970.

Bodiford, William M. *Sōtō Zen in Medieval Japan*. Honolulu: University of Hawai'i Press, 1993.

Bogel, Cynthea J. *With a Single Glance: Buddhist Icon and Early Mikkyō Vision*. Seattle: University of Washington Press, 2009.

Borgen, Robert. *Sugawara no Michizane and the Early Heian Court*. Cambridge: Council on East Asian Studies, Harvard University, 1986.

Boucher, Daniel. "The *Pratītyasamutpādagāthā* and Its Role in the Medieval Cult of Relics." *Journal of the International Association of Buddhist Studies* 14, no. 1 (1991): 1–27.

Bourdieu, Pierre. *Outline of a Theory of Practice*. Translated by Richard Nice. New York: Cambridge University Press, 1977.

Brackenridge, J. Scot. "The Character of Wei-Jin Qingtan: Reading Guo Xiang's *Zhuang zi*: Commentary as an Expression of Political Practice." Ph.D. diss., University of Wisconsin, 2010.

Brock, Karen L. "Awaiting Maitreya at Kasagi." In *Maitreya, The Future Buddha*, edited by Alan Sponberg and Helen Hardacre, 214–47. New York: Cambridge University Press, 1988.

Brook, Timothy. *Praying for Power: Buddhism and the Formation of Gentry Society in Late-Ming China*. Cambridge: Council on East Asia Studies, Harvard University, and Harvard-Yenching Institute, 1983.

Buffetrille, Katia. "One Day the Mountains Will Go Away .... Preliminary Remarks on the Flying Mountains of Tibet." In *Reflections of the Mountain: Essays on the History and Social Meaning of the Mountain Cult in Tibet and the Himalaya*, edited by Anne-Marie Blondeau and Ernst Steinkellner, 77–87. Vienna: Verlag de Österreichischen Akademie der Wissenschaften, 1996.

Campany, Robert. "Notes on the Devotional Uses of *Sūtra* Texts as Depicted in Early Chinese Buddhist Miracle Tales and Hagiographies." *Journal of the International Association of Buddhist Studies* 14, no. 1 (1991): 28–72.

Chikamoto Kensuke 近本謙介. "Bunji kara Kenkyū e: Tōdaiji shuto Ise sankei to Saigyō" 文治から建久へ—東大寺衆徒伊勢参詣と西行. *Junreiki kenkyū* 巡礼記研究 3(2006): 87–100.

———. "Kujōke-bon shoji engishū to Keisei no shosha katsudō: *Shozan engi* bunseki no tame no kiso sagyō to oboegaki" 九条家本諸寺縁起集と慶政の書写活動—『諸山縁起』分析のための基礎作業と覚書. In *Ōmine no kuden, engi keisei ni kansuru bunkengakuteki kenkyū: Shozan engi o chūshin ni* 大峯の口伝・縁起形成に関する文献学的研究—諸山縁起を中心に, edited by Kawasaki Tsuyoshi 川崎剛志, 30–9. Research report no. 14510477. Okayama: Shujitsu Daigaku, 2005.

———. "Nanto fukkō no keishō to tenkai: Keisei no kanjin o meguru futatsu no reitaku" 南都復興の継承と展開—慶政の勧進をめぐる二つの霊託. *Bungaku* 文学 11, no 1. (2010): 65–80.

Coleman, Simon, and John Eade, eds. *Reframing Pilgrimage: Cultures in Motion.* New York: Routledge, 2004.

Como, Michael. *Weaving and Binding: Immigrant Gods and Female Immortals in Ancient Japan.* Honolulu: University of Hawai'i Press, 2009.

Cranston, Edwin A. *The Gem-Glistening Cup.* Vol. 1 in *A Waka Anthology.* Stanford: Stanford University Press, 1993.

Davidson, Ronald M. *Indian Esoteric Buddhism: A Social History of the Tantric Movement.* New York: Columbia University Press, 2003.

Deal, William E. "The *Lotus Sūtra* and the Rhetoric of Legitimization in Eleventh-Century Japanese Buddhism." *Japanese Journal of Religious Studies* 20, no. 4 (1993): 261–95.

Derrida, Jacques. *Margins of Philosophy.* Translated by Alan Bass. Chicago: University of Chicago Press, 1982.

———. *Of Grammatology.* Translated by Gayatri Chakravorty Spivak. Baltimore: Johns Hopkins University Press, 1976.

Dolce, Lucia. "Reconsidering the Taxonomy of the Exoteric." In *The Culture of Secrecy in Japanese Religion,* edited by Bernard Scheid and Mark Teeuwen, 130–71. New York: Routledge, 2006.

Drummond, Donald Craig. "Negotiating Influence: The Pilgrimage Diary of Monastic Imperial Prince Kakuhō, *Omurogosho Kōyasan gosanrō nikki.*" Ph.D. diss., Graduate Theological Union, 2007.

Duthie, Torquil. "Envisioning the Realm: Kunimi in Early Japan." Paper presented at the Annual Meeting of the Association of Asian Studies, Chicago, March 2009.

———. "The Jinshin Rebellion and the Politics of Historical Narrative in Early Japan." *Journal of the American Oriental Society* 133, no. 2 (2013): 295–319.

———. *Man'yōshū and the Imperial Imagination in Early Japan.* Leiden: Brill, 2014.

Dykstra, Yoshiko K., trans. *Miraculous Tales of the Lotus Sutra from Ancient Japan: The Dainihonkoku Hokekyōkenki of Priest Chingen.* Honolulu: University of Hawai'i Press, 1987.

Eade, John, and Michael J. Sallnow, eds. *Contesting the Sacred: The Anthropology of Christian Pilgrimage.* Champaign: University of Illinois Press, 2000. Reprint edition.

Earhart, H. Byron. *A Religious Study of the Mount Haguro Sect of Shugendō: An Example of Japanese Mountain Religion.* Tokyo: Sophia University Press, 1970.

———. "Shugendō, the Traditions of En no Gyōja, and Mikkyō Influence." In *Tantric Buddhism in East Asia,* edited by Richard K. Payne, 191–205. Somerville, MA: Wisdom, 2006.

Ebersole, Gary L. *Ritual Poetry and the Politics of Death in Early Japan.* Princeton: Princeton University Press, 1989.

Elias, Norbert. *The Civilizing Process: Sociogenetic and Psychogenetic Investigations.* Translated by Edmund Jephcott. Rev. ed. Malden, MA: Blackwell, 2000.

———. *The Court Society.* Translated by Edmund Jephcott. Rev. ed. Dublin: University College Dublin Press, 2006.

Entrikin, J. Nicholas. *The Betweenness of Place: Toward a Geography of Modernity.* Baltimore: Johns Hopkins University Press, 1991.

Eubanks, Charlotte. *Miracles of Book and Body: Buddhist Textual Culture & Medieval Japan.* Berkeley: University of California Press, 2011.

Farris, William Wayne. *Heavenly Warriors: The Evolution of Japan's Military, 500–1300.* Cambridge: Council on East Asian Studies, Harvard University, 1996.

Faure, Bernard. *The Power of Denial: Buddhism, Purity, and Gender.* Princeton: Princeton University Press, 2003.

Ford, James L. *Jōkei and Buddhist Devotion in Early Medieval Japan.* New York: Oxford University Press, 2006.

Forte, Antonino, and Jacques May. "Chōsai." In *Hōbōgirin: Dictionnaire encyclopédique du boudhisme d'après les sources chinoises et japonaises,* edited by Sylvain Lévi, J. Takakusu, and Paul Demiéville, 5:392–407. Tokyo: Maison Franco-Japonaise, 1979.

Foucault, Michel. "Of Other Spaces." Translated by Jay Miskowiec. *Diacritics* 16, no. 1 (1986): 22–27.

Fowler, Sherry. "In Search of the Dragon: Mount Murō's Sacred Topography." *Japanese Journal of Religious Studies* 24, nos. 1–2 (1997): 145–61.

———. *Murōji: Rearranging Art and History at a Japanese Buddhist Temple.* Honolulu: University of Hawai'i Press, 2005.

Frey, Nancy Louise. *Pilgrim Stories: On and off the Road to Santiago; Journeys along an Ancient Way in Modern Spain.* Berkeley: University of California Press, 1998.

Friday, Karl F. *Hired Swords: The Rise of Private Warrior Power in Early Japan.* Stanford: Stanford University Press, 1992.

Fukunaga Mitsuji 福永光司. "Chūgoku shūkyō shisōshi" 中国宗教思想史. In *Chūgoku shūkyō shisō* 中国宗教思想, by Fukunaga Mitsuji 福永光司 et al., 1:3–158. Tokyo: Iwanami Shoten, 1990.

Fukuyama Toshio 福山敏夫. *Byōdōin to Chūsonji* 平等院と中尊寺. Nihon no bijutsu 日本の美術, vol. 25. Tokyo: Heibonsha, 1964.

———. *Jiin kenchiku no kenkyū* 寺院建築の研究. 3 vols. Tokyo: Chūō Kōron Bijutsu Shuppan, 1982–83.

Futaba Kenkō 二葉憲香. *Kodai bukkyō shisōshi kenkyū: nihon kodai ni okeru ritsuryō bukkyō oyobi han ritsuryō bukkyō no kenkyū* 古代仏教思想史研究—日本古代における律令仏教及び反律令仏教の研究. Kyoto: Nagata Bunshōdō, 1962.

Geertz, Clifford. "Centers, Kings, and Charisma: Reflections on the Symbolics of Power." In *Culture and Its Creators: Essays in Honor of Edward Shils,* edited by Joseph Ben-David and Terry Nichols Clark, 151–70. Chicago: University of Chicago Press, 1977.

Giebel, Rolf W., and Dale A. Todaro, trans. *Shingon Texts.* BDK Tripiṭaka 98. Berkeley, CA: Numata Center for Buddhist Translation and Research, 2004.

Glassman, Hank. *The Face of Jizō: Image and Cult in Medieval Japanese Buddhism.* Honolulu: University of Hawai'i Press, 2012.

Glassman, Hank, and Keller Kimbrough, eds. "Vernacular Buddhism and Medieval Japanese Literature." Editor's introduction. *Japanese Journal of Religious Studies* 36, no. 2 (2009): 201–8.

Goble, Andrew Edmund. *Kenmu: Go-Daigo's Revolution.* Cambridge: Council on East Asian Studies, Harvard University, 1996.

Gomez, Luis O. *The Land of Bliss: The Paradise of the Buddha of Measureless Light: Sanskrit and Chinese Versions of the Sukhāvatīvyūha Sutras.* Honolulu: University of Hawai'i Press, 1996.

Goodwin, Janet R. *Alms and Vagabonds: Buddhist Temples and Popular Patronage in Medieval Japan.* Honolulu: University of Hawai'i Press, 1994.

Gorai Shigeru 五来重, ed. *Yoshino, Kumano shinkō no kenkyū* 吉野・熊野信仰の研究. Sangaku shūkyōshi kenkyū sōsho 山岳宗教史研究叢書, vol. 4. Tokyo: Meicho Shuppan, 1975.

Gorai Shigeru 五来重 and Inoue Hiromichi 井上博道. *Yama no shūkyō: shugendō* 山の宗教—修験道. Kyoto: Tankōsha, 1970.

Grapard, Allan G. "Flying Mountains and Walkers of Emptiness: Toward a Definition of Sacred Space in Japanese Religions." *History of Religions* 21, no. 3 (1982): 195–221.

———. "Institution, Ritual, and Ideology: The Twenty-Two Shrine-Temple Multiplexes of Heian Japan." *History of Religions* 27, no. 3 (1988): 246–69.

———. "Linguistic Cubism: A Singularity of Pluralism in the Sannō Cult." *Japanese Journal of Religious Studies* 14, nos. 2–3 (1987): 211–34.

———. *The Protocol of the Gods: A Study of the Kasuga Cult in Japanese History.* Berkeley: University of California Press, 1992.

———. "Religious Practices." In Shively and McCullough, *Heian Japan*, 517–75.

Gregory, Peter N. *Tsung-mi and the Sinification of Buddhism.* Princeton: Princeton University Press, 1991.

Groner, Paul. *Ryōgen and Mount Hiei: Japanese Tendai in the Tenth Century.* Honolulu: University of Hawai'i Press, 2002.

———. *Saichō: The Establishment of the Japanese Tendai School.* Berkeley: University of California at Berkeley, Institute of Buddhist Studies, 1984.

Gyatso, Janet. *Apparitions of the Self: The Secret Autobiographies of a Tibetan Visionary.* Princeton: Princeton University Press, 1998.

———. "The Logic of Legitimation in the Tibetan Treasure Tradition." *History of Religions* 33, no. 2 (1993): 97–134.

Hakamada Mitsuyasu 袴田光康. " 'Kinpusen jōdo' keisei no kiban: 'Nichizō yume no ki' to Godaisan shinkō" 「金峯山浄土」形成の基盤—「日蔵夢の記」と五台山信仰. *Meiji Daigaku jinbun kagaku kenkyūjo kiyō* 明治大学人文科学研究所紀要 51 (2002): 53–88.

Hakeda, Yoshito S., trans. *The Awakening of Faith, Attributed to Aśvaghosha.* New York: Columbia University Press, 1967.

———, trans. *Kūkai: Major Works.* New York: Columbia University Press, 1972.

Halbwachs, Maurice. *On Collective Memory.* Edited, translated, and with an introduction by Lewis A. Coser. Chicago: University of Chicago Press, 1992.

Hamada Takashi 浜田隆. "Fujiwara no Michinaga no mitake mōde" 藤原道長の御岳詣. *Bukkyō geijutsu* 仏教芸術 168 (1986): 139–52.

Hardacre, Helen. "The Cave and the Womb World." *Japanese Journal of Religious Studies* 10, nos. 2–3 (1983): 149–76.

Hare, Thomas Blenman. "Reading, Writing, and Cooking: Kūkai's Interpretive Strategies." *Journal of Asian Studies* 49, no. 2 (1990): 253–73.

Hargett, James M. *Stairway to Heaven: A Journey to the Summit of Mount Emei.* Albany: State University of New York Press, 2006.

Harrison, Paul. "Is the *Dharma-kāya* the Real 'Phantom Body' of the Buddha?" *Journal of the International Association of Buddhist Studies* 15, no. 1 (1992): 44–94.

Harvey, David. *The Condition of Postmodernity: An Enquiry into the Origins of Cultural Change.* Cambridge, MA: Blackwell, 1989.

Hasegawa Kenji 長谷川賢二. "Chūsei kōki ni okeru jiin chitsujo to shugendō" 中世後期における寺院秩序と修験道. *Nihonshi kenkyū* 日本史研究 336 (1990): 31–59.

———. "Chūsei kōki ni okeru kenmitsu jisha soshiki no saihen: shugendō honzanha no seiritsu o megutte" 中世後期における顕密寺社組織の再編—修験道本山派の成立をめぐって. *Hisutoria* ヒストリア125 (1989): 56–75.

———. "Chūsei ni okeru Kumano sendatsu shihai ni tsuite" 中世に於ける熊野先達支配について. *Sangaku shugen* 山岳修験 14 (1994): 70–85.

———. "Shugendōshi no mikata, kangaekata: kenkyū no seika to kadai o chūshin ni" 修験道史のみかた・考え方—研究の成果と課題を中心に. *Rekishi kagaku* 歴史科学 123 (1991): 17–27.

Hashimoto Shinkichi 橋本進吉. *Denki tenseki kenkyū* 伝記典籍研究. Vol. 12 of *Hashimoto Shinkichi hakase chosakushū* 橋本進吉博士著作集. Tokyo: Iwanami Shoten, 1972.

Hashimoto Yoshihiko 橋本義彦. *Heian kizoku shakai no kenkyū* 平安貴族社会の研究. Tokyo: Yoshikawa Kōbunkan, 1976.

Hatta Tatsuo 八田達男. *Reigen jiin to shinbutsu shūgō: kodai jiin no chūseiteki tenkai* 霊験寺院と神仏習合—古代寺院の中世的展開. Tokyo: Iwata Shoin, 2003.

Hayami Tasuku 速水侑. *Heian kizoku shakai to bukkyō* 平安貴族社会と仏教. Tokyo: Yoshikawa Kōbunkan, 1975.

———, ed. *Inseiki no bukkyō* 院政期の仏教. Tokyo: Yoshikawa Kōbunkan, 1998.

Hayashiya Tatsusaburō 林屋辰三郎. *Kodai kokka no kaitai* 古代国家の解体. Tokyo: Tōkyō Daigaku Shuppankai, 1955.

Heian jidaishi jiten 平安時代史事典. Edited by Kodaigaku Kyōkai 古代学協会 and Kodaigaku Kenkyūjo 古代学研究所. 3 vols. Tokyo: Kadokawa Shoten, 1994.

Henderson, Gregory, and Leon Hurvitz. "The Buddha of Seiryōji: New Finds and New Theory." *Artibus Asiae* 19, no. 1 (1956): 4–55.

Hérail, Francine, trans. *Notes journalières de Fujiwara no Michinaga, ministre à la cour de Heian (995–1018).* 3 vols. Geneva: Droz, 1987–91.

Hino, Takuya. "The Daoist Facet of Kinpusen and Sugawara no Michizane Worship in the *Dōken Shōnin Meidoki:* A Translation of the *Dōken Shōnin Meidoki.*" *Pacific World,* 3rd ser., no. 11 (2009): 273–305.

Hirabayashi Moritoku 平林盛德. "Keisei shōnin den kō hoi" 慶政上人伝考補遺. *Kokugo to kokubungaku* 国語と国文学 47, no. 6 (1970): 35–46.

Hirabayashi Moritoku 平林盛徳 and Koike Kazuyuki 小池一行, eds. *Gojūonbiki sōgō bunin sōreki sōran: Suiko sanjūni-nen–Genryaku ni-nen (624-nen–1186-nen)* 五十音引

僧綱補任僧歴綜覧—推古卅二年–元暦二年(624年–1185年). Revised and expanded edition. Tokyo: Kasama Shoin, 2008.

Hiraoka Jōkai 平岡定海. *Nihon jiinshi no kenkyū* 日本寺院史の研究. Tokyo: Yoshikawa Kōbunkan, 1981.

Hirata Toshiharu 平田俊春. *Shisen kokushi no hihanteki kenkyū* 私撰国史の批判的研究. Tokyo: Kokusho Kankōkai, 1982.

Hobsbawm, Eric J., and Terence Ranger, eds. *The Invention of Tradition*. New York: Cambridge University Press, 1983.

Holt, John Clifford. *The Buddhist Viṣṇu: Religious Transformation, Politics, and Culture*. New York: Columbia University Press, 2004.

———. *Spirits of the Place: Buddhism and Lao Religious Culture*. Honolulu: University of Hawai'i Press, 2009.

Horiike Shunpō 堀池春峰. *Nanto bukkyōshi no kenkyū* 南都仏教史の研究. 2 vols. Kyoto: Hōzōkan, 1980–82.

Horikoshi Mitsunobu 堀越光信. "*Fusō ryakki*" 扶桑略記. In *Kokushi taikei shomoku kaidai* 国史大系書目解題, edited by Minagawa Kan'ichi 皆川完一 and Yamamoto Shinkichi 山本信吉, 2:331–69. Tokyo: Yoshikawa Kōbunkan, 2001.

———. "*Fusō ryakki* senja kō" 『扶桑略記』撰者考. *Kōgakkan ronsō* 皇学館論叢 17, no. 6 (1984): 23–56.

Horiuchi Noriyuki 堀内規之. *Saisen kyōgaku no kenkyū: inseiki shingon mikkyō no shomondai* 済暹教学の研究—院政期真言密教の諸問題. Tokyo: Nonburu, 2009.

Hosaka Saburō 保坂三郎. *Kyōzuka ronkō* 経塚論考. Tokyo: Chūō Kōron Bijutsu Shuppan, 1971.

Hotate Michihisa 保立道久. *Heian ōchō* 平安王朝. Tokyo: Iwanami Shoten, 1996.

———. *Ōgon kokka: higashi Ajia to Heian Nihon* 黄金国家—東アジアと平安日本. Tokyo: Aoki Shoten, 2004.

Huber, Toni. *The Cult of Pure Crystal Mountain: Popular Pilgrimage and Visionary Landscape in Southeast Tibet*. New York: Oxford University Press, 1999.

———. *The Holy Land Reborn: Pilgrimage and the Tibetan Reinvention of Buddhist India*. Chicago: University of Chicago Press, 2008.

Huey, Robert N. "The Medievalization of Poetic Practice." *Harvard Journal of Asiatic Studies* 50, no. 2 (1990): 651–68.

Hureau, Sylvie. "Buddhist Rituals." In *Early Chinese Religion, Part Two: The Period of Division (220–589 AD)*, edited by John Lagerwey and Lü Pengzhi, 1207–44. Leiden: Brill, 2010.

Hurst, G. Cameron III. *Insei: Abdicated Sovereigns in the Politics of Late Heian Japan, 1086–1185*. New York: Columbia University Press, 1976.

———. "Kugyō and Zuryō: Center and Periphery in the Era of Fujiwara no Michinaga." In Adolphson, Kamens, and Matsumoto, *Heian Japan: Centers and Peripheries*, 66–101.

Ihara Kesao 井原今朝男. *Nihon chūsei no kokusei to kasei* 日本中世の国政と家政. Tokyo: Azekura Shobō, 1995.

Ikawa Kazuko 猪川和子. "Sanbutsuji Zaō gongen zō to tainai nōnyū monjo" 三仏寺蔵王権現像と胎内納入文書. *Bijutsu kenkyū* 美術研究 251 (1967): 1–10.

———. "Zaō gongen zō to kongō dōji zō" 蔵王権現像と金剛童子像. *Bijutsu kenkyū* 美術研究 252 (1967): 1–12.

Inaba Nobumichi 稲葉伸道. *Chūsei jiin no kenryoku kōzō* 中世寺院の権力構造. Tokyo: Iwanami Shoten, 1997.

Inokuchi Yoshiharu 井口善晴. "Fujiwara no Michinaga no maikyō to Zaō gongen shinkō" 藤原道長の埋経と蔵王権現信仰. In *Kyōzuka kōkogaku ronkō* 経塚考古学論攷, edited by Andō Kōichi 安藤孝一, 3–23. Tokyo: Iwata Shoin, 2011.

Inoue Mitsusada 井上光貞. *Nihon kodai no kokka to bukkyō* 日本古代の国家と仏教. Tokyo: Iwanami Shoten, 1971.

Ishida Mosaku 石田茂作 and Yajima Kyōsuke 矢島恭介. *Kinpusen kyōzuka ibutsu no kenkyū* 金峯山経塚遺物の研究. Tokyo: Teishitsu Hakubutsukan, 1937.

Ishigami Eiichi 石上英一 and Katō Tomoyasu 加藤友康, eds. *Sekkan seiji to ōchō bunka* 摂関政治と王朝文化. Nihon no jidaishi 日本の時代史, vol. 6. Tokyo: Yoshikawa Kōbunkan, 2002.

Ivanhoe, Philip J., trans. *The Daodejing of Laozi.* Indianapolis: Hackett, 2002.

Jay, Nancy. *Throughout Your Generations Forever: Sacrifice, Religion, and Paternity.* Chicago: University of Chicago Press, 1992.

Kageyama Haruki 景山春樹. *Shintō bijutsu: sono shosō to tenkai* 神道美術—その諸相と展開. Tokyo: Yūzankaku Shuppan, 1973.

Kamens, Edward. "Dragon-Girl, Maidenflower, Buddha: The Transformation of a Waka Topos, 'The Five Obstructions.'" *Harvard Journal of Asiatic Studies* 53, no. 2 (1993): 389–442.

———. *Utamakura, Allusion, and Intertextuality in Traditional Japanese Poetry.* New Haven: Yale University Press, 1997.

———, trans. *The Three Jewels: A Study and Translation of Minamoto Tamenori's "Sanbōe."* Ann Arbor: Center for Japanese Studies, University of Michigan, 1988.

Kamikawa Michio 上川通夫. "Issaikyō to chūsei no bukkyō" 一切経と中世の仏教. *Nenpō chūseishi kenkyū* 年報中世史研究 24 (1999): 1–30.

———. *Nihon chūsei bukkyō keiseishi ron* 日本中世仏教形成史論. Tokyo: Azekura Shobō, 2007.

Kamiya Fumiko 神谷文子. "Jūgo seiki kōhan no Kōfukuji dōshū ni tsuite" 十五世紀後半の興福寺堂衆について. *Shiron* 史論 39 (1986): 30–48.

Kan Masaki 菅真城. "Hokkyō san'e no seiritsu" 北京三会の成立. *Shigaku kenkyū* 史学研究 206 (1994): 1–20.

———. "Inseiki ni okeru butsuji un'ei hōhō: sensō midokkyō o sozai toshite" 院政期における仏事運営方法—千僧御読経を素材として. *Shigaku kenkyū* 史学研究 215 (1997): 1–25.

Kanda, Christine Guth. *Shinzō: Hachiman Imagery and Its Development.* Cambridge: Council on East Asian Studies, Harvard University, 1985.

Kapstein, Matthew T., ed. *The Presence of Light: Divine Radiance and Religious Experience.* Chicago: University of Chicago Press, 2004.

Kase Fumio 加瀬文雄. "Fujiwara no Michinaga no bukkyō shinkō" 藤原道長の仏教信仰. *Fūzoku* 風俗 31, no. 3 (1993): 58–80.

Kashiharashi Shi Henshū Iinkai 橿原市史編集委員会, ed. *Kashiharashi shi* 橿原市史. Kashihara: Kashiharashi Yakusho, 1962.

Katsuura Noriko 勝浦令子. "Josei to kegare kan" 女性と穢れ観. *Bukkyō shigaku kenkyū* 仏教史学研究 51, no. 2 (2009): 1–20.

———. "Nana, hasseiki shōrai Chūgoku isho no Dōkyō-kei san'e ninshiki to sono eikyō: jingiryō sansaijō koki 'shōsan fujo mizaru rui' no saikentō" 七・八世紀将来中国医書の道教系産穢認識とその影響— 神祇令散斎条古記「生産婦女不見之類」の再検討. *Shiron* 史論 59 (2006): 1–29.

———. "Nihon kodai ni okeru gairai shinkō-kei san'e ninshiki no eikyō: honzōsho to mikkyō kyōten no kentō o chūshin ni" 日本古代における外来信仰系産穢認識の影響—本草書と密教経典の検討を中心に. *Shiron* 史論 60 (2007): 28–45.

Kawabata Shin 川端新. *Shōensei seiritsushi no kenkyū* 荘園制成立史の研究. Kyoto: Shibunkaku Shuppan, 2000.

Kawane Yoshiyasu 河音能平. *Tenjin shinkō to chūsei shoki no bunka, shisō* 天神信仰と中世初期の文化・思想. Vol. 2 of *Kawane Yoshiyasu chosakushū* 河音能平著作集. Kyoto: Bunrikaku, 2010.

Kawasaki Tsuyoshi 川崎剛志. "Inseiki ni okeru Yamato no kuni no reizan kōryū jigyō to engi" 院政期における大和国の霊山興隆事業と縁起. In *Chūsei bungaku to jiin shiryō, shōgyō* 中世文学と寺院資料・聖教, edited by Abe Yasurō 阿部泰郎, 401–25. Nagoya: Nagoya Daigaku Shuppankai, 2013.

———. "*Kumano engi:* kaidai, honkoku" 『熊野縁起』解題・翻刻. In *Ninnaji shiryō, daisanshū (engi hen)* 仁和寺資料, 第三集(縁起篇), edited by Abe Yasurō 阿部泰郎, 7–19. Nagoya: Nagoya Daigaku Bungaku Kenkyūka, Hikaku Jinbungaku Kenkyūshitsu, 2003.

———. "*Kumano gongen Kongō Zaō hōden zōkō nikki* to iu gisho" 『熊野権現金剛蔵王宝殿造功日記』という偽書. *Setsuwa bungaku kenkyū* 説話文学研究 36 (2001): 123–34.

———. "*Kumano Kinpu Ōmine engishū* kaidai" 『熊野金峯大峯縁起集』解題. In *Kumano Kinpu Ōmine engishū* 熊野金峯大峯縁起集, edited by Kokubungaku Kenkyū Shiryōkan 国文学研究資料館, 201–26. Kyoto: Rinsen Shoten, 1998.

———. "Muromachi zenki ni okeru Kumano sanzan saikō to bunka kōryū" 室町前期における熊野三山再興と文化興隆. In *Shugendō no Muromachi bunka* 修験道の室町文化, edited by Kawasaki Tsuyoshi 川崎剛志, 7–20. Tokyo: Iwata Shoin, 2011.

———. "Nihonkoku 'Kongōzan' setsu no rufu: inseiki, Nanto o chūshin ni" 日本国「金剛山」説の流布—院政期、南都を中心に. *Denshō bungaku kenkyū* 伝承文学研究 56 (2007): 12–22.

———. *Ōmine no kuden, engi keisei ni kansuru bunkengakuteki kenkyū: Shozan engi o chūshin ni* 大峯の口伝・縁起形成に関する文献学的研究—諸山縁起を中心に. Research report no. 14510477. Okayama: Shujitsu Daigaku, 2005.

———. "Reizan no jikū no saikōsaku: *Mino'odera engi* no shutsugen to sono yōha" 霊山の時空の再構築—『箕面寺縁起』の出現とその余波. Paper presented at "Religious Performance, City and Country in East Asia," symposium at University of Illinois, Champaign-Urbana, October 10, 2013.

Keenan, Linda Kleplinger. "En no Gyōja: The Legend of a Holy Man in Twelve Centuries of Japanese Literature." Ph.D. diss., University of Wisconsin, Madison, 1989.

Kertzer, David I. *Ritual, Politics, and Power.* New Haven: Yale University Press, 1988.

Kikuchi Hiroki 菊地大樹. *Chūsei bukkyō no genkei to tenkai* 中世仏教の原形と展開. Tokyo: Yoshikawa Kōbunkan, 2007.

———. *Kamakura bukkyō e no michi: jissen to shūgaku, shinjin no keifu* 鎌倉仏教への道—実践と修学・信心の系譜. Tokyo: Kōdansha, 2011.

Kim, Yung-Hee, trans. *Songs to Make the Dust Dance: The "Ryōjin Hishō" of Twelfth-Century Japan*. Berkeley: University of California Press, 1994.

Kimiya Yukihiko 木宮之彦. *Nissō sō Chōnen no kenkyū: shu toshite sono zuishinhin to shōraihin* 入宋僧奝然の研究—主としてその随身品と将来品. Tokyo: Kashima Shuppankai, 1983.

Kimoto Yoshinobu 木本好信. "Go-Nijō Moromichi no gishikikan ni tsuite" 後二条師通の儀式観について. In *Nihonkai chiikishi kenkyū* 日本海地域史研究, edited by Nihonkai Chiikishi Kenkyūkai 日本海地域史研究会, 47–62. Tokyo: Bunken Shuppan, 1985.

———. *Heianchō kanjin to kiroku no kenkyū: Nikki itsubun ni arawaretaru Heian kugyō no sekai* 平安朝官人と記録の研究—日記逸文にあらわれたる平安公卿の世界. Tokyo: Ōfū, 2000.

———. "Kanpaku Go-Nijō Moromichi no shūhen—kita mandokoro to himegimi o chūshin toshite" 関白後二条師通の周辺—北政所と姫君を中心として. *Nihon rekishi* 日本歴史 461 (1986): 90–96.

Kitamura Minao 北村皆雄, dir. *The Autumn Peak of Haguro Shugendō*. Tokyo: Visual Folklore, Inc., 2009.

Klein, Susan Blakeley. *Allegories of Desire: Esoteric Literary Commentaries of Medieval Japan*. Cambridge: Harvard University Asia Center for the Harvard-Yenching Institute, 2002.

Kleine, Christoph, and Livia Kohn, trans. "Daoist Immortality and Buddhist Holiness: A Study and Translation of the *Honchō shinsen-den*." *Japanese Religions* 24, no. 2 (1999): 119–96.

Kobayashi Yasuharu 小林保治. "Keisei" 慶政. In *Ningen* 人間, edited by Konno Tōru 今野達, Satake Akihiro 佐竹昭広, and Ueda Shizuteru 上田閑照, 215–40. Iwanami kōza Nihon bungaku to bukkyō 岩波講座日本文学と仏教, vol. 1. Tokyo: Iwanami Shoten, 1993.

Kodaigaku Kyōkai 古代学協会, ed. *Heiankyō teiyō* 平安京提要. Tokyo: Kadokawa Shoten, 1994.

Konno Toshifumi 紺野敏文. " 'Zaō gongen' no shutsugen" 「蔵王権現」の出現. *Kodai bunka* 古代文化 57, no. 7 (2005): 379–82.

Kōno Fusao 河野房雄. *Heian makki seijishi kenkyū* 平安末期政治史研究. Tokyo: Tōkyōdō Shuppan, 1979.

Kuroda Toshio 黒田俊雄. "The Imperial Law and the Buddhist Law." Translated by Jacqueline I. Stone. *Japanese Journal of Religious Studies* 23, nos. 3–4 (1996): 271–85.

———. *Kuroda Toshio chosakushū* 黒田俊雄著作集. 8 vols. Kyoto: Hōzōkan, 1994–95.

Kyōto Kokuritsu Hakubutsukan 京都国立博物館, ed. *Fujiwara no Michinaga: kiwameta eiga, negatta jōdo* 藤原道長極めた栄華・願った浄土. Kyoto: Kyōto Kokuritsu Hakubutsukan, 2007.

Kyōtoshi 京都市, ed. *Yomigaeru Heiankyō: Heian kento 1200 nen kinen* 甦る平安京—平安建都1200年記念. Kyoto: Kyōtoshi, 1994.

LaCapra, Dominick. "Rethinking Intellectual History and Reading Texts." *History and Theory* 19, no. 3 (1980): 245–76.

LaFleur, William R. *The Karma of Words: Buddhism and the Literary Arts in Medieval Japan.* Berkeley: University of California Press, 1983.

Lefebvre, Henri. *The Production of Space.* Translated by Donald Nicholson-Smith. Malden, MA: Blackwell, 1991.

Levering, Miriam. "Scripture and Its Reception: A Buddhist Case." In *Rethinking Scripture: Essays from a Comparative Perspective,* edited by Miriam Levering, 58–101. Albany: State University of New York Press, 1989.

Li, Michelle Osterfeld. *Ambiguous Bodies: Reading the Grotesque in Japanese Setsuwa Tales.* Stanford: Stanford University Press, 2009.

Li Yujuan (Ri Ikuken). 李育娟. "Kinpusen hiraisetsu to Ōe no Masafusa" 金峯山飛来説と大江匡房. *Kokugo kokubun* 国語国文 77, no. 2 (2008): 30–43.

Lindsay, Ethan Claude. "Pilgrimage to the Sacred Traces of Kōyasan: Place and Devotion in Late Heian Japan." Ph.D. diss., Princeton University, 2012.

Londo, William. "The 11th Century Revival of Mt. Kōya: Its Genesis as a Popular Religious Site." *Japanese Religions* 27, no. 1 (2002): 19–40.

———. "The Idea of Mappo in Japanese Religion and History." *Interdisciplinary Humanities* 24, no. 2 (2007): 115–25.

Lowe, Bryan D. "The Discipline of Writing: Scribes and Purity in Eighth-Century Japan." *Japanese Journal of Religious Studies* 39, no. 2 (2012): 201–39.

Mainichi Shinbunsha "Jūyō Bunkazai" Iinkai Jimukyoku 毎日新聞社「重要文化財」委員会事務局, ed. *Jūyō bunkazai* 重要文化財. 30 vols., plus supplements. Tokyo: Mainichi Shinbunsha, 1976.

Maki Michio 槇道雄. *In no kinshin no kenkyū* 院近臣の研究. Tokyo: Zoku Gunsho Ruijū Kanseikai, 2001.

Makransky, John J. *Buddhahood Embodied: Sources of Controversy in India and Tibet.* Albany: State University of New York Press, 1997.

Matisoff, Susan. "Barred from Paradise? Mount Kōya and the Karukaya Legend." In Ruch, *Engendering Faith,* 463–500.

Matsuda Hisao 松田寿男. *Niu no kenkyū: rekishi chirigaku kara mita Nihon no suigin* 丹生の研究—歴史地理学から見た日本の水銀. Tokyo: Waseda Daigaku Shuppanbu, 1970.

Matsumoto Kōichi 松本公一. "Go-Shirakawa-in no shinkō sekai: Rengeōin, Kumano, Itsukushima, Onjōji o megutte" 後白河院の信仰世界—蓮華王院・熊野・厳島・園城寺をめぐって. *Bunka shigaku* 文化史学 50 (1994): 112–29.

Matsunaga, Alicia. *The Buddhist Philosophy of Assimilation: The Historical Development of the Honji-Suijaku Theory.* Tokyo: Sophia University Press, 1969.

McCullough, Helen, trans. *Ōkagami, The Great Mirror: Fujiwara Michinaga (966–1027) and His Times, A Study and Translation.* Princeton: Princeton University Press, 1980.

McCullough, William H. "The Capital and Its Society." In Shively and McCullough, *Heian Japan,* 97–182.

McCullough, William H., and Helen Craig McCullough, trans. *A Tale of Flowering Fortunes: Annals of Japanese Aristocratic Life in the Heian Period.* Stanford: Stanford University Press, 1980.

McGuire, Mark, and Jean-Luc Abela, dirs. *Shugendō Now.* Montreal: Enpower Productions, 2009.

McGuire, Mark Patrick. "What's at Stake in Designating Japan's Sacred Mountains as UNESCO World Heritage Sites? Shugendo Practices in the Kii Peninsula." *Japanese Journal of Religious Studies* 40, no. 2 (2013): 323–54.

McKinney, Meredith, trans. *The Pillow Book.* New York: Penguin Classics, 2006.

McMullin, Neil. "The *Lotus Sutra* and Politics in the Mid-Heian Period." In Tanabe and Tanabe, *The Lotus Sutra in Japanese Culture,* 119–41.

———. "On Placating the Gods and Pacifying the Populace: The Case of the Gion 'Goryō' Cult." *History of Religions* 27, no. 3 (1988): 270–93.

Meeks, Lori. "The Disappearing Medium: Reassessing the Place of Miko in the Religious Landscape of Premodern Japan." *History of Religions* 50, no. 3 (2011): 208–60.

———. *Hokkeji and the Reemergence of Female Monastic Orders in Premodern Japan.* Honolulu: University of Hawai'i Press, 2010.

Merriam-Webster's Collegiate Dictionary. 11th ed. Springfield, MA: Merriam-Webster, Inc., 2003.

Mikawa Kei 美川圭. *Insei no kenkyū* 院政の研究. Kyoto: Rinsen Shoten, 1996.

———. *Shirakawa hōō: chūsei o hiraita teiō* 白河法皇—中世をひらいた帝王. Tokyo: Nihon Hōsō Shuppan Kyōkai, 2003.

Mills, D. E., trans. *A Collection of Tales from Uji: A Study and Translation of "Uji shūi monogatari."* Cambridge: Cambridge University Press, 1970.

Mitsuhashi Tadashi 三橋正. *Heian jidai no shinkō to shūkyō girei* 平安時代の信仰と宗教儀礼. Tokyo: Zoku Gunsho Ruijū Kanseikai, 2000.

Miyachi Naokazu 宮地直一, Yamamoto Nobuki 山本信哉, and Kōnō Seizō 河野省三, eds. *Ōharai kotoba chūshaku taisei* 大祓詞註釈大成. 3 vols. Tokyo: Naigai Shoseki, 1935–41.

Miyake Hitoshi 宮家準. *En no gyōja to Shugendō no rekishi* 役行者と修験道の歴史. Tokyo: Yoshikawa Kōbunkan, 2000.

———. *Kumano shugen* 熊野修験. Tokyo: Yoshikawa Kōbunkan, 1992.

———. *The Mandala of the Mountain: Shugendō and Folk Religion.* Edited and with an introduction by Gaynor Sekimori. Tokyo: Keiō University Press, 2005.

———. *Ōmine shugendō no kenkyū* 大峰修験道の研究. Tokyo: Kōsei Shuppansha, 1988.

———. *Shugendō: Essays on the Structure of Japanese Folk Religion.* Edited and with an introduction by H. Byron Earhart. Ann Arbor: Center for Japanese Studies, University of Michigan, 2001.

———. *Shugendō girei no kenkyū* 修験道儀礼の研究. Tokyo: Shunjūsha, 1971. Reprint, 1999.

———. *Shugendō shisō no kenkyū* 修験道思想の研究. Tokyo: Shunjūsha, 1985.

———. *Shugendō soshiki no kenkyū* 修験道組織の研究. Tokyo: Shunjūsha, 1999.

———. *Shūkyō minzokugaku* 宗教民俗学. Tokyo: Tōkyō Daigaku Shuppankai, 1989.

Miyake Toshiyuki 三宅敏之. *Kyōzuka ronkō* 経塚論攷. Tokyo: Yūzankaku Shuppan, 1983.

Miyazaki, Fumiko. "Female Pilgrims and Mt. Fuji: Changing Perspectives on the Exclusion of Women." *Monumenta Nipponica* 60, no. 3 (2005): 339–91.

Moerman, D. Max. "The Archaeology of Anxiety: An Underground History of Heian Religion." In Adolphson, Kamens, and Matsumoto, *Heian Japan: Centers and Peripheries*, 245–71.

———. *Localizing Paradise: Kumano Pilgrimage and the Religious Landscape of Premodern Japan*. Cambridge: Harvard University Asia Center, 2005.

Mollier, Christine. *Buddhism and Taoism Face to Face: Scripture, Ritual, and Iconographic Exchange in Medieval China*. Honolulu: University of Hawai'i Press, 2008.

Mori Katsumi 森克己 and Wada Hidematsu 和田英松, eds. *Kokusho itsubun (shintei zōho)* 国書逸文(新訂増補). Tokyo: Kokusho Kankōkai, 1995.

Mori, Mizue. "Ancient and Classical Japan: The Dawn of Shinto." In *Shintō: A Short History,* edited by Inoue Nobutaka, translated by Mark Teeuwen and John Breen, 12–62. New York: RoutledgeCurzon, 2003.

Morioka Miko (?) 盛岡美子. "Kakebotoke kigen kō" 懸仏起源攷. *Kōkogaku zasshi* 考古学雑誌 31, no. 6 (1941): 374–94.

Morrell, Robert E. "The Buddhist Poetry in the *Goshūishū*." *Monumenta Nipponica* 28, no. 1 (1973): 87–100.

———. *Early Kamakura Buddhism: A Minority Report.* Berkeley: Asian Humanities Press, 1987.

———, trans. *Sand and Pebbles ("Shasekishū"): The Tales of Mujū Ichien, A Voice for Pluralism in Kamakura Buddhism*. Albany: State University of New York Press, 1985.

———. "The *Shinkokinshū*: Poems on Śākyamuni's Teachings (Shakkyōka)." In *The Distant Isle: Studies and Translations of Japanese Literature in Honor of Robert H. Brower,* edited by Thomas Hare, Robert Borgen, and Sharalyn Orbaugh, 281–320. Ann Arbor: Center for Japanese Studies, University of Michigan, 1996.

Motoki Yasuo 元木泰雄. *Inseiki seijishi kenkyū* 院政期政治史研究. Kyoto: Shibunkaku Shuppan, 1996.

Murakami Senjō 村上専精, Tsuji Zennosuke 辻善之助, and Washio Junkei 鷲尾順敬, eds. *Meiji ishin shinbutsu bunri shiryō* 明治維新神仏分離史料. 5 vols. Tokyo: Tōhō Shoin, 1926–29.

Murdoch, James. *A History of Japan*. Vol. 1. New York: Ungar, 1964.

Nagasaka Ichirō 長坂一郎. *Shinbutsu shūgōzō no kenkyū: seiritsu to denpa no haikei* 神仏習合像の研究 —成立と伝播の背景. Tokyo: Chūō Kōron Bijutsu Shuppan, 2004.

Nagashima Fukutarō 永島福太郎. "Kasugasha Kōfukuji no ittaika" 春日社興福寺の一体化. *Nihon rekishi* 日本歴史 125 (1958): 13–19.

———. *Nara bunka no denryū* 奈良文化の伝流. Tokyo: Chūō Kōronsha, 1944.

Nagoyashi Hakubutsukan 名古屋市博物館 and Shinpukuji Ōsu Bunko Chōsa Kenkyūkai 真福寺大須文庫調査研究会, eds. *Ōsu Kannon: ima hirakareru kiseki no bunko* 大須観音—いま開かれる、奇跡の文庫. Nagoya: Ōsu Kannon Hōshōin and Arumu, 2012.

Naitō Sakae 内藤栄. "Kyōzō no seiritsu" 鏡像の成立. *Bukkyō geijitsu* 仏教芸術 206 (1993): 43–61.

Nakamura Gorō 中村五郎. "Kyōzuka to 10–12 seiki no shakai, shūkyō no dōtai: Kōyasan okunoin kyōzuka o kiten toshite" 経塚と10〜12世紀の社会・宗教の動態 —高野山奥之院経塚を起点として. *Nihon kōkogaku* 日本考古学 14 (2002): 53–70.

Nakamura, Kyoko Motomochi, trans. *Miraculous Stories from the Japanese Tradition: The "Nihon ryōiki" of the Monk Kyōkai*. Cambridge: Harvard University Press, 1973.

Namiki Katsuko 並木和子. "Sekkanke to Tenjin shinkō" 摂関家と天神信仰. *Chūō shigaku* 中央史学 5 (1982): 1–18.

Naniwada Tōru 難波田徹, ed. *Kyōzō to kakebotoke* 鏡像と懸仏. *Nihon no bijutsu* 日本の美術 284 (1990).

Nara Kokuritsu Hakubutsukan 奈良国立博物館. *Taimadera: gokuraku jōdo e no akogare, Taima mandara kansei 1250 nen kinen tokubetsuten* 當麻寺—極楽浄土へのあこがれ—當麻曼荼羅完成1250年記念特別展. Nara: Nara Kokuritsu Hakubutsukan, 2013.

Nara Sangaku Iseki Kenkyūkai 奈良山岳遺跡研究会, ed. *Ōmine sangaku shinkō iseki no chōsa kenkyū* 大峰山岳信仰遺跡の調査研究. Kashihara: Yura Yamato Kodai Bunka Kenkyū Kyōkai, 2003.

Nihon kokugo daijiten 日本国語大辞典. 14 vols. Tokyo: Shōgakkan, 2000–2.

Nihon rekishi chimei taikei 日本歴史地名大系. 50 vols. Tokyo: Heibonsha, 1979–2005.

Nishiguchi Junko 西口順子. *Onna no chikara: kodai no josei to bukkyō* 女の力—古代の女性と仏教. Tokyo: Heibonsha, 1987.

———. "Where the Bones Go." Translated by Mimi Hall Yiengpruksawan. In Ruch, *Engendering Faith*, 417–40.

Obeyesekere, Gananath. "The Great Tradition and the Little in the Perspective of Sinhalese Buddhism." *Journal of Asian Studies* 22, no. 2 (1963): 139–53.

Ōishi Masaaki 大石雅章. *Nihon chūsei shakai to jiin* 日本中世社会と寺院. Osaka: Seibundō Shuppan, 2004.

Oishio Chihiro 追塩千尋. "Kojimadera Shinkō no shūkyōteki kankyō: sekkanki nanto kei bukkyō no dōkō ni kansuru ichikōsatsu" 子島寺真興の宗教的環境—摂関期南都系仏教の動向に関する一考察. *Bukkyō shigaku kenkyū* 仏教史学研究 34, no. 2 (1991): 40–66.

Okada Shōji 岡田莊司. *Heian jidai no kokka to saishi* 平安時代の国家と祭祀. Tokyo: Zoku Gunsho Ruijū Kanseikai, 1994.

Oka Naomi 岡直己. *Shinzō chōkoku no kenkyū* 神像彫刻の研究. Tokyo: Kadokawa Shoten, 1966.

Okano Kōji 岡野浩二. *Heian jidai no kokka to jiin* 平安時代の国家と寺院. Tokyo: Hanawa Shobō, 2009.

Ooms, Herman. *Imperial Politics and Symbolics in Ancient Japan: The Tenmu Dynasty, 650–800*. Honolulu: University of Hawai'i Press, 2009.

Ortner, Sherry B. *High Religion: A Cultural and Political History of Sherpa Buddhism*. Princeton: Princeton University Press, 1989.

Orzech, Charles D. *Politics and Transcendent Wisdom: The Scripture for Humane Kings in the Creation of Chinese Buddhism*. University Park: Pennsylvania State University Press, 1998.

Ōsaka Shiritsu Bijutsukan 大阪市立美術館, ed. *Inori no michi: Yoshino, Kumano, Kōya no meihō tokubetsuten* 祈りの道—吉野・熊野・高野の名宝特別展. Osaka: Mainichi Shinbunsha and NHK, 2004.

Ōyodochō Shi Henshū Iinkai 大淀町史編集委員会. *Ōyodochō shi* 大淀町史. Ōyodo: Ōyodochō, 1973.

Payne, Richard K, ed. *Re-Visioning "Kamakura" Buddhism.* Honolulu: University of Hawai'i Press, 1998.

Piggott, Joan R., ed. *Capital and Countryside in Japan, 300–1180: Japanese Historians Interpreted in English.* Ithaca, NY: East Asian Program, Cornell University Press, 2006.

———. *The Emergence of Japanese Kingship.* Stanford: Stanford University Press, 1997.

———. "Tōdaiji and the Nara Imperium." Ph.D. diss., Stanford University, 1987.

Piggott, Joan R., and Yoshida Sanae, eds. *Teishinkōki: The Year 939 in the Journal of Regent Fujiwara no Tadahira.* Ithaca, NY: East Asia Program, Cornell University, 2008.

Pinnington, Noel John. "Models of the Way in the Theory of Noh." *Nichibunken Japan Review* 18 (2006): 29–55.

———. *Traces in the Way: Michi and the Writings of Komparu Zenchiku.* Ithaca, NY: East Asia Program, Cornell University, 2006.

Plutschow, Herbert E. *Chaos and Cosmos: Ritual in Early and Medieval Japanese Literature.* Leiden: Brill, 1990.

Pred, Allan. "Place as Historically Contingent Process: Structuration and the Time-Geography of Becoming Places." *Annals of the Association of American Geographers* 74, no. 2 (1984): 279–97.

Quinter, David. "Creating Bodhisattvas: Eison, *'Hinin,'* and the 'Living Mañjuśrī.'" *Monumenta Nipponica* 62, no. 4 (2007): 437–58.

———. "Invoking the Mother of Awakening: An Investigation of Jōkei and Eison's *Monju kōshiki.*" *Japanese Journal of Religious Studies* 38, no. 2 (2011): 263–302.

Rambelli, Fabio. *Buddhist Materiality: A Cultural History of Objects in Japanese Buddhism.* Stanford: Stanford University Press, 2007.

———. "Secret Buddhas: The Limits of Buddhist Representation." *Monumenta Nipponica* 57, no. 3 (2002): 271–307.

Reader, Ian. *Making Pilgrimages: Meaning and Practice in Shikoku.* Honolulu: University of Hawai'i Press, 2005.

———. "Review of Miyake Hitoshi, *Shūkyō minzokugaku.*" *Japanese Journal of Religious Studies* 17, no. 4 (1990): 433–38.

Reader, Ian, and Paul L. Swanson. "Pilgrimage in the Japanese Religious Tradition." Editor's introduction. *Japanese Journal of Religious Studies* 24, nos. 3–4 (1997): 225–70.

Rekishigaku Kenkyūkai 歴史学研究会 and Nihonshi Kenkyūkai 日本史研究会, eds. *Chūsei no keisei* 中世の形成. Nihonshi no kōza 日本史の講座, vol. 3. Tokyo: Tōkyō Daigaku Shuppankai, 2004.

Robson, James. *Power of Place: The Religious Landscape of the Southern Sacred Peak (Nanyue) in Medieval China.* Cambridge: Harvard University Asia Center, 2009.

Rong, Xinjiang. "The Nature of the Dunhuang Library Cave and the Reasons for Its Sealing." Translated by Valerie Hansen. *Cahiers d'Extrême-Asie* 11 (1999–2000): 247–75.

Rosenfield, John M. *Portraits of Chōgen: The Transformation of Buddhist Art in Early Medieval Japan.* Boston: Brill, 2011.

Roth, Carina. "Where Mountains Fly: The Honji-Suijaku Mechanism in Japan." *Études Asiatiques* 58, no. 4 (2004): 1073–83.

Roth, Carina, and Sandra Roth, dirs. *Where Mountains Fly.* Geneva, 2008.

Ruch, Barbara, ed. *Engendering Faith: Women and Buddhism in Premodern Japan.* Ann Arbor: Center for Japanese Studies, University of Michigan, 2002.

Ruppert, Brian D. *Jewel in the Ashes: Buddha Relics and Power in Early Medieval Japan.* Cambridge: Harvard University Asia Center, 2000.

———. "Royal Progresses to Shrines: Cloistered Sovereign, *Tennō,* and the Sacred Sites of Early Medieval Japan." *Cahiers d'Extrême-Asie* 16 (2006–7): 183–202.

———. "Saisen, 'Kōbō Daishi,' and the Dharma Prince Shukaku: The Shingon Culture of Learning, Lineage, and Sacred Works (Shōgyō) in the Insei Period." Paper presented at the Annual Meeting of the American Academy of Religion, Atlanta, November 2010.

Saitō Tōru 斉藤融. "Fujiwara no Michinaga no Kinpusen shinkō: kōshi tanjō kigan setsu ni taisuru gimon" 藤原道長の金峯山信仰—皇子誕生祈願説に対する疑問. *Nihon rekishi* 日本歴史 553 (1994): 11–29.

Saitō Toshihiko 斉藤利彦. "Issaikyō to geinō: Byōdōin issaikyōe to bugaku o chūshin ni" 一切経と芸能—平等院一切経会と舞楽を中心に. In *Issaikyō no rekishiteki kenkyū* (*Bukkyō Daigaku sōgō kenkyūjo kiyō, betten*) 一切経の歴史的研究(仏教大学総合研究所紀要, 別冊), edited by Bukkyō Daigaku Sōgō Kenkyūjo 仏教大学総合研究所, 77–156. Kyoto: Bukkyō Daigaku Sōgō Kenkyūjo, 2004.

Sakai Akiko 酒井彰子. "Chūsei Onjōji no monzeki to Kumano Sanzan kengyōshoku no sōshō: Jōjūin kara Shōgoin e" 中世園城寺の門跡と熊野三山検校職の相承—常住院から聖護院へ. *Bunka shigaku* 文化史学 48 (1992): 72–85.

Sakamoto Shōzō 坂本賞三. "Murakami Genji no seikaku" 村上源氏の性格. In *Kōki sekkan jidaishi no kenkyū* 後期摂関時代史の研究, edited by Kodaigaku Kyōkai 古代学協会, 299–329. Tokyo: Yoshikawa Kōbunkan, 1990.

Sakamoto Toshiyuki 阪本敏行. *Kumano sanzan to Kumano bettō* 熊野三山と熊野別当. Osaka: Seibundō Shuppan, 2005.

Salomon, Richard. "Why Did the Gandhāran Buddhists Bury Their Manuscripts?" In *Buddhist Manuscript Cultures: Knowledge, Ritual, Art,* edited by Stephen C. Berkwitz, Juliane Schober, and Claudia Brown, 19–34. New York: Routledge, 2009.

Sanford, James H., William R. LaFleur, and Masatoshi Nagatomi, eds. *Flowing Traces: Buddhism in the Literary and Visual Arts of Japan.* Princeton: Princeton University Press, 1992.

Sango, Asuka. "In the Halo of Golden Light: Imperial Authority and Buddhist Ritual in Heian Japan (794–1185)." Ph.D. diss., Princeton University, 2007.

Sansom, George. *A History of Japan.* 3 vols. Stanford: Stanford University Press, 1958–63.

Satō Fumiko 佐藤文子. "Ubasoku kōshin no jitsuzō to sono shiteki igi" 優婆塞貢進の実像とその史的意義. *Shisō* 史窓 50 (1993): 58–76.

Satō Kenji 佐藤健治. "Fujiwara no Morozane, Moromichi: ryōdenkasei no zasetsu" 藤原師実・師通—両殿下制の挫折. In *Ōchō no hen'yō to musha* 王朝の変容と武者, edited by Motoki Yasuo 元木泰雄, 229–48. Osaka: Seibundō Shuppan, 2005.

Satō Torao 佐藤虎雄. "Kinpusen no kenkyū: Kinpusen sōsōki ni tsuite 金峰山の研究—金峰山創草記について. In *Uozumi sensei koki kinen: Kokushigaku ronsō* 魚澄先生古稀記念, 国史学論叢, edited by Uozumi Sensei Koki Kinenkai 魚澄先生古稀記念会, 289–315. Kyoto: Daihō, 1959.

———. "Kongō Zaō gongen genryū kō" 金剛蔵王権現源流考. In *Nihon kodaishi ronsō: Nishida sensei shōju kinen* 日本古代史論叢—西田先生頌寿記念, edited by Kodaigaku Kyōkai 古代学協会 and Nishida Naojirō 西田直二郎, 267–83. Tokyo: Yoshikawa Kōbunkan, 1960.

Scheid, Bernard, and Mark Teeuwen, eds. *The Culture of Secrecy in Japanese Religion*. New York: Routledge, 2006.

Schuster, Nancy. "Changing the Female Body: Wise Women and the Bodhisattva Path in Some *Mahāratnakūṭasūtras*." *Journal of the International Association for Buddhist Studies* 4, no. 1 (1981): 24–69.

Seidensticker, Edward, trans. *The Gossamer Years: The Diary of a Noblewoman of Heian Japan*. Boston: Tuttle, 1964. Reprint, 2001.

Sekiguchi Makiko 関口真規子. *Shugendō kyōdan seiritsushi: Tōzan-ha o tōshite* 修験道教団成立史—当山派を通して. Tokyo: Bensei Shuppan, 2009.

Seki Hideo 関秀夫. *Kyōzuka no shosō to sono tenkai* 経塚の諸相とその展開. Tokyo: Yūzankaku Shuppan, 1990.

Sekimori, Gaynor. "Paper Fowl and Wooden Fish: The Separation of Kami and Buddha Worship in Haguro Shugendō, 1869–1875." *Japanese Journal of Religious Studies* 32, no. 2 (2005): 197–234.

———. "Sacralizing the Border: The Engendering of Liminal Space." *Transactions of the Asiatic Society of Japan*, ser. 4, vol. 20 (2006): 53–69.

———. "Shugendō: Japanese Mountain Religion—State of the Field and Bibliographic Review." *Religion Compass* 3, no. 1 (2009): 31–57.

———. "Varied Reactions to the Shinto-Buddhist 'Separation' Edicts as Seen at Shugendō Shrine-Temple Complexes, 1868–75." *Sangaku shugen* 山岳修験 special issue (2007): 45–55.

Sekine Daisen 関根大仙. *Mainōkyō no kenkyū* 埋納経の研究. Tokyo: Ryūbunkan, 1968.

Shahar, Meir. "The Lingyin Si Monkey Disciples and the Origins of Sun Wukong." *Harvard Journal of Asiatic Studies* 52, no. 1 (1992): 193–224.

Sharf, Robert H. *Coming to Terms with Chinese Buddhism: A Reading of the "Treasure Store Treatise."* Honolulu: University of Hawai'i Press, 2002.

———. "On the Allure of Buddhist Relics." *Representations* 66 (1999): 75–99.

Shen, Hsueh-Man. "Image in a Mirror, Moon in the Water: Liao Period Bronze Mirrors Incised with Buddha Images." *Orientations* 37, no. 6 (2006): 58–64.

———. "Realizing the Buddha's *Dharma* Body during the *Mofa* Period: A Study of Liao Buddhist Relic Deposits." *Artibus Asiae* 61, no. 2 (2001): 263–303.

Shiba Kayono 柴佳世乃 and Tonami Satoko 户浪智子. "Keisei *Kondō honbutsu shūjiki* o yomu: Keisei to Onjōji, Kujōke" 慶政『金堂本仏修治記』を読む—慶政と園城寺、九条家. *Chiba daigaku jinbun kenkyū* 千葉大学人文研究 38 (2009): 17–53.

———. "Keisei to Onjōji: Keisei *Miidera Kōjōin nado no koto, Taishi onsaku reizō nikki* o yomu" 慶政と園城寺—慶政『三井寺興乗院等事』『大師御作霊像日記』を読む. *Chiba daigaku jinbun kenkyū* 千葉大学人文研究 39 (2010): 69–104.

Shibata Minoru 柴田実, ed. *Goryō shinkō* 御霊信仰. Minshū shūkyōshi sōsho 民衆宗教史叢書, vol. 5. Tokyo: Yūzankaku Shuppan, 1984.

Shigeta Shin'ichi 繁田信一. *Onmyōji to kizoku shakai* 陰陽師と貴族社会. Tokyo: Yoshikawa Kōbunkan, 2004.

Shimizu Hiroshi 清水拡. *Heian jidai bukkyō kenchikushi no kenkyū: jōdokyō kenchiku o chūshin ni* 平安時代仏教建築史の研究—浄土教建築を中心に. Tokyo: Chūō Kōron Bijutsu Shuppan, 1992.

Shingonshū nenpyō 真言宗年表. Edited by Moriyama Shōshin 守山聖真. Tokyo: Kokusho Kankōkai, 1973.

Shinjō Mieko 新城美恵子. *Honzan-ha shugen to Kumano sendatsu* 本山派修験と熊野先達. Tokyo: Iwata Shoin, 1999.

Shinjō Tsunezō 新城常三. *Shaji sankei no shakai keizaishiteki kenkyū* 社寺参詣の社会経済史的研究. Tokyo: Hanawa Shobō, 1964.

Shirai Yūko 白井優子. *Inseiki Kōyasan to Kūkai nyūjō densetsu* 院政期高野山と空海入定伝説. Tokyo: Dōseisha, 2002.

Shively, Donald H., and William H. McCullough, eds. *Heian Japan*. Vol. 2 of *The Cambridge History of Japan*. New York: Cambridge University Press, 1999.

Shudō Yoshiki 首藤善樹. *Kinpusenji shi* 金峯山寺史. Yoshino: Kinpusenji, 2004.

Soja, Edward W. *Thirdspace: Journeys to Los Angeles and Other Real-and-Imagined Places*. Malden, MA: Blackwell, 1996.

Sonoda Kōyū 薗田香融. "Kodai bukkyō ni okeru sanrin shugyō to sono igi: toku ni jinenchishū o megutte" 古代仏教における山林修行とその意義—特に自然智宗をめぐって. In *Kūkai* 空海, edited by Takagi Shingen 高木訷元 and Wada Shūjō 和多秀乘, 40–65. Nihon meisō ronshū 日本名僧論集, vol. 3. Tokyo: Yoshikawa Kōbunkan, 1982 (article first published in 1957).

Spiro, Melford E. *Buddhism and Society: A Great Tradition and Its Burmese Vicissitudes*. 2nd ed. Berkeley: University of California Press, 1982.

Stone, Jacqueline I. *Original Enlightenment and the Transformation of Medieval Japanese Buddhism*. Honolulu: University of Hawai'i Press, 1999.

Strong, John S. *Relics of the Buddha*. Princeton: Princeton University Press, 2004.

Sugawara Shinkai 菅原信海. *Nihon shisō to shinbutsu shūgō* 日本思想と神仏習合. Tokyo: Shunjūsha, 1996.

Sugaya Fuminori 菅谷文則. "Kumano to Ōmine shinkō" 熊野と大峯信仰. In *Kumano gongen: Kumano mōde, shugendō* 熊野権現—熊野詣・修験道, edited by Wada Atsumu 和田萃, 69–104. Tokyo: Chikuma Shobō, 1988.

Sugaya Fuminori 菅谷文則, Maezono Michio 前園実知雄, and Saitō Kiyohide 西藤清秀. "Ōminesanji hakkutsu chōsa ni tsuite" 大峯山寺発掘調査について. *Bukkyō geijutsu* 仏教芸術 168 (1986): 117–26.

Sugiyama Nobuzō 杉山信三. *Inge kenchiku no kenkyū* 院家建築の研究. Tokyo: Yoshikawa Kōbunkan, 1981.

Suzuki Masataka 鈴木正崇. *Nyonin kinsei* 女人禁制. Tokyo: Yoshikawa Kōbunkan, 2002.

Suzuki Shigeo 鈴木茂男. *Kodai monjo no kinōronteki kenkyū* 古代文書の機能論的研究. Tokyo: Yoshikawa Kōbunkan, 1997.

Suzuki Shōei 鈴木昭英. "The Development of Suijaku Stories about Zaō Gongen." Translated by Heather Blair. *Cahiers d'Extrême-Asie* 18 (2009): 141–68.

———. *Shugen kyōdan no keisei to tenkai* 修験教団の形成と展開. Vol. 1 of *Shugendō rekishi minzoku ronshū* 修験道歴史民俗論集. Kyoto: Hōzōkan, 2003.

Swanson, Paul L. "Shugendō and the Yoshino-Kumano Pilgrimage: An Example of Mountain Pilgrimage." *Monumenta Nipponica* 36, no. 1 (1981): 55–84.

Taira Masayuki 平雅行. "Kyū bukkyō to josei" 旧仏教と女性. In *Josei to shūkyō* 女性と宗教, edited by Kojima Kyōko 児島恭子 and Shiomi Minako 塩見美奈子, 150–79. Nihon joseishi ronshū 日本女性史論集, vol. 5. Tokyo: Yoshikawa Kōbunkan, 1998.

Takayama Kyōko 高山京子. *Chūsei Kōfukuji no monzeki* 中世興福寺の門跡. Tokyo: Bensei Shuppan, 2010.

Tanabe, George J., Jr., and Willa Jane Tanabe. *The Lotus Sutra in Japanese Culture*. Honolulu: University of Hawai'i Press, 1989.

Tanabe, Willa Jane. "The Lotus Lectures: *Hokke Hakkō* in the Heian Period." *Monumenta Nipponica* 39, no. 4 (1984): 393–407.

———. *Paintings of the Lotus Sutra: The Relationship of Ritual, Text, and Picture*. New York: Weatherhill, 1988.

Teiser, Stephen F. *The Ghost Festival in Medieval China.* Princeton: Princeton University Press, 1988.

Teeuwen, Mark. *Watarai Shintō: An Intellectual History of the Outer Shrine in Ise.* Leiden: Research School CNWS, School of Asian, African, and Amerindian Studies, 1996.

Teeuwen, Mark, and Fabio Rambelli, eds. *Buddhas and Kami in Japan: Honji Suijaku as a Combinatory Paradigm*. New York: RoutledgeCurzon, 2003.

Teeuwen, Mark, and Hendrik van der Veere. *Nakatomi Harae Kunge: Purification and Enlightenment in Late-Heian Japan*. Munich: Iudicium, 1998.

Tenrishi Shi Hensan Iinkai 天理市史編纂委員会. *Kaitei Tenrishi shi, hon hen* 改訂天理市史, 本編. 2 vols. Tenri: Tenrishi Yakusho, 1976–79.

Thal, Sarah. *Rearranging the Landscape of the Gods: The Politics of a Pilgrimage Site in Japan, 1573–1912*. Chicago: University of Chicago Press, 2005.

Toby, Ronald P. "Why Leave Nara? Kammu and the Transfer of the Capital." *Monumenta Nipponica* 40, no. 3 (1985): 331–47.

Tokunaga Seiko 徳永誓子. "Kumano sanzan kengyō to shugendō" 熊野三山検校と修験道. *Nenpō chūseishi kenkyū* 年報中世史研究 27 (2002): 75–100.

———. "Shugendō seiritsu no shiteki zentei: geza no tenkai" 修験道成立の史的前提—験者の展開. *Shirin* 史林 84, no. 1 (2001): 97–123.

———. "Shugendō Tōzan-ha to Kōfukuji dōshū" 修験道当山派と興福寺堂衆. *Nihonshi kenkyū* 日本史研究 435 (1998): 27–50.

Tōkyō Kokuritsu Hakubutsukan 東京国立博物館. *Kyōzō* 鏡像. Tokyo: Tōkyō Kokuritsu Hakubutsukan, 1975.

Tōkyō Kokuritsu Hakubutsukan 東京国立博物館 and Kyūshū Kokuritsu Hakubutsukan 九州国立博物館, eds. *Kokuhō: daijinja ten* 国法, 大神社展. Tokyo: NHK Puromōshon, 2013.

Tomishima Yoshiyuki 冨島義幸. "Inseiki ni okeru Hosshōji kondō no igi ni tsuite" 院政期における法勝寺金堂の意義について. *Nihongaku kenkyū* 日本学研究 4 (2001): 23–56.

———. "Shirakawa: Inseiki 'ōke' no toshi kūkan" 白河—院政期「王家」の都市空間. In *Jikan to kūkan* 時間と空間, edited by Inseiki Bunka Kenkyūkai 院政期文化研究会, 169–209. Inseiki bunka ronshū 院政期文化論集, vol. 3. Tokyo: Shin'washa, 2003.

Tomishima Yoshiyuki 冨島義幸 and Takahashi Yasuo 高橋康夫. "Hosshōji no garan to kenchiku: sono enkaku saikō" 法勝寺の伽藍と建築—その沿革再考. *Kenchiku shigaku* 建築史学 26 (1996): 34–53.

Totman, Conrad. *The Green Archipelago: Forestry in Preindustrial Japan*. Athens: Ohio University Press, 1989.

Tsiang, Katherine R. "Embodiments of Buddhist Texts in Early Medieval Chinese Visual Culture." In *Body and Face in Chinese Visual Culture,* edited by Wu Hung and Katherine R. Tsiang, 49–78. Cambridge: Harvard University Asia Center, 2005.

Tsuji Hidenori 逵日出典. *Hachiman gūji seiritsushi no kenkyū* 八幡宮寺成立史の研究. Tokyo: Zoku Gunsho Ruijū Kanseikai, 2003.

———. *Narachō sangaku jiin no kenkyū* 奈良朝山岳寺院の研究. Tokyo: Meicho Shuppan, 1991.

Tsuji Zennosuke 辻善之助. "Honji suijaku setsu no kigen ni tsuite" 本地垂迹説の起源について. In *Nihon bukkyōshi no kenkyū* 日本仏教史之研究, 1:436–88. Tokyo: Iwanami Shoten, 1944.

Tsunoda Bun'ei 角田文衛. *Taikenmon'in Shōshi no shōgai: Shōtei hishō* 待賢門院璋子の生涯—椒庭秘抄. Tokyo: Asahi Shinbunsha, 1975.

Turner, Victor. "Pilgrimages as Social Processes." In *Dramas, Fields, and Metaphors: Symbolic Action in Human Society,* 166–230. Ithaca, NY: Cornell University Press, 1974.

Turner, Victor, and Edith Turner. *Image and Pilgrimage in Christian Culture.* 1978. New York: Columbia University Press, 1995.

Tyler, Royall, trans. *Japanese Tales.* New York: Pantheon, 1987.

———. "Kōfukuji and the Mountains of Yamato." *Nichibunken Japan Review* 1 (1990): 153–223.

———. "Kōfukuji and Shugendo." *Japanese Journal of Religious Studies* 16, nos. 2–3 (1989): 143–80.

———. "The Path of My Mountain: Buddhism in Nō." In *Flowing Traces: Buddhism in the Literary and Visual Arts of Japan,* edited by James H. Sanford, William R. LaFleur, and Masatoshi Nagatomi, 149–79. Princeton: Princeton University Press, 1992.

———, trans. *The Tale of Genji.* 2 vols. New York: Viking, 2001.

Tyler, Susan C. *The Cult of Kasuga as Seen through Its Art.* Ann Arbor: Center for Japanese Studies, University of Michigan, 1992.

Ueda Sachiko 上田さち子. *Shugen to nenbutsu: chūsei shinkō sekai no jitsuzō* 修験と念仏—中世信仰世界の実像. Tokyo: Heibonsha, 2005.

Uejima Susumu 上島享. *Nihon chūsei shakai no keisei to ōken* 日本中世社会の形成と王権. Nagoya: Nagoya Daigaku Shuppankai, 2010.

UNESCO. "Advisory Board Evaluation," World Heritage Site 1142. http://whc.unesco.org/archive/advisory_body_evaluation/1142.pdf.

———. "Sacred Sites and Pilgrimage Routes in the Kii Mountain Range." http://whc.unesco.org/en/list/1142.

Uno Shigeki 宇野茂樹. "Rengeōin: midō to sentaibutsu" 蓮華王院—御堂と千体仏. In *Go-Shirakawa-in: dōranki no tennō* 後白河院—動乱期の天皇, edited by Kodaigaku Kyōkai 古代学協会, 413–31. Tokyo: Yoshikawa Kōbunkan, 1993.

Ury, Marian, trans. *Tales of Times Now Past: Sixty-Two Stories from a Medieval Japanese Collection*. Berkeley: University of Califonia Press, 1979.

Ushiyama, Yoshiyuki 牛山佳幸. "The Historical Development of the Exclusion of Women from Sacred Places." *Acta Asiatica: Bulletin of the Institute of Eastern Culture* 97 (2009): 39–55.

von Verschuer, Charlotte. *Mono ga kataru Nihon taigai kōekishi—shichi–jūroku seiki* モノが語る日本対外交易史—七〜十六世紀. Translated by Kōchi Haruhito 河内春人. Tokyo: Fujiwara Shoten, 2011.

———. *Le riz dans la culture de Heian, mythe et réalité.* Paris: Collège de France, Institut des Hautes Études Japonaises, 2003.

Wada Atsumu 和田萃. *Kodai Nihon no girei to saishi, shinkō* 日本古代の儀礼と祭祀・信仰. 3 vols. Tokyo: Hanawa Shobō, 1995.

Wada Hisamatsu 和田英松. *Kokushi kokubun no kenkyū* 国史国文之研究. Tokyo: Yūzankaku, 1926.

Wakabayashi, Haruko Nishioka. *The Seven Tengu Scrolls: Evil and the Rhetoric of Legitimacy in Medieval Japanese Buddhism.* Honolulu: University of Hawai'i Press, 2012.

Wakamori Tarō 和歌森太郎. *Shugendōshi kenkyū* 修験道史研究. Tōyō bunko 東洋文庫, vol. 211. 1943. Tokyo: Heibonsha, 1972.

Wa-Kan Hikaku Bungakukai 和漢比較文学会, ed. *Sugawara no Michizane ronshū* 菅原道真論集. Tokyo: Bensei Shuppan, 2003.

Wakayamaken Kyōiku Iinkai 和歌山県教育委員会, ed. *Kōyasan okunoin no chihō: Kōyasan okunoin maizō bunkazai sōgō chōsa hōkokusho* 高野山奥之院の地宝—高野山奥之院埋蔵文化財総合調査報告書. Wakayamaken bunkazai gakujutsu chōsa hōkokusho 和歌山県文化財学術調査報告書, vol. 6. Wakayama: Wakayamaken Kyōiku Iinkai, 1975.

Watanabe Shōgo 渡辺章悟. *Daihannya to Rishubun no subete* 大般若と理趣分のすべて. Tokyo: Keisuisha, 1995.

Weber, Max. *The Theory of Social and Economic Organization.* Translated by A. M. Henderson and Talcott Parsons. New York: Free Press, 1997.

Yamada, Shōzen. "Poetry and Meaning: Medieval Poets and the *Lotus Sutra.*" In Tanabe and Tanabe, *The Lotus Sutra in Japanese Culture,* 95–118.

Yamagishi Tsuneto 山岸常人. *Chūsei jiin shakai to butsudō* 中世寺院社会と仏堂. Tokyo: Hanawa Shobō, 1990.

———. *Chūsei jiin no sōdan, hōe, monjo* 中世寺院の僧団・法会・文書. Tokyo: Tōkyō Daigaku Shuppankai, 2004.

———. "Hosshōji no hyōka o megutte" 法勝寺の評価をめぐって. *Nihonshi kenkyū* 日本史研究 426 (1998): 1–25.

Yamamoto Kenji 山本謙治. "Kinpusen hirai denshō to Godaisan shinkō" 金峯山飛来伝承と五台山信仰. *Bunka shigaku* 文化史学 42 (1986): 1–21.

Yamamoto Satsuki 山本五月. "Dōken (Nichizō) denshō no tenkai" 道賢（日蔵）伝承の展開. *Ajia yūgaku* アジア遊学 22 (2000): 90–99.

Yamamoto Yukio 山本幸男. *Shakyōjo monjo no kisoteki kenkyū* 写経所文書の基礎的研究. Tokyo: Yoshikawa Kōbunkan, 2002.

Yamanaka Yutaka 山中裕, ed. *Midō kanpakuki zenchūshaku, Kankō hachinen* 御堂関白記全註釈, 寛弘８年. Kyoto: Shibunkaku Shuppan, 2007.

Yamashita Katsuaki 山下克明. *Heain jidai no shūkyō bunka to on'yōdō* 平安時代の宗教文化と陰陽道. Tokyo: Iwata Shoin, 1996.

Yamato Bunkakan 大和文華官, ed. *Kyōzō no bi: kagami ni kizamareta hotoke no sekai: tokubetsu ten* 鏡像の美—鏡に刻まれた仏の世界—特別展. Nara: Yamato Bunkakan, 2006.

Yasuda Tsuguo 安田次郎. *Chūsei no Kōfukuji to Yamato* 中世の興福寺と大和. Tokyo: Yamakawa Shuppansha, 2001.

Yiengpruksawan, Mimi Hall. "The Eyes of Michinaga in the Light of Pure Land Buddhism." In Kapstein, *The Presence of Light*, 227–61.

———. *Hiraizumi: Buddhist Art and Regional Politics in Twelfth-Century Japan.* Cambridge: Harvard University Asia Center, 1998.

———. "The Phoenix Hall at Uji and the Symmetries of Replication." *Art Bulletin* 77, no. 4 (1995): 647–72.

Yokoyama Kazuhiro 横山和弘. "Shirakawa inseiki ni okeru hosshinnō no sōshutsu" 白河院政期における法親王の創出. Rekishi hyōron 歴史評論 657 (2005): 63–79.

Yoneda Yūsuke 米田雄介. "Eizanji no Kōfukuji matsujika o megutte" 栄山寺の興福寺末寺化をめぐって. In *Akamatsu Toshihide kyōju taikan kinen kokushi ronshū* 赤松俊秀教授退官記念国史論集, edited by Akamatsu Toshihide Kyōju Taikan Kinen Jigyōkai 赤松俊秀教授退官記念事業会, 347–60. Kyoto: Akamatsu Toshihide Kyōju Taikan Kinen Jigyōkai, 1972.

———. *Sekkansei no seiritsu to tenkai* 摂関制の成立と展開. Tokyo: Yoshikawa Kōbunkan, 2006.

Yoshida Kazuhiko吉田一彦. *Nihon kodai shakai to bukkyō* 日本古代社会と仏教. Tokyo: Yoshikawa Kōbunkan, 1995.

———. "Suijaku shisō no juyō to tenkai" 垂迹思想の受容と展開. In *Nihon shakai ni okeru hotoke to kami* 日本社会における仏と神, edited by Hayami Tasuku 速水侑, 198–220. Tokyo: Yoshikawa Kōkubunkan, 2006.

———. "Tado Jingūji to shinbutsu shūgō" 多度神宮寺と神仏習合. In *Isewan to kodai no Tōkai* 伊勢湾と古代の東海, edited by Umemura Takashi 梅村喬, 217–57. Tokyo: Meicho Shuppan, 1996.

Yoshikawa Shinji 吉川真司. *Ritsuryō kanryōsei no kenkyū* 律令官僚制の研究. Tokyo: Hanawa Shobō, 1998.

Yoshinochō Shi Henshū Iinkai 吉野町史編集委員会. *Yoshinochō shi* 吉野町史. 2 vols. Yoshino: Yoshinochō Yakusho, 1972.

Yü, Chün-fang. *Kuan-yin: The Chinese Transformation of Avalokiteśvara.* New York: Columbia University Press, 2001.

Zenitani Buhei 銭谷武平. *En no gyōja denki shūsei* 役行者伝記集成. Osaka: Tōhō Shuppan, 1994.

———. *Ōmine engi* 大峯縁起. Osaka: Tōhō Shuppan, 2008.

Ziporyn, Brook. *The Penumbra Unbound: The Neo-Taoist Philosophy of Guo Xiang.* Albany: State University of New York Press, 2003.

Zürcher, Erik. *The Buddhist Conquest of China: The Spread and Adaptation of Buddhism in Early Medieval China.* 2nd ed. Leiden: Brill, 1972.

Glossary-Index

Page numbers for figures are in italics.

Abe Yasurō 阿部泰郎, 189n56
Adamek, Wendi, 166
Adolphson, Mikael, 229
affective landscape, 20, 38; cultural memory, 19; of Kinpusen, 22, 56, 59; of pilgrims, 21, 56; spatial imaginary, 22; and women, 55
ajari. *See* esoteric master
Ākāśagarbha (Kokūzō 虚空蔵), 262
Amabenomine 海部峯, 39–40
amalgamation of *kami* and buddhas (*shinbutsu shūgō* 神仏習合), 67–68. See also *honji suijaku*
Amaterasu 天照 (sun goddess), 123, 246
Amida. *See* Amitābha
Amida kyō. See *Amitābha Sūtra*
Amitābha (Amida 阿弥陀), 45, 84, 93n92; at Hōjōji, 112, Pure Land of, 186
Amitābha Sūtra (*Foshuo Emituo jing* 佛説阿彌陀經; J. *Amida kyō*), 175, 178, 186, 200
Aogane-ga-mine 青金ヶ峰, 21–22n6
aristocratic pilgrims. *See* elite pilgrimage
Ashikaga 足利 shoguns, 282, 284
Ashikaga Takauji 足利尊氏, 283
Ashizuri 足摺 mountain hut, 147–48
Asia, 13, 43, 184
Association for Asian Studies, 135n10
Asuka 飛鳥 (capital), 100, 143
Atagoyama 愛宕山, 34n37, 278
Atsusada 敦貞 (Prince), 214
Atsuta 熱田 deity, 70
Avalokiteśvara (Kannon 観音), 45, 73n31, 75, 93n92, 95–96, 143; Ārya Avalokiteśvara, 95; Cintāmaṇi Avalokiteśvara, 95
Averbuch, Irit, 75
Āvici Hell, 47

Baopuzi 抱朴子, 28, 42
Benevolent Kings Sūtra (*Foshuo renwang bore boluomi jing* 佛説仁王般若波羅蜜經; J. *Bussetsu ninnō hannya haramitsu kyō*), 139, 165, 167, 170–72, 196, 217–18, 252
Benzaiten弁財天・弁才天, 254
bettō. *See* steward
Bhabha, Homi, 64; and third space, 23n7
Bialock, David, 28n19
Bokencamp, Steven, 135n10
Boucher, Daniel, 184

Harvard East Asian Monographs
(titles now in print)

7. Chao Kuo-chün, *Economic Planning and Organization in Mainland China: A Documentary Study, 1949–1957*
13. S. M. Meng, *The Tsungli Yamen: Its Organization and Functions*
31. Madeleine Chi, *China Diplomacy, 1914–1918*
36. Peter Frost, *The Bakumatsu Currency Crisis*
38. Robert R. Campbell, *James Duncan Campbell: A Memoir by His Son*
39. Jerome Alan Cohen, ed., *The Dynamics of China's Foreign Relations*
40. V. V. Vishnyakova-Akimova, *Two Years in Revolutionary China, 1925–1927,* trans. Steven L. Levine
41. Meron Medzini, *French Policy in Japan during the Closing Years of the Tokugawa Regime*
46. W. P. J. Hall, *A Bibliographical Guide to Japanese Research on the Chinese Economy, 1958–1970*
47. Jack J. Gerson, *Horatio Nelson Lay and Sino-British Relations, 1854–1864*
48. Paul Richard Bohr, *Famine and the Missionary: Timothy Richard as Relief Administrator and Advocate of National Reform*
50. Britten Dean, *China and Great Britain: The Diplomacy of Commercial Relations, 1860–1864*
51. Ellsworth C. Carlson, *The Foochow Missionaries, 1847–1880*
53. Richard M. Pfeffer, *Understanding Business Contracts in China, 1949–1963*
55. Ranbir Vohra, *Lao She and the Chinese Revolution*
60. Noriko Kamachi, John K. Fairbank, and Chūzō Ichiko, *Japanese Studies of Modern China Since 1953: A Bibliographical Guide to Historical and Social-Science Research on the Nineteenth and Twentieth Centuries, Supplementary Volume for 1953–1969*
61. Donald A. Gibbs and Yun-chen Li, *A Bibliography of Studies and Translations of Modern Chinese Literature, 1918–1942*
62. Robert H. Silin, *Leadership and Values: The Organization of Large-Scale Taiwanese Enterprises*
63. David Pong, *A Critical Guide to the Kwangtung Provincial Archives Deposited at the Public Record Office of London*

69. Eric Widmer, *The Russian Ecclesiastical Mission in Peking during the Eighteenth Century*
73. Jon Sigurdson, *Rural Industrialism in China*
74. Kang Chao, *The Development of Cotton Textile Production in China*
75. Valentin Rabe, *The Home Base of American China Missions, 1880–1920*
78. Meishi Tsai, *Contemporary Chinese Novels and Short Stories, 1949–1974: An Annotated Bibliography*
80. Endymion Wilkinson, *Landlord and Labor in Late Imperial China: Case Studies from Shandong by Jing Su and Luo Lun*
84. J. W. Dower, *Empire and Aftermath: Yoshida Shigeru and the Japanese Experience, 1878–1954*
85. Martin Collcutt, *Five Mountains: The Rinzai Zen Monastic Institution in Medieval Japan*
86. Kwang Suk Kim and Michael Roemer, *Growth and Structural Transformation*
89. Sung Hwan Ban, Pal Yong Moon, and Dwight H. Perkins, *Rural Development*
92. Edward S. Mason, Dwight H. Perkins, Kwang Suk Kim, David C. Cole, Mahn Je Kim et al., *The Economic and Social Modernization of the Republic of Korea*
93. Robert Repetto, Tai Hwan Kwon, Son-Ung Kim, Dae Young Kim, John E. Sloboda, and Peter J. Donaldson, *Economic Development, Population Policy, and Demographic Transition in the Republic of Korea*
94. Parks M. Coble, Jr., *The Shanghai Capitalists and the Nationalist Government, 1927–1937*
96. Richard Wich, *Sino-Soviet Crisis Politics: A Study of Political Change and Communication*
97. Lillian M. Li, *China's Silk Trade: Traditional Industry in the Modern World, 1842–1937*
98. R. David Arkush, *Fei Xiaotong and Sociology in Revolutionary China*
100. James Reeve Pusey, *China and Charles Darwin*
101. Hoyt Cleveland Tillman, *Utilitarian Confucianism: Chen Liang's Challenge to Chu Hsi*
102. Thomas A. Stanley, *Ōsugi Sakae, Anarchist in Taishō Japan: The Creativity of the Ego*
103. Jonathan K. Ocko, *Bureaucratic Reform in Provincial China: Ting Jih-ch'ang in Restoration Kiangsu, 1867–1870*
104. James Reed, *The Missionary Mind and American East Asia Policy, 1911–1915*
105. Neil L. Waters, *Japan's Local Pragmatists: The Transition from Bakumatsu to Meiji in the Kawasaki Region*
106. David C. Cole and Yung Chul Park, *Financial Development in Korea, 1945–1978*
107. Roy Bahl, Chuk Kyo Kim, and Chong Kee Park, *Public Finances during the Korean Modernization Process*
108. William D. Wray, *Mitsubishi and the N.Y.K., 1870–1914: Business Strategy in the Japanese Shipping Industry*
109. Ralph William Huenemann, *The Dragon and the Iron Horse: The Economics of Railroads in China, 1876–1937*
111. Jane Kate Leonard, *Wei Yüan and China's Rediscovery of the Maritime World*

117. Andrew Gordon, *The Evolution of Labor Relations in Japan: Heavy Industry, 1853–1955*
119. Christine Guth Kanda, *Shinzō: Hachiman Imagery and Its Development*
121. Chang-tai Hung, *Going to the People: Chinese Intellectual and Folk Literature, 1918–1937*
123. Richard von Glahn, *The Country of Streams and Grottoes: Expansion, Settlement, and the Civilizing of the Sichuan Frontier in Song Times*
124. Steven D. Carter, *The Road to Komatsubara: A Classical Reading of the Renga Hyakuin*
126. Bob Tadashi Wakabayashi, *Anti-Foreignism and Western Learning in Early-Modern Japan: The "New Theses" of 1825*
127. Atsuko Hirai, *Individualism and Socialism: The Life and Thought of Kawai Eijirō (1891–1944)*
129. R. Kent Guy, *The Emperor's Four Treasuries: Scholars and the State in the Late Chien-lung Era*
130. Peter C. Perdue, *Exhausting the Earth: State and Peasant in Hunan, 1500–1850*
131. Susan Chan Egan, *A Latterday Confucian: Reminiscences of William Hung (1893–1980)*
132. James T. C. Liu, *China Turning Inward: Intellectual-Political Changes in the Early Twelfth Century*
134. Kate Wildman Nakai, *Shogunal Politics: Arai Hakuseki and the Premises of Tokugawa Rule*
137. Susan Downing Videen, *Tales of Heichū*
138. Heinz Morioka and Miyoko Sasaki, *Rakugo: The Popular Narrative Art of Japan*
139. Joshua A. Fogel, *Nakae Ushikichi in China: The Mourning of Spirit*
140. Alexander Barton Woodside, *Vietnam and the Chinese Model: A Comparative Study of Vietnamese and Chinese Government in the First Half of the Nineteenth Century*
141. George Elison, *Deus Destroyed: The Image of Christianity in Early Modern Japan*
144. Marie Anchordoguy, *Computers, Inc.: Japan's Challenge to IBM*
146. Mary Elizabeth Berry, *Hideyoshi*
147. Laura E. Hein, *Fueling Growth: The Energy Revolution and Economic Policy in Postwar Japan*
148. Wen-hsin Yeh, *The Alienated Academy: Culture and Politics in Republican China, 1919–1937*
149. Dru C. Gladney, *Muslim Chinese: Ethnic Nationalism in the People's Republic*
150. Merle Goldman and Paul A. Cohen, eds., *Ideas Across Cultures: Essays on Chinese Thought in Honor of Benjamin L Schwartz*
151. James M. Polachek, *The Inner Opium War*
152. Gail Lee Bernstein, *Japanese Marxist: A Portrait of Kawakami Hajime, 1879–1946*
154. Mark Mason, *American Multinationals and Japan: The Political Economy of Japanese Capital Controls, 1899–1980*
155. Richard J. Smith, John K. Fairbank, and Katherine F. Bruner, *Robert Hart and China's Early Modernization: His Journals, 1863–1866*
157. William Wayne Farris, *Heavenly Warriors: The Evolution of Japan's Military, 500–1300*

159. James B. Palais, *Politics and Policy in Traditional Korea*
161. Roger R. Thompson, *China's Local Councils in the Age of Constitutional Reform, 1898–1911*
162. William Johnston, *The Modern Epidemic: History of Tuberculosis in Japan*
163. Constantine Nomikos Vaporis, *Breaking Barriers: Travel and the State in Early Modern Japan*
164. Irmela Hijiya-Kirschnereit, *Rituals of Self-Revelation: Shishōsetsu as Literary Genre and Socio-Cultural Phenomenon*
165. James C. Baxter, *The Meiji Unification through the Lens of Ishikawa Prefecture*
166. Thomas R. H. Havens, *Architects of Affluence: The Tsutsumi Family and the Seibu-Saison Enterprises in Twentieth-Century Japan*
167. Anthony Hood Chambers, *The Secret Window: Ideal Worlds in Tanizaki's Fiction*
168. Steven J. Ericson, *The Sound of the Whistle: Railroads and the State in Meiji Japan*
169. Andrew Edmund Goble, *Kenmu: Go-Daigo's Revolution*
170. Denise Potrzeba Lett, *In Pursuit of Status: The Making of South Korea's "New" Urban Middle Class*
171. Mimi Hall Yiengpruksawan, *Hiraizumi: Buddhist Art and Regional Politics in Twelfth-Century Japan*
173. Aviad E. Raz, *Riding the Black Ship: Japan and Tokyo Disneyland*
174. Deborah J. Milly, *Poverty, Equality, and Growth: The Politics of Economic Need in Postwar Japan*
175. See Heng Teow, *Japan's Cultural Policy toward China, 1918–1931: A Comparative Perspective*
176. Michael A. Fuller, *An Introduction to Literary Chinese*
177. Frederick R. Dickinson, *War and National Reinvention: Japan in the Great War, 1914–1919*
178. John Solt, *Shredding the Tapestry of Meaning: The Poetry and Poetics of Kitasono Katue (1902–1978)*
179. Edward Pratt, *Japan's Protoindustrial Elite: The Economic Foundations of the Gōnō*
180. Atsuko Sakaki, *Recontextualizing Texts: Narrative Performance in Modern Japanese Fiction*
181. Soon-Won Park, *Colonial Industrialization and Labor in Korea: The Onoda Cement Factory*
182. JaHyun Kim Haboush and Martina Deuchler, *Culture and the State in Late Chosŏn Korea*
183. John W. Chaffee, *Branches of Heaven: A History of the Imperial Clan of Sung China*
184. Gi-Wook Shin and Michael Robinson, eds., *Colonial Modernity in Korea*
185. Nam-lin Hur, *Prayer and Play in Late Tokugawa Japan: Asakusa Sensōji and Edo Society*
186. Kristin Stapleton, *Civilizing Chengdu: Chinese Urban Reform, 1895–1937*
187. Hyung Il Pai, *Constructing "Korean" Origins: A Critical Review of Archaeology, Historiography, and Racial Myth in Korean State-Formation Theories*
188. Brian D. Ruppert, *Jewel in the Ashes: Buddha Relics and Power in Early Medieval Japan*
189. Susan Daruvala, *Zhou Zuoren and an Alternative Chinese Response to Modernity*

191. Kerry Smith, *A Time of Crisis: Japan, the Great Depression, and Rural Revitalization*
192. Michael Lewis, *Becoming Apart: National Power and Local Politics in Toyama, 1868–1945*
193. William C. Kirby, Man-houng Lin, James Chin Shih, and David A. Pietz, eds., *State and Economy in Republican China: A Handbook for Scholars*
194. Timothy S. George, *Minamata: Pollution and the Struggle for Democracy in Postwar Japan*
195. Billy K. L. So, *Prosperity, Region, and Institutions in Maritime China: The South Fukien Pattern, 946–1368*
196. Yoshihisa Tak Matsusaka, *The Making of Japanese Manchuria, 1904–1932*
197. Maram Epstein, *Competing Discourses: Orthodoxy, Authenticity, and Engendered Meanings in Late Imperial Chinese Fiction*
199. Haruo Iguchi, *Unfinished Business: Ayukawa Yoshisuke and U.S.-Japan Relations, 1937–1952*
200. Scott Pearce, Audrey Spiro, and Patricia Ebrey, *Culture and Power in the Reconstitution of the Chinese Realm, 200–600*
201. Terry Kawashima, *Writing Margins: The Textual Construction of Gender in Heian and Kamakura Japan*
202. Martin W. Huang, *Desire and Fictional Narrative in Late Imperial China*
203. Robert S. Ross and Jiang Changbin, eds., *Re-examining the Cold War: U.S.-China Diplomacy, 1954–1973*
204. Guanhua Wang, *In Search of Justice: The 1905–1906 Chinese Anti-American Boycott*
205. David Schaberg, *A Patterned Past: Form and Thought in Early Chinese Historiography*
206. Christine Yano, *Tears of Longing: Nostalgia and the Nation in Japanese Popular Song*
207. Milena Doleželová-Velingerová and Oldřich Král, with Graham Sanders, eds., *The Appropriation of Cultural Capital: China's May Fourth Project*
208. Robert N. Huey, *The Making of 'Shinkokinshū'*
209. Lee Butler, *Emperor and Aristocracy in Japan, 1467–1680: Resilience and Renewal*
210. Suzanne Ogden, *Inklings of Democracy in China*
211. Kenneth J. Ruoff, *The People's Emperor: Democracy and the Japanese Monarchy, 1945–1995*
212. Haun Saussy, *Great Walls of Discourse and Other Adventures in Cultural China*
213. Aviad E. Raz, *Emotions at Work: Normative Control, Organizations, and Culture in Japan and America*
214. Rebecca E. Karl and Peter Zarrow, eds., *Rethinking the 1898 Reform Period: Political and Cultural Change in Late Qing China*
215. Kevin O'Rourke, *The Book of Korean Shijo*
216. Ezra F. Vogel, ed., *The Golden Age of the U.S.-China-Japan Triangle, 1972–1989*
217. Thomas A. Wilson, ed., *On Sacred Grounds: Culture, Society, Politics, and the Formation of the Cult of Confucius*
218. Donald S. Sutton, *Steps of Perfection: Exorcistic Performers and Chinese Religion in Twentieth-Century Taiwan*

246. Yongping Wu, *A Political Explanation of Economic Growth: State Survival, Bureaucratic Politics, and Private Enterprises in the Making of Taiwan's Economy, 1950–1985*
247. Kyu Hyun Kim, *The Age of Visions and Arguments: Parliamentarianism and the National Public Sphere in Early Meiji Japan*
248. Zvi Ben-Dor Benite, *The Dao of Muhammad: A Cultural History of Muslims in Late Imperial China*
249. David Der-wei Wang and Shang Wei, eds., *Dynastic Crisis and Cultural Innovation: From the Late Ming to the Late Qing and Beyond*
250. Wilt L. Idema, Wai-yee Li, and Ellen Widmer, eds., *Trauma and Transcendence in Early Qing Literature*
251. Barbara Molony and Kathleen Uno, eds., *Gendering Modern Japanese History*
252. Hiroshi Aoyagi, *Islands of Eight Million Smiles: Idol Performance and Symbolic Production in Contemporary Japan*
253. Wai-yee Li, *The Readability of the Past in Early Chinese Historiography*
254. William C. Kirby, Robert S. Ross, and Gong Li, eds., *Normalization of U.S.-China Relations: An International History*
255. Ellen Gardner Nakamura, *Practical Pursuits: Takano Chōei, Takahashi Keisaku, and Western Medicine in Nineteenth-Century Japan*
256. Jonathan W. Best, *A History of the Early Korean Kingdom of Paekche, together with an annotated translation of* The Paekche Annals *of the* Samguk sagi
257. Liang Pan, *The United Nations in Japan's Foreign and Security Policymaking, 1945–1992: National Security, Party Politics, and International Status*
258. Richard Belsky, *Localities at the Center: Native Place, Space, and Power in Late Imperial Beijing*
259. Zwia Lipkin, *"Useless to the State": "Social Problems" and Social Engineering in Nationalist Nanjing, 1927–1937*
260. William O. Gardner, *Advertising Tower: Japanese Modernism and Modernity in the 1920s*
261. Stephen Owen, *The Making of Early Chinese Classical Poetry*
262. Martin J. Powers, *Pattern and Person: Ornament, Society, and Self in Classical China*
263. Anna M. Shields, *Crafting a Collection: The Cultural Contexts and Poetic Practice of the* Huajian ji 花間集 *(Collection from among the Flowers)*
264. Stephen Owen, *The Late Tang: Chinese Poetry of the Mid-Ninth Century (827–860)*
265. Sara L. Friedman, *Intimate Politics: Marriage, the Market, and State Power in Southeastern China*
266. Patricia Buckley Ebrey and Maggie Bickford, *Emperor Huizong and Late Northern Song China: The Politics of Culture and the Culture of Politics*
267. Sophie Volpp, *Worldly Stage: Theatricality in Seventeenth-Century China*
268. Ellen Widmer, *The Beauty and the Book: Women and Fiction in Nineteenth-Century China*
269. Steven B. Miles, *The Sea of Learning: Mobility and Identity in Nineteenth-Century Guangzhou*
270. Man-houng Lin, *China Upside Down: Currency, Society, and Ideologies, 1808–1856*

271. Ronald Egan, *The Problem of Beauty: Aesthetic Thought and Pursuits in Northern Song Dynasty China*
272. Mark Halperin, *Out of the Cloister: Literati Perspectives on Buddhism in Sung China, 960–1279*
273. Helen Dunstan, *State or Merchant? Political Economy and Political Process in 1740s China*
274. Sabina Knight, *The Heart of Time: Moral Agency in Twentieth-Century Chinese Fiction*
275. Timothy J. Van Compernolle, *The Uses of Memory: The Critique of Modernity in the Fiction of Higuchi Ichiyō*
276. Paul Rouzer, *A New Practical Primer of Literary Chinese*
277. Jonathan Zwicker, *Practices of the Sentimental Imagination: Melodrama, the Novel, and the Social Imaginary in Nineteenth-Century Japan*
278. Franziska Seraphim, *War Memory and Social Politics in Japan, 1945–2005*
280. Cynthia J. Brokaw, *Commerce in Culture: The Sibao Book Trade in the Qing and Republican Periods*
281. Eugene Y. Park, *Between Dreams and Reality: The Military Examination in Late Chosŏn Korea, 1600–1894*
282. Nam-lin Hur, *Death and Social Order in Tokugawa Japan: Buddhism, Anti-Christianity, and the* Danka *System*
283. Patricia M. Thornton, *Disciplining the State: Virtue, Violence, and State-Making in Modern China*
284. Vincent Goossaert, *The Taoists of Peking, 1800–1949: A Social History of Urban Clerics*
286. Charo B. D'Etcheverry, *Love after* The Tale of Genji*: Rewriting the World of the Shining Prince*
287. Michael G. Chang, *A Court on Horseback: Imperial Touring & the Construction of Qing Rule, 1680–1785*
288. Carol Richmond Tsang, *War and Faith:* Ikkō Ikki *in Late Muromachi Japan*
289. Hilde De Weerdt, *Competition over Content: Negotiating Standards for the Civil Service Examinations in Imperial China (1127–1279)*
290. Eve Zimmerman, *Out of the Alleyway: Nakagami Kenji and the Poetics of Outcaste Fiction*
291. Robert Culp, *Articulating Citizenship: Civic Education and Student Politics in Southeastern China, 1912–1940*
292. Richard J. Smethurst, *From Foot Soldier to Finance Minister: Takahashi Korekiyo, Japan's Keynes*
293. John E. Herman, *Amid the Clouds and Mist: China's Colonization of Guizhou, 1200–1700*
294. Tomoko Shiroyama, *China during the Great Depression: Market, State, and the World Economy, 1929–1937*
295. Kirk W. Larsen, *Tradition, Treaties and Trade: Qing Imperialism and Chosŏn Korea, 1850–1910*
296. Gregory Golley, *When Our Eyes No Longer See: Realism, Science, and Ecology in Japanese Literary Modernism*

297. Barbara Ambros, *Emplacing a Pilgrimage: The Ōyama Cult and Regional Religion in Early Modern Japan*
298. Rebecca Suter, *The Japanization of Modernity: Murakami Haruki between Japan and the United States*
299. Yuma Totani, *The Tokyo War Crimes Trial: The Pursuit of Justice in the Wake of World War II*
301. David M. Robinson, ed., *Culture, Courtiers, and Competition: The Ming Court (1368–1644)*
302. Calvin Chen, *Some Assembly Required: Work, Community, and Politics in China's Rural Enterprises*
303. Sem Vermeersch, *The Power of the Buddhas: The Politics of Buddhism During the Koryŏ Dynasty* (918–1392)
304. Tina Lu, *Accidental Incest, Filial Cannibalism, and Other Peculiar Encounters in Late Imperial Chinese Literature*
305. Chang Woei Ong, *Men of Letters Within the Passes: Guanzhong Literati in Chinese History, 907–1911*
306. Wendy Swartz, *Reading Tao Yuanming: Shifting Paradigms of Historical Reception (427–1900)*
307. Peter K. Bol, *Neo-Confucianism in History*
308. Carlos Rojas, *The Naked Gaze: Reflections on Chinese Modernity*
309. Kelly H. Chong, *Deliverance and Submission: Evangelical Women and the Negotiation of Patriarchy in South Korea*
310. Rachel DiNitto, *Uchida Hyakken: A Critique of Modernity and Militarism in Prewar Japan*
311. Jeffrey Snyder-Reinke, *Dry Spells: State Rainmaking and Local Governance in Late Imperial China*
312. Jay Dautcher, *Down a Narrow Road: Identity and Masculinity in a Uyghur Community in Xinjiang China*
313. Xun Liu, *Daoist Modern: Innovation, Lay Practice, and the Community of Inner Alchemy in Republican Shanghai*
314. Jacob Eyferth, *Eating Rice from Bamboo Roots: The Social History of a Community of Handicraft Papermakers in Rural Sichuan, 1920–2000*
315. David Johnson, *Spectacle and Sacrifice: The Ritual Foundations of Village Life in North China*
316. James Robson, *Power of Place: The Religious Landscape of the Southern Sacred Peak (Nanyue* 南嶽*) in Medieval China*
317. Lori Watt, *When Empire Comes Home: Repatriation and Reintegration in Postwar Japan*
318. James Dorsey, *Critical Aesthetics: Kobayashi Hideo, Modernity, and Wartime Japan*
319. Christopher Bolton, *Sublime Voices: The Fictional Science and Scientific Fiction of Abe Kōbō*
320. Si-yen Fei, *Negotiating Urban Space: Urbanization and Late Ming Nanjing*
321. Christopher Gerteis, *Gender Struggles: Wage-Earning Women and Male-Dominated Unions in Postwar Japan*
322. Rebecca Nedostup, *Superstitious Regimes: Religion and the Politics of Chinese Modernity*

323. Lucien Bianco, *Wretched Rebels: Rural Disturbances on the Eve of the Chinese Revolution*
324. Cathryn H. Clayton, *Sovereignty at the Edge: Macau and the Question of Chineseness*
325. Micah S. Muscolino, *Fishing Wars and Environmental Change in Late Imperial and Modern China*
326. Robert I. Hellyer, *Defining Engagement: Japan and Global Contexts, 1750–1868*
327. Robert Ashmore, *The Transport of Reading: Text and Understanding in the World of Tao Qian (365–427)*
328. Mark A. Jones, *Children as Treasures: Childhood and the Middle Class in Early Twentieth Century Japan*
329. Miryam Sas, *Experimental Arts in Postwar Japan: Moments of Encounter, Engagement, and Imagined Return*
330. H. Mack Horton, *Traversing the Frontier: The* Man'yōshū *Account of a Japanese Mission to Silla in 736–737*
331. Dennis J. Frost, *Seeing Stars: Sports Celebrity, Identity, and Body Culture in Modern Japan*
332. Marnie S. Anderson, *A Place in Public: Women's Rights in Meiji Japan*
333. Peter Mauch, *Sailor Diplomat: Nomura Kichisaburō and the Japanese-American War*
334. Ethan Isaac Segal, *Coins, Trade, and the State: Economic Growth in Early Medieval Japan*
335. David B. Lurie, *Realms of Literacy: Early Japan and the History of Writing*
336. Lillian Lan-ying Tseng, *Picturing Heaven in Early China*
337. Jun Uchida, *Brokers of Empire: Japanese Settler Colonialism in Korea, 1876–1945*
338. Patricia L. Maclachlan, *The People's Post Office: The History and Politics of the Japanese Postal System, 1871–2010*
339. Michael Schiltz, *The Money Doctors from Japan: Finance, Imperialism, and the Building of the Yen Bloc, 1895–1937*
340. Daqing Yang, Jie Liu, Hiroshi Mitani, and Andrew Gordon, eds., *Toward a History beyond Borders: Contentious Issues in Sino-Japanese Relations*
341. Sonia Ryang, *Reading North Korea: An Ethnological Inquiry*
342. Susan Huang, *Picturing the True Form: Daoist Visual Culture in Traditional China*
343. Barbara Mittler, *A Continuous Revolution: Making Sense of Cultural Revolution Culture*
344. Hwansoo Ilmee Kim, *Empire of the Dharma: Korean and Japanese Buddhism, 1877–1912*
345. Satoru Saito, *Detective Fiction and the Rise of the Japanese Novel, 1880–1930*
346. Jung-Sun N. Han, *An Imperial Path to Modernity: Yoshino Sakuzō and a New Liberal Order in East Asia, 1905–1937*
347. Atsuko Hirai, *Government by Mourning: Death and Political Integration in Japan, 1603–1912*
348. Darryl E. Flaherty, *Public Law, Private Practice: Politics, Profit, and the Legal Profession in Nineteenth-Century Japan*
349. Jeffrey Paul Bayliss, *On the Margins of Empire: Buraku and Korean Identity in Prewar and Wartime Japan*
350. Barry Eichengreen, Dwight H. Perkins, and Kwanho Shin, *From Miracle to Maturity: The Growth of the Korean Economy*

351. Michel Mohr, *Buddhism, Unitarianism, and the Meiji Competition for Universality*
352. J. Keith Vincent, *Two-Timing Modernity: Homosocial Narrative in Modern Japanese Fiction*
354. Chong-Bum An and Barry Bosworth, *Income Inequality in Korea: An Analysis of Trends, Causes, and Answers*
355. Jamie L. Newhard, *Knowing the Amorous Man: A History of Scholarship on* Tales of Ise
356. Sho Konishi, *Anarchist Modernity: Cooperatism and Japanese-Russian Intellectual Relations in Modern Japan*
357. Christopher P. Hanscom, *The Real Modern: Literary Modernism and the Crisis of Representation in Colonial Korea*
358. Michael Wert, *Meiji Restoration Losers: Memory and Tokugawa Supporters in Modern Japan*
359. Garret P. S. Olberding, ed., *Facing the Monarch: Modes of Advice in the Early Chinese Court*
360. Xiaojue Wang, *Modernity with a Cold War Face: Reimagining the Nation in Chinese Literature Across the 1949 Divide*
361. David Spafford, *A Sense of Place: The Political Landscape in Late Medieval Japan*
362. Jongryn Mo and Barry Weingast, *Korean Political and Economic Development: Crisis, Security, and Economic Rebalancing*
363. Melek Ortabasi, *The Undiscovered Country: Text, Translation, and Modernity in the Work of Yanagita Kunio*
364. Hiraku Shimoda, *Lost and Found: Recovering Regional Identity in Imperial Japan*
365. Trent E. Maxey, *The "Greatest Problem": Religion and State Formation in Meiji Japan*
366. Gina Cogan, *The Princess Nun: Bunchi, Buddhist Reform, and Gender in Early Edo Japan*
367. Eric C. Han, *Rise of a Japanese Chinatown: Yokohama, 1894–1972*
368. Natasha Heller, *Illusory Abiding: The Cultural Construction of the Chan Monk Zhongfeng Mingben* 中峰明本 *(1263–1323)*
369. Paize Keulemans, *Sound Rising from the Paper: Nineteenth-Century Martial Arts Fiction and the Chinese Acoustic Imagination*
370. Simon James Bytheway, *Investing Japan: Foreign Capital, Monetary Standards, and Economic Development, 1859–2011*
371. Sukhee Lee, *Negotiated Power: The State, Elites, and Local Governance in Twelfth-Fourteenth China*
372. Ping Foong, *The Efficacious Landscape: On the Authorities of Painting at the Northern Song Court*
373. Catherine L. Phipps, *Empires on the Waterfront: Japan's Ports and Power, 1858–1899*
374. Sunyoung Park, *The Proletarian Wave: Literature and Leftist Culture in Colonial Korea, 1910–1945*
375. Barry Eichengreen, Wonhyuk Lim, Yung Chul Park, and Dwight H. Perkins, *The Korean Economy: From a Miraculous Past to a Sustainable Future*
376. Heather Blair, *Real and Imagined: The Peak of Gold in Heian Japan*

Harvard East Asian Monographs

377. Emer O'Dwyer, *Significant Soil: Settler Colonialism and Japan's Urban Empire in Manchuria*
378. Martina Deuchler, *Under the Ancestors' Eyes: Kinship, Status, and Locality in Premodern Korea*
379. Joseph R. Dennis, *Writing, Publishing, and Reading Local Gazetteers in Imperial China, 1100–1700*
380. Cathy Yeh, *The Chinese Political Novel: Migration of a World Genre*
381. Noell Wilson, *Defensive Positions: The Politics of Maritime Security in Tokugawa Japan*
382. Miri Nakamura, *Monstrous Bodies: The Rise of the Uncanny in Modern Japan*
383. Nara Dillon, *Radical Inequalities: China's Revolutionary Welfare State in Comparative Perspective*